PRADHAN MANTRI TO PRADHAN SEWAK

PRADHAN MANTRI TO PRADHAN SEWAK

Modi's Quest for a Vibrant India

Compiled and Edited by

Amit Garg

Shib Ram Roy

GYAN

ISBN : 978-81-212-1301-1

Price : ₹ 450

First Published, 2015

Published by

Gyan Publishing House
23, Main Ansari Road, Darya Ganj
New Delhi-110002
Ph. : 23242060, 23261060
Fax : 011-23285914
E-mail: books@gyanbooks.com
Website : www.gyanbooks.com

Printed at : G. Print Process, Delhi

Cataloging in Publication Data—DK

Courtesy: D.K. Agencies (P) Ltd. <docinfo@dkagencies.com>

Garg, Amit, author.

Pradhan mantri to pradhan sewak : Modi's quest for a vibrant India / Amit Garg, Shib Ram Roy.

pages ; cm

ISBN 9788121213011

1. Modi, Narendra, 1950- 2. Prime ministers—India—Biography. 3. India—Politics and government—21st century. 4. India—Foreign relations—1984- 5. India—Economic policy—21st century. I. Roy, Shib Ram, author. II. Title.

DDC 954.0532092 23

Dedicated to India's Visionary Prime Miniter Narender Modi

New Immaculate Conception

Inevitability of NaMo : History was scripted in the forecourt of Rashtrapati Bhawan on the evening of 26th May 2014 as Narendra Modi took oath as the Prime Minister of India after a historic mandate from the people of India. In Modi, the people of India see a dynamic, decisive and development-oriented leader who has emerged as a ray of hope for the dreams and aspirations of a billion Indians. His focus on development, eye for detail and efforts to bring a qualitative difference in the lives of the poorest of the poor have made him a popular and respected leader across the length and breadth of India.

Modi's life has been a journey of courage, compassion and constant hardwork. At a very young age he had decided to devote his life in service of the people. He displayed his skills as a grassroots level worker, an organiser and an administrator during his 13 years long stint as the Chief Minister of his home state of Gujarat, where he ushered a paradigm shift towards pro-people and pro-active good governance.

India's choice of the man of the year was inevitable, where the elite, the crowd and the media converged on one choice: Narendra Modi. What is missing is the need for a critique of a different kind — to demystify him.

Year endings, like year beginnings, are predictable in terms of rituals. People want to celebrate the ending of the year and the media want to ensure that such endings are memorable spectacles. Each year needs a memorial to itself. The year should be full of turmoil and must appear to be like a race ending in a staggering triumph. The victor is the hero, the man of the year. It's a combination of a mythical figure, part Greek legend, part Olympic winner. In 2014, the man of the year is inevitable. Demographically and symbolically, the elite and the crowd have converged on one choice. In fact there is no other; 2014 offers us the inevitability of Namo.

To me, as a spectator, as a critic, as a citizen, it's not the choice that matters. He dominates all, but the logic of the argument goes deeper. While one reads leading magazines and major columnists, one senses the rhetoric around him that puzzles, intrigues, and finally disturbs.

Identifying with power: Modi's rise has been laudatory. He is a self-made man obsessed with power. The contrast, by now latent, is an almost forgotten Rahul Gandhi. Rahul is adolescent, casual, a man who inherited power only to squander it.

The media and the middle class were tired of a diffident India ... It wanted a winner; a stalwart who would understand and transform India from civilisation to a modern empire.

They have a tremendous need to be close to power. They are enamoured with the possibility of power. The ruler and the regime is someone they need to identify with. By now, the narrative has moved a second step. The semiotic alters and the photographs mark a different time; the man is no longer an aspirant and is presented as a leader among other leaders. He is not carping about history but making it. He is presented as a statesman changing the world; a focussed reformer who doesn't want to be distracted or diverted by trivia, those little sour grape stories about educational snafus and conversion narratives is at the Olympus of policy. He evokes leadership. His body language is muted. Appearing at home in the corridors of power he walks with Putin, Obama, as one among equals. He is ritually correct and precise.

He has realised that politics is a costume ball and is immaculately dressed for it. He knows he cannot wear either dull khadi or a predictable western suit but has to convey unity in diversity, blending the ethnic, the national, the *swadeshi* and the global to stir expectations. India seems to have found the leader it is looking for. his noisier incarnations. He has not abandoned them but outsourced them to Mohan Bhagwat, Amit Shah and to the Vishwa Hindu Parishad. He can keep eyes on them.

The Indian dream: As a presence, he conveys a blend, at one level he appears unique but he also suggests shades of Nehru, Patel, Vajpayee, Malaviya, and by invoking all, has combined the nostalgia for all of them. He is projected as a man of all seasons and sensitivities.

The media and the middle class were tired of a diffident India, and with an India that was a perpetual also-ran in international politics. It wanted a winner; a stalwart who would understand and transform India from civilisation to a modern empire. He is emperor Modi of an India that always wanted to be acknowledged by the rest of the world. Gradually, one realises that all these writings are catering to a psychological deficit. He is not the individual Modi but the collective Rorschach of a people. He is the projection of the Indian dream and the media is merely spelling out the dream's performance, not as his achievement in policies but as rhetorical acts of the imagined that he seems so desperate for. He is the man of the year because every man as He is man of the year.

Style dominates content and in fact style in its density is presented as the equivalent of content. This is no one-act play but it is an India that has projected its epic self on the global stage. Our elite realises that the old catechism of Non-alignment and third world-ism is the voice of the weak. What one is looking for is a new machismo. Not the brutal bully boy machismo of the streets but a muscular disciplined machismo which speaks a managerial, ethnocratic and nationalist idiom which both small town aspirant and diaspora understand. The diaspora is a major part of India and the global age and represents the Indian success story abroad. It is easier to be patriotic in New

Jersey and New York as the Indian flag flutters proudly and makes them feel glad to be Indians in America. The Madison Square Garden meeting was a performance and fulfils the diasporic need of the American senators paying court to their leader.

As one studies the photo of Modi, one realises that his icon ideal and image are a collective fantasy of India as a decisive, modern crowd, and respected nation. He is the mirror in which the middle class, tired of the Congress's indifference, salutes itself. India feels global and contemporary as he jokes with Obama or shows Xi Jinping around.

A need to demystify: One also realises that grandeur is the perfect moment for sanitisation. Modi is cleaned of his past. In fact, his past is now enacted by characters around him. Let us be clear; even if he wishes to do something and the wish list is genuine, he is hampered by two sets of forces. First, his past is alive in the present in the shape of the Rashtriya Swayamsevak Sangh and the Bharatiya Janata Party. They would like to leave their own stamp on history. Second, governance involves more than one man's leadership. A cleanliness drive itself is mere whitewash when it comes to reforming governance.

We have a crowned king and have decided that the king can do no wrong. In many ways, he is the new Sardar with a patriotic fervour who has already been granted his place in history; unlike the old Sardar, he will need no compensatory statue. He represents the new idea of agency in Indian history as India exorcised itself of its current past. The media, as high hybrids of change, have performed the ritual role brilliantly. He is the new Immaculate Conception.

Contents

Preface

'It is an opportunity to change our fate and of our nation ....
Glory to Mother India! Glory to Her children!

The Congress-led UPA Government sapped genuineness from governance; authenticity from administration and mere enactment without action. Consequently, it couldn't deliver the desired goods for the people of India. The previous government has reduced a polity of promises and not performance. It represents an economy of deficit, a work culture of delays and an asset-base of deficiency. To say the least, Congress-led UPA has made India a global synonym for 'corruption, scandals and stagnation'. To make it even worse, the years of long suffering compelled us to witness utter decision and policy paralysis, sluggish economic growth, unprecedented price rise and unstable currency.

The following demands need an urgent and viable solutions, i.e., economy including agriculture, energy, environment, natural resources, education and health, employment, external and internal threats to security, empowerment, governance and erosion of moral and societal values.

If India ought to survive as nation, which it had to, among the comity of nations, its voice heard for creating a peaceful and egalitarian world order, it should take up challenges with urgency and determination and provide proper solutions for most opportune time. It is a pity that the present set up have demoralised leadership presiding over the state apparatus, incompetent enough to handle the present problems. What is needed today is to arrive at a consensus about the 'Idea of India' and redesign approach in consonance with the seeking and preference towards the Indian people.

The situation in the country is deteriorating rapidly. Delay in resolving the crisis could be dangerous. We ought to take lessons from history, recognise the vitality and resilience of India, and utilise its strength; we should analyse its weaknesses that led to this abysmal fall. We had to pick up the thread from where the continuum of our civilisational consciousness was lost and reorient the polity in consonance with those strong points of Indian psyche, which will be the engine for our future glory. Let's keep the windows open and have somewhat clear understanding of global scenario. How can we assimilate the best of the technological advancements, without destroying uniqueness?

India has tremendous potential; she has the ability to achieve the cherished goal in making the nation a 'super power', provided her leaders introspect to accomplish the task. What we need is a political party committed to deliver. We need a leadership with strong determination and political will.

As the great sage Swami Vivekananda had said, *"All power is within you. You can do anything. Believe in that."* Yes, the power lies in the people, in the inner sanctum sanctorum of Mother India. What is needed is to ignite the spark and Mother India would rise in her full glory.

This is the commitment of BJP-led NDA government at the Centre to the Nation and to the People. The party under the charismatic leadership of Narendra Modi got a massive mandate. We are optimistic that it would leave an indelible mark and work whole-heartedly for a stable, strong, visionary and progressive India.

As Sri Ma Sarada spouse of the most revered and admired Sri Ramakrishna Paramahansa had once said that India had become the symbolic representation of all the difficulties of modern mankind, but India will also be the land of her resurrection to higher and truer life. We believe, Modi will leave no stone unturned to fulfill the dreams of 1.60 billion Indians.

Today, India is blessed with the rare capacity and opportunity of Democracy, Demography and Demand. If we could consolidate and harness them, we should reach the heights which India deserves. The biggest reason for the sorry state of affairs is bad intentions on the part of those, who have ruled the country for six decades. And that is where it would show the first difference.

For the BJP-led government, the goal of the policies and practices would be—

Ek Bharat, Shreshtha Bharat!

Even after nearly seven decades of our independence from the grip of the oppressed and ruthless British, the country has not been able to realise its inherent vitality, the sense of time and the will to act. As a result, in spite of being the oldest civilisation and a young Republic, we are engulfed by a multi-dimensional crisis. A crisis, which has encompassed all walks of life. The rising disparities, social and communal divide and terrorism leading to a fractured society has been worsening the situation rapidly. The present crisis is the result of this confusion and disconnect from the seekings and sensibilities of the people. This is worse confounded by the weak and spineless leadership of the UPA Government. The tragedy is further heightened by their failure to diagnose the malady and find the remedy. Instead of creating a socio-economic and political paradigm of governance drawn from the civilisational consciousness of India, the leaders tried to follow whatever was being practiced in the Western country.

It's an irony that, we have wasted more than half of a century. Many countries, even with smaller size and lesser resources have surpassed us in development parameters. Another reason for this is that the governance in these decades was marred by lack of trust, leading to excessive controls. It was also marked by lack of openness in the government and the lack of people's participation. This has led to concentration of power in a few hands and lack of transparency breeding corruption and nepotism on a massive scale.

The so-called 'liberalisation' came into being in 1990s. It was presumed to be a half-hearted approach. It didn't work because the rest of the eco-system remained the same. However, the beginning of the 21st century showed some light under the NDA rule. India started being reckoned as an economic superpower. The six-year rule of NDA had given the nation many firsts, building her image among the international community.

However, many of the hopes, potentials and projects have not been fully realised in the subsequent years. The situation started worsening and missed a historic opportunity when UPA returned to power in 2004.

The people of India were fed up with cynical politics and endemic corruption of the erstwhile govetrnment, gave an unprecedented mandate in favour BJP and its allies. Narendra Modi deserved encomiums from all quarters. His decisive leadership helped his party regain the power at the Centre for new beginning and new hope.

Mentioning past deserves equal importance if we see it in real perspective. We find India as the most ancient civilisation of the world. She has always been looked upon by the world as a land of wealth and wisdom. India has been credited to have developed, apart from philosophy and mathematics, science and technology of a very high order. She had attracted scholars from all over the world. Al-Andalusi, a Spanish scholar in the 11th century, in his monumental work 'Tabaqat al-Umam' had discussed the state of science in different countries. He writes, "The first nation to have cultivated science is India... India is known for wisdom people. Over many centuries, all the kings of the past have recognised the ability of Indians in all branches of knowledge." Andalusi further states, "Indians, as known to all nations for many centuries, are the metal (essence) of wisdom, the source of fairness and objectivity. They are the people of sublime pensiveness, universal apologues and useful and rare inventions."

India's contribution to the march of civilisation goes back to several thousand years before the Christian era. From the Vedas to Upanishads and Gautam—the Buddha and Mahavira—the 24th Jain Tirthankara and then to Kautilya and Chandra Gupta and down up to the eighteenth century, India was respected for her flourishing economy, trade, commerce and culture. It had an international outreach from Korea to Arabia, from Bamiyan to Borobudur and beyond. Before the advent of Britishers, Indian goods were internationally recognised for their quality and craftsmanship. India had a much bigger role and presence in industry and manufacturing than any nation in Europe or Asia. She had a well-developed banking system and equally renowned businessmen, along with its financiers, who were contributing to create flourishing and progressive economy.

According to Sunderland, India was also one of the greatest shipbuilding nations and consequently had an access to international markets. Indian prosperity held the world enthralled. It was this wealth which attracted the foreigners—from Alexander to the Britishers. Historical records establish the level of progress and prosperity attained before the advent of Europeans. Indian advancement in mathematics, astronomy, physics and chemistry along with the biological sciences has been well-recognised. India was a land of abundance, prosperity, affluence, a land of sharing and caring living in perfect harmony and peace with the nature. From ancient times, almost all religions practiced in different parts of the world, have existed peacefully in India and will continue to do so. India thus provides the most ennobling experience in spiritual co-existence.

The BJP's prime ministerial candidate Narendra Modi recognises that no nation could chart out its domestic or foreign policies unless it has a clear understanding about itself, its history, its roots, its strengths and failings. In a highly mobile and globalised world, it is imperative for a nation to know its roots that provide sustenance to its people.

Indian freedom struggle, which was inspired by Tilak, Gandhi, Aurobindo, Patel, Bose, Bhagat Singh and others, had a clear vision of the civilisational consciousness of India. These leaders had directed the freedom movement, keeping the Indian ways and thoughts reflecting in their action. They had a vision to reconstruct the political and economic institutions of India as a continuum of civilisational consciousness, which made India one country, one people and one nation.

After achieving independence, the leaders at the helm of affairs lost the spirit and the vision, which the freedom movement had evoked. They discarded the vision and adopted the institutional framework of administration created by the Britishers which was quite alien to India's world-view. It is unfortunate that these leaders could not comprehend India's inner vitality, which was the main force responsible for India's survival despite several attacks and prolonged foreign rule and thus, failed to rekindle the spirit of India.

Now, it's time for the new Prime Minister of India Narednra Modi to gain the confidence of electorate who reposed their faith on his charismatic leadership on the spirit of the democratic value and the path would be *Sabka Saath and Sabka Vikas.*

This book is based on the ethos and spirit of Prime Minister Narendra Modi's development plank and Make in India Drive. His meteoric success in the Indian politics, termed as 'phenomenon'. It was evident during the 2014 General Elections, when the BJP-led NDA got absolute majority and the BJP itself got a clear majority on its own.

Notwithstanding his stupendous success in Gujarat as a successful CM, Namo caught the attention of the people of India with such short period of time that made the all opposition parties including Congress awestruck. They were simply clueless and bereft of ideas. What went wrong especially the Congress-led UPA, who were annihilated?

In this discourse, the successful implementation of Gujarat Model in the context of India and PM Modi's dream to take the nation to the next level is discussed. Apart from reviving economy, taming inflation, the border issues with Pakistan and China are the major concern. Though Modi government had started a noble attempt to call the SAARC heads of the governments in his official swearing ceremony, still it would need extraordinaire yet cautious efforts to have a durable and robust foeign policy for peaceful relation with China and Pakistan. Aside, India has to make strenuous efforts to establish good relation with US and other foreign countries.

Other factors like internal security (Maoist and Terrorism), education and creating job oportunities, FDI, problems in social sectors and promoting agriculture, power, transport, industry and trade have been discussed keeping with the pace of the present government's flag-ship programmes. In that context, this book is very useful and readable for all.

1 Humble Beginning

Overview

Narendra Damodardas Modi, popularly known as Narendra Modi a believer in the true philosophy of Hinduism and a member of the RSS is the 15th and current Prime Minister of India. Modi, a leader of the BJP, served as the chief minister of Gujarat from 2000–14. He is currently the Member of Parliament (MP) from the Varanasi parliamentary constituency.

Modi was a key strategist for the success of BJP during 1995 and 1998 Gujarat state electioneering. He became Chief Minister of Gujarat in October 2001 and served longer in that position than anyone else to date. Modi was a major campaign figure during the 2009 general election, when the BJP-led National Democratic Alliance lost to the Congress-led UPA. He led the BJP in the 2014 general election, which resulted with an outright majority for the party in the Lok Sabha (the Lower House of the Indian Parliament) – the last time that any party had secured an outright majority in the Lok Sabha was in 1984.

His administration has been criticised for the incidents surrounding the 2002 Gujarat riots. However, Modi has been praised for his economic policies, creating an environment for a high rate of economic growth in Gujarat. But his administration has been criticised for failing to make significant positive impact upon the human development of the state.

Early Life

Narendra was born on September 17,1950 to a family of grocers, belonging to the backward Ghanchi-Teli (oil-pressing) community, in Vadnagar in Mehsana district of erstwhile Bombay Province (present-day Gujarat), India. He was the third of four children born to Damodardas Mulchand Modi and his wife, Heeraben. The Modi family originally hailed from the Navdotra village in Banaskantha distict. In the latter years of nineteenth century, a person by the name of Maganlal Ranchhoddas left home to set up a grocery store in

Vadnagar. Maganlal had a son, Mulchand, who took over his father's small shop. Moolchand's son, Damodardas, was born in 1915. Modi was the third of six children born to Damodardas Mulchand Modi and his wife, Heeraben.

Modi's Siblings

All the Modi children were born in a neighbourhood in Vadnagar, where many other families belonging to Modi community have lived. The eldest brother, Som, born in 1944, became a sanitary inspector in the public health department. Now, a retired health oficer and runs an old-age home in Ahmedabad. The second borther, Amrit, born in 1946, became a turner in a private company in Odhav. His only sister, Vasanti, was born in 1955 and his two younger brothers, Prahlad and Pankaj were born in 1955 and 1958 respectively but neither of them went for higher studies. Pankaj runs a fair price shop in Ahmedabad. He is also an activist fighting for the interests of fair-price shop owner. Pankaj works in the state information department, Gandhinagar.

Decrepit House

The house Narendra was born in and brought up was built by brick and mud. It was forty feet long and twelve feet wide, and had three rooms. The front-room served as a bedroom and sitting room. The same room, partitioned off with a sheet, doubled up as a bathing area. The room aside served as a kitchen and prayer room, where the idols and photos of household deities were kept in a little nitche. Drinking water was stored in the kitchen corner. The third adjacent room was used to store dung cakes and wood that fired the hearth. It was not unusual for three rooms to be filled with smoke at the time of cooking. As none of the rooms had windows, the house was dark and soiled. A kerosene lamp had to be kept lit throughout the day, which added to the smoky atmosphere within the house. The only opening was the main door that led out to an extremely narrow lane. The heat was unbearable during summer. The flooring was made of bamboo which his mother has covered with mud and cow dung. There was no bathing and toilet facility. The entire family had to go out in the fields to relieve themselves. They went to nearby lake to bathe, wash their clothes and enjoy swimming. Water for cooking and drinking had to be fetched from a well nearby. Even though, these daily chores made life full of struggle for his family, still they emerged unscathed.

School and College Life

Narendra did his primary school-level education at a government-run institution. He enrolled later in the Bhagavatcharya Narayancharya High School (BNHS). He helped his father sell tea at Vadnagar railway station. As a child and as a teenager, he ran a tea stall with his brother near a bus terminus. In 1967, he completed his schooling in Vadnagar, where a teacher described him as being an average student, but a keen debater with an interest in theatrics. That interest has influenced how he now projects himself in politics. At the age of eight, Modi came in contact with RSS. He began attending its local *shakhas* where he came in contact with ***Lakshmanrao Inamdar***, popularly known as ***Vakil Saheb***, who is known as his political ***guru*** and mentor. Inamdar inducted Modi as a *Balswayamsevak*, a junior cadet in RSS. During his morning exercise session at the Keri pitha *shakha*, he also came in contact with

Vasant Gajendragadkar and Nathalal Jaghda, Jan Sangh leaders, who later founded the BJP's Gujarat state unit in 1980. Modi's parents arranged his marriage as a child, keeping with the traditions of Ghanchi caste. He was engaged at the age of 13 to Jashodaben Chimanlal. The couple got married by the time he was 17. They spent very little time together and were soon estranged. Modi often decided to pursue an itinerant life. The marriage as such never consummated. Modi kept the marriage secret for most of his career, acknowledging the existence of his wife when filing his nomination for a parliamentary seat in the 2014 general elections.

According to Kishore Makwana's *Common Man Narendra Modi,* published in 2014, after leaving home at 17, he went to Ramakrishna Mission Ashram in Rajkot and then to the Belur Math near Kolkata. Later, he went to Guwahati, joined another ashram, established by Swami Vivekananda in Almora, in the Himalayan foothills. Two years after, he returned to Vadnagar, after a brief halt at house, Modi left again for Ahmedabad, where he lived and worked in a tea stall run by his uncle. He again came in contact with Lakshmanrao Inamdar, who was then based at Hedgewar Bhavan, the RSS headquarters in the city. He worked in the staff canteen of Gujarat State Road Transport Corporation, until he became the full–time *pracharak* (campaigner) for RSS in 1970. In 1978, Modi graduated with an Extramural degree through Distance Education in political science from Delhi University. In 1983, while remaining as a *pracharak* in the RSS, he completed his Master's degree in political science from Gujarat University. He continues to visit Belur Math and talks about his reverence for the Ramakrishna Mission.

His Mentors

Mentors Role in Shaping His Career: A lot of people in the RSS have done a good job for him in his formative years. A few key persons from Sangh pariwar have played a significant role in shaping his skill, character and personality. They nurtured him with utmost care by extending him support so that some day he could take the mantle of the country. It is true that Modi's deep involvement in the ethos of Saffron spirit has made him a force to reckon with when he was summoned to Delhi to take the responsibility of the BJP party in the capacity of a national general secretary. The then prime minister of India Atal Behari Vajpayee and his deputy L.K. Advani realised his tremendous potential as he had the knack of transforming adversity to the benefit of the party. After serving the party in various roles including the party spokesman, he was assigned the difficult task of taking the job of chief ministership of Gujarat from Keshubhai Patel when the south-western border state was passing through the crisis due to internal feud. After that he did not look back. Now, he is elected Prime Minister of India after serving Gujarat as the longest ever chief minister. It is important to mention how his career was built brick by brick in his formative years in the RSS. His single-minded devotion and involvement in the safron outfit with dedicated persons of Sangh pariwar. It is also important to note how the RSS taught him the management skills.

RSS Teaches Management Skills

Where did Gujarat's longest-serving chief minister pick up his dazzling style of governance? He is though by most in India's industry, and increasing numbers of the population in general, to possess a *mantra* of unusual management, if not unique and effective. According to Modi, his training was in the management school presuming to be as good as Harvard and Stanford. Modi sketches the characters of men who taught him what he knew, after he joined the RSS as a child and their manner of functioning and credits them for his success.

India's identity cannot be limited to the style of government, its politics and its power. We must also consider its cultural heritage for wholesome picture. India's *rishis,* saints and *sadhus, acharyas* and *dharma-gurus*, wise men and scientists, teachers and those who serve society have appreciated contributed to its identity. For thousands of years, in one form or another, this tradition has come down and benefitted. For generations, this has been so. It is true even today in our modern times. If we are observant, we can spot selfless men, making their quiet contribution in some corner of our blessed land. In 20th century India, one significant effort was mounted for service to the nation. This was the RSS. Dr Hedgewar founded the institution and began the work of serving the motherland through character-building in society.

Today, the finest management lessons are taught in places like IIM, Harvard and Stanford. Specific skills and character-forming things are being taught. We must place these institutions and their western models against the RSS's Indian model and study the similarities and differences. The institution's speciality owes to penance, faith, commitment, sacrifice, persistence and acquiring power or influence. As a *Swayamsevak* of the RSS, Modi was fortunate to have imbibed these values. Modi says, for sure what was best in him, finest in him, was due in larger part to training with the RSS. In this cultural journey, there are many men, small in the eyes of the world but giants in reality, whom he has had the opportunity and privilege to learn from. Their affection, their abilities helped him along. For lack of time, he failed to pay his respects to men through reminiscence. What they have done—without expectation of anything, having offered life and all its years to our society—this tradition of theirs is not very well-known in society. It is very rare that these men and their work are being noticed. The fragrance of their efforts perfumes the air we breathe.

Organisation Skill

Little is known of the two years that Narendra spent travelling, probably in the Himalayas. He resumed selling tea upon his return. He left home for second time, went to Ahmedabad to uncle, Babubhai, who ran a canteen at the state transport office. He served there for a while, determined to be some use. In his spare time, he attended discourses on social, political and spiritual matters. However, they did not impress him. It was at this point in life that he inclined fully towards the RSS, with which he was familiar since childhood.

True that the RSS came into existence in 1925, but it had not spread its wings in Gujarat. The Vadnagar *sakha* was set up in 1944. The *sakha* ran very well between 1944 and 1948. Following the assassination of Mahatma Gandhi in 1948, its reputation took a nose dive. The development did not stop of RSS-run *sakhas*. He never heard anyone discuss Mahatma Gandhi's murder. The most talked about name within the RSS was that of Chhatrapati Shivaji. Amongst such activities, the RSS received massive support because of ideological appeal. In a sense, it was Baroda that was the epicentre of the RSS. The organisation had witnesed lot of upheavel with changing hands of its reign, Madhkarrao Bhagwat—a *prant-pracharak* (full-time worker) took the charge and laid the foundation of the RSS in the state. Rajpal Puri, a doyen from Sindh province, succeeded Bhagwat in the wake of partition. He did not last long, but was succeeded by Laxmidhar Inamdar. He led the outfit in Gujarat for three long decades and made it a force to reckon with. It was Inamdar who came to be known as Vakil Saheb and trained Narendra in the early years of his apprenticeship in the hierarchy. Indeed, being influenced by the ideas and philosophy of Vakil Saheb, Narendra went on to become his *manas putra.* Though, Narendra was already familiar with the RSS even before Inamdar enetered his life. It was Inamdar who turned out to be a decisive influence in Narendra's life.

In 1971, when Narendra proved his sense of commitment to values through *Satyagraha* as a possible solution to the problems; the case of Bangladesh and the struggle of East Bengal Muslims and Hindus against the tyranny and genocide by the Pakistani army mobilised him. He was arrested and sent to Tihar Jail, but released thereafter. In 1972, he started working as an RSS *pracharak* formally. Narendra left his uncle to work under Vakil Saheb. He used to do all kinds of activities ranging from cooking to scavenging. It was around that time he started developing interest in studying seriously on the advice from Vakil Saheb. He got admitted to Open Delhi University and graduated in due course. Narendra was assigned additional duties of routine correspondence of the Sangh at *prantik prant* office. After a year, he was given the responsibility of helping the families of *Swayamsevaks* reaching Ahmedabad for medical treatment in the wake of riots.

A workaholic, Narendra was entrusted with the duty of journey reservation for Sangh officials, who were on tour for organisational work. This called for constant communication with rail and bus transport officials and soon, he was on the firendliest man with all of them. In this process, he learnt one of the most important lessons—how to get things done. He organised the Gujarat *sammelan* of VHP under the guidance of Vanikarji which enriched his organisational skill.

Almost every kind of work was a learning experience for Narendra. He always preferred to observe, analyse and added to his valuable study of human character. His eagerness to accept challenge, anew always stood him apart from the rest. His life was full of struggle from the beginning. Perseverance, organising skill and analytical mind facilitated him to take a giant stride in his political career. Until he became a full–time *pracharak* (propagandist) of the RSS in 1970, he worked in the staff canteen of Gujarat State Road Transport Corporation. He had been involved with the RSS as a volunteer from the age of eight and had come into contact with Vasant Gajendragadkar and Nathalal Jaghda, leaders of the Jan Sangh who later founded the BJP's Gujarat state unit. After Modi had received some training in Nagpur, which was a pre-requisite for taking-up an official position in the Sangh Parivar, he was made incharge of Sangh's student wing ABVP in Gujarat. Modi was responsible for vigil and covert distribution of pamphlets during the Emergency.

Early Political Career

Narendra became a member of the RSS after the Indo-Pakistani War of 1971. The RSS had launched ABVP under the guidance of Prof Balraj Madhok in 1948 which helped Jan Sangh sprout. In the meantime, few political parties are formed like MGIP (Maha Gujarat Janata Parishad, PSP (Praja Socialist Party) and Swatantra Party. These parties had limited support and could not do much. The fact that RSS had a distinct ideology went beyond the immediacy of gaining independence from British, which made it survive. The RSS, ABVP survived along with Jan Sangh because of its strong and self-sustaining Hindu society. Modi's interest was noticed in social work. He took part in *go-raksha* movement in 1967. He participated in movements' against inflation, price rise and issues affecting common man. His role as a *pracharak* gained gound when Jan Sangh spread its wing.

Through Navnirman movement in Gujarat, Jan Sangh gave a tough time to ruling Congress-I at that time under the leadership of Jayaprakash Narayan (JP), whom Narendra met and understood his ideals and views and his spending with the magnetic personality like JP stood him in a good stead. Jayprakash Narayan was a civil servant (IAS) of 1952 cadre; Navnirman movement was so massive that forced then chief minister of Gujarat to resign. The first ever non-Congress-I government was formed with Babubhai Jashbhai Patel as the chief minister in early 1975.

Indira Gandhi clamped the Emergency in 1975. All hell broke across the entire country. Leading opposition leaders Jayaprakash Narayan, L.K. Advani, Charan Singh and A.B. Vajpayee were imprisoned. The RSS geared up to fight against odds. Under Laxmanraoji Inamdar, it was decided that an underground movement mobilised to fight the situation. The RSS Swayamsevaks spread them throughout the state with the message of non-violent resistance.

Like other RSS workers, Narendra went into hiding. He met with the chairman of Socialist Party George Fernandes. He had been assigned the job of taking care of *Swayamsevaks* and others in the Sangh parivar. An underground worker, he had to do various disguises frequently. On one occasion, he donned the garb of a *sanyasi* and on another he grew a beard and look like a Sikh with long hair and turban. He played safe and familiarised himself with the role he would assign beforehand. It was difficult for an underground worker to meet someone in jail. He managed to act as a consort to a lady who frequented the jail and succeeded to meet Shanker Singh Veghela and Vishnu Pandya. His toughest task was raising funds to help the families of RSS. The elite were not ready to help, but the common men came forward with meagre. And many apolitical persona opposed the Emergency were willing to donate on a regular basis. Narendra apart from bringing out Muktwani—a small underground newspaper, published full-length commentaries on the state Emergency and the philosophy of democracy. Few articles which created ripples in the political world were published under great risk. These include *Story of two emergencies, Twenty-one point deceptions, Emergency X-rayed, Proposed constitutional reforms, Review of a decade, When disobedience to law is a duty, Indian press gagged, Anatomy of fascism and nail Indira's lies.*

Narendra needed the support of families who had no fear of consequences. He spotted such families throughout the state. It was an experience which helped him a lot in his later part of the political career. Those who came forward to help were firm believers whose real cause was struggle for values. People trusted leaders like Jayaprakash Narayan, Sarvodya workers and the RSS workers, who they believed were above political ambition.

During those 21 months of Emergency, the distance between the Sarvodaya and the Sangh found lessened. The proces that started with the Navanirman movement gained teeth during the emergency. Narendra did what he was asked. He has proved to be a disciplined soldier during 21 months emergency for the RSS. After the turbulent period, the startling announcement of the Lok Sabha polls came on Janurary 18th, 1977. The Indian National Congress was defeated. The very next day the Emergency was lifted and hundred RSS workers across the country were freed. Narendra experienced hardship and the real face of political ambience. This was the first decade of his public life and the third decade of Gujarat as a state. He had written a book on the history of Gujarat, titled '*Sangharsh maa Gujarat*' (Gujarat in Hardship) during the Emergency.

During anti-Emergeny, one of the duties Narendra had been allocated was to maintain links between Indians abroad and visist home. He became a *vibhag pracharak* in 1978, at relatively young age. The *vibhag* consisted of six districts, namely rural Vadodara, Panchmahal, Dahod, Anand, Kheda and Vadodara city. At the same time, he was appointed as a *praant padadhikari* (regional head) and was allocated the responsibility of *praant sabha vyavastha pramukh* (joint president of regional organisations). Narendra's talents as an organiser were being recognised. Withing two years, he was apponited *sambhag pracharak*, with jurisdiction over the vibhags of Surat and Vadodara, while his field extended from central and south Gujarat's Kheda districts to Valsad's Umergaon.

Following the death of Prant pracharak Keshavrao Deshmukh on March 2nd, 1981, Narendra was asked to stay at Gujarat headquarters at Ahemdabad to maintain close liasion with Akhil Hind Vidyarthi Parishad, Bharatiya Kisan Sangh, Vishwa Hindu Parishad, Samutkarsh and its publications wing, and the weekly *Sadhana*. The top echelons of the RSS were very pleased with 31-yr-old Narendra's dedication and efficiency. Whatever task he undertook, he completed with full vigour and zeal. A dam on the Machchu River in Morbi broke in 1979 and nearly 1800 people died and the whole city was devastated. The Sangh started massive relief work which lasted almost a year. He ensured the satisfactory rehabilitation work on time.

Sanskardham is a secondary school with a difference. This school offers a comprehensive training and development programme for students. Skills are not taught in isolation but in a holistic way. Everything is planned and designed in such a manner that there is ample room for a child to learn to be expressive. A school based on thoughts and ideas of Vakil Saheb's dream. Apart from the prescribed curriculum, there were other activities that keep the students active –yoga, karate, music, moral education, horse-riding, computer skills and so on. Right from the beginning, Narendra was involved with the growth and operation of the school.

Sanskardham was Narendra's tribute to his mentor and preceptor, Vakil Saheb. He wrote two inspirational songs tuned and sung during opening stint.

In 1977 general elections, the rise of the Janata Party were hailed by most Indians, especially those who had suffered greatly during the Emergency, as a 'revolution by the ballot box'. The Janata government did not last long due to internal-bickerings at the hands of Morarji Desai with successor Charan Singh. Charan Singh did not even attend the Lok Sabha. His premiership lasted for a mere 24 days as Indira Gandhi withdrew her support.

The infighting in the Janata Party at the Centre led to its fall, in Gujarat the intra-party feud rarely came to the fore. Indira Gandhi avenged the Janata Party on returning to power and ordered the dissolution of assemblies in nine states. When the elections were held in 1980 in Gujarat, the Congress party regained power. The Janata Party barely managed to get 22 seats.

BJP Formed: Seeing this change within a short period, Jan Sangh decided to retain its indentity, rechristened as—Bharatiya Janata Party (BJP) in 1980. Keshubhai Patel took the reign as president of the Gujarat unit.

The Congress government in Gujarat introduced a reservation policy. The chief minister Madhavsinh Solanki classified 82 castes and communities as socio-educational. It recommended five steps for their advancement reservation of ten per cent seats in educational institutes and government jobs. It led to agitation and massive riots as the upper castes became highly embarrassed. Inflation and price rise aggravated the situation. Consequently, furious riots erupted from one end of Gujarat to another.

A serious tragedy took place in 1984. Indira Gandhi was assassinated by her own bodyguards. The entire nation was convulsed with grief and anger. More than five thousand Sikh men, women and children were massacred across the country, more so in New Delhi. Rajiv Gandhi was brought to power on sympathy vote. The Congress captured 24 out of 26 seats the Lok Sabha, while BJP won just two seats in Gujarat. The anti-reservation was resumed in full cry. It soon converted into anti-Muslim inferno. The state was in full turmoil. Some 237 people were killed and a thousand were injured. Production loss and property damages worth over Rs 2200 cr were reported. Communal hatred expected to disappear after independence, erupted with unabated fury. More than 30 thousands riots took place across the country where the Congress party was in power. The Congress party bore the brunt of unabated communal frenzy, price rise and corruption. It lost to the Janata Dal-BJP alliance in 1990, headed by Chimanbhai Patel in saddle.

By 1992, the people took note of Narendra as a political force to reckon with in Gujarat. The US government invited him to the country as a youth leader. The party recognised his organisational skills and Narendra was summoned to Delhi and asked to take over organising the party as Secretary. In a sense, Narendra had come of political age. He took over his duties in right earnest. In 1992, the assembly elections were to be held in five states—UP, MP, Rajasthan, Himachal Pradesh and Assam. Outside Gujarat, this was Narendra's first political task. It was a great learning experience for him. It exposed him to geopolitical leadership of different states. Every task that he was given, found converted into a capacity-building exercise for the party.

The years of Congress rule in Gujarat were marked by inefficiency and recklessness. At the end, the man who was to bring peace and normalcy therein was one reviled by the English media in recent history—Narenda Modi.

Emergency: The Prime Minister Indira Gandhi declared a state of the Emergency for 27 months. Political opponents were jailed and political outfits including RSS were outlawed. Modi went underground and evaded arrest occasionally disguised as a Sikh, a saint, an elderly man distributing booklets against the Central government in Delhi. He kept constant vigil by covert distribution of Sangh's pamphlets.

Modi participated in the movement against the Emergency under

Jayaprakash Narayan. He was made the general secretary of the Gujarat Lok Sangharsh Samiti. He was to co-ordinate between the state and activists. He wrote a book titled *Sangharsh ma Gujarat* (Gujarat's struggle) in Gujarati which chronicles events, anecdotes personal experiences. The RSS outfit annointed Modi to the BJP in 1985. Shankersinh Vaghela and Keshubhai Patel were the heavy weights in Gujarat unit, when Modi rose to prominence after organising Murli Manohar Joshi's Kanyakumari-*Srinagar Ekta Yatra* (Journey for Unity) in 1991. In 1988, Modi was elected as organising secretary of BJP's Gujarat unit, marking his formal entry into mainstream politics. As secretary, his electoral strategy was central to BJP's victory in the 1995 state elections.

In November 1995, Narendra was elected National Secretary of BJP. He was transferred to New Delhi where he was responsible for the party activities in five states namely Haryana, Himachal Pradesh, Punjab, Chandigarh and Jammu and Kashmir. Vaghela defected from BJP after he lost 1996 Lok Sabha elections. Modi was elevated as the general secretary in May 1998. He favoured supporters of Patel against those loyal to Vaghela, in an attempt to end up the factional division within the party in shortlisting candidates for 1998 assembly polls. His strategies were credited as being kingmaker to win elections.

Role in Gujarat: As a youth, he became a member of the ABVP, a student body involved in anti-corruption. After having worked for full time, he was nominated as its representative in the BJP. Modi was a campaigner during his college years and took the task of encouraging party members. Partnering with Shankersingh Vaghela, Modi began a strong cadre-base organisation in Gujarat. He came from a humble background with unique lifestyle. He had the reputation of being workaholic and introvert. He has tried to change his image from that of a Hindu Nationalist politician to that of sincere and able administrator.

The party began getting political attention and formed a coalition government in April 1990. The BJP returned to power in 1995. Modi was responsible for the Somnath to Ayodhya Rath Yatra followed by trek from Kanyakumari in the South to Kashmir in the north. A careful observation of his rise to the national podium would evince how he remained glued to his fundamentals—continuing agitation during nationwide Emergency, organising Murli Manohar Joshi's Ekta Yatra (journey for unity), and impressing everyone with electoral strategy ahead of the 1995 state elections. As BJP made inroads, Modi relished his newly ordained post. The workaholic and loyal 'sevak' moved to manage the activities acros five states—Haryana, Punjab, Chandigarh, Jammu and Kashmir and Himachal Pradesh through three summers.

Babri Masjid Demolished: In 1992, Chimanbhai Patel was the chief minister of Gujarat. He had a good rapport with the Union government, P.V. Narasimha Rao. He emerged as a bulllwark blocking BJP's avalanche. It was during his tenure the Babri Majjid was demolished in 1992.

The repurcussions in Gujarat was terrible. The maniacal Hindu-Muslim riot broke out all over the state. Surat was the worst affected by the horrific bloodbath. Chimanbhai came to be widely suspected of being in league with shaddy characters with blew of allegations of him being corrupt. Amidst growing lawlessness, a senior Congress-I worker, lawmaker Rauf Walilullah was murdered in broad day light. Things inevitable happened which changed the state of development, Chimanbhai died of massive heart attack in 1994 and the senior most members in the cabinet Chhabildas Mehta assumed office. Narendra Modi was ready to face the elections in 1995 Assembly polls. To gain an upper hand at the polls, the BJP had decided to train workers at every level. In a large-scale training programme, about 1.5 lakh workers, who had to handle about 28,000 polling booths, were given rigorous training on how to handle voters with unexpected problems. The programme was highly sucessful due to his multiple skills.

Having done poorly in the elections in various states, 1995 assembly pols in Gujarat turned out to be a major success for the BJP. The factionalism in the Congress party in the state also a factor and the entry of BSP, led by Mayawati did not make it easier for the Congress. BJP won 121 out of 182 seats. It was a quantum jump in popularity for the party. Never before in history had any party made ventured. BJP won in almost 98 per cent units and some districts panchayat elections, the party's victory was hundred per cent. Media and political analysts named Modi 'the architect of BJP's victory' in Gujarat in Assembly and the local elections. However, BJP's very success turned out to be a problem in the portrayal of Charishmatic leader.

The BJP was formed in 1980 when the post of general secretary was abolished in Jan Sangh. The post was revived to strenghthen the party and Narendra, the organising secretary of the Gujarat unit, being a *pracharak*, streamlined the party machinery. There were apparently personality clashes. Kanshiram Rana preferred Suresh Mehta as state general secretary; RSS took it as an afront to its authority. The situation compelled Rana to renominate Narendra for the same post and was endorsed by party president L. K. Advani.

Keshubhai was elected as CM of Gujarat. Intra-rivalry in the party mobilised Shankarsinh to project Narendra in bad light. But that did not deter his spirit. He continued to be busy to train party workers as a part of the organisational work. As many as ten thousand elected representatives received training for Municipl elections. In the Municipal Corporations elections, BJP won six seats and eighteen of the nineteen Zila Parishad Boards and in Surat, the party won all the seats. The feud in the party continued between Shankarsinh and Keshubhai. Narendra was made a scapegoat for this discontentment which forced him to resign. The rift widened. Shankarsinh, who had perosnal clout, political skill and enviable public relations, failed to abide by party discipline. He defected from the parent party to form Rashtriya Janata Party (RJP). His action proved reasonable for all revolts. Dragging Narendra's name was just a ploy by Shankarsinh to achieve his own goal.

Narendra had been appointed National general secretary of the BJP on November 20 in 1995. Since then Delhi became his centre of work. In 1996, under Advani's leadership a team was formed in which Narendra was given the tough assignment. His main responsibility was organising the party in Haryana, Himachal Pradesh, Chandigarh, Punjab and Jammu and Kashmir. Being a true workaholic, he enoyed it. He kept moving from one place to another, met people and organised meetings. The party provides him the task of preparing workers. In the subsequent assembly polls for all the states, the BJP was to succeed beyond estimation. He was quite clear about one thing—the need for discipline. Such was the devotion to work that in a span of two years, he took over Maha Mantri at the national level on May 1998. He rose to the occasion as courageous, effective and daring.

In the capacity of a national general secretary, Narendra worked diligently at organising his party in five states. The *Chittisinghpura massacre,* shooting to death of 36 Sikhs on 20th March, 2000, in the Anantnag district of the State of Jammu and Kashmir in India when the ex-president of US Bill Clinton visited the state, shook the nation. The Indian government asserts the role of an Islamic Fundamentalist militant group Lashkar-e-Taiba which is based in Muridke in Pakistan and is listed on US State Department list of Foreign Terrorist Organisations, Mohammad Suhail Malik of Sialkot, Pakistan. Narendra as a party in-charge of the area went to the Valley to see whether he could extend possible help to the victims' family. It proved his attitude on a fatalistic approach where nothing mattered except doing his duty.

Narendra was doing his job to the best possible way what he could in the capacity of a party in-charge in five states. In Punjab, he spent about six months when Municipal Corporation elections were due in Chandigarh. It helped the BJP capture 17 seats out of 20 and MP of that area—Pawan Kumar commented that despite there was no presence of the Sangh, BJP if gained such a good success, it was due to the untiring efforts of Narendra Modi.

The Kargil War: Kargil War was an armed conflict between India and Pakistan. It took place between May and July 1999 in the Kargil district of Kashmir and elsewhere along the Line of Control (LOC). The conflict is also referred to as Operation Vijay, Indian operation to clear the Kargil sector.

The cause of the war was infiltration of Pakistani soldiers and Kashmiri militants on the Indian side of the LOC, the *de facto* border between the states. Pakistan blamed the fighting entirely on independent Kashmiri insurgent. The documents left behind by casualties and later statements by Pak Premier and Chief of Army Staff showed the involvement of Pak paramilitary forces, led by General Altaf Rasheed. The Indian Army, supported by the Indian Air Force, recaptured majority of positions on the Indian side infiltrated. The Pakistani forces withdrew from the remaining Indian positions along the LOC after international parleys.

Narendra's obsession with duty motivated him to carry out unusual plans. He happened to be in Kargil when the war broke but stayed in and made carryon baggage. He did not do it for the sake of leadership but volunteered the cause on being 'son of soil'. During that crucial period, he took the onus of addressing the media. He grabbed this opportunity and emerged as good debater in various TV sessions quite non-challantly. Narendra was in demand during Agra summit between the Prime Minister Atal Behari Vajpayee and Pakistan's president Parvez Musharraf won the confidence for his good media handling at the time of Kargil conflict to prove his responsibility.

The National Democratic Alliance (NDA) is a centre-right coalition of Indian political parties. The BJP led thirteen constituent parties, formed its first government in 1998 and the coalition was in power till 2004, it was left to Narendra to invite the chief ministers of all BJP-ruled states to come to Delhi for the oath-taking ceremony. At that time, Narendra did a remarkable job and earned applaud for his organisation skill with the BJP performed well in the elections, he was sought after by many internatonal capitals. A Foreign Minister of a Commonwealth country inviting the General Secretary of the BJP was an unusual act in any case. Narendra visited Brisbane, Australia in 2000-01, at the invitation of Foreign Minister Alexander Donner, where the CHOGM

(Commonwealth Heads of Government Meeting) was going to be held later in the year. He met leaders of the Labour Party and the Liberal Party, and discussed the working of the political system in Australia with them. He discussed prospects of joint ventures between the two countries with Donnner. The latter appreciated the growing power of India in Information Technology (IT), bio-technology and yoga. Australia had made a good progress in the field of eco-tourism and he also visisted Frazer Island to make a study on this subject.

Narendra visited Malaysia in 2001. The Prime Minister of Malaysia Dr Mahathir Mohammed, and president of the United Malays National Organisation (UMNO), the ruling party of the country, in a rare gesture, he was invited to the National Assembly on UMNO. A pact was signed between the two countries to construct railway line therein at expenditure of $18 billion.

Gujarat Earthquake: Earthquake shook on January 26, 2001, 52nd Republic Day, and lasted for over two minutes. The epicentre was about 9 km south-southwest of the village of Chobari in Bhachau Taluka of Kutch district. The quake reached a magnitude of between 7.6 and 7.7 on the Richter scale. The quake took toll around 20,000 people (including 18 in south eastern Pakistan), injuring another 167,000 and destroyed nearly 400,000 homes. This was an intraplate quake, one that occurred at a distance from an active plate boundary, so the area was not well prepared. The shock waves spread to 700 km, affecting 21 districts rendering 600,000 people homeless. The Gujarat society organised a vegetarian food fete in Malacca for raising funds for quake victims. When Modi visited Malaysia a sum of 40,000 Malaysian Ringgit was raised on the occasion and it was donated to the CM's Relief Fund in Gujarat.

BJP Spokesman

Narendra Modi met PM Atal Bihari Vajpayee for 30 minutes to discuss about the fallout of Agra summit. He, along with some other BJP officials, has been given the task of explaining the government's position to the media. About the fall out of Agra summit, Modi says, "What transpired at the meeting is a confidential matter between Prime Minister Vajpayeeji and myself. Hence, I cannot talk about it. As far as his mood is concerned I think one need not go into this matter."

Vajpayee on the defensive, he says, "Defensive and offensive are subjective terms. Atalji is not merely a politician, but also a statesman. He was very clear about what he was doing before extending an invitation to the Pakistan president. The very fact that Musharraf had to go back without signing any agreement clearly shows that Atalji was not on the defensive, but on the offensive." Musharraf was the architect of Kargil war. Atalji told him bluntly that India has the capacity to deal with terrorism despite Pakistan's presence. This was done to send a signal to the terrorist outfits in Pakistan that when it comes to dealing with them, India will not hesitate to crush them.

No pact on Agra summit, he says 'No minister in the Union Cabinet acted as a stumbling block. Pakistan has thrown this idea to keep the Indian media busy.' Neither the Government of India nor the BJP has said that the talks have failed. In our considered opinion the journey has just begun. As far as the agreements are concerned, we have the agreements signed between India and Pakistan at Simla and Lahore respectively'.

We should not forget that the creation of Pakistan began on the basis of a campaign of hatred. Even today the politicians of Pakistan survive on this. We want to raise the hopes for peace and development in the citizens of Pakistan. Pakistan should realise it would benefit more by having friendly relations with India than in a confrontation. In a peace process, there will be ups and downs. But we should carry on with the work. On final agreement, he says, 'This is not true.' Indirect hints have been thrown that a minister in the Union Cabinet did not want the draft agreement to be signed and hence he acted as a stumbling block. No minister in the government would do such a thing. Pakistan has thrown this idea so that the India media is kept busy in trying to figure out which minister was playing spoilsport.

'Neither the Government of India nor the BJP has said that the talks have failed. In our considered opinion the journey has just begun.' It was not proper on the general's part to have played games with the media. We have been told by some editors that they were not even aware that it was being telecast live on Pakistan television. When two heads of states hold talks, you do not go to the media to score a point or two. If General Musharraf thought he could solve the Kashmir problem through press conferences, then he is welcome to hold 1,000 press meets. He would still be at square one.

Narendra during in an interview to the party journal *BJP Today* said that this meeting is more important for Pakistan. Its policy makers have to utilise this opportunity. In the last fifty years, whether at Tashkent, Shimla or Lahore, Pakistan has got a lot of opportunities to project itself as a peace-loving nation. But, it has lost all these chances. Since an anti-terrorism mood has been sweeping the nations of the world, Pakistan has become isolated. It has still to establish its credibility in the international community. Modi caught the attention of the media in Delhi as General Secretary and spokesman of the BJP. He was invited, for instance, by *Sify.com* to talk about his understanding of a roadmap towards India of his dreams on the country's 55th Independence Day. He made remarkable observation.

He said that unfortunately it is being perceived now that the sense of service and duty to the nation that had permeated the freedom movement about the rights, almost to the total neglect of the duties and responsibilities towards the nation. His appeal to the media was that they must work out a system where at least at every two days in a week, they will desist from reporting the activities of politicans in the newspapers. A moratorium of ten years is imposed on the practice of naming a government building or street or road after a politician who dies in harness. We are living in the IT age. For me, it does not mean Info-tech it also means 'India Tomorrow'. About the *Mahakumbh Mela* his views is that the Indians are quite capable of meeting any challenge provided, they are motivated and inspired. Over twelve million people attend the *Mahakumbh* daily, the number of people who gather at the banks of the River Ganga, equals the entire population of Australia. It is mircale of organisational acumen and it is a pristine example of human management.

As far as Narendra is concerned, **nothing is impossible. After all, the word 'impossible' itself contains 'I am possible'**.

During a conference of Modi commuity in Rajasthan, Modi said that he is the son of this *samaj*. He has been a member of RSS since his childhood. The outfit taught him *Hindutva.* It has been a part of me since then. A man becomes great on the sttrength of the *samaj*. If the *samaj* is not with him he cannot be great. To use *samaj* for politicking purposes do not help. The platform of the *samaj* should be used to enhance the strength of *samaj*. If we make a strong resolve to become economically, educationally and socially, we will forge ahead. For that we have to nurture good human beings to form a good society. By imparting good education, we can educate the entire *samaj*. In politics, work for left out and neglected is to build a good platform.

Narenda was shifted to Delhi and stayed in the national capital between 1995 and 2001, since he was the general secretary of the party except during the 1999 elections. He won the confidence of top hierarcies of the party by doing a good job. Obviously, it was expected a bigger responsibility will fall on him.

Incidentally, the condition of BJP in Gujarat was quite grim despite getting absolute majority in the 1999 assembly elections. The government and party appeared to separate entities and used to passing the bucks to each other when they failed to deliver. The people of the state felt cheated. During that turmoil, the party needed someone who could reinculcate a sense of discipline and unity in the hopes of rejuvenating the party and organisation. The situation had come to such a pass that in 2000-01, the party could not win a single bye-election in the state. Even the party lost to Congress in local polls which forced the party to think and act according to the need.

At this crucial juncture, a man who could set the matters right was no other than Narendra, who was shifted to Delhi due to internal bickerings in the Gujarat state-party almost six years back. The then Prime Minister of India, A.B. Vajpayye asked him to take the mantle from Keshubhai. He has to prepare for contesting the elections. So far he has helped others to fight in elections but now has to contest in the polls. A reluctant Narendra denied the offer and said to Atalji that he would look after the party affairs in Gujarat. He would stay there for ten days in a month and rest of the period he would be in the national capital for executing his job as a general secretary. He told that he was not fit for the job. L.K. Advani later gave him a call and told him about the party's decision.

CM of Gujarat

Eventually, an unenthusiastic Narendra conceded to the demand of the party high-command and accepted the offer. Since then he came over to Gujarat and involved the affairs of the state. Narendra, who was a national general secretary of the party and the RSS strongman, took oath of the chief ministership from Keshubhai Patel. It was seconded by Suresh Mehta on October 7th, 2001. The occasion was very emotional. He touched the feet of Kushabhahu Thackery and warmly embraced Madan Lal Khurana, Rajendersinh Rana and others to herald a new beginning. He was the 14th chief minister of the state. A mere Sangh *pracharak* had become a CM—a record of its kind.

Modi made his priorities clear after taking the mantle as the subsequent assembly polls in the state only 500 days and 12,000 hours away. Efficiency, integrity and discipline would be the sole criteria. The ministers in the state cabinet accused of corruption and incompetence would get the boot. Within this short period, his team would have to strive hard to fulfill the expectations of the people and ensure a victory for the BJP in the 2002 asssembly polls. He raised a new slogan in the state–*Aapanu Gujarat, Aagavu Gajuarat* (Our Gujarat, unique Gujarat).

In 2001, Keshubhai Patel's health was failing. The BJP had lost seats in the by-elections. Allegations of abuse of power, corruption and poor administration were being made. Patel's standing had been damaged by his administration's handling of the Bhuj Earthquake of 2001. As a result, the BJP's national leadership sought some new candidate for the office of chief minister. Modi, who had aired his misgivings about Patel's administration, was chosen as a replacement. L.K. Advani, a senior leader of the BJP, did not want to ostracise Patel. He was worried about Modi's lack of experience in governance. Modi declined an offer to be Patel's deputy chief minister, informing Advani and Atal Bihari Vajpayee that he was "going to be fully responsible for Gujarat or not at all". Modi was appointed the Chief Minister of Gujarat, on October 7th, 2001 with the responsibility of preparing the BJP for elections in December 2002. As Chief Minister, Modi's ideas of governance revolved around privatisation and small government, which stood at odds with what political commentator Aditi Phadnis has described as the "anti-privatisation, anti-globalisation position" of the RSS.

First Term (2001–2002)

On February 27th 2002, a train with several hundred passengers including large numbers of Hindu pilgrims was burned near Godhra, killing around 60 people. Following rumours that the fire was carried out by Muslim arsonists, anti-Muslim violence spread throughout Gujarat. Estimates of the death toll ranged from 900 to over 2,000, while several thousand more people were injured. The Modi government imposed a curfew in major cities, issued shoot-at-sight orders and called for the Army to prevent the violence from escalating. However, human rights organisations, opposition parties, and sections of the media accused Gujarat's government of taking insufficient action against the riots and even condoning it in some cases. Modi's decision to move the corpses of the *Kar Sevaks,* who had been burned to death in Godhra to Ahmedabad had been criticised for inflaming the violence.

In March 2008, the Supreme Court asked the state government to re-investigate nine cases in the 2002 Gujarat riots, including the Gulbarg Society incident, and constituted a Special Investigation Team (SIT) to probe the cases afresh. Responding to a petition from Zakia Jafri, widow of Ehsan Jafri, who was killed in the Gulbarg Society massacre, the Supreme Court in April 2009 asked the SIT to probe her complaint alleging that Modi and another minister had been complicit in the killing. The SIT questioned Modi on March 2010, and in May 2010 presented its report before the Court, stating that it found no evidence to substantiate the allegations. In July 2011, the *amicus curiae* Raju Ramachandran submitted his final report to the Supreme Court, stating that Modi could be prosecuted based on the available evidence, contrary to the position of the SIT. Ramachandran's report was criticised by the SIT for relying on the testimony of Sanjiv Bhatt, who, it said, had fabricated the documents used as evidence. The Supreme Court handed the matter to the magistrate court, and left it to the SIT to examine Ramachandran's report. The SIT submitted its final report in March 2012, seeking closure of the case, against which Zakia Jaffri filed a protest petition. In December 2013, the magistrate court rejected the protest petition and accepted the clean chit given to Modi by SIT stating that there was no evidence against Modi in the case.

In 2012, Maya Kodnani, a former minister in Modi's Government from 2007-09, was convicted of having participated in the Naroda Patiya massacre during the 2002 riots. She was the first female and the first MLA to be convicted in a post-Godhra riots case. While initially announcing that it would seek the death penalty for Kodnani, Modi's government eventually pardoned her in 2013 and settled for a prison sentence.

2002 Election

In the aftermath of violence, there were widespread calls for Modi to resign from his position as chief minister of Gujarat. These came from both within and outside the state, including from the leaders of the Dravida Munnetra Kazhagam and the Telugu Desam Party, which were allies in then BJP-led NDA government at the Centre. The opposition parties stalled the national parliament over the issue. In April 2002, at the national executive meeting of BJP at Goa, Modi submitted his resignation; however, it was rejected by the party. On July 19th, 2002, Modi's cabinet had an emergency meeting and offered its resignation to the Governor of Gujarat, S.S. Bhandari, and the assembly was dissolved. In the subsequent elections, the BJP, led by Modi, won 127 seats in the 182-member assembly. Modi made significant use of anti-Muslim rhetoric during his election campaign, though he later denied it.

Second Term (2002-07)

Despite allegations of using anti-Muslim rhetoric during campaign, Modi's emphasis shifted during his second term from Hindutva to the economic development of Gujarat. Modi's decisions curtailed the influence of organisations of the Sangh Parivar such as the Bharatiya Kisan Sangh (BKS) and the Vishva Hindu Parishad (VHP), which had become entrenched in Gujarat after the decline of Ahmedabad's textile industry. Modi dropped Gordhan Zadafia, an ally of his former Sangh co-worker and VHP state Chief Praveen Togadia, from the cabinet ministry. When the BKS launched farmers' agitation, Modi ordered their eviction from houses provided by the state government. Modi's decision to demolish 200 illegal temples in Gandhinagar deepened the rift with VHP. Various organisations of the Sangh were no longer consulted nor informed of Modi's administrative decisions prior to enactment.

The changes brought by Modi in the period 2002-07 have led to Gujarat being called an attractive investment destination. Aditi Phadnis writes that, "there was sufficient anecdotal evidence pointing to the fact that corruption had gone down significantly in the state... if there was to be any corruption, Modi had to know about it". Modi started financial and technology parks in the state. During the 2007 Vibrant Gujarat summit, real estate investment deals worth INR6.6 trillion were signed in Gujarat.

Despite his focus on economic issues during the second term, Modi continued to be criticised for his relationship with Muslims. Atal Bihari Vajpayee, then Prime Minister of India, who had asked Modi not to discriminate between citizens in the aftermath of the 2002 Gujarat violence and had pushed for his resignation as Chief Minister of Gujarat, distanced himself from Modi and reached out to North Indian Muslims before the 2004 elections to the Lok Sabha.

2007 Election

In the run up to the assembly elections in 2007 and the general election in 2009, the BJP stepped up its rhetoric on terrorism. On July 18th, 2006, Modi criticised the Indian Prime Minister, Manmohan Singh, "... for his reluctance to revive anti-terror legislations" such as the Prevention of Terrorist Activities Act. He asked the national government to allow states to invoke tougher laws in the wake of the 2006 blasts in Mumbai. Around this time Modi frequently demanded the execution of Afzal Guru, a collaborator of the Pakistani jihadists who had been convicted of terrorism for his involvement in the 2001 Indian Parliament attack. As a consequence of the November 2008 Mumbai attacks, Modi held a meeting to discuss security of Gujarat's 1,600 km (990 miles) long coastline which resulted in the Central government authorisation of 30 high–speed surveillance boats. In July 2007, Modi completed 2,063 consecutive days as chief minister of Gujarat, making him the longest-serving holder of that post. The BJP won 122 of the 182 seats in the state assembly in the 2007 election, and Modi continued as chief minister.

Third Term (2007–12)

Development Projects: Successive BJP governments under Patel and Modi supported NGOs and communities in the creation of infrastructure projects for conservation of groundwater. Gujarat is a semi-arid state and, according to Tushaar Shah, was "... never known for agrarian dynamism". By December 2008, 500,000 structures had been constructed, of which 113,738 were check dams. While most check dams remained empty during the pre-monsoon season, they helped recharge the aquifers that lie beneath. The 60 of the 112 *tehsils* found to have over-exploited the groundwater table in 2004 had regained normal level by 2010, meaning that Gujarat had managed to increase groundwater levels at a time when they fall in other Indian states. As a result, production of genetically-modified Bt cotton, which could now be irrigated using tube wells, increased to become the largest in India. The boom in cotton production and utilisation of semi–arid land saw the agriculture growth increase to 9.6 per cent during 2001-07. Though public irrigation measures in the central and southern areas, such as the Sardar Sarovar Project, have not been as successful, for the decade 2001–10, Gujarat recorded agricultural growth of 10.97 per cent, the highest among Indian states. However, sociologists believed the growth under the Congress government during 1992–97 was 12.9 per cent. The Modi government succeeded in bringing electricity to every village, although Dipankar Banerjee believes 170 of them had been electrified under the previous Congress administration. Modi changed the system of power distribution, with significant impact on farmers. The Jyotigram Yojana scheme, where the agricultural electricity supply was rewired to separate from other supplies. The electricity was rationed to fit scheduled demand for irrigation, resulting in cost reduction. Initial farmer protests died down when benefitted farmers found more regular supply. An assessment study found corporations and large farmers had significantly benefitted with least impact on small farmers and labourers.

In his third term, Gujarat International Finance Tec-City project was considered as Modi's pet projects. The first phase, which encompassed two skyscrapers, GIFT One and Two, was completed in 2012.

Gujarat's Development

Modi's government has worked to brand Gujarat as a state of dynamic development, economic growth and prosperity, using the slogan "Vibrant Gujarat". However, critics have pointed to Gujarat's relatively poor record on human development, poverty alleviation, nutrition, and education. The state is 13th in India for poverty, 21st for education, 44.7 per cent of children under five are underweight and 23 per cent are undernourished putting the state in the "alarming" category on the India State Hunger Index.

In contrast, officials from the state claim that Gujarat outperformed India as a whole in the rates of improvement of multiple human indicators, such as female education, between 2001 and 2011. The school drop-out rates declined from 20 per cent in 2001 to 2 per cent in 2011, and that maternal mortality declined by 32 per cent from 2001 to 2011. Additionally, the Indian Supreme Court, in a review of the Land Acquisition Act, 1894, identified Gujarat as being one of the few states from there were no complaints of forcible land acquisition.

Political scientist Christophe Jaffrelot asserts the development has been limited to the urban middle class, while rural dwellers and lower castes have become increasingly marginalised. Gujarat ranked, 10th among the 21 Indian states in the Human Development Index, which he attributes to the lower development in rural Gujarat. The number of families living below poverty line has increased, and particularly rural adivasi and dalits have become increasingly marginalised. In July 2013, Economics Nobel Laureate Amartya Sen criticised Modi's governance record and said. Gujarat's "record in education and healthcare is pretty bad". However, economists Arvind Panagariya and Jagdish Bhagwati state that social indicator improved from much lower baseline than other Indian states. The performance in raising literacy rates has been superior to other states, and the 'rapid' improvement of health indicators in Gujarat as evidence that "its progress has not been poor by any means."

Fourth Term (2012-14)

In 2012 Gujarat legislative assembly elections, Modi won from the constituency of Maninagar with majority of 86,373 votes over Sanjiv Bhatt's wife, Shweta from Indian National Congress. The BJP won 115 of the 182 seats, continuing the majority that the party has had throughout Modi's tenure, and allowing the party to form the government, as it has in Gujarat since 1995.

In later by-elections, the BJP won an additional four assembly seats and two Lok Sabha seats that were all held by the Indian National Congress prior to by-elections, even though Modi never campaigned for its candidates. This brought the number of seats held by the BJP in the state assembly up to 119. In 2013, the Wharton India Economic Forum (WIEF) at the Wharton School of the University of Pennsylvania cancelled a keynote video-conference speech by Modi after some Indian-Americans lobbied against Modi. After being elected as Prime Minister, Modi resigned from the post of chief minister on May 21st, 2014, and his MLA seat from the Maninagar constituency, after an emotional speech Anandiben Patel was chosen as his replacement.

International Diplomacy

Modi made visit to countries such as Russia, China, Singapore and Japan to woo foreign investment. He visited China in November 2006 to study the

Special Economic Zones that were about to be implemented in Gujarat. He again visited in September 2007 and later in November 2011. A month after his visit of 2011, the Chinese Government released 13 diamond traders from India who had been jailed by the Shenzhen Customs, which Modi attributed to his diplomatic efforts and statesmanship.

Modi's relation with Western nations was a troubled one. His role in the 2002 Gujarat riots resulted in a boycott by the UK, the US and the EU. He was barred from entering the United States under a provision of the Immigration and Nationality Act. He is the only person to have ever denied a visa to the US. The UK as well as the European Union refused to deal with him about the perceptions of his role. However, as Modi emerged as a national leader, the UK and the EU lifted their boycotts in October 2012, and March 2013 respectively.

Modi met the South Korean ambassador in Gandhinagar. In 2011, the Karachi Chamber of Commerce and Industry, impressed with the development, invited him to visit Pakistan and address prominent business leaders. They asked him to consider a flight between Karachi and Ahmedabad, on account of the historical cultural and economic relations between the two regions of Gujarat and Sindh. Modi wanted to help Pakistan out of its power crisis, especially in Sindh, suggesting Pakistan follow the 'Gujarat Model' – Gujarat Solar Park and Kalpasar Project. In April 2014, in a move described as "unexpected", senior Pakistani diplomats said to *The Daily Telegraph* that Modi is their preferred choice for the next Prime Minister of India," as he could provide the strong leadership necessary for peace talks".

Although boycotted by Western nations, Modi visited Japan in 2012. According to Ryohei Kasai, research fellow at the Centre for South Asian Studies, Gifu Women's University, Japan, "There is a growing interest in Modi in Japan with much anticipation that he will reshape India by revitalising its economy and better governance. Japan has an excellent relationship with him. Not only have successive Japanese ambassadors to India been regular guests in 'Vibrant Gujarat' investors' summit (organised biennially) but Japanese private companies also made a big amount of investment in the state."

Personality and Image

Modi is a vegetarian. He has a frugal lifestyle with a personal staff of three. He is a workaholic and an introvert. He writes poems in Gujarati. As a speaker, he is known as a crowd-puller. In the critical opinion of Somini Sengupta, writing for *The New York Times* in a 2009 article on the Supreme Court's ordering of an investigation into Modi's role in the 2002 Gujarat riots, "Mr Modi has assiduously sought to reinvent himself from a scruffy mascot of Hindu nationalism to a decisive corporate-style administrator". He emerged as social media savvy politician. He is currently the fourth most followed leader in the world with over five million on Twitter. His interaction on Google Hangouts on 31st August, 2012 made Modi the first Indian politician to interact with netizens through live chat on the internet.

Modi has been labelled by the media and some articles in peer-reviewed journals as a controversial, polarising and divisive figure, but British economist Jim O'Neill, author of the BRIC report, wrote on his blog that Modi is "good on economics", one of the things that "India desperately needs in a leader". In August 2013, financial analyst Chris Wood, chief strategist of CLSA, wrote in his weekly Greed and Fear that "the Indian stock market's greatest hope is the emergence of Gujarat Chief Minister Narendra Modi as the BJP's prime ministerial candidate".

Awards and Recognitions

The national and international organisations recognised his meritorious services and confered upon him many rewards. Gujarat Ratna by Shri Poona Gujarati Bandhu Samaj at Ganesh Kala Krida Manch on celebration of centenary year. E-Ratna award by the Computer Society of India. In a nationwide survey conducted in 2007 by India Today magazine, Narendra Modi was declared the Best Chief Minister in the country. Asian Winner of the FDI Personality of the Year award for 2009 by FDI magazine. In March 2012, Modi appeared on the cover of the Asian edition of *Time,* one of India's few politicians to have done so. Modi was featured in *Time's* 2014 edition among 100 most influential people in the world.

2 Decisive and Responsible Leadership

Introduction

Besides being a revered orator, voracious reader and a prolific writer, Narendra Modi is also a caring son and a man with his brand of humour. Those who have associated with him for long believe the idea of power excites him. Next time you wonder how he could garner so much of national attention, think of this. He underwent a rigorous training in the US on public relations and image management. On brand building, Modi believes there's no greater inspiration than Mahatma Gandhi. His eulogies endorses, "He spoke of *Ahimsa* but carried a stick. He never wore a cap but the world wears a *Gandhi topi*." Modi's careful metamorphosis from a Hindutva party man to a pro-development leader and change-maker speaks volumes for image-building ability. His two-year long escapade into the Himalayas mingling with *yogis*, *sadhus* gave him a fair understanding of Hinduism. That partly explains why people listen to him in rapt attention when he talks of ideologies.

Narendra Modi had to face lot of difficulties when he became Gujarat CM. A severe earth-quake and the unforgettable Gujarat carnage did not dampen his spirit. He brought Gujarat out of quake-ridden phase with his good oraganisation skill and innovative policies to rehabilitate and reconstruct the state within short span of time. He faced the serious legal stumbling block over Gujarat riots quite non-challantly. Slowly and steadily he caught the imagination of the Gujaratis by transforming the state into a developed state by dint of his perseverance, dynamic leadership and devoted organisation skill. His mantra was the development and good governanace and that helped him won the confidence of minorities.

Gujarat ki Gaurav

Driven to excel Gujarat's success has not been confined to the industrial sector alone, the convincing data show that the state has reduced poverty and malnutrition, sex ratio has improved, and the quality of education is also gets a new impetus. With the bid by Gujarat Chief Minister Narendra Modi for the office of the prime minister of India in full swing, attacks on the Gujarat story have intensified. Given the narrowing of the contest to one between Modi and the Congress, one would expect the critics to compare the accomplishments of the former in Gujarat to the latter's nationally. But no critic would hazard such a comparison. The data leave little room for anyone to credibly question the superior performance of Gujarat in industrialisation, agricultural development, and overall growth. Therefore, critics have invented the argument that thanks to its long-standing entrepreneurial tradition, Gujarat has always grown fast. But if so, why is Rajasthan not a powerhouse of growth despite its legendary Marwari entrepreneurs? Attracted by the superior business environment, in fact, those entrepreneurs have, migrated to Gujarat. The claim that Gujarat has always grown fast also turns out to be false.

Child Malnutrition: Gujarat has been widely admonished for child malnutrition. Estimates based on the more up-to-date data from the Integrated Child Development Services (ICDs) paint a very different picture. The Comptroller and Auditor General of India estimates Gujarat cut the proportion of underweight children between 2006-07 and 2010-11 by a gigantic 32 per cent. The corresponding reduction was 9 per cent at the national level and just two per cent in Kerala. The state officials believe an additional reduction of 14 per cent in 2011-12 and 2012-13.

***Muslim Poverty*:** At 7.7 per cent, Gujarat boasts the lowest poverty ratio for Muslims in rural areas. The state also counts among the seven states with lower poverty ratio for Muslims than Hindus in rural and urban areas combined. It has achieved this distinction by cutting poverty among Muslims by 23.3 per cent in rural areas and 27.7 per cent in urban areas since 2004-05.

Female Infanticide/ Foeticide: The state launched the 'Save the Girl Child Campaign'. A recent Sample Registration System report attributes female foeticide rose from 865 per 1,000 during 2004-06 to 903 during 2008-10. The corresponding increase at the national level was much smaller, from 892 to 905.

Primary Education: Anticipating the damage on input norms in the Right to Education (RTE) Act, Gujarat has adopted the most innovative methods. These rules limit the requirement for the recognition of as yet unrecognised schools to 8 sq ft of area per student plus 60 sq ft for the teacher in each classroom. More importantly, continued recognition is based on a formula that assigns 30 per cent of the weight to the level of learning outcomes and an additional 40 per cent to the improvement in those outcomes. The formula assigns input norms just 15 per cent weight. Many states use onerous input norms in the RTE Act to shut down low-budget private schools with superior learning outcome but inferior facilities, Gujarat has chosen to reward schools that deliver superior learning outcomes.

Many Faces of NaMo

On November 18th, 2012 audiences in cities around Gujarat were treated to a political spectacle. Modi made a speech from a studio in Gandhinagar, his likeness, in the form of four 3D holograms, was beamed simultaneously down onto stages in Ahmedabad, Vadodara, Rajkot and Surat. The holograms waved and walked forward fuzzily, like ambassadors from the starship enterprise.

"Today marks a huge achievement for Gujarat," the 3D *avatars* said, praising the technology, licensed for India from UK-based company Musion by Enchant 3D, a wholly owned subsidiary of film-maker Mani Shankar's Kasu Mani Enterprises.

The four *avatars* of Modi assured Gujaratis to have embraced the unflattering nicknames the Congress party had lately bestowed on him ahead of the 13, 17 December state assembly election. They said they were proud to be called "Hanuman's monkey" and "Ganapati's mouse." "I have got the chance to serve Gujarat. The six crores Gujaratis are like Ram to me, I am their Hanuman," the Modi said, weaving each new identity into a mantle of apparent humility with practised ease before the appreciative crowd. The show, according Shankar, was a runaway success: "More than the technology, a lot of credit for the success of the shows goes to Modi for his commanding presence and great oratory skills." Shankar was anxious to redress rumours about him had been slimmed in his hologramic form: "Although some people feel Modi appears slimmer than in real life, it is not so," he said. "The 3D is a true-to-life image of Modi." Not everyone was charmed. Modi's predecessor as chief minister, and now Gujarat Parivartan Party president, 84-year-old Keshubhai Patel, slammed his rival's "illusionary campaign" as a desperate and wasteful publicity stunt that would cost about Rs 200 crore. Congress leaders protested that the Election Commission ought to probe the source of the funds.

The BJP refused to reveal how much money the hologram technology had cost, but it did not seem deterred; a little over a week later, 26, 3D Modis addressed audiences in specially constructed theatres around the state. It was the last in a run of publicity stunt over the past couple of months, beginning with the October launch of a TV channel named after Modi. NaMo's programming is interspersed with bulletins on Modi's life and opinions. Its name uses the kind of Hollywood-style elision usually reserved for film stars (NaMo also means "bow down" in Gujarati).

Candidate Modi

Ahead of the elections in Gujarat, Modi was on a campaign overdrive—touring constituencies, meeting voters, staring down at passers-by from gigantic cutouts (some as large as 100 ft tall) or grinning back at people from masks that first became popular during the last state elections in late 2007.

However, although the 62-year-old politician may be seeking re-election for what will be his fourth term as chief minister, it was evident that had an eye on bigger prize. On the campaign trail, he persistently addressed national issues. He squared up to Congress party president Sonia Gandhi and prime Minister Manmohan Singh. Indeed, several senior leaders of the BJP have said enough to indicate an endorsement of Modi as the party's prime ministerial candidate in the next general elections. Another sweeping win for Modi in 2012 would fuel these aspirations, but it would also be a victory for the public relations machine that has created new identity after identity for one of the few state-level politicians who is a household name all over India.

In Gujarat, Modi and the BJP are inseparable—a conflation that Modi encourages. A recent BJP radio and TV advertisements called Modi no manas (Modi's man), asked voters to pick the BJP if they believe in Modi. "Do you want to leave the man who has spent sleepless nights working for your prosperity and risk your future?" One farmer asks another in the ad. "I am Modi's man. Are you?" "So am I" replies the second farmer, earnestly.

At a rally on November 29, Modi asked his audience to vote for any BJP candidate, keeping in mind that, in doing so, they would be casting a ballot for him. The success of this conflation between man and party adds up to one of the most powerful political brands India has ever seen, and Modi is hyper-conscious and controlling of his image, say some of his colleagues, who are curiously reluctant to take credit for any campaign initiative, instead insisting that every idea came from Modi himself. If Modi's public image has been less than consistent over the 11 years he has held the top job in Gujarat, that is no accident, according to political scientists and advertising gurus who have watched him go through a series of metamorphoses depending on the needs of the moment. "Modi's changing image is in part responding to changing India," said Mona Mehta, professor of political science at the Indian Institute of Technology (IIT), Gandhinagar. From Hindutva party man, to aggressor of Muslim minorities, to development guru, to entrepreneur, to tech-savvy changemaker, Modi's face has come to mean different things to different people. An Advertising executive Piyush Pandey believes him to have managed to hold up a mirror to Indian society, and show it what it thinks it wants, at that time, in that place.

"Any brand, human or not human, is decided by its target audience," Pandey said. "I guess the brand Modi is a result of what the people think of him in terms of his achievement. Everything is dependent on delivery." Pandey is the executive chairman and national creative director at Ogilvy and Mather (O&M) India, which was involved in the promotional campaign of Gujarat by the state tourism department featuring Bollywood actor Amitabh Bachchan.

Politician Modi

Modi's first stint as chief minister of Gujarat began in 2001. The BJP decided to replace Keshubai Patel for the post. Modi was a little known party politician, and his first months as chief minister were uneventful. Then, in 2002, violence broke out in the state after a train carrying Hindu pilgrims was torched by a mob of Muslims in Godhra. The backlash was a series of riots that killed about 2,000 people, mostly Muslims, according to activist groups; although the state government put the death toll at 1,200, of which at least 900 people were Muslims. Those riots came to define Modi, who activists claim turned a blind eye to the violence. Investigators have since cleared him of wrongdoing, though other members associated with the ruling party and outfits of Sangh Parivar, as the Rashtriya Syayamsevak Sangh and its affiliates are known, were indicted.

Modi's image as a protector of Hindus may have been built accidentally. It endorsed him a thumping victory at the polls. His 2002 victory garnered 127 of the total 182 assembly seats, the biggest ever victory for the BJP in Gujarat. However, his Hindutva politics were not sustainable in the long run. He was forced to temper his leanings to the Hindu right with a new image.

"Modi realised that to be a successful politician he had to distance himself from his communal roots," said the social scientist Shiv Visvanathan. "He had to preserve the flavour but alter the contents. Modi's politics demanded that he distance himself from BJP politics. From a *Swadesi Pracharak* arose Modi, the moderniser. A modernist cannot look anti-Muslim," said Visvanathan. "He cannot look like some right-wing ideologue that belongs to some bygone era."

Modi's repositioning of his image as a man with an entrepreneurial spirit who would bring business to Gujarat was a natural step, according to Mehta. "In India now, Hindutva is not in vogue and Modi seems to know that. Besides his national aspirations, his image is also keeping in mind that 43 per cent of the Gujarat voters are urban, who want development," said Mehta.

Business-friendly Modi

Modi is today seen as a clean, efficient and no-nonsense administrator, an image that has been cultivated by sending messages to the right kind of audience, according to a senior official, who did not want to be named, from an advertisement company that has been working on the Vibrant Gujarat project. Gujarat has been among the more industrialised states in the country, on account of the enterprising the Gujaratis, but Modi built on this success until he managed to become the face of Gujarat's development.

Things didn't start well. At an industry event in New Delhi in 2003, a couple of industrialists openly criticised the Gujarat riots and asked whether he could win back investor confidence. Modi's response was the Vibrant Gujarat Investors Summit, a biennial event wherein businesses indicate their desire to invest in the state and sign agreements with government. To date, five such summits have been held, agreements indicating investments of about Rs 39.5 trillion have been signed and about Rs 3.5-4 trillion of this money has actually been invested in the state.

Not everyone is taken in by this idea. "Modi is a good brand manager and an excellent propagandist. He is not a statesman; his political philosophy is of majoritarianism," said Achyut Yagnik, an Ahmedabad-based social scientist and the author of 'The Shaping of Modern Gujarat'. "His development agenda is one-dimensional, profiting many large industries. A lot of small and medium scale industries in Gujarat have been losing ground by his development agenda."

"He has risen from the fire. It is quite natural that his pro-development image would have been an antidote to his communal image," said a senior bureaucrat working in the Modi government, who wished to remain unidentified. "A politician's image-building exercise is very different than that of a Bollywood film star. It takes a long time and cannot be achieved overnight."

If not overnight, however, the transformation of Modi's image from Hindu leader to big-business man happened extremely fast. By 2007, Vibrant Gujarat had become a platform for industrialists to come and shower praises on the chief minister and the work done by his government. Influential business leaders like Ratan Tata, Mukesh Ambani, Sunil Bharti Mittal and Anil Ambani became mouthpieces for Modi's development plans. After his easy win in the 2007 elections, Ambani and Bharti suggested him to be the next prime ministerial candidate.

His sway among the rich and powerful added to Modi's credibility. In 2008, Modi boasted that it cost him only an SMS worth one rupee to bring in investment of about Rs 2,000 crore to Gujarat, referring to Tata Motors Ltd's Nano factory, which moved from West Bengal to Gujarat after Modi sent a text to Ratan Tata, then chairman of Tata Group. Ghanshyam Shah, a political scientist and former professor in Jawaharlal Nehru University, said that the association between Modi and the state he runs works both ways. If Amitabh Bachchan is campaigning for tourism in Gujarat, it is seen that he is campaigning for Modi, he said. Conversely, if praise for Gujarat is synonomous with praise for Modi, then any criticism of him was seen as a criticism of Gujarat.

Techno Modi

According to Shah, Modi is a man with a mission. The vacuum in the BJP leadership and United Progressive Alliance upheld him a chance to project as national leader.

"In 2008, there was a hoarding in Vadodara by the BJP on how Gujarat will show the way to India to become a pollution-free country by use of CNG," Shah said. "This ad gave the first direct indication of Modi's national ambition. In 2009, L.K. Advani was the prime ministerial candidate of the NDA, contesting from Gandhinagar seat. A role reversal carried away as the campaign was led by Modi."

Modi has a sense of a messiah about him, said Shah. He is able to make a direct connection with his audience to the detriment of his own party at times. An early riser, Modi, who as an RSS *pracharak* (propagator) handled media interaction before joining BJP, spends a considerable amount of time each morning and read what the media has written about him and Gujarat. He is very careful, said a person close to the chief minister. His PR is tightly handled. APCO Worldwide promotes the Vibrant Gujarat summit. The agency also works on getting interviews for the chief minister with international publications. He became one of the few politicians to feature on the cover page of *Time Magazine* in March 2012.

"Modi has an in-depth understanding of media and how it works," said a BJP party official who refuses to be identified "In 2007, Modi was touring a rural village of Gujarat addressing on local issues in Gujarati. He changed his speech to Hindi when he came to know that a national channel had come to cover him and spoke on some national issues that were played by the national channel throughout the day."

In an interview with *The Economist* this year Modi defended himself against allegations that he behaved like a dictator. "I'm telling you, the essence of democracy is criticism," he said. "I always welcome criticism. I am against the allegations. What we hear is not a criticism, it is an allegation... So we must differentiate what is criticism and what is allegation. You have every right to do the criticism. I am beneficiary because of the criticism," he said.

"Modi may be taking advice from many people formally or informally," said the government official quoted earlier in the story, "But, you've also got to realise the fact he is a man who is seen as a contender to the top post in the world's largest democracy. It's not surprising whether the world media shows interest in him."

Modi's oratory skills have a lot in the making of his image. His rustic humour and puns frequently get laughs from his audience. He was targeting Manmohan Singh during October 2013 rally, calling him the Prime Minister Maun (silent) Mohan Singh, and mocking his lack of response to allegations of corruption at the highest levels.

Modi has a team of professionals working on his website. It gives regular update about him and his governance. He has a million followers on Twitter, although there have been allegations that many of these are robotic users, not real people. According to Faker App, a tool developed in the UK that allows users to check their follower quality, Modi's account has 51 per cent fake and 36 per cent inactive users.

He is as good at ignoring issues as taking them on. On August 31, a trial court ordered a life sentence for former Gujarat minister and BJP member of the legislative assembly Maya Kodnani in a riot case, Modi answered questions such as governance, administration and food on Google+ Hangout, a live video chat, anchored by actor Ajay Devgn. Conscious about his dressing style, Modi gets his clothes crafted at Jade Blue, an Ahmedabad-based retail store chain. The shop has a popular in-house brand called 'Modi Kurta'. According to the unnamed BJP official quoted earlier, Modi has also had a hair transplant.

Modi Sahib

Modi has attempted to patch up relations with the Muslim community in his state. In 2011, soon after the Supreme Court refused to pass an order on Modi's alleged inaction during the riots, he embarked on a Sadbhavna Mission—seen as an attempt to appease Muslims, who would be a crucial vote bank in any national level race.

"Modi is getting more and more powerful," said Rahul daCunha, MD and creative head of daCunha Comminucations. "He has his PR machinery planned, with holograms. If he has to succeed at a national level, no brand Modi will succeed if he cannot convince Muslims that he has their interests at heart."

Few are convinced about his intentions honourable, however. "The Sadbhavna performance was for the outside world and not for Gujarat," says Shiv Visvanathan. "Everything else might work, except his body language, which is not pro-Muslim." According to Visvanathan, the success of Modi's image redesign lies in the fact that the more fabricated he is, the more authentic he looks. The chief minister's olive branch to the Muslims is purely on his own terms, said Mehta. "So it means that Muslims even today can't get houses in a Hindu locality in Ahmedabad. The outside world may believe that Modi has changed. Gujarat is still deeply sympathetic to the Hindutva core of Modi. In his list of candidates declared for the upcoming elections, he has not fielded one Muslim candidate. The Hindutva ideology is very much there. Modi is trying to blend with developmentalist politics, including anti-corruption."

At a time when the Central government is struggling with its policies and facing corruption charges, Modi's authoritarian ways may seem an antidote for the lack of oversight percieved as the root of the corruption scandals. Visvanathan believes his frequent travels to China cast him as the man who can take India's reply to its rival and lead development and international co-operation. However, his potential as an international ambassador for India remains tarnished by the 2002 riots. Several US Congressmen urged secretary of state Hillary Clinton to continue to deny Modi a visa—his application was turned down by the Bush administration in 2005 in view of the allegations of crimes against humanity made against him.

Juggling these various positions requires a steady nerve, said one media expert, who did not want to be identified; Modi is caught in an image trap. "If he does something to appease Muslims, he is criticised by the right-wing parties where he has his political roots. If he attempts to become Hindutva poster boy, his national image of being an inclusive leader may get damaged."

Whatever the temporary efficacy of Modi's various images revamps, many remain sceptical that he can muster enough universal appeal to make a credible candidate for national office. "Being a national leader is beyond public policy and governance," said Visvanathan. "Modi does not seem to be democratic enough to lead the nation... his vocabulary does not seem to go beyond two words—security and development. A prime minister's image is far more complex."

His colleagues in the party may be beginning to sense this weakness. "There has already been a lot of dissent within the party," she said. "His dictatorial image is against the plural fabric of the nature of Indian society. A lot of authoritative figures like Indira Gandhi have been efficient. But efficiency is not the sole criteria for democratic India today."

Model Gujarat

The economy of Gujarat has significant agricultural as well as industrial production within India. Gujarat controls some of the largest businesses in India. Major Agricultural produce of the state include cotton, groundnuts (peanuts), dates, sugar cane, milk and milk products. Industrial products include cement and petrol. The world's largest ship breaking yard is in Gujarat near Bhavnagar at Alang. Reliance Petroleum, one of the group companies of Reliance Industries Limited founded by Dhirubhai Ambani operates the oil refinery at Jamnagar which is the world's largest grass roots refineries. The company has planned another SEZ (Special Economic Zone), in Jamnagar.

Gujarat ranks second nationwide in gas-based thermal electricity generation with national market share of over eight per cent and second nationwide in nuclear electricity generation with national market share of over one per cent. Legatum Institute's Global Prosperity Index 2012 has recognised Gujarat as the highest-scoring among all States of India on matters of social capital. The State ranks 15th in a list of 142 nations worldwide and actually ranks higher than several developed nations.

The state Gujarat maintains a variety of industries, the principal ones being general and electrical engineering and the manufacture of textiles, vegetable oils, chemicals, soda ash, and cement. New industries include the production of fertilisers and petrochemicals. Major resources produced by the state include cotton, peanuts, dates, sugarcane, and petrol. The state is rich in calcite, gypsum, manganese, lignite, bauxite, limestone, agate, feldspar and quartz sand and successful mining of these minerals is done in their specified areas. Gujarat produces about 91 per cent of India's required amount of 628+9 soda ash and gives the country about 66 per cent of its national requirement of salt. Chemical Industries in Gujarat count for more than 35 per cent of Indian Chemicals production.

Gujarat has per-capita GDP significantly above India's average. Kalol Khambat and Ankaleshwar are today known for their oil and natural gas production. 'Dhuvaran' has a thermal power station, which uses coal, oil and gas. The Tarapur nuclear station in Maharashtra supplies the remaining power. Also on the Gulf of Khambat, 50 kilometres southeast of Bhavnagar, is the Alang Ship Recycling Yard (the world's largest). General Motors produces the

'Astra' car at Halol near Vadodara. Jalalpur is a large town of Gujarat, where several small and large textile industrial units have been established. Surat, a city by the Gulf of Khambat, is a hub of the global diamond trade.

Gujarat emerged as a leader in various industrial sectors—textiles, engineering, chemicals, petrochemicals, drugs and pharmaceuticals, dairy, cement and ceramics, gems and jewellery, etc. Post-liberalisation period saw Gujarat's State Domestic Product (SDP) rising at an average growth rate of 14 per cent per annum in real terms (from 1994–2002).

Ahmedabad, Ankleshwar and Vapi are the hub of Chemical Industries in the state, having number of manufacturing units (private as well as state owned) manufacturing dyes, specially chemicals, agro chemicals, pesticides, pigments, colours etc. Rajkot city is the hub of manufacturing companies manufacturing auto components, auto engines, CNC machines, forging and casting parts etc. The state operating companies like GNFC, GSPC, GSFC, and GMDC are a few among flagship companies of the state.

Gujarat augmented power generation capacity by as much as 35 per cent of augmentation during the period 1995–96 and 2000–01. The private sector producers (IPPs) have contributed significantly. The liquid cargo (chemicals) handling port at Dahej set up in joint sector become operational. At an investor's summit entitled Vibrant Gujarat arranged between January 10, 2007 to January 13, 2007, at Science City, Ahmedabad, the state government signed 104 Memorandum of Understanding for Special Economic Zones totaling worth Rs. 2.5 trillion. However, most of the investment was from domestic industry. Gujarat is the main producer of tobacco, cotton and groundnuts in India. Other major crops produced are rice, wheat, jowar, bajra, maize, tur and gram. Gujarat has an agricultural economy; the total crop area amounts to more than one-half of the total land area.

Animal husbandry and dairying have played a vital role in the rural economy of Gujarat. Dairy farming, primarily concerned with milk production, functions on a cooperative basis and has more than a million members. Gujarat is the largest producer of milk in India. Amul milk co-operative federation products are well-known all over India and is Asia's biggest dairy. Among livestock raised are buffalo and other cattle, sheep, and goats. As per the results of livestock census 1997, there were 209.70 lakh livestock in Gujarat state. As per the estimates of the survey of major livestock products, during the year 2002–03 the Gujarat produced 6.09 million tonnes of milk, 385 million eggs and 2.71 million kg of wool. Gujarat also contributes inputs to industries like textiles, oil and soap. The state has a large tourist potential. Gujarat Tourism projects it as seventh largest state in India.

3 Nomination to Coronation

Introduction

After serving fourth consecutive term to become the longest serving chief minister of Gujarat, the sociable and gracious Narendra Modi, nurtured and motivated by the RSS has changed his focus from the state to the mainstream politics. Through his good organising and persuasive skill, he drew the attention of the top leaders like A.B. Vajpayee and L.K. Advani and others in the BJP proving his loyalty and credibility in the role of a national general secretary. At the instance of the then Prime Minister of India A.B. Vajpayee, he took the reign of Gujarat, when the state was passing through a difficult period due to internal bickerings, corruption and prejudices. He took the command and injected a new spirit in the saffron outfit riding on the wave of his Hindutva ideology.

Despite facing two serious tragedies in the forms of a severe earth-quake in 2001 and the subsequent worst-ever communal carnage-Gujarat riot, he controlled the situation with his superb administrative skill. Later, his Gujarat model of development and good governanace enabled the largest western border state to occupy the top slot in GDP and made him a forced to reckon with for the national politics.

In the last part of the UPA-II, the people of India were fed-up for endemic corruption, cynisim in politics and back-breaking inflation; the clamouring for Modi was hot up in the BJP, supported by the RSS and other Hindu organisations. The party felt that at this crucial juncture, the fiery and dynamic leader like Narendra Modi only could lead BJP in the 2014 general elections. Of course, he had made his presence felt in 2009 general polls in the national level albeit the desired success. Close to the heels of such an encouraging scenario, Rajnath Singh replaced Nitin Gadkari for the party president and that paved his way to the national politcs. First, he was appointed as the chairman of BJP's campaign committee for 2014 Lok Sabha elections to set the momentum and later he was nominated for the prime ministerial candidate.

Chairman of Campaign Committee

Putting an end to national speculation, the BJP president Rajnath Singh announced Modi as the Chairman of the party's Campaign Committee for 2014 general elections. Singh made the announcement at the end of the two-day executive meeting at the Goa conclave.

Modi was recently appointed a member of the party's parliamentary board. Stating that Modi will lead BJP to victory in the elections, Rajnath Singh said that the party has taken the decision with consensus. From corruption to mis-governance, this country has been let down by the present government.

Earlier Developments: The BJP President said that all senior leaders were being consulted on the issue and sought to downplay reservations of senior party leader L.K. Advani on declaring Modi as prime ministerial candidate. Party sources said Rajnath Singh met Sushma Swaraj in a bid to pave the way for the announcement. He had earlier met Advani and party leader Murli Manohar Joshi. They said Rajnath Singh may also decide to make an announcement on Narendra Modi after consulting members of the board individually.

Prime Ministerial Candidate

Fitting Birthday Gift for Narendra: After months of deliberations and dilly-dallying, the country's principal opposition party, the BJP, finally appointed Narendra Modi as its Prime Ministerial candidate for the 2014 elections, leaving the party patriarch L.K. Advani sulking. More significantly, Shiv Sena and the BJP allies in the National Democratic Alliance (NDA) also put a seal of approval on Modi. BJP's big announcement is surely a perfect birthday gift from the party to its most successful, dedicated and dynamic leader, as it came a day ahead of his birthday on September 17. The development is also significant as it not only puts to end months of speculation, media hype and *hoopla*, war on social networking websites, the blame game but also the bitter game to sabotage Modi's chances of becoming the PM nominee. It not only cements the Gujarat Chief Minister's colossal status within the party and outside but also indicates the end of BJP veteran L.K. Advani's domination in the party, which he had built along with Atal Behari Vajpayee from the scratch and transformed it into a prominent national party.

With the BJP and the RSS sealing Modi's name for the top job, the Advani era, during which the party went on to become a national political force to reckon with riding on the 'Rath', finally came to an end. Gujarat's impressive economic record and his resounding victory in last year's Assembly election third in a row had catapulted Modi miles ahead of other top PM hopefuls within the party and it was then hoped that party veteran Advani will probably subside gracefully from the scene, paving way for his one-time protégé.

Considering Modi's background as the hard-boiled RSS man it was almost clear that he would face little opposition from his colleagues in BJP. The party's major worry at that time was whether there will be consensus over Modi—a highly polarising figure—among the NDA constituents (JD-U, Shiv Sena and SAD). The party went into a huddle weighing the pros and cons of naming Modi ahead of the crucial assembly elections in many states and the 2014 polls. As the things unfolded, the JD-U, under influence of 'secular' Bihar Chief Minister Nitish Kumar, parted ways with the BJP, saying that Modi as

NDA's choice for PM's job was not acceptable to them. Initially shattered by the split, the BJP and its ideological fountainhead, the RSS, then brainstormed on the issue and finally decided to back Modi as its biggest bet for 2014. Having survived this crisis, the party faced another major one when party patriarch Advani expressed his strong opposition to naming Modi as the party's official candidate for the PM's post.

Advani's first major act of rebellion against the ascension of Modi came to fore in June, when he resigned from all party posts after the Gujarat Chief Minister was picked up as the BJP's campaign-in-charge for 2014 polls. However, intervention by the RSS persuaded him to return to the party-fold. But this was not the end of the BJP's dilemma as the battle for one-upmanship and the prime ministerial ambition harboured by many, primarily the 85-year-old Advani, kept the central leadership on the edge.

The old guard of the party, through a coterie of his close aides, led a strident but largely ineffectual campaign against the man who he once mentored. The ageing leader, whose "inner conscience" prevented him to support Modi, allegedly predicted a "political disaster" if the BJP named the Gujarat leader as its presumptive prime minister. Advani also wanted to BJP to postpone announcement on Modi till Assembly elections are over in MP, Rajasthan, Delhi and Chhatishgarh. Advani probably thought that delaying a decision on Modi will allow him to push Shivraj Singh Chauhan, who has thrown his political weight to win the MP assembly polls for a third time in a row—something that would put him on equal footing with Modi.

With the party's chief patron Advani not relenting, the BJP and the RSS bigwigs recently went into a huddle for two days for evolving a coordinated strategy on "ideological matters" ahead of the next year's elections and, most importantly, decide the political future of Modi. It was probably during this session that the RSS empowered BJP president Rajnath Singh to go ahead and declare Modi as the party's unanimous choice for 2014 polls. The BJP's ideological mentor believed that Modi's surging popularity among party workers could extend to voters and thus wanted him to be declared the right man for the right job at the earliest.

However, the big cause of concern for Rajnath Singh and the RSS was not letting the party approach the game-changer 2014 polls as a divided house and that's why the two wanted Modi to be declared a consensus candidate to counter criticism from rivals. Finally, after relentless persuasions, the RSS and the BJP chief managed to convince Advani to give up, respecting "the people's mood, cadres' enthusiasm and the situation in the country that favoured Modi's immediate elevation. By quelling the dissent and taking Advani on board (though reluctantly), Rajnath Singh has for the time being averted a big crisis amid hopes that Modi's "coronation" would give a much-needed thrust to the party ahead of the 2014.

But the task is yet not over for the "party with a difference" as it is yet to be seen whether Modi will actually manage to oust Congress in 2014 and bring his party back to the centre stage. The Modi factor and the Muzaffarnagar riots have heavily polarised the electorate, especially in UP, and if the sentiment persists till 2014 and leads to strict voting on communal lines, the political landscape of India will surely change thereafter. However, at this juncture, Modi has a tough task of keeping the party intact and preparing a blueprint for BJP's success in 2014.

Role in the Decisive LS Polls

Narendra Modi in his message gave a clarion call to the countrymen being the prime ministerial candidate just prior to the 2014 general elections. The victory in the polls is not about winning or losing but ensuring a bright future for India. It is about sowing the seeds for a *'Bhavya and a Divya Bharat'*, marked by good governance, freedom from corruption, youth's employment and *ek bharat and shrestha bharat*. He deserves credit for leading an election campaign that was unprecedented for leading an amazing campaign, an innovative and sustained campaign in an election ever.

Waged Battle Single-handedly

Modi waged the battle for BJP virtually single-handedly, addressing 440 rallies across the length and breadth of the country since his anointment as the party's prime ministerial candidate in September while most other national leaders of the party largely confined themselves to their constituencies.

Modi revealed the figures himself in his blog posting after campaigning for the nine-phase Lok Sabha elections drew to a close.

"Friends in the party told him that he addressed rallies and programmes in almost 5,800 locations, covering a distance of over 3 lakh kilometers. The number of rallies he addressed in this campaign season is 440, including the Bharat Vijay Rallies that he began with the blessings of Maa Vaishno Devi on March 26, 2014," Modi said.

BJP chief Rajnath Singh — who contested from Lucknow—was the only other top leader to have addressed over a 100 BJP rallies in different states in the past few months. Senior leaders L.K. Advani, Sushma Swaraj, Arun Jaitley and Murli Manohar Joshi stayed put in their own constituencies for most of the election campaign. Since the polling in their constituencies was in the later phases of the long-drawn election, the party could not optimally utilise their services. Nitin Gadkari, former party chief, did chip in by addressing some rallies, but only after polling got over in his seat Nagpur on April 10. As such, most of the credit for giving a push to 'Modi wave' goes to the PM candidate himself. Other BJP programmes such as *Chai pe Charcha*, 3D hologram addresses and use of social media, were also centered on Modi and controlled by his close team. This had invited criticism from some quarters that the campaign is too Modicentric and even veterans like former prime minister Atal Bihari Vajpayee were not celebrated during the campaign.

Call it a lack of demand from party candidates or their falling political fortunes, senior leaders like Advani, Swaraj and Joshi have not had much of a presence in the BJP campaign even as Modi even held rallies in Tamil Nadu for newly acquired NDA allies like DMDK, MDMK and others. Advani, who was the presumptive prime minister for BJP in the 2009 Lok Sabha elections, spent most of his time in Gandhinagar during the 2014 elections. This came as a surprise to many within the party and outside as he had hardly campaigned for himself in the previous elections. According to his office, Advani did address BJP rallies in West Bengal, Bihar, Uttarakhand, Tamil Nadu, Madhya Pradesh and Kerala. He spent a day each in these states and the rallies went virtually unnoticed. Swaraj, considered close to the Advani camp antagonistic to Modi, chose to confine to her constituency Vidisha for much of the Lok Sabha elections. She campaigned in a few seats of Madhya Pradesh, and spent a day each in Haryana and Delhi. Once polling was over in Vidisha on April 24, in the sixth phase of the nine phase elections, Swaraj visited Telangana, Gujarat and Uttarakhand for a day each and spent a couple of days in Bihar and Uttar Pradesh. Jaitley, considered close to Modi, did not budge from his constituency Amritsar even on April 7, the day BJP manifesto was released in the Capital. Faced with a tough fight as Congress fielded former Punjab chief minister Amrinder Singh against him, Jaitley decided to focus on his own seat.

With just days to go for the first phase of Lok Sabha polls, BJP's PM pick Narendra Modi has scaled up his target to 300 seats and invoked the stability card, saying only a government which has a strong mandate can deliver and command respect. Addressing a rally in Bareilly on April 2, 2014, Modi said Congress was plotting and praying to ensure the next government turned out to be a weak one, stressing that a PM can be effective only if he has the backing of 300 or more MPs. "*300 se jyada MP leke baithe hue PM ki baat duniya bhi theek se sunegi* (The world will pay attention to a PM who has more than 300 MPs by his side)," he said.

Modi invoked the stability card when he addressed a rally at Rewa in MP later in the day. Contending that a stable government was essential for development, he said, "No PM will be able to drive if people's mandate translates into a car with only three wheels. It is necessary that a four-wheeled government is selected to scale new heights of development."

The switch from a conservative 272—the magic figure in the 543-strong Lok Sabha—to an ambitious 300 attracted the attention of many in political circles, and left them wondering about the possible motivation. The last 72 hours have seen Modi casting himself as "future PM", and his setting sights higher could be part of the same strategy to fire-up the base and throw the opponents off-balance. It could also be meant to tap into the anxiety that an unstable government will hurt the prospect of economic recovery—a worry which may lead the fence-sitters to back the frontrunner. Importantly, considering that "stability" has for long been Congress's theme, Modi's pitch also marked an audacious attempt to snatch the plank from his chief rival.

Muslim Mantra and Mission 272

The recently concluded meeting of the BJP's 2014 election campaign committee sprang many surprises. First, the meeting saw BJP patriarch L. K. Advani, whose acrimony with Narendra Modi had recently brought the saffron party on the verge of a split, praising the Gujarat Chief Minister Narendra Modi and secondly, the party shifting its focus to the Muslim community for the first time since the A.B. Vajpayee era. The main Opposition has probably realised that it needs to impress the Muslim community, or at least a section of it, if it has to dislodge the Congress from power in 2014 General Elections. With the BJP top brass goading its office bearers to focus on booth-level activity and include all sections of society, the message is clear—the party now wants to get back to the basics to defeat the Congress by wining 272+ seats in the next Lok Sabha elections. But, the moot question is whether BJP will be successful in its mission 272 and whether BJP willgo for Muslim votes strategy; make any difference and help it win maximum number of seats in Parliament to oust arch-rival Congress from power?

With the Janata Dal (United) parting ways with BJP over Modi and the Shiv Sena and SAD of Punjab still in dilemma over the Gujarat CM, the apex

BJP leadership is aware of the challenges it faces in materialising its dream to defeat Congress. The party is aware that getting allies on board would be a difficult task for the BJP with Modi at the helm of its affairs. Modi—the four-time Chief Minister of Gujarat and the party's biggest bet for 2014—too clearly knows that the parliamentary elections cannot merely be won on sentiments and macro issues.

And that's the reason, why the hardline leader has asked his supporters and the BJP cadre to focus on local issues related to each constituency and every individual in order to prepare the party for what is surely going to be the mother of all elections. As part of this new strategy, the BJP will take concerted attempts to woo the Muslim voters, probably telling them that it's not a party against minorities, and attract the young voters in the age group of 18-24 years.

The BJP's apparent softening of stance towards Muslims is a significant move since the party never openly brainstormed on winning crucial minority votes since the tenure of A.B. Vajpayee during which the party had experimented with a *'Himayat Yatra'*. It too was not on a major scale as the BJP cadre was not involved. The initiative was led by a select group of Muslim leaders. Sometime back, L.K. Advani too had advocated the need for reaching out to Muslims and removing their misconceptions that it was a party of majority Hindus. In this context, Modi's gameplan to take Muslims on board by giving them party tickets in the local body polls in Gujarat is a well thought-out move aimed at including the minorities at the ground level.

As expected, Modi's appeal to open party's doors for Muslims has evoked sharp reactions from the Congress. It hit back saying that the party is just fooling the minorities and they would get nothing by sticking to the BJP. By chanting the Muslim mantra, the BJP leadership is also aiming to woo those secular Hindu voters, who never approved the communal riots in Gujarat after the Godhra incident. If the minorities too vote in favour of a 'changed' BJP, then it would be a major gain for the 'Team Modi'.

Devising a strategy to win Muslim votes and actually getting their support are two different things. Securing the minorities' support won't be an easy task for the BJP. It has no other option than to rely on the 'Narendra Modi' factor in the high-stake 2014 polls. Modi's impressive track record, the success of Gujarat model and, more recently, the international community's softening of stance on a communal and a polarising Modi can work in the party's favour. There is no doubt that the BJP's task won't be an easy one.

The other factor which will benefit the BJP is the rising unpopularity of the Congress-led UPA government among the common people. It was especially due to spiralling prices of the essential commodities, slew of corruption cases and various scams in Manmohan Singh's two tenures. Increasing confrontation with China, the beheading of Indian soldiers along LoC and repeated ceasefire violations by the Pakistan Army and the Centre's failure to give a befitting response to our hostile neighbours only added to people's perception that the ruling disposition is effective in managing national security.

Not to forget, Modi has come a long way from being a 'minority-basher' to being a powerful mass leader and a successful administrator. His repeated success in Gujarat is a firm pointer which seldom could be overlooked. Modi's detractors in Congress and within his party have now realised that his constant criticism over the 2002 communal riots will be of no use and can be counter-productive. The disappointing economic situation has hit the common man most and left no breathing space for him. The *Aam Admi* has realised that the present Congress disposition has nothing new to offer and that's where Modi's clean image and his mass appeal could do the trick.

There is no doubt that the BJP under Modi faces a colossal task of winning the bigger game of 2014, it also appears confident that its new avatar would probably change the political landscape of the country.

The BJP's prime ministerial candidate Narendra Modi did a fine job with his good oratorial skill and charishmatic leadership and single handedly waged a lone battle to give his party long-cherished desire to get majority of its own.

Main reasons of NDA's thunderous victory

Upper Caste- Advantage BJP: As expected and as indicated by Lokniti's surveys, the 2014 elections saw a massive consolidation of the upper caste support in favour of the BJP and its allies only due to Modi's dynamic leadership. The BJP-led alliance managed to secure 56 per cent of the upper caste votes, which is a thirty per cent point increase compared to the 2009 Lok Sabha elections. The Congress and its allies have lost approximately 19 per cent. In 2009, the upper caste vote was almost equally shared by the UPA, NDA and the regional parties.

NES data suggests that the upper caste voters have shifted towards the BJP in a big way in the Hindi heartland—Bihar and Uttar Pradesh. The BJP consolidated position among the upper castes in Bihar as the party gained an advantage of 14 per cent in 2014 compared to 2009. These votes seem to have shifted from the Congress to the BJP alliance. The Bihar story extends to Uttar Pradesh as well. In 2009, two out of four upper caste votes went to the BJP. This time three out of four upper caste voters have supported the BJP and allies. On the other hand, the Congress and allies saw a considerable decline of 15 percentage points among these groups from 2009 to 2014. The non-BJP and non-Congress regional players considerably lost their support among upper castes. The data clearly shows an acceleration of the upper caste votes toward the BJP. Although upper castes have been the traditional stronghold of the BJP, they deserted the party in 2009, shifting towards the Congress and allies in some States and strong regional players in others. These votes have moved back to the BJP in 2014. In this election, if one is looking for en bloc voting in any social section, the case of upper castes is perhaps the most prominent instance of that. This development is politically significant. It symbolises the success of a renewed social coalition that the BJP attempted this time, in Bihar and Uttar Pradesh. In Bihar, its alliance with the Lok Janshakti Party seems to have benefitted among the upper as well as lower castes rather than alienating with any of these sections. The successful coalition not only has a possibility of reversing the patterns in the wake of Mandal agitation. The verdict in 2014 may revive traditional patterns of upper castes presiding over social coalitions in these states.

Seismic Political Shift

Narendra Modi thundered to victory on May 16, 2014 in India's election, trouncing the Congress, led UPA in a seismic political shift that gives the

Hindu nationalist and his party a mandate for sweeping economic reform. Modi's landslide, the most resounding election victory India has seen in 30 years, was welcomed with a blistering rally on India's stock markets and raucous celebrations at offices across the country of his BJP, where supporters danced, let off fireworks and handed out sweets. The BJP achived parliamentary majority, giving the 63-year-old former tea-seller ample room to advance reforms started 23 years ago by current Prime Minister Manmohan Singh but which stalled in recent years.

Manmohan Singh's Congress suffered its worst wipeout, a big boost to Modi's goal of ending the dominance of the Nehru-Gandhi family that has governed for most of the 67 years of independent India. Singh, whose party looked set to win less than 50 of the 543 parliamentary seats at stake, congratulated Modi with a telephone call. Party president Sonia Gandhi and her son Rahul quickly conceded defeat. The desire for change has been so strong that voters put aside concerns about Modi's Hindu-centric politics. "India's economy was in the doldrums. We have hope that he'll lift up the economy, that he'll create jobs," said Shailesh Jha, 29, embracing a jubilant group of friends at the BJP's Delhi headquarters. In Washington, the Obama administration congratulated Modi and the BJP. He said he would be granted a visa for US travel. Washington denied Modi a visa in 2005 over sectarian riots in Gujarat three years earlier, when he had become state chief minister.

BJP Gets Majority

The BJP, led by its prime ministerial candidate Narendra Modi, won the Lok Sabha elections, with 282 seats on its own. The alliance it leads—National Democratic Alliance (NDA)—has 336 seats in the lower house of the Parliament. This is the highest number of seats won by any party on its own since the 1984 LS elections, when the Congress, led by then PM Rajiv Gandhi won a landslide victory. The 1991 Congress government was a minority one, and the party had just 244 seats in the Lok Sabha.

Crushing Win Leaves Rivals Broken

Modi's landslide victory in polls has swept aside the long-dominant Congress party and left many of the most high-profile politicians clinging on for dear life after staggering electoral losses. Modi's campaigners hailed the tidal wave of support for the Hindu nationalist who demolished rivals ranging from India's top low-caste politician to its most famous anti-corruption activist and a widely admired chief minister. Nitish Kumar, former CM of Bihar, whose government was feted for engineering a turnaround in the once crime-wracked state, resigned after his party was decimated. His Janata Dal (United) party won just two seats while BJP swept the state, one of the country's most populous and poorest, taking 22 seats.

The result as an all-India tsunami in favour of the BJP, was signifying that most people voted for a change at the Centre, ignoring the otherwise strong track record of regional leaders like Nitish Kumar. With the exception of a handful of states in southern and eastern India, which have long lacked a significant Congress or BJP presence, the anti-incumbent vote went to Modi. Kumar's loss at the hands of former BJP allies came less than a year after he cut ties with the party over its decision to field Modi, a popular but divisive figure, as a prime ministerial candidate. He said Modi's role as chief minister of western Gujarat state during religious riots in 2002 would alienate voters. More than 1,000 people, mainly Muslims, were killed in the clashes.

The Modi landslide also buried other rivals, including "Dalit Queen" Mayawati, a former chief minister of Uttar Pradesh state and champion of India's low-caste Dalit community previously known as "untouchables". Her Bahujan Samaj Party won no seats in the electorally pivotal state. Moreover, Modi's success at painting himself as a unifying leader left scant room for opponents, who traditionally relied on votes from specific castes, communities and religions. B.G. Verghese, of the New Delhi-based Centre for Policy Research, said, "Modi first played the orthodox Hindu card but later changed gears, appealing to moderates as well as lower-caste Hindus, many of whom switched loyalties and voted for him."

The gamble paid off spectacularly in Uttar Pradesh, where the BJP increased its 2009 tally sevenfold, winning 71 of 80 seats and isolating usually dominant caste-focused regional parties. Besides Mayawati, Mulayam Singh Yadav's Samajwadi Party, which has relied on rural, low-caste votes, also saw its strength plummet. Sunil Khilnani, director of King's College London's India Institute, likened the impact to "a democratic asteroid that wiped out many old habits".

"We enter a new, less predictable phase of Indian democracy, as more citizens slip loose from their caste, religious or political traditions to vote as individuals", Khilnani wrote in *The Times of India*.

The Modi juggernaut flattened old and new parties alike—from the Congress, which traces its history to the 19th century, to the upstart Aam Aadmi (Common Man) Party, led by anti-corruption activist Arvind Kejriwal. The results plunged the Congress into its worst crisis in years, leaving party leaders reeling after their seat count slid to 44 from 206 in 2009. The Congress campaign targeted Modi's controversial past, but his economic record in Gujarat, which boomed during his stint as chief minister, won over voters. Millions approved of his pledge to reproduce those policies at the national level and revive the ailing economy. Congress's failure underlined the party's urgent need to look beyond the Nehru-Gandhi family, which has produced three premiers but whose scion, 43-year-old Rahul Gandhi, failed to convince voters he was fit to lead India. And Kejriwal, whose early success at targeting young Indians frustrated over unemployment and corruption saw him become Delhi chief minister, also suffered defeat due to the BJP blitz.

Performs Puja at Varanasi Temple: A hero's welcome was accorded to Narendra Modi in New Delhi after he thundered to victory in India's LS polls, trouncing the ruling Congress in a seismic political shift that gives his party a mandate for sweeping economic reform. A brass band struck up early in the morning at the capital's airport as crowds awaited the arrival of Modi from Gujarat, where the night before he had addressed a sea of jubilant supporters chanting his name.

After the meeting in Delhi, Modi headed straight for the holy city of Varanasi which he wrested from BJP's Smriti Irani and AAP's Arvind Kejriwal. Modi reached Varanasi in the evening. Kashi Vishwanath Temple was his first stop. At the temple, he performed the '*rudravishi puja*' to Lord Shiva.

Stupendous Ascension

After the declaration of election results on 16th May, 2014, Modi met the President of India Pranab Mukherjee on 20th May where Mukherjee invited Modi to form the next government. The BJP had won 282 seats and their alliance NDA won a total of 336 seats in the 543-seat Lok Sabha, the strongest mandate since the 1984 elections where Indian National Congress had won. The BJP then announced that Modi will be sworn in on 26th May, 2014 at 6 pm.

Sworn in as PM

On a hot and dusty evening, with temperatures reaching 40°C but with none of the rain that had been forecast, more than 4,000 guests watched Modi and his ministers swear their oaths of office before President Pranab Mukherjee. The ceremony capped an extraordinary rise from humble origins in a provincial town in Gujarat, 600 miles from Delhi, through decades as an organiser with a hardline conservative revivalist organisation and then long years behind the scenes in the BJP, which he now leads. However, his resounding victory in the recent polls and the crushing majority now commanded by the BJP give Modi huge authority. The Congress party, which has dominated Indian politics since the country won independence from Britain in 1947, has been reduced to a historic low of 44 of the 543 seats. The party's key leaders, including Sonia and Rahul Gandhi, attended the ceremony. Modi's decision to invite regional leaders to the ceremony surprised many. Nawaz Sharif, elected prime minister of Pakistan for the third time last year, was among eight leaders of the South Asia Association for Regional Cooperation (SAARC) invited to attend. Analysts hailed a bold step to launch a policy of regional engagement.

All SAARC Heads of Govts Attended

Afghanistan – President Hamid Karzai accepted the invitation to attend the ceremony. He is bound to leave the office post the ongoing presidential elections. But his acceptance is seen as Afghanistan's interest in working with India in future. Media also noted that his either successors Abdullah Abdullah and Ashraf Ghani Ahmadzai are pro-India.

Bangladesh - Shirin Sharmin Chaudhury, the speaker of Jatiyo Sangshad, (the House of the Nation) accepted the invitation on behalf of the Prime Minister Sheikh Hasina as Hasina had a pre-planned visit to Japan.

Bhutan - Prime Minister Tshering Tobgay attended the ceremony and planned to have a discussion on bilateral relations of the two countries on 27 May.

Maldives - Maldivian President Abdulla Yameen Abdul Gayoom attended the ceremony.

Mauritius - Mauritius Prime Minister Navin Ramgoolam agreed to attend the ceremony.

Nepal - Nepal Prime Minister Sushil Koirala accepted the invitation.

Pakistan - Indian politicians reacted strongly after Nawaz Sharif accepted the invitation to the swearing-in ceremony on May 24. National Conference's (NC) Omar Abdullah was glad that the Pakistan PM had accepted the invitation to Modi's swearing-in. He said that this will mark a new beginning in Indo-Pak ties. Key NDA ally Shiv Sena, which has been vocal against Pakistan for "sponsoring" terrorism in India-Pakistan has come out opposing the invite to the Pakistan Prime Minister. The invitation has aroused hope among the people in India and Indian Muslims, especially, are construing it as portend of a happy turn of events. Pakistani journalists and politicians however have welcomed the decision of their Prime Minister Nawaz Sharif to visit India and attend the ceremony swearing Narendra Modi in as the Prime Minister of India.

Sri Lanka - President Mahinda Rajapaksa's invitation and attendance to the ceremony came under heavy criticism amongst Tamil Nadu politicians. The All India Anna Dravida Munnetra Kazhagam (AIADMK) and NDA ally Marumalarchi Dravida Munnetra Kazhagam (MDMK) leaders have spoken against the Narendra Modi government's decision to invite the Sri Lankan president. MDMK chief Vaiko met even with Modi to try to change his mind about the invitation while the Congress leaders were one with the MDMK and the AIADMK opposing the invitation. Amid strong opposition from all quarters to Prime Minister designate Narendra Modi's invite to Sri Lankan President Mahinda Rajapaksa for his swearing-in, CPI(M) said the Centre should utilise this occasion for resolving the Lankan Tamils issue. A Tamil students group called Delhi Tamil Youth Forum staged a protest in the streets of Delhi to register their anger against the incoming Government's decision to extend invitation to Sri Lankan President, Mahinda Rajapaksa day before the swearing ceremony. Due to Modi's goodwill and peaceful approach, Indian Fishermen were released by Pakistan and Sri Lanka. Pakistan only released 151 fishermen on 25th May from the Malir jail in Karachi and Nara jail in Hyderabad in Sindh province which was welcomed by the PM-designate Modi. Modi welcomed this move by the swearing-in ceremony invitee nations.

4 Top Challenges Ahead

Introduction

Seemingly untiring, dedicated and determined Narendra Modi faced and overcame the relentless campaign of denigration, of distorted charges and that would have sunk most, apart from the concerted campaign by intelectuals, members of the media, which seemed intent to either have him sent to jail or make him a demon, a monster in the eyes of the electorate. But what a victory, he has scored. And India has shown what a vibrant democracy it is. A *chaiwalah*, shouting at a ralway platform *chai, garam chai,* becomes Prime Minister of a country of 125 crore people!

Economist Jagdish Bhagwati comments, Modi is 'people's Prime Minister for his humble origin and subsequent struggle for sheer survival in the cauldron of high-intensity politics. His candidature for the coveted post orginited from the lower strata of the party as he was not the original choice of top echelons of BJP. It was essentially due to pressure coming from myriads of ordinary activists. He was the people's choice to lead. No, other PM nominee was targetted so badly nor has been facing the rigour of judicial scrutiny. He survived all these attempts to stride a giant leap. The stunning election victory of the BJP has far-reaching implications for the country's socio-cultural, political and economic life. As the Sangh Parivar-driven Namo takes charge as PM in time of neo-liberalism, what are the challenges before him?

Modi got an astounding mandate. After getting the historic victory, expectations of every single citizen of the country are also running sky high. From common households to most sophisticated investors in the financial markets, everyone is expecting things to change for the better. Challenges are numerous for Modi and he needs to set his priorities right. Government's performance on these fronts will decide success or failure of the BJP-led NDA government. Especially, the young voters, who have pinned a high hope on him and looking forward with a new hope to get, addressed the unemployment problems by creating ample job opportunities. The most serious problem Namo is facing to revive the economy which is in complete shambles. In this chapter, the focul points which Modi government has to face to do justify the faith of the electorate, who gave him a positive mandate in the hope of seeing a vibrant and prosperous India.

Put India on Path towards Prosperity

Although India's sputtering economy was the dominant issue in the campaign, Modi's victory implies a significant transformation ahead for India's foreign policy as well. In short, an era of timidity and hesitation, bordering on paralysis, under the Congress-led UPA has ended. There is no shortage of external challenges facing India's new government. Upon assuming office in 2004, the UPA frittered away the positive national-security and foreign-policy position that the previous BJP government had achieved, neglecting key partnerships as it struggled to work effectively in the face of chronic infighting.

For example, the Communist-led Left Front, part of the UPA, foiled the implementation of the momentous civil nuclear deal with the United States and consistently undermined the creation of a balanced nuclear-liability bill. Indeed, that bill is still languishing—a situation that Modi should rectify soon. Economic diplomacy will undoubtedly play a central role in Modi's efforts. After all, India's international prominence is based largely on its economic potential. Among India's top priorities should be measures to strengthen its relationships in its immediate neighbourhood. Modi has already highlighted the imperative of making the South Asian Association for Regional Cooperation a "living body," instead of the moribund group that it was under Congress.

To this end, the relevant parties must abandon the usual saber rattling, and implement confidence-building measures. This logic likely drove Modi's decision to invite SAARC leaders—including Pakistan's Nawaz Sharif—to witness his swearing in as prime minister. To build on this, Modi should work to expand intra-regional trade linkages and foster person-to-person connections.

Of course, economic cooperation and development will be impossible without sustained peace—and that will not be easy to achieve in a region beset by deep-rooted tensions, including between India and Pakistan, and the threat of state-sponsored terrorism. Making matters worse, India and China are locked in a longstanding border dispute. Add to that the turmoil in the nearby Middle East—exacerbated by America's withdrawal from Iraq and Afghanistan and India's security situation is not immediately conducive to harmony and cooperation. A more peaceful and prosperous future will demand a clear and credible strategic vision from Modi, including a zero tolerance approach to terrorists and their sponsors. At the same time, with the United States retreating from the Middle East, India must take responsibility for the security of its interests in the region, such as by developing a blue-water naval capacity to secure its maritime energy-trade routes.

This imperative is one of the factors linking India and Japan. As many Indian strategists have noted, Japanese Prime Minister Shinzo Abe may embody the kind of self-confident and decisive leader that Modi aspires to become. Increased investment and defence cooperation with Japan will add much-needed substance to India's "Look East" policy, which could be advanced further by implementing long-planned projects with Bangladesh,

Myanmar and Thailand, as well as by building road and maritime infrastructure and strengthening trade links.

Engagement with the Association of Southeast Asian Nations—something that the Congress government was always reluctant to pursue—must also become a priority, if only to ensure regional stability. India's membership in the ASEAN + 6-led Regional Comprehensive Economic Partnership was a step in the right direction, but much more needs to be done. But India's most important partnership remains that with the US. The problem is that former Prime Minister Manmohan Singh did not seem to recognise this, leading to a growing divide that has cost India dearly. And Modi's relationship with the US has not been entirely positive, either, owing to American officials' decision to deny him a visa following the deaths of many Muslims during riots a decade ago in Gujarat, where he was chief minister.

Given the bilateral relationship's economic and strategic importance, Modi must reinvigorate ties, and quickly. For starters, he must work with the US to address commercial and economic issues, including American concerns over India's weak intellectual-property protection and fears within India's information-technology industry regarding proposed US immigration reform. Success will require both sides' patience and willingness to compromise, bolstered by confidence-building measures. India could initiate realistic tax reforms, such as eliminating transfer-pricing and retroactive taxation. India's relationship with Russia—as well as with the US and even Israel– is to allow for increased foreign investment in domestic defence industries, including more co-production initiatives. Indeed, according to former US Under-Secretary of Defence Ashton Carter, stronger military co-operation and increased technology transfer is the most effective approach to deepening US—India ties. Why not adopt the same approach to strengthen India's relationships with Germany, France, the United Kingdom and Japan?

Modi faces major foreign-policy challenges. But, with a clear, confident vision and credibility-enhancing policies, he has a rare opportunity to put India firmly on the path towards peace and prosperity.

Key Issues Need to Address

The man who made nearly many Indians, hit by corruption and trying to cope up with spiralling inflation, believe in the jargon that good days are ahead. The BJP central leadership, its parent body 'the RSS', its strategists, its workers and supporters may be elated that their months-long hard work is now bearing rich dividends. Modi, who criss-crossed the country to ensure his party's victory, has little time to rejoice as he is clearly aware of voters' high expectations from him and the challenges he faces in reviving the fortunes of the country. Here are some of the major challenges, which Modi faces as Prime Minister and key issues, which he needs to address.

Economy: Throughout his election campaign, Modi had attacked the Congress-led UPA government of failing to curb inflation, preventing corruption and retarding the economic growth rate of the country. In this context, bringing economy back on track, accelerating growth rate, increasing foreign exchange reserves, attracting more and more Foreign Institutional Investors, containing the burgeoning fiscal deficit and, above all, infusing a sense of optimism in the market will be the first and foremost challenge before the Modi government and it will face its first credibility test with markets when he delivers a budget by June or July that will need to show the country can realistically contain its fiscal deficit.

Foreign Policy: The main opposition party has always attacked the Congress-led UPA government for its weak and directionless foreign policy, and its soft approach towards terrorism. Though the BJP's election manifesto speaks very little in this regard, it is quite certain that India's foreign policy will undergo a "sea change" under the Modi government. Modi's regular criticism of the UPA government for its soft response to terrorist attacks emanating from Pakistan and to Chinese incursions into the Indian Territory has created a perception that the new regime will be tough in its dealing with Pakistan and would not succumb to China's bullying tactics. Modi himself gave an indication in this regard in a recent interview when he said that talks with Pakistan can't continue amid bomb blasts and gunshots. It will not be wrong to presume that the Modi government envisages a bigger role for military in shaping India's national security and formulating doctrines, and a greater say for states in the government's formulation and execution of foreign policy.

Minorities: Despite concerted efforts by the BJP central leadership to woo the minorities, the Muslims in India still see the party dominated by Modi-an aggressive, authoritarian and polarising leader—with scepticism. A vigorous campaign by rival parties raking up the issue of 2002 communal riots in Gujarat during their poll campaign has further instilled anxiety in the minority community about the new Modi government. Modi urgently needs to change this perception. He needs to make minorities feel safe and realise that they are equal partners in India's growth story and they enjoy equal rights as all Indians. Though Modi has fallen short of saying 'sorry' for the Gujarat carnage, he and the apex BJP leadership have taken significant steps towards repairing the bridge with the minorities while sticking to the party's Hindutva agenda.

The Balancing Act: Even before Modi was declared the BJP's PM nominee, it was said that he needs to fear his own party colleagues more than his rivals in other parties. This holds true with the emergence of several power centres in the party. A section of leaders in VHP and RSS have opposed Modi, who is seen as a ruthless, authoritarian and an uncompromising leader who demands 100 per cent loyalty. Modi has faced criticism for wiping out his opponents, silencing his critics and even sidelining party veterans, including Sushma Swaraj and LK Advani (who was forced to bless him under intense RSS pressure) in order to fulfill his political ambitions. Though the party has put up a united front, the reports of Advani sulking over Modi's nomination as PM candidate, the controversy over his choice of seat to contest Lok Sabha elections, the debate over "Modi bigger than party" indicate that keeping the party intact will be a big challenge before Modi. Modi needs to learn how to cohabit with adversaries.

As a four-time elected Chief Minister of Gujarat, Modi has made development and clean governance as the hallmark of his leadership, so he is often seen with scepticism whether he will execute the RSS's Hindutva agenda after becoming the Prime Minister. Hence, maintaining a fine balance between his constitutional obligations as the Prime Minister and the expectations of the RSS will be yet another test of the man, who has often said that development is his only agenda.

Coalition Arithmetic: Modi's detractors always say that he lacks the charisma of Atal Bihari Vajpayee, widely regarded as the embodiment of consensus among BJP top leaders. Though Vajpayee too had RSS ideologue Govindacharya as his bitter critic, he was a master craftsman when it came to building working relationships with his foes. The poet-politician, who was an excellent orator too, not only tolerated Advani - a leader of his stature - but also managed to cobble up a good equation with NDA allies to run a smooth coalition government.

An Inspiring Cabinet: Whatever critics say about Modi, this is also true that he is a workaholic leader, who has no single case of corruption against him. Gujarat's progress and prosperity have made his "Gujarat Model of Development" a talking point. He needs to maintain the same tempo while in the Centre too and for this he would need a loyal and committed team, which will discharge duties with honesty and maintain the sanctity of posts. Hence, a strong and inspiring Cabinet is a must for 'Prime Minister' Modi. However, in doing so, he will have to "accommodate" everyone, while also maintaining cordial ties.

Emerges as Symbol of Hope

Narendra Modi has proved in letter and spirit what Napoleon Bonaparte said: "Impossible is a word to be found only in the dictionary of fools... Victory belongs to the most persevering." The BJP's primeministerial candidate has made history. He termed this historic win as a victory of people of India and the Indian democracy with an assurance to the 125 million people". Modi has emerged as a symbol of hope for the youth of this country. People have posed unwavering confidence in his leadership. He will now have to meet their expectations by taking some radical measures to ensure political stability, economic growth and transparency in governance — the three promises he made to the people during his hectic whirlwind campaign throughout the length and breadth of the country in the last more than six months.

Reviving Economy: Reviving growth and checking inflation is the primary mandate that the people have given to the government. It has to be understood though that there is no magic wand to achieve these goals, and it will take time to put in place some of the institutional changes that are necessary for a return to high and sustained growth rates. However, a number of challenges lie ahead, the biggest of them, without doubt, being the state of the economy. To use a term that has increasingly been employed in this context, the economy is in a state of paralysis. So what are the most important steps that the government needs to take to help the economy recover from this paralytic state? To answer this, it is important to understand how the current state of affairs came about.

The Reforms Era: In the first slew of economic reforms post-liberalisation, the traditional industrial and services sectors within the economy gained a lot of freedom. Earlier these sectors faced legal and policy constraints as the industrial licensing policy, tariff and quota restriction on import of raw materials and intermediate goods, blocked growth. The 1993 reforms removed most of these constraints. The average per capita growth rate of the economy going up from less than two per cent to more than four per cent per year, in 2004 second growth boom with per capita growth rates increasing to more than six per cent per year. The momentum in the minerals sector came from exports, as global demand and the price of minerals were very high during this period. In the real estate and the telecom sectors, growth resulted directly from increased middle class incomes due to the first growth boom. The impetus in construction was the result of conscious policy decisions of the government that wanted to push for big infrastructure projects. The mineral sector completely under the public sector catered largely to domestic demand consciously opened up to big private investment and exports. The real estate sector, with almost entirely of small players, saw a number of large private investments. In the telecom sector, the nature of the market ensured that only big players could participate. Even in the construction sector, some of the big projects like airports needed huge investment and big businesses.

Paralysis and Backlash: The reforms of the 1990s, which focussed on removing constraints on activity. There insufficient to provide broad-based, corruption-free growth in the sectors. Each of these sectors needed a different governance structure and set of regulations. Those were not put in place before the sectors started growing at a very rapid rate. The regulatory failures during second growth boom led to strong institutional and political backlash since 2010. The media raised issues of corruption and crony capitalism. Civil society got involved and voiced on the need for alternative regulatory institutions like the Lokpal. Finally, the courts passed orders and the verdicts criticised the government decisions. It yielded to policy paralysis.

From agents of economic growth—bureaucrats and private investors, once the courts gave adverse rulings on the decisions taken by some bureaucrats, the bureaucracy as a whole became jittery about taking decisions. Sometimes it deferred matter to them to the extent that projects simply ground to a halt. Private investors, on the other hand, found out formal and informal understanding. The political classes were not as secure as they had thought them to be. Especially, in the face of court cases and popular political uprising like the one in Singur, uncertainty crippled both the bureaucracy and private investors led to the collapse of investment and growth rates.

Bureaucracy and Business: Against this backdrop, what should do to bring back growth? The first thing that it needs to do is to move the economy out of this paralytic state. It has to attempt to rejuvenate both the bureaucracy and the private investor on a priority basis, but these are complex institutional problems. Mere right intent may not be enough, unless the nature of the problem is well understood. Take the case of the bureaucracy. The government should ensure that the bureaucracy does not become a part of any deal with the business class. It can lead to decisions that are not in the best interests of the country. Strong penalties ought to be levied for any malpractice by bureaucrats. However, if the government adopts an approach that strongly penalises the bureaucracy for any outcome that is less than satisfactory, then this may lead to a very risk-averse bureaucracy, which also hampers vibrant decision-making. In effect, the government needs to put in place a system which can differentiate between the deliberate malpractice of the bureaucracy and poor decisions that it may occasionally take even with the best of intentions.

The crony-capitalism associated with the second growth boom resulted in all sorts of informal deals between the political and the business class, which initially raised investor confidence in this period, but later led to a breakdown in confidence when the deals were challenged by 'accountability institutions' like the Comptroller and Auditor General of India (CAG), the Central Bureau of Investigation (CBI) and the courts. Any future relationship between the political class and the business elite has to be based on formal rather than informal deals. This will not only help investments become less costly due to a fall in transaction costs but also assure investors that these deals will not be reneged in future. Ultimately, investor confidence can be brought in. In practical terms, this means that sectors which are prone to high rents and crony capitalism need to have more appropriate regulatory mechanisms. This will encourage investment and growth without causing future political backlash. Once these sectors are taken care of, the investment climate will no longer be held hostage to investor paralysis. It is then that the government can shift focus to structural factors like infrastructure, etc.

Tackling Inflation: Tackling inflation has been partly demand-driven and partly structural, due to supply bottlenecks. In India, in the last few years, the structural part drives inflation, particularly food. While the Reserve Bank of India (RBI) and monetary policy ensures that inflation does not lead to hyperinflation, unless the problem in the food sector, we will keep on having high inflation rates. Hence, interest rates will not to come down lending to hampering growth. It is widely discussed that farmers are not getting adequate returns from the prices they get. Consumers ought to pay high price in the retail market. The government needs to collect data on a real-time basis about various stages of the agricultural pricing process. It should be right from the farm up to the retail market, to identify about the problem. Once there is an adequate understanding, the government can take appropriate measures to minimise. These measures have to involve the enabling of more competition at some level of wholesale business, after the produce leaves the farm, but before it reaching the retail market. Reviving growth and checking inflation is the primary mandate that the people of India have given to this government. It has to be understood though that there is no magic wand to achieve these goals, and it will take time to put in place some of the institutional changes that are necessary for a return to high and sustained growth rates. If the government succeeds in putting these changes in place and reviving growth, it would have successfully dealt with its biggest challenge.

Tackling India's Economic Headwinds: Indian economy declined every quarter since the end of 2010-11, i.e., for the last 12 quarters. The industrial sector has shown negative or near zero rates of growth. The services sector, the engine of growth for the economy, has experienced declining rates of growth. So has agriculture. This has led to sluggish employment generation. The problem has been compounded by capital intensive nature of current investment using less labour and more capital. Employment hardly grows with ouput rise. People are forced to work in the informal sector at low wages coupled with high persisting inflation, under economic distress and political unrest.

Increase in Inequality: The rate of investment declined from 38 per cent in 2007-08, up in 2009-10, but was down to about 32 per cent. It is still high compared to the figure of around 20-23 per cent in the 1990s. It rapidly increased in the 2000s leading to the boom of 2003-08. The rapid increase in investment was engineered by allowing national income to shift rapidly in favour of high savers. Those who have high property incomes ought to save more. This was evident from the direct tax data which showed that corporate tax collections boomed after 1999. This trend has led to a rapid increase in inequality. A slow rise in mass consumption leads to the growth. The investment rate declined after 2010-11. The rate of growth of the economy fell. Investment in the economy depends on private investment, foreign and domestic and on public investment. There has been a problem with each of them.

Discredited Model of Investment: The situation has been aggravated by developments on the external and the fiscal fronts. The green shoots in the United States did not bloom, Eurozone went into a double dip recession, and Japan continued its sluggish growth and the Chinese and the other BRICS economies slowed down. Thus, the growth rate of exports has been low. But, imports rose sharply due to the high import bill for petro products and the increase in the gold import bill. The consequence has been a high trade deficit and CAD and a decline in demand in the economy. This has also been accompanied by a reduced inflow of foreign investments so that the value of the rupee *vis-à-vis* the dollar declined sharply in the last few years. This added to the imbalance on the external front with speculation and a flight of capital aggravating it. The threat by credit rating agencies to downgrade the country has been looming large which could lead to an increase in cost of borrowing abroad and a rise in CAD.

Foreign investment has slowed down but it only constitutes around 10 per cent of the total investment in the economy. The bulk of investment is internal and this has slowed down due to several factors. One of them has been the unravelling of scams since 2009, and the subsequent intervention of courts. This has impacted the confidence of the business community which was used to employing crooked means to manage its investments and the markets. After the court interventions, there have been question marks over many decisions like allotment of spectrum, coal blocks and iron ore mining. This has unnerved businessmen who have lost the confidence that they can manage the business environment the old way.

Their confidence has also been shattered by widespread public protest against large-scale acquisition of land needed for major projects. This goes back to the days even before Singur. Resistance has continued in Jaitapur, Kudankulam, POSCO, and Tata Mundra and so on. Some big ticket investment projects like the $12-billion project by the Mittals have been called off. The problem remains unresolved because the public perceives a loot of natural resources—land, air, water, spectrum, forests and mines—at its expense. So, the execution of big projects has slowed down. The private corporate sector has been flush with funds which it has not invested due to the uncertainty and sluggish demand in the economy. In brief, the slowdown in internal investment is a result of the discredited model of investment in the country which has been based on collusion between businessmen, politicians and the bureaucracy. Thus, for different reasons, both foreign and domestic private investment has slowed down.

The last element, public investment has also slowed down because of policy paralysis in the government and even more importantly due to the sharp cutback in Plan size in each of the last five years so as to keep the fiscal deficit down; compared to budget estimates, the actual has been less by Rs 5 lakh crore in these five years. This has led to a slowdown in investment in infrastructure and an aggravation of shortages.

Because of the slowdown in the economy, tax revenue increase has suffered. That is why the fiscal deficit has tended to increase. To keep it in check, the Plan size has been curtailed. But that sets up a vicious negative cycle. As the economy slows down, the threat of a downgrade by credit rating agencies increases, revenues of the government rise less and the deficit tends to rise, both of which lead to a loss of confidence and a further slowdown.

Can the new government tackle the difficult economic situation? Prime Minister Narendra Modi is reputed to be a "man of action" but the issue here is what action? The corporate sector has backed him in the hope that he will reverse the misfortunes of industry. The stock markets have risen sharply in the last few weeks. Can the new government simultaneously fulfil the hopes of business and those of underemployed youth hoping for a miracle?

Improving Investor Confidence: The rise in the stock markets signals the flow of funds from FII. It does not mean that foreign direct investment will suddenly increase. There is the danger of a speculative bubble building up—as in the past—which could collapse and adversely impact the investment climate. This could be triggered by the continuing easing of the Fed intervention in the US—something that is ongoing. Any increase in foreign investment is a small part of total investment. It cannot be the major stimulus needed. Domestic investment—public and private—needs to be revived. Large investment remains hamstrung by environmental and other clearances. There are difficulties in land acquisition unless laws are changed but that would take time. Transparency in business decisions is needed to revive investment. The only thing that can be done soon is to increase public investment, especially in rural areas where infrastructure is woefully inadequate.

Schools, dispensaries, roads, telecom, water, small irrigation are badly needed in rural India. This has the potential to create lots of jobs. Unlike big investments it would be much less expensive in urban areas because land is expensive. It would benefit more people, and slow down the expensive and environmentally damaging urbanisation. But this requires efficient governance. In brief, the problems of the economy stem from the macro-economic imbalances and corruption. Unless they are addressed, the economy will not recover. The need today is not only for decisive leadership but also for a new, holistic macro-economic approach—a break from the UPA's policies.

5 Time for Bold Reforms

Introduction

Often change comes from an individual level. The individual is the catalyst. Others are inspired, a movement begins, and change happens. Whether it has to do with cleaning up our environment, our education system, our tolerance towards religious, ethnic, and different societal groups—the message is clear: the change has to come from within the system.

We lament at India being labelled a third world country. We lament that despite having the world's 10th largest nominal GDP, we rank 133 in GDP per capita, and the country's ranking is likely to slip to 145 next year. We do not even know the poverty rate of our country because there is no standard way to measure it. While overall poverty seems to be on a decline on a year to year basis, the percentage of people in abject poverty is on the rise.

India is the world's largest democracy, and while democracy has its limitations, its ultimate purpose is to give power to the people. We, as Indian citizens, can create the change we want. It is our time to act. Manipulations need to be replaced with excellence. Our education system will not fix itself; it must fixed by us, as a collective society. Individuals need to rise up and take charge. Teenagers need to be inspired by the Ratan Tatas and Elon Musks of the world. Narendra Modi, who is now at the helm, promises to make an impact in the spectrum of the national politics in view of giving the country a responsible, stable and decisive leadership and so, five years from now, when we judge his act as a Prime Minister, we should not just look at what was done by the government to help the country. We should instead ask ourselves: what did I do to help the country?

Pundits argued that the era of majority governments was over. The present government thought outside the box and dared to change lives of the people for better. People responded and delivered what pundits predicted as impossible. They gave BJP an absolute majority in the Lok Sabha. To accomplish the mission, the government ought to formulate some innovative policies to reform the system.

Unity in Diversity

The Modi-led government believes in India being one country, one people and one nation. It recognises the importance of diversity in Indian society, and the strength and vibrancy it adds to the nation. It believes in the principle of unity in diversity. India constitutes of all its' people, irrespective of caste, creed, religion or sex. It constitutes of all the communities - ethnic, social and cultural groups and also our culture, which is defined by tolerance and co-existence. The hallmark of India is "Unity in Diversity". It constitutes of each and every inch of our land, its natural resources and mental and physical energy we possess. It constitutes of all the institutions made in the past and present. For Nrendra Modi, the only philosophy and religion of a government should be India First; the only epic of a government should be India's Constitution; the only power of a government should be the power of the people; the only prayer of a government should be the welfare of its people; the only way of a government should be *'Sabka Saath, Sabka Vikas'*.

System Reform

Administrative reforms will be the main priority for the ruling government at the Centre. It should execute through an appropriate body under the PMO. It should have transparency in decision-making process. It should be citizen friendly, corruption free and accountable. Every effort will be made to meet the development aspirations of the people. It should make the government agencies accountable to the citizens. It had to set-up an effective Lokpal institution. Corruption at any level should be dealt with firmly and swiftly.

From birth certificate to school admission, from setting up business to paying of taxes, our present systems complicate the lives of our own people. Reforms as such will make it easy in terms of access, efficiency and delivery.

Following Specific Action will be Initiated: Digitisation of government records will be taken up on top priority so that they are easily accessible; performance review, social and environment audit would be mandated for all government schemes and programmes; open up government to draw expertise from the industry, academia and society into the services; government will be redefined by elimination of whatever is obsolete in laws, regulations, administrative structures, practices and would be purposive.

It will generate *Kartavya Bhavna* among public servants as lives and productivity of people is dependent on the quality and efficiency of public services. On the whole, hallmarks of our governance model would be: People-centric, policy driven, time-bound delivery, minimum government, maximum governance and e-governance: easy, efficient and effective.

The government believes that IT is a great enabler for empowerment, equity and efficiency. India is the IT capital for the whole world, except benefits of IT have not percolated down. This will be a high priority area for the government that IT touches the lives of ordinary men and women. It has been known for good governance through e-governance. It will nurture a Digital India—making every household and every individual digitally empowered. Information Technology has made it possible to make information and services reach to the ordinary men and women even in remote areas, easily and effectively. Availability of information is the key to empowerment of the stakeholders. It will reduce the scope for discretion and manipulation.

The government ought to focus on increasing the penetration and usage of broadband across the country. Deployment of broadband in every village would be a thrust area. Leverage technology for e-governance and engage proactively with the people through social media for effective public grievance redressal, IT-based jobs need to be guaranteed in rural and semi-urban areas. Technology enabled products should be affordable for students. Technology should unburden reading of books on children. Institutions and schools should be enabled in a phased manner.

Digital learning and training need to be used extensively. A mission mode project under the 'National Rural Internet and Technology Mission' should use of tele-medicine and mobile health-care for rural health-care. IT should be used for agriculture for real time information; Self-help Groups; retail trade and SMEs; and rural entrepreneurs. National e-Governance plan should cover every government office from the centre to the panchayats. The 'E-Gram, Vishwa Gram' scheme in Gujarat is expected to be implemented nationwide. Promote e-Bhasha—National Mission for the promotion of IT in Indian Languages. SC/ST, OBCs and other weaker sections of the society ought to be brought within the ambit of IT enabled development. IT should protect India's priceless cultural and artistic heritage. It includes digitisation of all archives and museology, through 'open source' and 'open standard' software. Digitisation of all government work reduces corruption and delays. High-speed digital highways will unite the nation. Technology could reduce transmission and distribution losses. Mobile and e-Banking ensures financial inclusion. The government aims to make every household digitally literate with a goal to make India the Global Knowledge hub, with IT being a major driver and engine of growth.

Institutional Reform

The importance of Institutional Reform is utmost importance. It will improve the working efficiceny administrative, judicial, police and electoral sectors.

Administrative: Today, people of this country are frustrated with the present system. Our administrative set up should be people-centric, responsive and result-oriented. The government is expected to bring the following reforms:

The administration and its members should be made truly accountable. It will be so to their tasks as well as the people through rigorous evaluation process. Good performance will be rewarded. Non-performers will be given opportunities and training support. Rationalisation and convergence among the ministries, departments and other arms of the government will to focus on delivery. Government will draw expertise from the industry, academia and society. Services of youth in particular will be tapped to contribute in governance with fellowship and internship programmes.

Judicial: The government is committed to ensure Justice for All — justice which is prompt and accessible. Understanding that Justice Delayed is Justice Denied, it will adopt a multi-pronged approach to address the high pendency of cases in our judicial system. The government will accord high priority to judicial reforms. It will appoint judges; fill the vacancies, open new courts, set up a mechanism for speedy clearance of backlog of cases at various levels.

A mission mode project for vacancies in the judiciary is on. It should double the number of courts and judges in the subordinate judiciary. National Judicial Commission will shortlist judges in higher judiciary. A fund for modernisation of courts will improve the operational efficiency. A separate class of courts for cases involving specified commercial laws will be set up fast track the litigation process and reform the criminal justice system to make dispensation of justice simpler, quicker and more effective and after examining the recommendations of earlier reports on this subject.

Development Agenda

Initiate the computerisation and networking of courts all over the country; extend fast track courts to all layers of the judiciary; expand alternative dispute redressal mechanisms through Lok Adalats and Tribunals; implement the National Litigation Policy in letter and spirit to reduce average pendency time of cases; review and reduce significantly the number of cases, in which the Government is a litigant in the next five years; periodically review and refine/ scrap outdated laws. Create courts specially equipped to deal with IPR cases; give special emphasis to the development of Alternate Dispute Resolution mechanisms – like Lok Adalats, Arbitration and Conciliation centres.

Set up a comprehensive National e-Library, empowering Lawyers. Aim to enhance the number of women in the Bar as well as Bench, reducing the gender gap in judiciary. Evolve a national network of specialised universities having expertise in complementary domains like Forensics, Arbitration, IPR, International Law, etc. Develop India into a Global Hub for Arbitration and Legal Process Outsourcing. The government will simultaneously reform the legal system to make it more accessible to the common man. For that it will undertake a comprehensive review of the legal system to simplify complex legislations–converge overlapping legislation, as well as remove contradictory and redundant laws. Establish an institutional mechanism to periodically review. Let that give suggestions for refining our laws. Simplify legal procedure and language. Make legal information open and freely accessible. Run legal awareness programme. Introduce the programme in school curriculum, making the common man aware of his rights and duties.

Police: The country's police forces are entrusted with the crucial responsibility of maintaining law and public order. It forms one of the central pillars of our democracy. The government will work with the states to empower them with the authority, independence and resources necessary to deliver.

Roll out a comprehensive strategy for bringing the Indian Police at par with international standards. Facilitate training and capacity building of Police forces. Modernise the police force, equip them with latest technology. Initiate the networking of police stations across the country for intelligence sharing and crime control. Strengthen the investigations; make them swift, transparent, fair, clear and decisive. Act as an inescapable deterrent to wrong-doers and a protective shield to the innocent.

Develop specialised expertise in investigation; through continuous training. It should be especially so in evolving competencies. Overhaul our intelligence set up. Focus on co-ordination and integration of human and technological Intel. Comprehensively gear it towards collecting real time, specific and actionable inputs. Modernise prison system with technology and infrastructure. Let that strengthen the security as well human rights and correctional dimensions. Work towards evolving common national standards and protocols. Train and technologically enable the police to track, pursue, as well as prevent cyber crime.

Bring Coastal States on a common platform. Discuss about the issues of marine policing. Reinterpret the age-old concept of community policing in modern times. Evolve ways for the police to reach out to the people. Build bonds of trust and friendship—including spreading out into areas of public safety and public wellness. Give special emphasis for improving the working conditions and welfare of police personnel.

Electoral: Initiate electoral reforms to eliminate criminals. It will seek, through consultation with other parties. Evolve a method of holding Assembly and Lok Sabha elections simultaneously. Apart from reducing election expenses for both political parties and government ensure stability for state governments. Revise the expenditure limits realistically.

Widen the Platform: Certain segments of India have been historically disadvantaged. It is due to lopsided development approach and skewed allocation of resources. These continue to lag behind the rest of the country in socio-economic indicators despite abundant natural resources and talent. Our demographic dividend is not being fully actualised. It is the duty of the government to enable every Indian to realise his or her full potential, ensure equitable growth and development. Empower each and every Indian through health and education. Increase opportunities by making Job creation central to our economic model. Ensure a basic level of infrastructure to all - Hhme, electricity, water, toilets and access.

Poor and Marginalised – Bridge the Gap: The real test of the success of any development process lies in the happiness of common man. The fruits of growth and development must reach the weakest, most deprived and remotest of people. *Antyodaya* - uplifting the poorest of the poor - extreme poverty and malnutrition should be treated as a National priority.

The Government will Take the Following Steps: Strengthen delivery of poverty alleviation programs through convergence, transparency and efficiency. Identify 100 most backward districts. Bring them at par with other districts through priority and integrated development. Strengthen the natural resource base of the people to tide over natural calamities. Aim to gainfully employ rural poor in agriculture and allied activities. Enable the urban poor to develop skills availing opportunities. Facilitate partnership across all levels of government, civil society, academic and financial institutions.

Time for Bold Steps

It is now PM Modi-led government's turn to rise to the expectations of the electorate. Ministers and bureaucrats work long hours, six days a week. Transparency rose with no signs of bribes are being taken to swiftly clear large projects. Pundits claim the Central government cannot make major changes to existing labour and land legislations. We have sought stealthy avenues to land and labour market reforms, through delegation of authority to states and tweaking of rules and regulations. Rajasthan's CM Vasundhara Raje Scindhia initiated a set of reforms viz., the Factories Act of 1948, Industrial Disputes Act of 1947 and Contract Labour Act of 1971. However, it could not improve marginally the lives of youth and unemployed, underemployed. For the laws or Act ratified takes their own time to get into practice, domestic norms are so, the laws framed during the first generation yield fruits to the third generation. But, the cost of project, technological development and the impact of world economy rob the outcome for charm the laws/Acts was made.

A huge momentum for change has infused a level of energy and dynamism at all levels of bureacracy. The ministers, bureaucrats and the people of India are ready for change. Why not clean up labour and land laws for all of India through central legislation? Why hold the vast majority of workers toiling in the informal sector hostage to the privileged status of a tiny elite labour force?Let us think equally big about private sector "projects" in manufacturing. Think about Foxconn, a manufacturing firm in China that assembles products for international brand names such as Apple and Dell of the United States and Nintendo and Sony of Japan. Foxconn alone employs 1.3 million workers and pays its workers $3 per hour (yes, per hour, not per day). Why can India not have Foxconn 10 years from now?

The President's address has made a roadmap to tackle the slowing of the economy, boost heavy investment in infrastructure and governance reforms. Tying in with what Modi said on the need for speedy decision-making, there will also be mention of zero tolerance towards terrorism and corruption. The address will stress on "...streamlining government processes, especially in infrastructure projects, a prime reason seen as reason for slowdown of the economy."

PM Development Agenda

The Indian President Pranab Mukherjee sets the Tone: The Indian President Pranab Mukherjee shared the Narendra Modi government's agenda for the country from the economy to the environment, from minorities to terrorism, a series of programmes on a variety of issues facing the country. He also spelled out the new government's stance on thorny issues like bilateral ties with Pakistan, water-sharing, FDI etc. Also mentioned Modi's much talked about 'minimum government, maximum governance', establishment of IITs and IIMs in every state, revival of economy, provision of housing and power for all by 2022 and zero tolerance for terrorism and concluded his speech by mentioning 'democracy, demography and demand'—three focus areas for development Prime Minister Modi has always stressed on.

Stable Govt: This has been an election of hope. It marks a turning point in the evolution of our democratic polity. The surge in aspirations and the belief that these could be realised through democratic processes, has been amply reflected in the record 66.4 per cent participation by voters, and a clear verdict in favour of a single political party after a gap of nearly 30 years. The electorate transcended the boundaries of caste, creed, region and religion to come together and vote decisively in favour of Development through Good Governance.

The country needed a strong and stable government that could provide effective leadership. The people have voted for a united, strong, and modern

India - *"Ek Bharat-Shreshtha Bharat"*. The government will work to fulfill these aspirations; with the involvement of all the 125 crore people of this great country.

The government is committed to nurturing the right environment for actualising this mandate of the people. For this, it pledges itself to the principle of *'Sabka Saath, Sabka Vikas'*; which can be fulfilled only through your active participation. We will work together to re-establish the credibility of the institutions of democracy. The government will function on the mantra of 'Minimum Government, Maximum Governance'. In all our actions, we will be guided by the core values of our great civilisation.

Policy for Poor: The government is dedicated to the poor. Poverty has no religion, hunger has no creed, and despair has no geography. The greatest challenge before us is to end the curse of poverty in India. It will not be satisfied with mere "poverty alleviation"; and commits itself to the goal of "poverty elimination". With a firm belief that the first claim on development belongs to the poor; the government will focus its attention on those who need the basic necessities of life most urgently. It will take necessary steps to provide security in its entirety to all citizens; through empathy, support and empowerment.

Food Inflation: There would be an emphasis on improving the supply side of various agro and agro-based products could prevent hoarding and black marketing. It will reform the Public Distribution System, incorporating best practices from the States. It is committed to improving the quality of life in our villages, through empowered Panchayati Raj institutions. A substantial part of investment will focus on creating community assets and improving basic infrastructure such as roads, shelter, power and drinking water. It will strive to end the rural-urban divide guided by the idea of Rurban; providing urban amenities to rural areas while preserving the ethos of the villages.

Agriculture: It is the source of livelihood for majority of our people. In the recent past, our farmers have been under severe stress with hopelessness to immolate. It is committed to reversing this unfortunate trend. It will increase investment in agriculture, both public and private, especially in Agri-infrastructure. Farming had to be into a profitable venture through scientific practices and Agro-technology. It will address issues pertaining to pricing and procurement of agricultural produce, crop insurance and post-harvest management. Productivity of Animal Husbandry will be increased. It will incentivise the setting up of food processing industries. The review of existing co-operative sector laws might remove anomalies and lacunae. A National Land Use Policy which will facilitate scientific identification of non-cultivable land and its strategic development.

Water Security: Each drop of water is precious. The government is committed to complete the long pending irrigation projects on priority. The 'Pradhan Mantri Krishi Sinchayee Yojana' with the motto of *'Har Khet Ko Paani'* is expected to support people. There is a need for seriously considering all options including linking of rivers, where feasible; for ensuring optimal use of our water resources to prevent the recurrence of floods and drought. By harnessing rain water through *'Jal Sanchay'* and *'Jal Sinchan'*, we could nurture water conservation and ground water recharge. Micro irrigation ought to be popularised to ensure 'Per drop-More crop'.

Education: India is the world's oldest civilisation. Today it is also a country with the largest population of the youth. We must equip and nurture youth with right kind of education, skill-set and opportunity to reap this demographic dividend. Youth Development could be translated into Youth-led Development and set up Massive Open Online Courses and virtual classrooms. It will formulate a National Education Policy aimed to meet the challenges posed by lack of quality, research and innovation in our educational institutions. IITs and IIMs have to be established in every state. In order to empower school teachers and students, a national e-library will be established. With the motto of *"Har Haath Ko Hunar"*, the government will strive to break the barriers between formal education and skill development, and put in place a mechanism to give academic equivalence to vocational qualifications. With the goal of skilled India, government will also launch a national multi-skill mission.

Sports: The children and youth of the country need avenues of recreation. It will develop them constructively and keep them fit. National Sports Talent Search System could facilitate development and promotion of Indian sports, particularly rural sports. Sports could be popularised by making it an integral part of the school curriculum and providing educational incentives. The country needs a holistic health care system, universally accessible, affordable and effective. To achieve this objective, it will formulate a New Health Policy and roll out a National Health Assurance Mission is expected to promote Yoga and AYUSH. Health care needs to involve professionals; health education and training. AIIMS like those institutes will be established in every state in a phased manner.

Swachh Bharat Mission: The people must not tolerate the indignity of homes without toilets and public spaces littered with garbage. Waste management and sanitation across the nation a "Swachh Bharat Mission" could be tribute to Mahatma Gandhi on his 150th birth anniversary to be celebrated in the year 2019. Keeping in mind welfare of the people belonging to the Scheduled Castes, Scheduled Tribes, Other Backward Classes and the weaker sections of our society; it will take steps to create an enabling eco-system of equal opportunity in education, health and livelihood. It is committed to launch a dedicated "Van Bandhu Kalyan Yojana". Electrification of tribal hamlets and connecting them with all-weather roads will be a priority area.

Minority: The minorities' equal partners in India's progress. The government will especially strengthen measures to spread modern and technical education among minority communities and a National Madarsa Modernisation Programme will be initiated. The welfare and rehabilitation of specially-abled people is integral to the government's vision of a caring society. It will take steps to provide dignity of life to them by facilitating their participation in all walks of life. Steps will be taken to identify their special needs and to provide institutional care to them.

Role of Women: It recognises the important role our women play in the development of our society and growth of the nation. It is committed to providing 33 per cent reservation to them in the Parliament and State Legislative Assemblies. With a commitment of *'Beti Bachao - Beti Padhao'*, the government will launch a mass campaign for saving the girl child and enabling her education. It will structure a comprehensive scheme, incorporating best practices from States in this regard. In the recent past, the country has witnessed some gruesome incidents of violence against women. The government will have a policy of zero tolerance for violence against women, and will strengthen the criminal justice system for its effective implementation.

India is a Federal Polity. The federal spirit has been diluted. The States and the Centre should function as an organic Team India. In order to actively engage with the States on national issues, the government will reinvigorate fora like the National Development Council and the Inter-State Council. The Centre will be an enabler in the rapid progress of States through Co-operative Federalism. State-specific development models will be developed taking into account the special needs and unique problems of coastal, hilly and desert areas. The highest priority will be accorded to bring eastern region of the country on par with west in terms of physical and social infrastructure. It is committed to address the issues on development of Andhra Pradesh and Telangana. The government will lay special emphasis on improving intra-region connectivity and border infrastructure in the north-east as well as in Jammu and Kashmir. The issue of infiltration and illegal immigrants in the region will be tackled on priority and fencing work pending along north-east border will be completed. Efforts will be made to ensure Kashmiri Pandits return to land of ancestors with full dignity, security and assured livelihood.

Lok Pal: The government is committed to provide clean and efficient administration focussed on delivery. The institution of Lok Pal is important to curb corruption. It will endeavour to formulate rules in conformity with the Act. It will take steps to build the confidence and morale of our bureaucracy; enabling with freedom to work, welcoming innovative ideas. It will stress on putting in place transparent systems and time-bound delivery of government services. The systems and processes will be revisited to make them citizen-friendly, corruption-free and accountable. Efforts will be made to eliminate obsolete laws, regulations, administrative structures and practices. Rationalisation and convergence among ministries, departments and other arms of government will be ensured to have focussed delivery. Digitisation of government records will be done for improving accessibility.

E-governance brings empowerment, equity and efficiency. It has the power to transform peoples' lives. IT will be used to drive re-engineering of government processes to improve service delivery and programme implementation. We will strive to provide Wi-Fi zones in critical public areas in the next five years. It will rollout broad band highway to reach every village and make schools e-enabled in phased manner. Technology will be used to prepare our children for a knowledge society. The national e-governance plan will be expanded to cover every government office from the centre to the panchayat for variety of services to citizens.

Social Media will be used as a tool for; participative governance, directly engaging people in policy-making and administration. It is determined to rid the country of the scourge of corruption and the menace of black money. The government has already constituted a SIT to unearth black money stashed abroad. This will be followed up vigorously by proactively engaging with foreign governments. The government will adopt a multi-pronged approach to clear backlog of cases in the judicial system. It will progressively modernise courts to improve operational efficiency, and reform the criminal justice systems to make dispensation of justice simpler, quicker and more effective. It will initiate a mission mode project for filling vacancies in the judiciary and for doubling the number of courts and judges in the subordinate judiciary in a phased manner. The government will give special emphasis to the development of Alternate Dispute Resolution mechanisms.

Our GDP growth has been less than five per cent. Tax collection has declined. Inflation continues to be at an unacceptable level for past two years. We will work together to usher our economy into a high growth path, rein in inflation, reignite the investment cycle, accelerate job creation and restore the confidence of the domestic as well as international community in our economy.

Induct GST: The government will create a policy environment which is predictable, transparent and fair. It will embark on rationalisation and simplification of the tax regime to make it non-adversarial and conducive to investment, enterprise and growth. It will make every effort to introduce the GST while addressing the concerns of States. Reforms will be undertaken to enhance the ease of doing business. A policy of encouraging investments, including through FDI; will be allowed in sectors that help create jobs and assets. For rapid creation of jobs in the manufacturing sector, the government will promote labour-intensive manufacturing. Employment opportunities will also be expanded by promoting tourism and agro-based industries. It will transform Employment Exchanges into Career Centres - connecting our youth with job opportunities in a transparent and effective manner through technology, through counselling and training. The government will strengthen the pension and health insurance safety nets for labour force of all categories accessing to modern financial services. It needs to transform ourselves into a globally competitive manufacturing hub powered by Skill, Scale and Speed. The government will set up world class investment and industrial regions, particularly along the Dedicated Freight Corridors and Industrial Corridors spanning the country. It will encourage the domestic industry to innovate and collaborate internationally. It will strive to move towards a single-window system of clearances both at the Centre and at the States through a hub-spoke model.

Global Trade: Erstwhile procedures will be simplified and trade infrastructure strengthened to reduce transaction time and costs. The SSI and Handicraft sectors will be enhanced technological, marketing and investment support. Export potential of this sector will be encouraged. Every effort will be made to improve the working conditions of weavers. A task force will review and revive our MSME sector. Robust infrastructure is one of India's major impediments. The government will chalk out an ambitious. A fast-track, investment friendly and predictable PPP mechanism will be put in place. Modernisation and revamping of Railways is on top of the infrastructure agenda, through a Diamond Quadrilateral project of high speed trains. The country will have a network of freight corridors with specialised Agri-Rail networks for perishable agricultural products. Investment in railways will be increased using innovative financing methods. Expansion of railways in Hilly States and Northeast region and modernisation of rail safety systems will be prime focus areas. It will encourage R&D and high level local manufacturing for railway systems. A fast, time-bound and well-monitored programme for execution of the National Highways programme will be initiated, to overcome the stagnancy of past few years. Low cost airports will be developed to promote air-connectivity to smaller towns. The government will evolve model of Port-led development. The government will modernise existing ports and developing new world class ports. We will connect the ports with the hinterland through road and rail. Inland and coastal waterways will be developed as major transport routes.

National Energy Policy: National Energy Policy will focus on development of energy-related infrastructure, human resource and technology. Electricity generation capacity through conventional and non-conventional sources will be substantially augmented. The national solar mission will connect households and industries with gas-grids. Reforms in the coal sector will be pursued with urgency for attracting private investment in transparent manner. The international civil nuclear agreements will be operationalised and nuclear power projects for civilian purposes will be developed. The government will build 100 cities focussed on specialised domains, equipped with world-class amenities. Integrated infrastructure will be rolled out in model towns to focus on cleanliness and sanitation. Every family will have a pucca house with water connection, toilet facilities, 24×7 electricity supply and access by 2022.

Sustainability: The government will sustain at the core of planning process. The environmental conservation can go hand in hand with development. Environment and forest clearance systems will be made more predictable, transparent and time-bound. Simultaneously, an effective system will be developed for sound appraisal processes and strict compliance of clearance conditions, especially those relating to rehabilitation of displaced communities and regeneration of forests. Cleaner fuels will be promoted to bring down pollution levels in our cities. The government will earnestly take up mitigation works to meet the challenges posed by climate change and will closely work with the global community. Conservation of Himalayan ecology will be a priority area through the national mission.

Natural Resources: The government will formulate clear and transparent policies on allocation of critical natural resources such as coal, minerals and spectrum. River Ganga is a part of our rich cultural heritage, a symbol of faith and the lifeline for millions. It continues to remain polluted with many stretches becoming dry in lean season. Necessary steps will be taken to ensure a perennial, clean and pristine Ganga.

Our rich cultural heritage is the very foundation on which rests the unity of our diverse nation. Indian languages are repositories of rich literature, history, culture, art. A national mission "e-Bhasha" will develop digital vernacular content and disseminate our classic literature in different languages. It will provide the required resources for maintenance and restoration of national heritage sites. The government will initiate a mission mode project to create 50 tourist circuits around specific themes. A National Mission for beautifying and improving the amenities and infrastructure at pilgrimage centres of all faiths will be launched. The government will encourage and incentivise private sector investments, domestic and foreign, in science and technology and in high-end research. It will build world class centres in the fields of nanotechnology, material sciences, thorium technology, brain research, stem cells, etc. The institute Technology for Rural Development and a Central University of Himalayan Studies will change the scenario.

Internal Security: The government will maintain utmost vigil in the area of internal security. A policy of zero tolerance towards terrorism, extremism, riots and crime will be pursued. The states will be assisted for modernising police infrastructure and equipment to tackle new forms of terrorism including narco-terrorism and cyber threats. The state governments will be consulted to effectively curb incidents of communal violence and the challenges from left-wing extremism. It will take steps to equip the security forces with the latest technology. It will carry out reforms in defence procurement to increase efficiency and economy. It will encourage domestic industry, including the private sector; to have a larger share in design and production of defence equipment. We will introduce policies to strengthen technology transfer, including through liberalised FDI in defence production. With readily available skilled human resource, India can emerge as a global platform for defence manufacturing including software, which will strengthen our defence and spur industrial development as well as exports. The country is proud of its Armed Forces. They serve the nation with professionalism, dedication and valour; securing our nation and supporting relief and rescue operations in the wake of disasters and calamities. We will strengthen defence preparedness by modernising our Armed Forces and addressing the shortage of manpower on priority. Recognising the importance of coastal security, government will set up a National Maritime Authority. It will do everything to repay the debt of our brave and selfless soldiers. It will appoint a Veterans Commission to address their grievances, so that they know that we don't stop caring for them when they retire from active service. The government will build a National War Memorial will honour the gallantry of our soldiers very soon. One Rank- One Pension scheme will be made through.

India's Foreign Policy: The government will engage with other countries on the strength of our values with pragmatism, leading to a doctrine of mutually beneficial relation. It is committed to build a strong, self-reliant and self-confident India; regaining rightful place in the comity of nations. It sent a unique and bold signal to the South Asian region and the world, by inviting neighbours to the swearing-in ceremony of the new Cabinet. We are grateful to them for accepting the invitation at such a short notice. Their participation not only added sheen, but also represented a celebration of democracy in the region. This shows government's commitment and determination to work towards building a peaceful, stable and economically inter-linked neighbourhood which is essential for the collective development and prosperity of the South Asian Region.We will further work together with South Asian leaders to revitalise SAARC for regional co-operation as a united voice on global issues. It emphasises that the future of shared prosperity can stabilise the region, which requires sensitivity to security concerns of terrorism to neighbours.

It will engage energetically with other neighbours in our region, including China, with whom it will work to further develop our Strategic and Co-operative Partnership. It will strive to make progress in the many initiatives that are ongoing with Japan, especially in the field of building modern infrastructure in our country. Russia remains a privileged and strategic partner and government will build further on the firm foundations of this relationship. India and the United States have made significant progress in developing strategic partnership over the years. Government will bring a renewed vigour to our engagement and intensify it in all areas, including trade, investment, science and technology, energy and education. India also values its broad-based cooperation with Europe. The government will make concerted efforts to achieve progress in key areas with the European Union as well as its leading members. Our softpower potential needs to integrate it into our external interchange, with particular emphasis on our rich spiritual, cultural and philosophical heritage. The government will revive Brand India riding on our strengths of 5T's: Tradition, Talent, Tourism, Trade and Technology.

Indian Diaspora had been a source of great pride. They have done pioneering work in diverse fields, held the highest public offices and worked hard to support localities and families in India. They have contributed immensely to their adopted country. They also carry a little flame of India in their hearts that can light up the promise of change in our country. A hundred years ago, in 1915, India's greatest Pravasi Bharatiya, Mahatma Gandhi, returned home and transformed the nation's destiny. The next Pravasi Bharatiya Diwas in January 2015 will thus be a special occasion. As we celebrate the centenary of Gandhiji's return to India. We would take steps that would deepen every NRI (Non-resident Indian) with India for development. The people of India have given a clear mandate. They want to see a vibrant, dynamic and prosperous India. They want to see a resurgent India regaining admiration and respect from international community. They want quick results, brimming with hope and expectation. With three Ds of Democracy, Demography and Demand on our side, India is poised to actualise these aspirations. We must rise to the occasion to fulfill these great expectations. We shall say with confidence and pride that we have done it after sixty months.

Opportune Time for Reform

The Modi government is proceeding apace to rein in petroleum subsidies, which have been a major fiscal headache for successive governments. First, it turned to the task of wiping out under-recoveries on diesel and freeing its pricing. Secondly, the direct benefit transfer scheme for cooking gas is being rolled out across cities. Another recent step is the decision to do away with the supply of subsidised kerosene through the public distribution system (PDS). Just as in the case of cooking gas, the idea behind stopping subsidised kerosene supply through the PDS is to ensure that subsidies are targeted at those who deserve them and that leakages are plugged. It is estimated that as much as 40 per cent of the subsidised kerosene supplied through the PDS is diverted, mainly to adulterate diesel. The government's decision to stop PDS supply appears well-founded. According to 2011 Census data, kerosene is no longer a fuel of choice for cooking but is used mainly for lighting. Cooking gas has replaced kerosene in urban and semi-urban areas as per the Census; biomass is the cooking fuel of choice in rural areas, with less than 2 per cent of rural households using kerosene as a medium. Armed with these findings, the government now wants to move to a cash transfer system for rural households that deserve subsidy.

The move will help the government cut down kerosene subsidy to about a fifth of what prevails now. According to data from the Petroleum Ministry, kerosene subsidy, shared between the government and the oil companies, was

Rs31,250.47 crore in 2013-14. This will come down to Rs.5,852.14 crore in the next year following the latest move. The decision, while helping to cut the Central budget deficit, shifts the onus to the States, which will now have to identify households that use the fuel for lighting. The choice will be between direct transfer of cash subsidy to these households on a regular basis, or upfront subsidy for them to install solar lighting systems. With the kerosene subsidy issue thus addressed, the government should now turn its attention to cooking gas subsidy. The fuel is also used by the middle-class and the rich who do not deserve the subsidy. With oil prices sliding, the time is opportune for the government to align cooking gas prices to the market without much pain being felt by consumers. Those found deserving of subsidy can be taken care of by the direct cash transfer mechanism. The time is also ripe for the government to attempt some serious reform of the pricing policies of the oil companies, which are rather opaque at this moment. The policy of linking pricing of fuels such as petrol, diesel and cooking gas with their respective landed costs needs review.

Land Acquisition Law Through Ordinance

The Narendra Modi government is set to unleash several big-ticket announcements over the next few weeks, starting with changes in the land acquisition law through an ordinance, setting the stage for the budget that will be unveiled at the end of February 2015 by finance minister Arun Jaitley. Unable to get parliamentary approval because it does not have the numbers in the Rajya Sabha, the government used the ordinance route to raise the foreign investment limit in the insurance sector to 49 per cent from 26 per cent signalling its determination to push through with reforms even at the cost of a political backlash. The government has been emboldened by the latest electoral win in Jharkhand and poll results in Jammu & Kashmir to pursue policy changes amid criticism from some quarters that it has not done enough in this regard since coming to power in May.

"There are a few more steps in the offing," said a senior government functionary, indicating that the reform momentum will be maintained. The direct benefit transfer scheme, aimed at ensuring that subsidies are sent to the bank accounts of beneficiaries, is set to be launched nationwide from January 1 following a pilot. The move could be followed up with the weeding out of some who have hitherto been beneficiaries of various welfare programmes.

There has been a clamour for changes in the land acquisition rule that came into force on January 1 because it has led to a complete halt in development. No land has been acquired for public purposes under the new law because of some of its draconian provisions, stalling industrial development that was already squeezed by the previous government's inability to get projects off the ground. The Right to Fair Compensation and Transparency in Land Acquisition, Rehabilitation and Resettlement Act 2013 was enacted by the previous United Progressive Alliance government after violent protests over land being taken away from farmers for various projects.

The government has already indicated its unhappiness with provisions of the law that have stalled land acquisitions. "Discussions are on... draft is being finalised," a senior government official said. "Ordinance could be taken up by the cabinet soon." The government favours expansion of the list of exempted sectors under the land law to include defence, education and health care and infrastructure while leaving compensation unchanged.

Modi calls for International Yoga Day

Yoga got a strong leg up on the world stage when Prime Minister Narendra Modi called for observing an International Yoga Day, describing the ancient science as "India's gift to the world." Modi's unexpected reference to yoga during his UN General Assembly speech came when he was talking about climate change and going back to basics. Yoga is not just about fitness or exercise, it is about changing one's lifestyle, Modi said, plugging for ancient practice that was introduced to the west by Modi's spiritual inspiration, Swami Vivekananda.

Yoga is enjoying rising popularity in the United States and has now become a multi-billion dollar business, but its link to India is often understated. Modi's public reference on the world stage to India's gift is possible meant to remind international audience of this link. Some organizations have been celebrating World Yoga Day since 2007 (the next one is on February 22, 2015), but it has no official sanction. Modi has said he is fortunate to have been introduced to the world of yoga and pranayama at a young age and it helps him synchronize the heart, mind, and body. India's Prime Minister has been keeping a nine-day Navratri fast during which time he subsists only on a liquid diet, mostly lemon juice, but he showed no sign of fatigue during his 30-minute speech that was delivered in a strong voice, without once pausing to even sip water. New York City itself is something of a yoga capital in the US, with enthusiasts promoting the science in public places such as Times Square and Central Park.

6 Economic Revival

Introduction

The people of India have decisively voted for a change under the dynamic leadership of Narendra Modi. The verdict represents the exasperation of people, status-quo. India unhesitatingly desires to grow. The government is duty bound to usher in a policy regime for macro-economic outcome of higher growth, lower inflation, sustained level of external sector balance and a prudent policy stance.

Worst Slowdown in 25 Years

The big challenge for the government will be to generate enough job opportunities. Some 10 million people enter the country's work force every year. India needs to grow eight per cent each year to prevent demographic disaster. The government will focus on bringing economy to the seven per cent.

Reduce Inflation: The government should be focussed on reducing inflation so that a sustainable environment can be created for growth. India's aggregate subsidy (including state and central government) is close to four per cent of GDP. $70-80 billon of excess cash prevails in the system without output. This extra cash creates excess demand leading to higher inflation. The government needs to prune the excess cash by cutting down subsidies. The government will bring down diesel subsidy to zero plugs in the deficiencies in the PDS and manage its food stocks better.

Improve Productivity: The incremental capital output ratio has halved over the course of five years. A large number of projects have stuck due to various reasons. If the government clears these projects things may improve. India needs quick executive decision through suave engagement with states.

Deleverage the Private Sector: The private sector debt has gone up. The government needs to transfer this debt from the private sector to the public sector. The government can fix this by ensuring that real rates are positive. Positive real rates will attract domestic savings to financial assets from physical assets. It will ultimately increase the deposit ratio of banks and create capacity in the banking system. Simultaneously, the government ought to recapitalise public sector banks. Positive real rates attract domestic investment to equity markets. The corporates could raise equity from markets. The stage is already set. The equity markets have turned positive. The window for equity issuance is open the state owned banks can now raise capital from the market.

Following steps should be taken to revive the moribund economy:

1. *Tame Inflation*: It is the top priority for the government, especially controlling food inflation that affects all the people, in particular the poor. The supply side needs to be tackled urgently. There should be a crackdown on hoarding. For longer-term, critical agriculture reforms, ignored for long, are required.

2. *Stimulate Growth:* It's important to not just pull the economy out of the worst phase of growth in a decade but take it back to 8-9 per cent levels to generate jobs. It's important to boost the manufacturing sector with easier clearances and easy access to finance.

3. *Control Subsidies and Rein in Fiscal Deficit*: The politics of entitlement and free flow of subsidies has taken a severe toll on government finances. Lower spending will translate into lower borrowings and create room for borrowing by the private sector.

4. *Boost Exports*: Rein in current account deficit (CAD) and maintain a stable rupee. The only way to bridge CAD is to boost exports. With demand remaining weak in the US and Europe, transaction costs need to be cut and other steps are requires to make exports competitive.

5. *Create Conditions for Lowering Interest Rates and Boosting Investments.* A curb on the inflation rate and a smaller borrowing programme will create conditions for RBI to reduce rates. At the same time, steps are required to boost FDI.

6. *Revisit BJP's Opposition to FDI in Multi-brand Retail.* Despite fears of this affecting our small shopkeepers, the experience worldwide is that robust chains of multi-brand retail outlets create jobs and cut out profiteering middlemen, as a result of which, prices actually come down. It also doesn't kill small neighbourhood shops.

7. *Scrap/amend Laws that are Inhibiting Foreign Investments*. A good example would be the retrospective tax law which was slapped on Vodafone, and alarmed global business.

Two Years to Repair, Three Years for Growth

The new government has to take a series of valuable steps to regain investor confidence. Fiscal consolidation has to be kept firmly in sight as part of its plan to mend the economy in the next two years. An aggressive push for growth in the remaining three years may complete the term. The government had to focus on a concrete plan to fix the struggling economy inherited with two consecutive years of growth below five per cent. No fiscal or monetary lever could stimulate economic expansion.

The first task is addressing inflation, so growth has to be revived without compromising on the fiscal consolidation. Quality fiscal consolidation will be the underlying theme. The target for next year's deficit will be narrower than the 4.5 per cent of GDP achieved last year. However, the government does not want the burden to be excessive. It is not likely to increase any taxes in the name of fiscal consolidation. There may be additional spending from the abolition of the diesel subsidy through monthly increases in the retail price and the restructuring of social sector schemes. A monthly price increase mechanism for cooking gas could also be introduced.

Growth-oriented Policies

G-20 is an Organisation of Developed and Emerging Economy: The Finance Secretary Arvind Mayaram is confident that this will be growth-oriented reform process could put the economy on a high-growth path. It is in line with the G-20 objective of strong, sustainable and balanced growth. Mayaram said at the G20 deputies' meeting in Australia, "Reform measures will be presented by the finance minister in the forthcoming budget which he couldn't speedy at this stage."

As for diesel, that will likely be completely deregulated in the coming months. The government has to foot a bill of about Rs 1 lakh crore on account of various subsidies including oil, food and fertiliser for the fourth quarter of the previous financial year. Global rating agencies will be closely watching the budget for reform signals. India's sovereign credit outlook for India will not depend on whether the new government keeps its fiscal deficit target for 2014-15 below or above 4.1 per cent of GDP set by the previous government. The recent Iraq crisis may have made the new government's task more difficult. It has curtailed the already constrained fiscal space. It will hold back from spending on the social sector or infrastructure to boost growth and lift people out of poverty. Our policy actions, excluding on infrastructure and trade, are expected to provide an additional 0.8 per cent growth rather than the targetted 2 per cent. The investment includes infrastructure that we need to put our heads together to come up. It will be replaced with new and additional policy actions to unlock our growth potential.

Cautious Start

The budget 2014-15 was caught up between high hopes and hard decisions. The Finance Minister Arun Jaitley in his budget speech said, "The prevailing economic situation presents a great challenge. It calls for a conscious choice to be made by all of us. Should we allow this drift to carry on and watch helplessly? Should we allow our future to suffer because of our indecisiveness? Should we be victims of mere populism or wasteful expenditure?" In such a challenging situation instead of going for Big Bang changes, he has opted for a Balancing Act between Ensuring Growth and Controlling Inflation, Industry and Agriculture, Populism and Pragmatism, Urbanisation and Rural Development. The Finmin encourages Indigenous Entrepreneurship and creating Conducive Environment for Investment in select sectors. While retaining the Stamp Modi of addressing high aspirations, he has cleverly played within the limitations of the fiscal restraint. Therefore, despite divergent views about presentation, details and specificities, all over budget is positively received. The maiden budget of the new government presented bears the stamp of Modinomics, because the announcements made by the Finance

Minister Arun Jaitley were in line with the vision and promises made by Narendra Modi during his election campaign.

The Finance Minister has sought to retain money into the wallet of the common man with personal tax proposals. These include raising the personal income tax exemption limit to Rs. 2.5 lakh from the existing Rs. 2 lakh. For senior citizens, it will go from Rs. 2.5 lakh to Rs. 3 lakh. In addition, investments up to Rs. 1.5 lakh, instead of the present Rs 1 lakh, will receive relief under Section 80C of the Income Tax Act. The deduction for interest payment on self-occupied house property will go up to Rs 2 lakh from the existing Rs. 1.5 lakh. The Budget's stated intent is to lay down broad policy indicators to enable the government deliver goods on big-bang economic reforms, lower inflation, provide jobs, empathetic governance, augment infrastructure and basic amenities. The Finance Minister did not disturb the previous government's schemes and projects including MGNREGA, the National Livelihood Mission and Industrial Corridors.

Roadmap to Stable Economy

The Finance Minister Arun Jaitley said the government will retain the fiscal deficit at 4.1 per cent of GDP against the target of 3 per cent. He believed fiscal prudence could lead to fiscal consolidation and discipline, while presenting 2014-15 Budgets in New Delhi. Jaitley said fiscal deficit would be brought down to 3.6 per cent (2015-16) and 3 per cent (2016-17). It touched a high of 5.7 per cent (2011-12), down 4.8 per cent (2012-13) and to 4.5 per cent (2013-14). The reduction was achieved by reduction in expenditure rather than realising higher revenues. Jaitley said two years of low GDP growth has brought standstill. A moderate increase in indirect taxes and large subsidy burden has kept the buoyant.

"There is a need to revive growth, particularly in manufacturing sector and infrastructure. A "turnaround" in the current account deficit (CAD) situation (2013-14) brought down GDP to 1.7 per cent (2013-14), from a record 4.7 per cent (2012-13). We must continue to be watchful about the CAD," he said.

2014 has been the year of Challenges and Reforms for India

2014 was one of the most challenging years for India. For two consecutive years our GDP growth was sub 5 per cent. Employment generation had declined, the revenue buoyancy was low and the country had become investment starved.

The 2014 general election results brought in an air of freshness. After thirty years, the Indian electorate gave a majority to a single party in the Lok Sabha. The Government led by Prime Minister Narendra Modi promised to be decisive and firm. The popular expectation was that the Government would usher in an era of reforms and growth. In the past seven months, the Government has undertaken more reform oriented measures than any Government in recent memory. Some of the steps are as under:

Outlining the vision of co-operative federalism through the creation of successor to the Planning Commission. The new structure would provide an alternative to the command and control economy. Building a national consensus and introducing a bill to amend the constitution to implement the Goods and

Services Tax (GST). Opening the gates of investment by raising FDI limits in the insurance, defence and the railways. The FDI conditions in real estate have been liberalised.

Issuing an ordinance to amend the complicated procedures of the land acquisition law. The new law facilitates development but balances it with higher compensation, relief and rehabilitation measures for the farmers. Compensation and RNR package has been made entirely applicable to the thirteen exempted laws. Clearing up the mess in the coal and power sector, a law has been introduced to facilitate a transparent and non-discretionary method of allocation of coal blocks, enabling commercial mining to enhance the potential of the sector. This will cut down power cost and increase generation. Deregulation of diesel prices and facilitating the opening up of petrol and diesel sector to private investment.

Raising the gas prices while maintaining a balance between cost to the consumers and the need of gas exploration in the country. Moderating inflation and particularly inflation in agricultural items. Replacing the model of cooking gas subsidy to direct transfer so deserving consumers get benefit and leakages in subsidy are plugged to the benefit of the exchequer. Unleashing an era of financial inclusion, providing Pradhan Mantri Jan Dhan Yojana where over 10 crore accounts of the weaker sections have been opened. The DBT cash benefits will be transferred to this account. Account holders have an accidental, LIC policy and overdraft facility. Launching flagship programmes such as Swachch Bharat Abhiyan, Digital India and Skilled India so that the real image and potential of India is explored. Facilitating States like Rajasthan to usher in an era of labour law reforms. Major tax rebates given to tax payers by raising the income tax limit, and providing incentives on both savings and housing investments. Rationalizing tax management to end the image of India having an ultraaggressive tax policy.

Resolving of pending disputes through appropriate mechanisms so that our tax structures do not become a disincentive against investments. Giving major tax rebates to the manufacturing sectors which is facing a slowdown. Undertaking various banking sectors reforms such as recapitalisation of banks, professionalising managements, bringing Government equity to 52 per cent and allowing greater autonomy to banks and financial institutions. Undertaking major steps to unearth black money, both domestically and that lying in foreign bank accounts. Assessment of assesses with illegal foreign accounts available with the government in India to be completed by 31st March, 2015 and prosecutions launched against those against whom evidence is available. Amending provisions of the Companies Act to add to ease of doing business in India. Giving major boost to tourism by introduction of e-visa. Various measures for trade facilitation by allowing 24 × 7 custom clearance on 17 airports and 18 seaports. Despite major reforms steps taken, there are still challenges which economy faces. Investment needs to be enhanced and encouraged. Infrastructural spending has to be stepped up. Manufacturing sector has to be given a major push. This has to be done through encouraging public and private investment. This is our resolve for the upcoming year. siness Gets Back its Buoyancy

The NDA government returned to power when the economy was facing serious challenges: The GDP grew at sub-five per cent for two consecutive years. Inflation was above the RBI's comfort zone. The investor and consumer confidence had been shaky. The business sentiment perked up and factory order books improved as reflected in the HSBC Purchasing Managers Index up 53 in July as against 51.5 in June. The GDP during April-June hung around 5.7 per cent, the highest in ten quarters. The excise duty concessions were extended to boost demand in the passenger vehicle and some other sectors. The passenger vehicle sector seems to have made u-turn with July showing a positive growth in sales for the third month.

The 2014-15, Union Budget promised India would no longer resort to retrospective taxation. It was a long-standing and significant grievance of investors. The government took steps to make the tax regime more predictable and investor-friendly through advanced rulings and dispute settlements mechanism. There was an intention for subsidy reforms for the plugging of leakages in the delivery system. The government followed up the austerity measures from the Expenditure Reforms Commission. The commission set up a committee to review the economic cost of foodgrains payable to the highly inefficient Food Corporation of India. The relaxed the FDI cap in defence and introduced a Bill in Lower House for insurance sector. The opening up of these sectors is likely to generate enhanced investment, especially in defence manufacturing. The FDI conditions for the development of housing were also relaxed. The price rise, particularly in food items, the government announced a price stabilisation fund set up with a Rs 500-crore corpus. In consultation with the States, it threatened to make hoarding a non-bailable offence. An export curb on onions and other items prone to seasonal increases in prices hiked allocations from the buffer stocks of rice to the poor. It released wheat supplies from its granaries into the open market for stabilising cereal prices. The wholesale price inflation swinging between seven to nine per cent (2011-13) reached 5.19 per cent in July. Retail inflation fell from 8.6 per cent in April to 7.96 per cent in July, despite poor monsoon.

Make in India: FM Pledges to Remove Barriers to Businesses

The government on Dec 29, 2014 pledged to remove entry barriers to business and ensure a competitive tax regime to push manufacturing growth under its "Make in India" programme, even as it blamed high interest rate for slowdown. The programme aims at manufacturing low-cost quality products both for domestic as well as export market, finance minister Arun Jaitley said here. Criticising the monetary policy of RBI governor Raghuram Rajan, he said high interest rate is the "singular factor" which responsible the slowdown in manufacturing sector.

"The entry point into the manufacturing sector itself has to be eased. Our initial barriers have to be lowered and perhaps even removed. If we keep the doors closed, investments won't come in," he said at a "Make in India" event.

He further said there is a need to ensure liquidity in the markets. "We need to ensure capital is available, we need to ensure that those sectors which are starving we are in a position to provide adequate capital to those industries." The success of bankers' retreat with Prime Minister Narendra Modi later this week and the "Make In India" campaign will give a fillip to manufacturing, he added. Jaitley also rejected Rajan's criticism of Modi's pet programme "Make in India", saying that it is about manufacturing of quality products at low costs and it was not relevant whether they are sold in India or abroad.

"Whether 'Make in India' is made for consumers within India or outside is not so relevant. The principle today says that consumers across the world like to purchase products which are cheaper and are of good quality. They hire services which are cheaper and good quality," Jaitley said.

Earlier this month, Rajan had sounded a word of caution about the new government's "Make in India" campaign, saying it assumes an export-led growth path of China and it should rather be "Make for India" with a focus on manufacturing products for the domestic market. The RBI governor had said he was "cautioning against picking a particular sector such as manufacturing for encouragement, simply because it has worked well for China. "India is different, and developing at a different time, and we should be agnostic about what will work".

Stressing on the importance of domestic manufacturing, Jaitley said: "... if we lose out on cost, quality then we would be threatened with a situation where in we would become nation of traders rather than nation of manufacturers."

Tax Reforms

Taxes are important for every economy. It funds government expenditure on security and welfare of people. In the interim Budget (2014-15) the UPA had set revenue collection target for direct and indirect taxes. The government retains these targets and shall endeavour to achieve. The impact of tax changes proposed has been factored into the Budget Estimates (2014-15). Nonetheless, we propose to introduce measures to revive the economy. Promote investment in manufacturing sector and rationalise tax provisions to address the problem of inverted duty structure in certain areas, and give relief to individual taxpayers and certain sectors of economy.

Tax Administration

The sovereign right of the government to undertake retrospective legislation is unquestionable. However, this power has to be exercised with extreme caution and judiciousness keeping in mind the impact of each such measure on the economy and the overall investment climate. This government will not ordinarily bring about any change retrospectively which creates a fresh liability. Eerybdoy is aware that consequent upon certain retrospective amendments to the Income Tax Act 1961 through the Finance Act 2012, a few cases have come up in various courts and other legal fora. The cases are at different stages of pendency and will reach logical conclusion. At this juncture, we would like to convey to the investors' community at large that we are committed to provide a stable, predictable taxation investor-friendly regime. We have decided that fresh cases arising out of retrospective amendments of 2012 in respect of indirect transferers will be scrutinised by a high-level committee to be constituted by the CBDT before any action is initiated in such cases. It is hoped that the investor community within and abroad would repose confidence on our stated position and participate in the Indian growth with renewed vigour.

Other Tax Related Measures

Advance Rulings: Tax demand of more than Rs. 4 lakhs crore is under dispute and litigation before various courts and appellate authorities. The new government proposes to make certain legislative and administrative changes. Currently, an advance ruling can be obtained about the tax liability of a non-resident from the Authority for Advance Rulings. This facility is unavailable to resident taxpayers except public sector undertakings. It proposes to enable resident taxpayers to obtain an advance ruling in respect of income tax liability above threshold to strengthen the authority by constituting additional benches.

As an administrative measure, Govt. proposes to set up a high level committee to interact with trade and industry on a regular basis. It will ascertain areas where clarity in tax laws is required. The Central Board of Direct Taxes and the Central Board of Excise and Customs shall issue appropriate clarifications, wher necessary, on the tax issues within a period of two months.

Transfer pricing is a major area of litigation for resident and non-resident taxpayers. The government has proposed certain changes in its regulations. These measures would go a long way in improving the confidence of taxpayers and would provide certainty and clarity in tax laws.

Goods and Services Tax (GST)

The debate whether to introduce a Goods and Services Tax (GST) must come to an end. Some states have been apprehensive about surrendering their taxation jurisdiction. Others want to be adequately compensated. The matter has been discussed with the states both individually and collectively. Govt. shall approve the legislative scheme, enabling the introduction of GST. This will streamline the tax administration, avoid harassment of the business and result in higher revenue collection for the centre and the states. Govt. assures states that the Centre will be more than fair in dealing with them.

Milestone for Tax Reform

Implementation of the long-pending GST will be a key milestone for the economic reform process as it would improve tax administration and mobilise resources. Tax reform would also be critical for improving the ease of doing business. The introduction of GST will have a significant bearing on the resource-raising potential of state governments, besides being an important tax reform measure. Replacing existing indirect taxes, the GST will create a national market. It eliminates cascading taxes and aligns imports and exports. The move will improve competitiveness of production and exports.

"CII strongly advocates early implementation of GST. It would increase GDP growth by about 1.5 per cent and hopes that the suggestion in the survey on a single-rate GST would be fast-tracked," said Ajay S Shriram, president. The Direct Tax Code (DTC) would be critical for clean modern replacement of the existing laws. Issue related to compensation to states and the demand to keep petroleum products and entry tax out of the purview of GST need to be sorted out.

Tough Decisions to be Taken: The government at the Centre can take bold steps: *First*, there is no need for miserliness with the states in terms of giving them so-called compensation to persuade them to sign up for the GST. A few tens of thousands of crores in payment to states to cover estimate of losses through the GST, as well as generously settling earlier VAT and sales tax claims, would be a masterstroke. States are likely to use these funds to cover up their battered balance sheets; the combined fiscal deficit of the Central and state governments are unlikely to explode.

Second, the officials must be duty-bound to implement the law fairly *via-a-vis,* tax-paying citizens. It should not be the job of government officials to hound citizens for taxes.

Third, the government should make a one sentence announcement that the notorious "Vodafone" amendment will be made prospective one.

Fourth, a settlement commission is expected to resolve speedily and decisively a host of legal wrangles that have accumulated under previous dispensations. This would include matters like transfer pricing claims, on site-offshore revenue splits and other issues that have bedevilled tax administration and made it hostile to business and entrepreneurship.

Reviving the Investment Climate: "Reviving the investment climate" is one of its main priorities and this one decision of forbearance in litigation can single-handedly unleash the animal spirits of investments like no other, annouces by the government.

The Big Brother rating agencies happy had been habitual in postponing government payments. State governments, municipalities, oil companies and fertiliser companies that are asked to wait for payments in turn delay making payments to their supply chain; literally, thousands of suppliers and vendors to the government face endless delays in getting legitimate payments. This has several perverse effects on the economy. Many firms, especially smaller ones, go under; banks that have financed the so-called "risk-free" government receivables get stuck with bad loans. The overall effect of such capricious delays is to paralyse an economy in a gridlock mode. Making a set of large one-time payments to eliminate arrears will definitely blow up the fiscal deficit.

In recent years, concern for fiscal rectitude has forced the government to go in for public-private partnerships in the area of infrastructure. Many PPP projects are stuck in legal quagmires; it will take time for a new and hopefully fair and transparent system to emerge. In the meantime, infrastructure should not wait. The government should go ahead with state-funded infrastructure delivered by a competent and autonomous set of state institutions. This is based on the hope, perhaps optimistic, that the new government can pull off such an effort competently. This may be bad for the fiscal deficit, but may end up being anti-inflationary from supply side. If these risks create trouble, let us remember that it is not Year 1, but Year 5 that counts for a re-election. By that time, the risks would have paid off and India will be in double-digit growth mode.

Tax Exemption Limit Raised to Rs. 2.5 Lakh

The Finance Minister Arun Jaitley raises tax exemption limit to Rs 2.5 lakh from Rs. 2 lakh, providing a relief of Rs. 5,000. With the view to provide relief to small and marginal and senior citizen, and propose to increase the personal income tax exemption limit by Rs. 50,000 from Rs. 2 lakh to Rs. 2.50 lakh in case of individual tax payer below the age of 60 years. The proposal, according to an estimate, is likely to be benefit about 2 crore tax payers. Similarly, tax exemption limit raised from Rs. 2.5 lakh to Rs. 3 lakh for senior citizens. Jaitley does not propose to make any change in the rate of surcharge for either corporates or individual. The education cess for them shall continue at three per cent.

Thus, the tax on income from Rs. 2.5 lakh to Rs. 5 lakh is retained at 10 per cent, up to Rs. 10 lakh at 20 per cent and above Rs. 10 lakh at 30 per cent. Noting that households are main contributors to savings. The investment limit under

80C has been raised to Rs. 1.5 lakh from the existing Rs. 1 lakh to encourage savings. Investment in Public Provident Fund up to Rs. 1.5 lakh would now be exempt from tax. This was earlier pegged at Rs. 1 lakh. Tax deduction limit raised on account of interest of housing loan in case of self occupied property to Rs 2 lakh from Rs 1.5 lakh.

The increase in basic exemption limits and under Section 80C have been long-standing demands of taxpayers given that inflation has eroded the value of the current limits. Analysts, while commending the overdue concessions, point out the Minister could have been a little more generous. The Section 80C limit could have been hiked by Rs. 1 lakh (as opposed to Rs. 50,000 now) given that the government is keen to divert household savings to financial instruments from physical assets. For those who travel abroad, the Finance Minister has added an additional incentive in the form of a higher baggage allowance which goes up from Rs. 35,000 to Rs. 45,000.

Inflation

RBI Role to Control Inflation

The Reserve Bank of India (RBI) Governor Raghuram Rajan is expected to join hands with the government to bring down high inflation. The plan to curb food inflation seems sensible. The public's inflation is expectated to fall. Indian bond yields fell in anticipation of RBI to stabilise the economy. The benchmark 10-year bond yield fell 4 basis points to 8.61 per cent, following RBI Governor's comments. The apex bank has raised interest rates three times by a total of three-quarters of a percentage point in an attempt to curb persistently high inflation. Consumer price inflation (CPI) picked up in April, while wholesale inflation moderated but remained at elevated. Rajan is a former International Monetary Fund (IMF) chief economist and is widely viewed as India's most capable technocrat. He is expected to win the respect of investors for his handling of a currency crisis that hit Asia's third-largest economy last year. The RBI chief said he was worried about non-performing assets in the banking sector, but wanted to redress the grievance.

Centre-State Co-ordination

To deal with Hoarders and Black-marketeers to Check Inflation: PM Narendra Modi sought co-ordination between the centre and states on contingency plans. He asked states to set up fast-track courts to check hoarders and black-marketeers. He directed that adequate water, power and seed supply should be ensured to the farmers' so that the production is not affected due to scant rainfall.

The Agriculture Ministry has firmed up a contingency plan for more than 500 districts. The Prime Minister directed officials of maximum possible use being made of the existing water resources through rainwater harvesting. He emphasised on ensuring adequate power and seed availability for agricultural sector, and directed that NREGA be used to generate rural employment, if necessary. The country has received 45 per cent less rainfall in the first spell till June 17. Met deparment has forecast monsoon to be below normal at 93 per cent of the long period average. Rising prices of essential food items like vegetables, fruits and cereals pushed up wholesale price index based inflation to five-month high of 6.01 per cent. Price of potatoes and onion has risen to about Rs 25-30 per kg in the national capital.

India Inc Supports Modi's Vision

The Prime Minister Narendra Modi endorsed efforts to improve farm productivity, rein in price rise and impart skills to youth will transform the nation in the days to come. PM sought agriculture productivity through modern farm techniques and university-farmer collaboration hold the key to check price rise. He said the foremost priority of his government would be uplift of the poor and ensuring that nobody is without a house with water, electricity and toilet by 2022, when the country celebrates 75th year of independence. India Inc endorses his dream of providing housing with modern amenities, including electricity, broadband connectivity, sanitation and educational reach. Emphasising the importance of increasing farm productivity, Modi said there is a need for use of modern technique in the agriculture sector because farm land is shrinking with rising population.

According to CII, the existing educational framework needs to be overhauled to provide skills training to the vast majority of our labour force. Having an employment ready workforce is an imperative for meeting the aspirations of the youth for social stability. The party manifesto had listed many steps to contain inflation, price stabilisation fund, setting up of special courts to deal with hoarding and black marketing, unbundling of the Food Corporation of India (FCI) and establishment of national agriculture market.

Price Rise: Runaway food inflation crippled household budgets. It contributed to the overall inflationary trend under the Congress-led UPA's watch. The food and nutritional security of millions is threatened. The committee headed by Narendra Modi, submitted a report on food inflation.

Making India Inc. Accountable

It is not the responsibility of the government alone to act in order to curb corruption; corporate firms need to be proactive as well in checking fraudulent financial practices.

The winter session of Parliament witnessed a noisy debate on the black money controversy. Governments of all hues have disappointed the Indian janata on the issue of black money and the failure is often associated with a perceived nexus between politicians and big business, weak laws and poor enforcement. At the G20 summit in Brisbane, Prime Minister Narendra Modi had made statements regarding getting international cooperation to bring the unaccounted wealth of Indian individuals and organisations back from global tax havens, but back home these have not inspired much confidence.

A recent report from the Organisation for Economic Cooperation and Development (OECD) hints at multinational companies using internal loans and complex financial structures as a strategy for tax evasion. The OECD report raises several concerns relating to the erosion of the tax base in countries due to multinational companies adopting such practices. The Global Financial Integrity Report, released in December 2013, shows that 60 per cent of black money generated in developing countries such as India happens because of corporate tax evasion. In this report, India figures among the six Asian countries that are in the top 15 exporters of illicit capital, mostly due to trade-based money laundering. The report further says real GDP growth is significantly related to driving the flow of illicit money.

What that means is that greater economic growth and greater international trade is only likely to increase illicit capital flows out of the country. A 2012 White Paper on Black Money brought out by the Finance Ministry had observed that in India, more than 60 per cent of global trade is carried out by associated enterprises of multinational enterprises, with shifting of taxable income from high-tax to low-tax jurisdictions in these enterprises being a favoured method for minimising tax liability.

While the current discourse has largely focussed on the question of bringing back illicit money that has already been transferred discreetly to Swiss banks, there is also need for concentrating attention closer home and looking at ways to strengthen vigil mechanisms that will ensure the accountability of corporate firms in India. The Switzerland envoy's comments that India must show proof of fraud before seeking information on black money stashed in Swiss banks point to the absence of a healthy monitoring mechanism to curb fraudulent financial transactions at home.

Supply side of corruption: Corruption, which includes concerns pertaining to black money, has a supply side to it as well. The moment we take cognisance of this, it would become evident why checking corruption at the source is crucial for addressing present concerns. It is not the responsibility of the government alone to act in order to curb corruption; corporate firms need to be proactive as well in checking such practices.

The 2014 Global Fraud Survey conducted by Ernst & Young's (EY) Fraud Investigation and Dispute Services (FIDS) wing shows that "unethical behaviour" persists among Indian businesses with practices to win/retain businesses ranging from offering entertainment, making cash payments, giving personal gifts and misstating company's financial performance. A whopping 71 per cent of participants in the survey said at least one of these practices for winning/retaining businesses was "justified" in India. Further, to the question whether bribery/corruption happens widely in businesses in India, 68 per cent of the participants answered in the affirmative. The report further shows that 71 per cent of Indian participants had not received any anti-corruption training and 53 per cent also reported the absence of whistle-blowing hotlines for monitoring compliance with anti-corruption laws in India. In another 2014 survey by EY FIDS on the compliance with the whistle-blowing framework provided under the Companies Act, 2013, only 13 per cent of the respondents indicated that their whistle-blowing frameworks were fully compliant with what was required by law. The survey also stated that only 22 per cent of the respondents had implemented the framework because they considered the structured mechanism integral to their business operations. The principal respondents of this survey comprised senior executives in business functions, including internal audit and legal compliance, representing Indian enterprises with domestic operations as well as Indian subsidiaries of MNCs.

Arpinder Singh, Partner and National Leader at EY FIDS, who oversaw the surveys, said, "While many organisations had a whistle-blower policy in place, half of the respondents offered only one channel for reporting of complaints — which is more a 'tick in the box' approach than actually reaping the real benefits of a whistle-blowing framework. This shows that while organisations are taking the initial steps to be compliant, they still have a long way to go in establishing a robust whistle-blowing framework."

What we can infer from this is there is not enough incentive for reporting of financial malpractice among Indian enterprises at present. Since its revision, the Companies Act 2013 has introduced a provision for mandatory vigil mechanism to monitor fraudulent practices, and also ensured the appointment of independent directors, who must "ascertain and ensure" that the company has an "adequate and functional" vigil mechanism and that the interests of the person using this mechanism are protected.

Whistle-blowing frameworks within companies cannot be an answer for addressing ongoing black money-related concerns since the matter largely falls within the realm of banking and taxation. But they help in pressuring companies to comply with anti-fraud mechanisms mandated by law.

Speaking from a Companies Act perspective, Mr. Singh said that specific revisions as well as additional guidance focussed on vulnerable industries such as gems and jewellery, real estate, NGOs, etc., which are currently unregulated from an anti-money laundering perspective, call for strengthening compliance to the monitoring framework. Having a reporting mechanism to an independent body such as the Financial Intelligence Unit (FIU), under the Ministry of Finance, could also be considered as a good starting point, he added.

Lessons from the US

The anti-fraud mechanisms available in the United States have saved millions of dollars of losses to the government there. These offer valuable lessons for India. Andrew Beato, chair, False Claims Act and Whistleblower Practice Group at Stein Mitchell Muse Cipollone and Beato LLP, said the False Claims Act in the US allows citizens to report instances of abuse of public money for personal gain. "For every dollar that the US government invests in implementing this law, they earn back 20 dollars," he said. To cover tax frauds, the US Internal Revenue Service runs a separate whistle-blower programme. He cited the example of Bradley Birkenfeld, the whistle-blower in the tax evasion case involving Swiss global financial services company UBS AG in which cross-border fraud by American citizens to the tune of $780 million was exposed. The IRS whistle-blower programme helped Mr. Birkenfeld win $104 million from the tax authorities in return for his services. Mr. Beato, who had represented the case of the Ranbaxy whistle-blower Dinesh Thakur in the US courts, said that the absence of a comparable mechanism in India to safely report corporate fraud compelled Indian citizens to turn to the US to report such practices.

In an interview published in The Hindu on December 3, Switzerland's envoy to India Linus von Castelmur had remarked that India must show proof of fraud before seeking information from them on the illegal wealth of Indians held in their banks. The envoy's comments draw attention to the perils of not having a healthy monitoring mechanism to curb fraudulent financial transactions in India. The hard lesson for India remains that curbing financial fraud, like charity, has to begin at home.

Promises to Rein in Prices

Vowing to control inflation, PM Modi said improving agriculture productivity through modern farm techniques and university- farmer collaboration hold the key to check price rise. Replying to the motion of thanks to President's address in Lok Sabha, Modi said his government's top priority is to provide every citizen with a house that has running water, electricity and toilet. No person should go to bed hungry, he said while stressing the government's resolve to bring food prices under check.

The retail inflation accelerated to a three-month high of 8.59 per cent in April, mainly due to increasing prices of vegetables, fruits and milk. "We have promised to control inflation. We are determined achieve this target," he said. "We will do this (control inflation) not only because it is our election promise but we want every poor to have access to food," he said, adding that "this is our collective responsibility.

Govt. May do Away with LPG Subsidy for Rich

The government is considering doing away with the LPG subsidy for the well-off, Union Finance Minister Arun Jaitley said recently.

"The next important decision India will have to take is whether people like me...(are) entitled to get our LPG subsidy," he said at the HT Leadership Summit. "I think the sooner we are able to take these decisions as to who is entitled to these subsidies, of course some people would be, the better it would be for our system. These decisions are all on our agenda," he added.

Currently, 12 cylinders are available to consumers at a subsidised rate of Rs 414 each (in Delhi). Any requirement beyond this will have to be purchased at the market price of Rs 880 per 14.2—kg cylinder. Jaitley said: "Once political leadership, particularly the man on the top, has decisiveness, the most complicated of the decisions will also become simple.

"One does not have to wait for years to decide on coal blocks or what to do with spectrum or natural resources, or with diesel pricing or with gas pricing."

Some of these decisions had been complicated over the years, but the new government wasted no time and simply took a call on them he said, adding that "I think that's the agenda we continue to follow". Jaitley further said that India is at a crucial stage "where we must not exhaust our patience" as global investors are looking at the country with renewed interest. After coming to power, the Narendra Modi-led government deregulated diesel prices and linked them to the market rate. Earlier, the government used to provide subsidy on diesel. Jaitley said he was "almost ready" with the proposal on the Goods and Services Tax and was confident that the Constitution Amendment Bill on it would be introduced in the next session. Referring to long-pending insurance bill, he said "we are on the verge" of opening the sector a little more. The Bill proposes to increase foreign direct investment limit in the insurance sector to 49 per cent from the current 26 per cent.

Poor to Gain from per-kg LPG subsidy

The big bang reforms rolled out by the Modi government in the oil and gas sector further opened it up to the private sector, but also aimed to make subsidies more accessible to the poor. Instead of a per-cylinder basis, LPG subsidy will be provided on a per-kg basis. As a result of the government's decision on reforms in the oil and gas sector, LPG subsidy will for the first time become available to slum dwellers and migrant labourers as it will apply to all purchase of LPG irrespective of cylinder size. Earlier smaller sized cylinders were excluded from the subsidy. The subsidy will be provided through direct cash transfers to plug leakages.

"The shift to per-kg basis will make the subsidy available to the poor who are truly deserving of the benefit but never manage to get gas connections and are forced to buy small sized unsubsidised cylinders from the market," a finance ministry source said. The decision to completely de-control diesel prices will pave the way for private companies including Reliance and Essar to resume retail operations that they had shut 12 years back and bring fresh investors in to the sector, the official said.

"The diesel decontrol along with the already in place petrol prices deregulation creates a level playing field for private investors vis-a-via government-owned oil companies... this will attract investments into retail and even refining and exploration and will revive a key energy sector boosting growth," he said.

Cash Transfers Can Work Better Than Subsidies

With oil prices falling, it was perhaps a good time to fade out fuel subsidies. All subsidies are inefficient and distortionary, and most are regressive. The same could be said of costly public works schemes as well. By contrast, the debate on direct benefit transfers has moved into a more sensible phase, with the posturing criticism of a couple of years ago rather muted. In that context, perhaps it is time for a more dispassionate discussion. Two pilot schemes conducted in Madhya Pradesh, in which thousands of men, women and children in nine villages received a modest basic income, paid each month, in cash, unconditionally, for 18 months. The effects were evaluated by a series of surveys, comparing what happened to the recipients with what was happening to thousands of non-recipients in 13 other villages. The amount of money provided was modest, about a third of subsistence. But what we wanted to find out was whether, as scornful sceptics had claimed, people would waste the money or by contrast be able to use it rationally to improve their lives.

We made sure to issue no guidance as to how to spend the money. The only insistence was that recipients should open bank or cooperative accounts within three months of starting to receive the monthly payment. This showed that financial intermediation can be achieved effectively when there are incentives to do so. No less than 96 per cent of all recipients had opened accounts by the end of three months.

"Surveys conducted among people in Madhya Pradesh's villages, who received a modest basic income as cash transfers, showed that beneficiaries were quite capable of making rational decisions that improved their lives"

As for the claim that villagers would waste the money, the evidence gathered through three rounds of detailed surveys showed that people were quite capable of making rational decisions that improved their lives and their communities. Some critics claim India could not afford to provide all its citizens with a basic income. That conveniently overlooks the fact that a vast amount is spent on schemes that never reach the intended beneficiaries. Every informed policy-maker and social scientist knows that.

Providing people with a modest basic income instead of subsidies would actually save public revenue. We know that most of the money spent on the Public Distribution System is wasted, leaving villagers to rely on stale wheat or rice. The system also acts as a deterrent to local food production. Of course, if the state throws vast amounts at even a chronically inefficient scheme, some of it will get through. But it is dumb. Be that as it may. What the pilots have shown is something we had not fully anticipated. Unlike subsidies or public works, the basic income transfers have the potential to be transformative. If the government is setting up a Policy Commission in which one of the four pillars is to focus on Direct Benefit Transfers, it should start by considering this point.

Effects of basic income: The point is that the basic income has three types of effect. First, it improves personal and community welfare. The evidence from the pilots showed improvements in child nutrition, schooling attendance and performance, health and healthcare, sanitation and housing. It also has desirable equity outcomes, since it benefitted women more than men, the disabled more than others, the least secure and lowest income groups more than others.

However, what should please my fellow economists is that it also stimulates growth. While discussing economic growth, there is a tendency to concentrate on corporations and big industrial sectors, and to see villages as zones of stagnation. However, in the villages receiving the basic incomes, economic activity increased, new small-scale businesses sprung up, work and labour increased — contrary to critics who claim that giving people cash would induce idleness — and more equipment and livestock were bought. Although child wage labour declined, the overall increase in work and labour was shown by way of a shift from casual wage labour to more secondary activities. Other studies have tended to concentrate on people's main activity. Had we done that, we would not have picked up the phenomenon that, in a rational risk-reducing way, households tended to diversify into more secondary activities.

The key point here, however, is that the cash transfers should not be depicted simply as welfare expenditure. That is bad economics and poor accounting. Yet it is the third dimension that really makes the policy transformative. One way of putting it is to say that the emancipatory value of the basic income is greater than the monetary value. Money itself is a scarce commodity in Indian villages, and, as with any scarce commodity, this drives up the price. Moneylenders and landlords can easily put villagers into debt bondage and charge exorbitant rates of interest that families cannot hope to pay off. What we found is that many recipients used the cash to make savings, putting themselves in a better position to avoid highly costly short-term borrowing in emergencies. In effect, the liquidity lowered their cost of living and reduced the monopoly power of the moneylenders. Indeed, in a survey of impressions after the pilot had ended, several respondents told us that the only people who were unhappy about the experiment had been the moneylenders. How tragic. The emancipatory effect helped make the welfare and growth effects more sustainable. So, the scheme had a combination of positive effects, not just one. Now, government should be encouraged to make haste slowly. Launch several pilots in a few low-income areas in which the design could vary. There are good reasons for believing that making cash transfers universal within communities would save money in administrative and other costs, and induces more positive economic and social outcomes than selective or targeted schemes. Among other reasons is that they induce collective action for community benefits. It is also important to consider the potential role of intermediary non-government bodies. They can play a strong role in encouraging beneficial outcomes and help overcome the tendency for vulnerable people to remain vulnerable.

Above all, however, policymakers should learn to trust people whom they claim to serve. A growing danger in social policy is that it will veer towards social engineering, through sophistry and tighter conditionalities. Freedom matters, and so does the challenge of transformation.

Foreign Direct Investment (FDI)

The government will promote Foreign Direct Investment (FDI) selectively in sectors with the larger interest of economy. FDI in several sectors helps in promoting domestic manufacture and job creation. Barring the multi-brand retail sector, FDI will be allowed in sectors where needed for job and asset creation, infrastructure and acquisition of niche technology and specialised expertise. It will protect the interest of small and medium retailers, SMEs and those employed by them. The FIPBs (Foreign Investment Promotion Board) functioning shall be made more efficient and investor-friendly.

India today needs a boost for job creation. Our manufacturing sector in particular needs a push for job creation. India is the largest buyer of defence equipment in the world. Our domestic manufacturing capacities are at a nascent stage. We buy substantial part of defence requirements directly from foreign players. Companies controlled by foreign governments and foreign private sector supply considerable outflow of foreign exchange. Currently, we permit 26 per cent FDI in defence manufacturing. The composite cap of foreign exchange is being raised to 49 per cent with full Indian management and control through the FIPB route. The Insurance sector is investment starved. The composite cap in the sector is proposed to be increased up to 49 per cent from the current level of 26 per cent, with full Indian management and control, through the FIPB route. To encourage development of Smart Cities, which will provide habitation for the neo-middle class, requirement of the built up area and capital conditions for FDI is being reduced from 50,000 square metres to 20,000 square metres and from $10 million to $5 million respectively with a three year post completion lock in. Projects which commit at least 30 per cent of the total project cost for low cost affordable housing will be exempted from minimum built up area and capitalisation requirements, with the condition of three years lock-in. FDI in the manufacturing sector is today on the automatic route. The manufacturing units will be allowed to sell its products through retail including E-commerce platforms without any additional approval.

PM will Review FDI

Narendra Modi claimed that the economic policy of his government will be pro-people and in favour of India's business interest. He also said that there was a need to review FDI with a different perspective.

"We have to protect the manufacturing sector of India. If we are unable to protect manufacturing sector and small scale industries then our youth's future will be destroyed," he claimed. Speaking on FDI, Modi said that not just retail logic, but manufacturing logic must also be kept in mind. "We have to protect small scale industries and have a holistic approach towards FDI. "PSUs should be allowed to recover from debts. They should not be branded as loss-making entities. Centre has to take states on board in the matter of general sales tax or GST." "There is no 100-day model of governance, take stock of our economic policies after five years. "We will not reduce subsidies and no crony capitalism will be tolerated."

Black Money

The new government is committed to initiate the process of tracking and bringing back black money stashed in foreign banks and offshore accounts. A Task Force shall recommend amendments to existing laws or enact new laws thereupon. The process of bringing back black money will be put in motion on priority. It will proactively engage with foreign governments to facilitate on information sharing.

A Real Tall Order

A Special Investigative Team (SIT) will probe instances of illicit accounts of Indians outside India. How to get accurate estimates of the amount of capital flight (CF) is a question of uncertainty, given varying estimates of Indians' illicit wealth abroad, this is easier said than done. A key component of CF is trade misinvoicing (TM). For any given country X CF through TM occurs in two instances: one, when the stated value of country X's exports to country Y are lower than the—freight and insurance adjusted—value of country Y's imports from country X. This is called under-invoicing of exports.

Two, when the stated value of country Y's exports to X are lower than the freight and insurance adjusted value of country X's imports from country Y, this is called over-invoicing of imports. The magnitudes of these two differences are added to obtain total value of CF through misinvoicing. This exercise is then repeated for all trading partners of country X. The sum, so obtained, is stashed in tax havens overseas and is a loss to country X.

We got the data for our analysis from UN COMTRADE Standard International Classification (SITC) Rev. 3, websites of MIT and IMF E-library. For the period 1988-2012, we could obtain data only for 17 trading partners of India: United Arab Emirates (UAE), Brazil, Switzerland, China, Germany, France, the UK, Hong Kong China, Indonesia, Italy, Japan, South Korea, Kuwait, the Netherlands, Singapore, United States and South Africa.

From an aggregate outflow of $1.12 billion in 1988, CF fell to $544.8 million in 1989 and further to $62.48 million in 1990. There was an inflow of just over $8 million in 1991 and an outflow of $60.16 million in 1992 followed by a substantial inflow of $872.8 million in 1993. There was an outflow of $97.23 million in 1994 followed by two big inflows: $1.5 billion in 1995 and $1.74 billion in 1996. In 1997, there was an outflow in excess of $1.7 billion which increased sharply to $5.1 billion in 1998 and $6.4 billion in 1999. In 2000 CF fell sharply to just over $1.5 billion, rose to $3.1 billion in 2001 but fell to $ 1.8 billion in 2002. In 2003 CF rose to $3.35 billion. In 2004, there was a huge structural break and CF jumped sharply to over $8.2 billion. Magnitudes of CF have been very high since 2004. Over $7.65 billion in 2005, over $11.9 billion in 2006, over $9.87 billion in 2007 and a staggering amount—nearly $40 billion—in 2008. In 2009 CF came down to just under $10 billion, but rose sharply to over $27 billion in 2010 and over $33 billion in 2011 before falling to just over $17 billion in 2012.

Over the period 1988-2012, the cumulative outflow from India due to misinvoicing was in excess of $186 billion. This is an astonishing figure. To put this amount in perspective, according to the website of the Ministry of Finance at the end of December 2013, India's short-term external debt was $92.7 billion, less than half of total capital flight through misinvoicing in the period 1988-2012.

SIT on Black Money: The government gave the go ahead for setting up a Special Investigation Team (SIT) to bring black money back stashed abroad. The committee will be headed by retired Supreme Court judge, Justice MB Shah. Though, the probe into black money was a challenging task, he was hopeful that results will start coming soon. Various probes have been handled in the past following the SC directive. The probe could be streamlined with members from other official agencies. SIT will be monitoring the investigations and ensure that the entire gamut is covered.

The committee will also have former SC judge Justice Arijit Pasayat as the vice chairman. He will be assisted by the Revenue Secretary, directors of CBI, Intelligence Bureau, Research and Analysis Wing and Enforcement Directorate, the CBDT Chairman and an RBI deputy governor. Justice Pasayat believes it as a sensitive assignment and a challenging job. The massive job involves lot of international transaction. The apex court has imposed confidence on us. We will do whatever possible and will not hesitate to take any action. The apex court appointed two judges and granted the governmentsome time till to set up the SIT.

Indian Money Rises to Over Rs 14,000 Cr

The funds held by Indians rose by over 40 per cent during 2013, up from about 1.42 billion Swiss francs at the end of previous year, as per the Swiss National Bank data. Indians' money in Swiss banks has risen to over two billion Swiss francs (nearly Rs 14,000 crore). Despite a global clampdown is against the famed secrecy wall of Switzerland banking system. The funds held by Indians with banks in Switzerland rose by over 40 per cent during 2013. Up from about 1.42 billion Swiss francs at the end of previous year, as per the latest data released today by the country's central banking authority Swiss National Bank (SNB). In contrast, the money held in Swiss banks by their foreign clients from across the world continued to decline and stood at a record low of 1.32 trillion Swiss francs (about $1.56 trillion or over Rs 90 lakh crore) at the end of 2013. During 2012, the Indians' money in Swiss banks had fallen by over one-third to a record low level. The total Indian money held in Swiss banks included 1.95 billion Swiss francs held directly by Indian individuals and entities, and another 77.3 million Swiss francs through 'fiduciaries' or wealth managers at the end of 2013.

Govt Submits 627 Names of Foreign Account Holders to SC

The Govrnment submitted a list comprising names of 627 Indians with foreign bank accounts in a sealed cover to the Supreme Court in an attempt to recover black money stashed abroad. Attorney general Mukul Rohatgi handed over three sets of documents to the apex court. The Centre said roughly half of them were resident Indians who could be prosecuted. The rest were NRIs who could not be prosecuted against under Indian tax laws, the attorney general, appearing on behalf of the Centre, said. The court did not open the sealed envelope and sent it to its special investigation team tasked to bring back black money. The move comes a day after the Supreme Court reprimanded the Modi-led government for "providing a protective umbrella to foreign bank account holders?"

The AG also brought up the double taxation avoidance agreement-related confidentiality clause which impeded Centre's desire to make all names public. He said the Centre did not want to have any say in what the apex court intended to do with these 627 names, but said the Union government's bilateral and international treaty obligations had to be addressed. The Supreme Court had ordered the Centre to furnish in sealed cover names of all Indians holding accounts abroad hinting that it suspected the Modi government's intent to get into the bottom of black money stashed abroad and taking steps to bring it back. "Whatever information you have received from foreign countries, pass it on to us. We will ask the CBI or some other agency to investigate and give us a report. Don't ask us to modify the earlier order (to reveal all the names). We will not change a word of it (the order). We take the responsibility of investigating the entire issue. We will ensure confidentiality of investigation," a bench comprising Chief Justice H L Dattu and Justices Ranjana P Desai and Madan B Lokur had said.

India Misses the Global War Against Tax Evasion

The Supreme Court's fiat to the government to disclose the names of all Indians holding bank accounts abroad, in a sealed envelope, may force India to renege on a commitment it had made to join the global war against tax evasion. That is unfortunate. The court has said it cannot change an earlier order directing the government to disclose names of persons who have bank accounts abroad but with no evidence of tax evasion in India.

So, India will skip a crucial meeting organised by the Organisation for Economic Cooperation and Development (OECD), a club of rich countries, in Berlin today. Many countries gathered there will ink a new pact to boost worldwide efforts to crackdown on tax evasion. The pact, known as automatic information exchange, is part of the OECD's campaign to end base erosion and profit shifting by multinational companies. Effective information sharing will come in handy to establish audit trails in a globalised economy in which MNCs undertake complex deals to escape taxes. The OECD has developed the new standard on automatic information exchange based on a mandate from the G20 that has been turning the heat on tax havens. Many developed countries, starved of revenues with their economies slowing down, hope to recover money to meet their spending needs through such novel efforts. Rightly, India aspired to be an early adopter along with rich countries and, surprisingly, some tax havens such as Cayman Islands and Jersey, marking a step towards more transparency.

Tax Havens should Provide Information on Black Money

As India makes attempts to recover black money from abroad, Prime Minister Narendra Modi asked every country, especially tax havens, to provide information for tax purposes in accordance with treaty obligations. Raising the pitch on the black money issue, Modi in his intervention at the summit of the Group of 20 industrialised and major emerging economies called for close global coordination to address the challenge posed by it. He voiced India's support for a new global standard on automatic exchange of tax information, saying it would be instrumental in getting information relating to unaccounted money hoarded abroad and enable its eventual repatriation. He also extended India's backing for all initiatives to facilitate exchange of information and mutual assistance in tax policy and administration. The Prime Minister made the remarks at the plenary session on the subject of "Delivering Global Economic resilience" on the second and final day of the summit held at the Brisbane Exhibition and Convention centre.

He also expressed the hope that Base Erosion and Profit Sharing (BEPS) system would fully address concerns of developing and developed economies. BEPS is a technical term referring to the effect of tax avoidance strategies used by multinational companies on countries' tax basis. BEPS is known more commonly as "Transfer pricing" This term is used in a project headed by the OECD that is said to be an attempt by the world's major economies to try to rewrite the rules on corporate taxation to address the widespread perception that the corporations don't pay their fair share of taxes. The Prime Minister also said that increased mobility of capital and technology have created new opportunities for avoiding tax and profit shifting. Modi underpinned the need for the world community to take coordinated decisions although each country has its domestic priority. "Need for policy coordination among major economies remains strong," he said.

"Close coordination is important not just for addressing the challenge of black money but also security issues like terrorism, drug trafficking and arms smuggling," he said. Touching upon the resilience of the financial system in the world, said it will also depend on cyber security.

Repatriation of Black Money 'A Key Priority'

Prime Minister Narendra Modi unequivocally said that repatriation of black money kept abroad is a "priority" for his government, as he sought close global coordination to achieve this objective. Raising the black money issue at an informal meeting of leaders of the five-nation BRICS bloc, he set the tone on this key issue ahead of the G20 Summit in the wake of his commitment to bring back every penny of black money stashed abroad.

"Repatriation of black money kept abroad is a key priority for us," he said the BRICS leaders. Calling for close coordination on the issue of black money kept abroad, he also said this unaccounted money is also linked to security challenges. As India makes attempts to retrieve the black money, PM has already made it clear that close co-operation to retrieve the black money from abroad is a key issue for him. The G-20 host Australia vowed a "very aggressive" crackdown on tax avoidance. India is also seeking strong action by the Group of 20 industrialised and emerging economies against tax havens.

"A key issue for me would be to highlight the importance of international cooperation against black money," Modi had said, as he is set to renew the country's commitment at the G20 summit to a global response to deal with cross border tax avoidance and evasion. India is also expected to urge the G20 to pressure tax havens into revealing more information on black money from

India to help retrieve this illegal money. Besides Modi, Chinese President Xi Jinping, Russian President Vladimir Putin, South African President Jacob Zuma and Brazilian President Dilma Rousseff, were the other leaders who took part in the informal interaction. "Namaste! Leaving for my first programme, the Informal BRICS meeting," Modi tweeted ahead of the meeting.

- We can promote new models of governance and financing, while maintaining the highest banking standards. We should also make it more participatory. We need to work towards their early implementation. We propose that we should set the target of 2016 for inauguration of this Bank.
- We hope to ratify the agreement by the end of the year. We would soon nominate our candidate for the post of the Presidency. The Contingent Reserve Arrangement is also a very timely initiative.
- The work on the Reinsurance pool among BRICS is also a welcome one. We hope that our officials will be able to come up with a concrete proposal by the next year.
- These measures send a strong message to the rest of the world about the efficacy of BRICS.
- Besides these, we have started work on many other proposals that would deepen our relations and enhance our cooperation in all spheres.

Cabinet Approves GST Constitutional Amendment Bill

The Union Cabinet on Dec 17, 2014 approved the Constitutional Amendment Bill on Goods & Services Tax (GST), inching closer to the rollout of an ambitious indirect tax reform expected to raise revenues and boost growth . The government aims to implement GST by April 1, 2016 and has been working overtime to get states on board. The tax reform is a centrepiece of the Narendra Modi government's economic agenda. Sources said the government hopes to introduce the bill in the Winter Session 2014 of Parliament. It may be introduced in the Rajya Sabha soon. The tax reform measure has missed several rollout dates in the past due to lack of consensus between the Centre and states on a host of issues and the government is keen to get the bill approved in the current session.

The Centre managed a breakthrough after finance minister Arun Jaitley assured the states of a fair deal. Sources said initially, petroleum will be kept out of GST but will be included in the new tax set up once states come on board. It may take two years but the government hopes to include it in the years ahead. Alcohol too is expected to be kept out of the comprehensive levy. Additionally, the Centre has devised a levy of one per cent above the GST rate on select items and is assuring the states full compensation for revenue loss for three years, followed by 75 per cent in fourth year and 50 per cent in the fifth. The Centre does not see a significant amount of compensation to be paid as it expects collections through GST to be better due to fewer exemptions and a gain from service tax. Experts cheered the Cabinet nod to the GST bill.

"Cabinet clearance assumes greater importance as there were few doubts after the recent empowered committee meeting wherein it seemed that consensus between Centre and states still eluded on few critical points," said Pratik Jain, partner, indirect tax at consultancy firm KPMG , India.

"Now with the bill all set to be presented in the current session of Parliament, it would be seen as enormously positive towards GST implementation from April 1, 2016. However, it would be important for all stakeholders to ensure that GST covers all transactions including petroleum, real estate and electricity in due course, if not immediately," he said. The finance ministry had swung into action after state finance ministers rejected the draft GST Constitutional Amendment Bill saying the provisions did not take into account their concerns and staunchly opposed the move to include petroleum under the GST ambit. The states also said the bill does not address their concern on the issue of entry tax. In a bid to bridge the trust deficit between the states and the Centre, Jaitley had approved the release of Rs 11,000 crore as compensation for loss on account of central sales tax which had been pending since 2010. He had also vowed to pay the pending amount as he moved to ensure that the states come on board for rolling out the tax reform measure, which has the potential to add significantly to government revenues and overall economic growth.

Corruption

Corruption is a manifestation of poor Governance. It reflects the bad intentions of those sitting in power. All pervasive corruption under the Congress-led UPA has become a 'National Crisis'. The PM Modi will establish a system, which eliminates the scope for corruption. We will do this through: public awareness, technology enabled e-Governance, minimising the discretion in the citizen-government interface, system-based, policy-driven governance, making it transparent, rationalisation and simplification of the tax regime—which is currently repulsive for honest tax payers. Simplification of the processes and procedures at all levels—bestowing faith in the citizens, institutions and establishments.

The Jan Lokpal Bill, also referred to as the Citizen's Ombudsman Bill, is an anti-corruption Bill drafted and drawn up by civil society activists in India seeking the appointment of a Jan Lokpal, an independent body to investigate corruption cases. This bill also proposes improvements to the Lokpal and Lokayukta Bill 2011, which was passed by Lok Sabha in December 2011.

The Jan Lokpal Bill aims to effectively deter corruption, compensate citizen grievances, and protect whistle-blowers. The prefix Jan (translation: citizens) signifies that these improvements include inputs provided by "ordinary citizens" through an activist-driven, non-governmental public consultation.

The word Lokpal was coined in 1963 by late L.M. Singhvi, a Member of Parliament during a debate. To draw the attention of the government, a focussed campaign "India Against Corruption" (IAC) was started in 2011. Anna Hazare is the head of civil society and the IAC movement. Through these collaborative efforts till August 2011, IAC was able to upload the 23rd version of the Jan Lokpal Bill draft. As of January 2014, the Delhi State Government, led by CM Arvind Kejriwal was preparing to adopt the Jan Lokpal Bill, but was unable to introduce it to the house, resigning moments later.

The Lokpal Bill was first introduced by Advocate Shanti Bhushan in 1968 and passed by the 4th Lok Sabha in 1969. But before it could be passed by Rajya Sabha, the Lok Sabha was dissolved and the bill lapsed. Subsequent versions were re-introduced in 1971, 1977, 1985, 1989, 1996, 1998, 2001, 2005 and in 2008, but none of them were passed. In 2011, during the Parliament's Winter Session, the Lok Sabha passed the controversial Lokpal Bill, but could not be passed by Rajya Sabha due to shortage of time in the winter session of 2011. The Government tabled the Lokpal Bill in the Rajya Sabha on 13th December 2013 and the debate was adjourned till 16th December 2013. The Lokpal Bill was finally passed on 17th 2013 in the Rajya Sabha. It was passed in the Lok Sabha on 18 December 2013.

Diesel Prices Regulated

In the biggest wave of economic reforms since coming to power, the NDA government de-regulated the price of diesel and announced a new price for domestically-produced natural gas. The Government also announced the re-launch of the UPA's flagship Direct Benefit Transfer Scheme for liquefied petroleum gas to benefit consumers denied subsidy for want of an Aadhaar number. With the Cabinet decision, the price of diesel, like petrol, would now stand linked to the market without any government intervention, with retail rates reflecting price changes in the global market. On gas pricing, the Government surprised analysts — who had been predicting revised prices in the range of $ 6-7/mmbtu (million metric British thermal units) — by fixing the price at $ 5.61 per mmbtu, 75 per cent lower than the rates proposed by the Rangarajan Committee under the UPA Government. The immediate impact on diesel will be a reduction in prices by Rs 3.37 a litre (ex-Delhi) with effect from midnight. Speaking on the Cabinet decision deregulating the price of diesel, Union Finance Minister Arun Jaitley said, "Henceforth, like petrol, the price of diesel would be linked to the market and therefore depending on whatever is the cost involved …the consumers will have to pay." He was speaking to presspersons following the Cabinet meeting. On gas pricing, the major modification to the Rangarajan formula was the removal of the Japanese and Indian LNG import components. The move will fetch the exchequer additional revenue of Rs. 3,800 crore in higher royalties, 80 per cent of which will accrue to government companies. In a related decision, the Cabinet approved a Petroleum Ministry note giving leeway in the production sharing contract that companies sign with the government, to monetise hydrocarbon discoveries faster. Cairn, Gujarat State Petroleum Corporation and ONGC will be among the immediate beneficiaries of the removal of red tape in the hydrocarbon exploration processes.

Insurance

Approves Ordinance to Hike FDI in Insurance to 49pc

Government approved promulgation of an Ordinance to hike Foreign Direct Investment (FDI) cap in the insurance sector to 49 pc from 26 pc, as the legislation could not be passed in Winter session of the Parliament in 2014. The Cabinet has cleared the Ordinance on insurance sector," sources said after the meeting of the Union Cabinet headed by Prime Minister Narendra Modi here. The Insurance Bill, which has been pending since 2008 in the Rajya Sabha, seeks to increase the composite foreign investment limit in insurance companies to 49 per cent from current level of 26 per cent. The 49 per cent cap would include both FDI and foreign portfolio investments.

The proposed hike in foreign investment limit to 49 per cent in the insurance sector has potential to attract up to USD 7-8 billion (about Rs 50,000 crore) from overseas investors, giving a major boost to the segment. The total capital deployed in the private life insurance sector is close to Rs 35,000 crore. At FDI at 26 per cent, foreign equity is close to Rs 8,700 crore. The Insurance Laws Amendment Bill, 2008 could not be taken up for discussion despite being approved by the Select Committee of the Upper House because of the uproar by opposition parties over the conversion and other issues. The government has blamed political obstructionism for the disruption of Rajya Sabha, where the ruling NDA does not have a majority. There are 52 insurance companies operating in India, of which 24 are in the life insurance business and 28 in general insurance business. In addition, GIC is the sole national reinsurer.

Investments

Strategies to Revive Investment Flows

The PMO asked economic ministries to come up with strategies to revive investment flows into the country on a war-footing. A first step in this direction could be liberalising foreign direct investments in defence, with Prime Minister Narendra Modi backing indigenous production of defence equipment using cutting-edge technology. Nripendra Misra, principal secretary therein address the meeting of the secretaries from core economic ministries to discuss steps to expedite investment flows into India.

"There was a general brainstorming on some of the immediate steps that could help, such as resolving conflicts between investors and the government," the official said. Though officials were tight-lipped about the specific deliberations at the meeting, the foreign direct investment policy in the defence sector is learnt to have been discussed.

A proposal for the cabinet to change the policy is expected to be taken up soon, following Modi's signal to allow higher FDI than the present thresholds of 26 per cent and 49 per cent (on a case to case basis)—as long as such investments involve transfer of technology and create domestic production facilities and local jobs. "Why should we import defence equipment? We dream of an India that is self-sufficient in producing defence equipment using the latest technology," Modi said at the launch of mega-aircraft carrier INS Vikramaditya in Goa. The secretaries were asked to revert with some big ideas on turning the investment tide to help the economy recover from one of its most difficult phases. A publicity campaign to remind global investors about India's attractive market opportunities was on the cards.

To Boost Household Savings: The government could increase encourage people to save after the RBI and stock market watchdog Sebi made a strong pitch for raising the limit to encourage financial savings to wean people away from gold. Massive curbs on gold drastically reduced imports. It helped narrow current account deficit to about 2 per cent of GDP in 2013-14. The policymakers are worried that calibrated reduction in import duty on gold that is set to begin this budget could increase demand for gold again. Higher financial savings are needed to lower interest rates and fund massive infrastructure investment that the government has planned. Economists say tax benefits will encourage financial savings.

The regulators have asked the government to raise the 80C exemption limit, under which Rs 1 lakh is reduced from total income for the purpose of calculating tax. Individuals can claim tax exemption for investing in provident fund, national savings certificate, five-year fixed deposits, repayment of principal amount of home loans, children's tuition fee, public provident fund, some mutual funds and premium paid on a life insurance policy as part of the 80C basket. The total estimated tax revenue loss on account of this incentive in 2012-13 was Rs 30,662 crore. "A number of instruments have been added to this basket but without raising the limit. Some more space is thus required to be created," said the official. For instance, over the years, spending on school fee and housing loan principal have been included in the basked, leaving less room for financial savings. One of the options is to increase the limit by creating an addition for infrastructure bonds, which was the case earlier. Sebi has suggested that the Rajiv Gandhi Equity Savings Scheme be done away with as it has not taken off. The finance ministry believes the scheme needs a total revamp. It is complicated and has failed to meet the objectives introduced for. The previous UPA government had announced the RGESS in the 2012-13 budget, offering 50 per cent tax rebate to new retail investors who invest up to Rs 50,000 directly in equities and whose annual income is below Rs 12 lakh.

FII Inflows hit $20-billion Mark in First Half of 2014

Overseas investors pumped in a staggering over-$20-billion into the Indian market in the first half of the year. The net investments by foreign investors into equity markets stood at $9.96 billion (Rs 59,795 crore) during January-June 2014. The same for debt markets was at $10.42 billion (Rs 62,834 crore) taking the total to $20.4 billion (Rs 1.23 lakh crore). Market analysts believe foreign investors to have been betting on the Indian market mainly on hope of reform-orientation. The inflows are expected to surge further as the verdict met overseas investors' expectations in the Lok Sabha polls. "Moreover, foreign investors continued their positive bias towards Indian markets after elections as well primarily on reforms oriented decisions taken by the new government," an analyst said. FIIs (Foreign institutional Investors), the main driver of the equity market, have helped in pushing up the benchmark BSE Sensex by over 20 per cent in the first six-month of the year.

Foreign investors had made a net investment of Rs 62,288 crore into the country's securities market in 2013 (January-December). This included a net investment of Rs 1.13 lakh crore in equities, while they pulled out a net amount of Rs. 50,848 crore. From the beginning of June, FIIs along with sub-accounts and qualified foreign investors have been clubbed together by market regulator SEBI to create a new investor category called Foreign Portfolio Investors. The strong inflows in the recent months have taken the cumulative net investments of foreign investors into India to $191 billion, while their investments in rupee terms is Rs. 9 lakh crore level. This is based on the data since November 1992 when foreign investors began investing into Indian markets and includes about $156 billion investments into equities and further about $35 billion in debt markets.

How to Make the Most of Investment Opportunities in 2015

At the stroke of midnight on 31st December each year, the air ripples with a rare magic. Happiness hangs heavy and hope swirls down with snow to encrust all. The failures and despondency of the previous year melt away, while nostalgia is tinged with lessons learnt in the past year. We go through this smorgasbord of feelings each year, much like our readers. We rejoice at having dispensed the advice that helped you with your finances, we despair over the developments that were not in investors' interests, and we resolve anew each year to guide our readers the best we can. In many ways, 2014 was a landmark year. It marked a turning point for the global and domestic markets after several years of gloom and unnerving uncertainty.

Even as the world economy stabilised, on the domestic front, the new government at the Centre ushered a refreshing spell of revival and hope. As macro and micro indicators swung towards optimism, we also detected a need for caution. Still, there's much to look forward to in 2015 in every aspect of personal finance, ranging from stocks, mutual funds and banking to gold, real estate and insurance. As we herald another year, we try to capture the economic outlook for you. Combining the forward look with a backward glance, we shall take you through the major developments in all the sectors. We also highlight their impact and the lessons these hold for you in the next 12 months. And as you start the new year, remember that happiness and riches are yours for the taking if you plan well, adopt a disciplined approach to finances—and take our advice.

7 Nation First and Universal Brotherhood

Introduction

A resurgent India must get rightful place in the comity of nations and international institutions. The vision is to fundamentally reboot and reorient the foreign policy goals with content and process. It will locate global strategic engagement in a new paradigm and on a wider canvass. It is not just limited to political diplomacy, but includes our economic, scientific, cultural, political and security interests. The regional and global cash in on the principles of equality and mutuality, it anticipates stronger India with its voice heard in the international fora.

Political stability, progress and peace in the region are essential for south Asia's growth and development. The predecessor government has failed to establish enduring friendly and co-operative relations with neighbours. India's relations with traditional allies have turned cold. India and her neighbours have drifted apart. The absence of statecraft has never been felt so acutely. India is seen to be floundering, whereas it should have been engaged with the world on confidence. The collapse of Indian economy has contributed to the sorry state of foreign affairs in no small measure.

India has failed to duly appreciate the full extent and gamut of soft power potential. There is a need to integrate our soft power avenues into our external interchange. It could harness and focuss on the spiritual, cultural and philosophical dimensions. India has always played a major role in world affairs, offering a lot to the World. This has been its tradition since time immemorial. Her magnetic power of India has always been in its ancient wisdom and heritage, elucidating on principles like harmony and equity. This continues to be equally relevant to the world in present phase of soft power.

India was reckoned not only as mentor but also a vibrant trading society. Our ancestors used to trade with foreign nations through the routes of sea, centuries ago. This was based on the strength of our business acumen and integrity, our products and crafts. The symbols of our ancient civilisations stand as a testimony to our architectural and urban planning excellence. We ought to revive Brand India with the help of our strengths of Five T's: Tradition, Talent, Tourism, Trade and Technology.

Robust Foreign Policy

The government has focussed on six top priorities for robust foreign policy. The MEA will build a strong, self-reliant and self-confident India, regaining its rightful place in the comity of nations. In this, the ruling government will be firstly guided by our centuries old tradition and foreign policy will be based on best National interests. It will create a web of allies to mutually further our interests. We will leverage all our resources and people to play a greater role on the international high table.

1. *India's lacklustered ties with the US:* The MEA needs to infuse life into it by making it more transactional and business-like. The civil nuclear liability law needs to be amended to open India to nuclear energy industry, fix the retroactive taxes to revive business sentiment in the US and explain her stand on IPR in pharma.

2. *India's big challenge is China:* The powerful neighbour China's rise and aggression causes' anxiety. It will reduce if China is seen to be developing a stake for India. The way to do away is to push its investment in India and develop a genuine economic partnership. The MEA has to help the security establishment overcome its fear about China.

3. *Look east policy has petered out.* The economic and strategic moorings are in Asia. The MEA will have to look at advance Indian interests in Asia, countries like Vietnam, Indonesia, Singapore as well as Australia —who are anxious about China's territorial moves.

4. *Inviting all neighbours for his swearing-in:* The Prime Minister Modi has made a fine beginning by inviting all neighbours for his swearing-in. It's a gesture to indicate that we want better ties with them. India's arrogance as Big Brother in south Asia has brought these ties to a low from which they can only grow. Pakistan has been told upfront that terror and trade can't coexist. Nawaz Sharif needs to make it apparent that he is trying to contain the terror operatives in Pakistan.

5. *SAARC countries look-up to India:* This needs to be exploited by Sushma Swaraj-led MEA with a genuine appreciation of requirements of our neighbours as well as their political sensitivities, as a regional bloc, South Asia is the least integrated in the world. Injecting faith and trust by opening up trade and business would change the situation.

6. *Building trade missions:* Key embassies could facilitate Indian economic interests. A good way to approach this would be to absorb the international trade division of commerce ministry into the MEA.

The equations ought to be mended through pragmatism. A doctrine of mutually beneficial and interlocking relation should be based on enlightened national interest. It will champion uniform international opinion on issues like terrorism and global warming. India ought to engage proactively on its own with countries in the neighbour and beyond. It will continue our dialogue, engagement and cooperation, with global forums like BRICS, G-20, IBSA, SCO and ASEM. The states need to be encouraged to play a greater role in diplomacy; actively build relations with foreign countries to harness mutual cultural and commercial strengths, under the direction of the Union government. The NDA will expand and empower its pool of diplomats, ensure the country's message conveyed to the world. The NRIs, PIOs and professionals settled abroad are a vast reservoir to articulate the national interests and affairs globally. This resource ought to be harnessed for strengthening Brand India. India shall remain a natural home for persecuted Hindus. They shall be welcome to seek refuge at home.

Move Diplomacy into High Gear

India needs more personnel and specialists to make its foreign policy proactive and productive. Economic considerations must take primacy in foreign policy. The ministry of external affairs summoned its envoys posted in the neighbourhood for a conclave on India's regional policy. The external affairs minister engaged ambassadors posted in Saarc countries, Central Asia, China, Myanmar and Iran to discussed ways and means to advance India's priorities. Improving regional co-operation and connectivity have become the key thrust areas. Diplomats were expected to be mindful of the wider security challenges. Identifying policy priorities swerving the government to discern where political intervention is required to make progress.

The envoys spelt out the need for confidence-building initiatives. The prime ministerial visit to Nepal, the Teesta water-sharing agreement with Bangladesh and pressing on with India-Pakistan trade are a few. The envoys will have alerted New Delhi to China's increasing footprint across the region. China's trade volume with Bangladesh is more than India, so also its investments in Myanmar, Afghanistan and Central Asia. The MEA envoys will soon convey India's presence in the region fades in comparison with the number of personnel that Beijing devotes at home and away on foreign affairs. India's lack of capacity in this area has been well known, but the situation has barely improved. The MEA has around 900 officers on its rolls. China is said to have 4,200. Britain, Germany and France each have more than 6,000 officers. Indian diplomats plod on with unmanageable remits as a result. Joint secretaries handle several key countries at once. They deal with one major visit or a crisis, like the one currently about Indian nationals being abducted in Iraq. Every other issue ceases to become priority. The MEA does remarkably well under the circumstances. The tendency to operate always in a frantic mode hurts its ability to effectively and thoughtfully pursue India's interests. The government must cut through bureaucratic resistance mobilise IFS recruitment. They should focus particularly on inducting professional talent through lateral entry. The MEA must have a range of mid-career and senior specialists. These include strategic analysts, economists, linguists and experts from other fields. The United States has done this for decades, enriching both government and academia.

Main Challenges: India needs to rethink her unipolar strategy. Modi's decision to invite South Asian leaders to his swearing-in ceremony signals the new government's desire to reboot its Asian engagement. Even before he took the oath of office, it was clear that Asia is going to be high on his foreign policy agenda. Japan is likely to be Modi's first foreign visit as Prime Minister, followed by China.

The Prime Minister enjoys close ties with Japan's Premier Shinzo Abe. He visited Japan five times as chief minister of Gujarat. He attended the BRICS summit where he met the leaders of the emerging powers. He met China's President Xi Jinping and Russia's president Vladimir Putin.

Unipolar Mentality: India should overcome its unipolar mentality. It will be much the same way it as the Cold War mentality, and prepare itself for more dynamic world order and the 'Asian century'. The term 'Asian century' came up as a passing reference at the December 1988 meet between the late Chinese leader Deng Xiaoping and the then Indian premier late Rajiv Gandhi. Deng told Gandhi that many people attribute the next century as the 'Asian century'. The phrase eventually became a popular geo-strategic term. It refers to the steady rise of China and the fast-changing equations in global power politics. It is believed that Chinese seem to have realised the real potential of the Asian century much earlier. India, the third largest Asian economy, failed to structurally reorient her engagement with the Asia anew.

China gave foremost importance to economic development. It restrained its strategic play within Asia, apparently in a bid to emerge as a dominant player. The changes India made in its post-Cold War foreign policy were largely aimed in accommodating itself within a unipolar world. The policy-makers in New Delhi believed the world had changed for good. The global domination of the US was there to stay. This policy shift actually improved India-US ties. It did little to strengthen India's geo-political standing in Asia, where China was steadily expanding its reach. Nouriel Roubini, a noted economist who advised Bill Clinton foresaw the biggest geo-political risk of times was the rise of China. China emerging as a regional power in Asia, tensions between Beijing and its neighbours were on the rise. US President Barack Obama had unveiled earlier plans to "pivot" to Asia to "contain" China. Japan, upset over China's muscle-flexing in the region, demonstrated itself to end the "passive diplomacy". It projected in the region as a counter-point to Beijing. The US plan is to stitch together a broader alliance in Asia that could check China. It encouraged the changes in Japan's foreign and security policy thinking. The US foresaw Japan as a major partner in the pivot, expecting India to join this alliance. This coincides with another pivot, that of Russia. Putin recently clinched a $400 billion gas deal with China. Russian energy giant Gazprom is to supply natural gas to China National Petroleum Corp for 10 years. The deal not only intensifies energy cooperation between the two countries. It takes bilateral relations between the world's fastest-growing major economy and an ambitious former superpower to new high. The two rival blocs have one theatre and multiple players. It is a Cold War like situation in Asia.

India cannot sidestep this scenario while crafting the contours of its new Asian engagement. One way or the other, it will have to respond to the boiling geo-political competition in the continent. She can however, take a cue from the Gandhi-Deng summit of 1988. If the ongoing century belongs to Asian, India should radically realign her foreign policy priorities and extend foremost importance to stability in Asia. The rise of China has already turned Asia into a hotbed of geopolitics. The US and Russia are already present in the region. The blocs will want India to join them, and selecting one over the other as a move to not only jeopardise India's interests but also Asian security.

New Delhi's decision to back Tokyo in her territorial dispute with China was a move in such direction. Such acts would only antagonise China. Choosing the middle path while simultaneously strengthening partnership with other Asian powers is a difficult job that needs imaginative diplomacy, but it will pay off in the long term. It is possible only if India places Asian stability at the centre of her foreign policy agenda. Perhaps, that happens to be the greatest challenge before the new government. SAARC members' countries face challenges in tackling international issues plaguing collectively. The government's main priority is to project the strength of India abroad and improve her international relation. The government has made a beginning in improving ties with the neighbourhood. It would next improve ties with strategic partners, and after that with India's extended neighbourhood.

Indian Premier told his Pakistani counterpart Nawaz Sharif that if bomb blasts continue, then peace talks between the two countries will be lost in the din. Talks and good relations can be successful and right only when terrorism is stopped. If bomb blasts continue, then the talks will be lost in the din. The Indian referred on the topic of speedy trial of the 26/11 terror attack accused. The Indian Foeign Secretary claimed India have raised the issue of detention of her fishermen with Sri Lankan President Mahinda Rajapaksa, she said. "We also raised the issue of 13th Amendment; expect the issue specifically of Kachchatheevu.

Brings Style to Substance in Foreign Police

Meticulous to a fault, the Japanese dislike sudden changes in his programmes. Yet, when Narendra Modi arrives, a day earlier to the heritage temple city of Kyoto made them euphoric.

"Amid the B2B [business to business] and G2G [government to government] [interactions], he spelt out H2H [heart to heart] relationship, who helped organise his international visits when he was the state Chief Minister.

Modi has introduced a leitmotif, bringing style to the substance of foreign policy. Most of his announcements were in continuation of those during the visits of erstwhile premiers. Every major newspaper in the hill nation, spoke of "Modi operandi" and "Modi magic mantra." The agreement went from water sharing to construction projects. In Japan too, agreements on the Mumbai-Delhi and Chennai-Bangalore industrial corridors, the IREL-Toyota Tsusho rare earth deal and the nuclear agreement of 2010 brought the nation euphoric with Japanese ties. Modi has relegated the External Affairs Ministry as a policy-maker. Each decision — let it be the invitation to SAARC leaders, cancellation of talks with Pakistan, prioritising of the neighbourhood with visits to Bhutan and Nepal or the refusal to sign the WTO agreement — bears Modi's mark. His interactions with one twenty world leaders so far appended the summit-style of his diplomacy to resolve issues.

Modi, no doubt relied on multiple inputs from other Departments. In Nepal, local industrialist advised him; on the US visit to forget he is known to have delegated his public appearances in New York to NRI community groups; and in Japan, he took many of his ideas on the Kyoto initiative and boosting business sentiment from think tanks that specialise on India-Japan ties. In all of these, he has made it clear he intends to communicate directly, dropping national and regional journalists from his plane. The PM's only interactions on the ground have been an interview to a Japanese media delegation ahead of his visit there.

He received Australian Prime Minister Tony Abbott to finalise an agreement for Uranium. He pursued back-to-back engagements with Chinese President Xi Jinping and US President Obama. His speech at the United Nations General Assembly refelcted his personal opinion coupled with foreign policy plans for the future. Modi signed power sharing agreements with Nepal to the border areas and water-sharing agreements with Bangladesh. Sri Lanka will require some attention, despite Pakistan and Afghanistan being embroiled in political turmoil. He met SAARC leaders at the Kathmandu summit. It may be best to judge how far his government has come at that point, as he comes full circle, engaging the very same leaders of the neighbourhood as he began his promising tenure with.

Time for Refurbishing SAARC

Dr Subramanian Swamy told a Chinese government-backed meeting to India prioritises ties with South Asian countries and neighbours in her foreign policy. The Indian Premier focussed on "refurbishing" SAARC's organisational structure to make the "weak" body more effective. Dr Swamy, invited to address the "World Peace Forum" at Beijing's Tsinghua University, said any further evolution of SAARC calls for the United States and China, currently observers, to have a greater role in the deliberation.

"PM Narendra Modi has made it clear that in foreign policy, neighbours come first," he said, with SAARC countries—whose leaders were invited to Mr Modi's swearing-in—being followed by Asia and then the United States in terms of emphasis. "Mr Modi overruled people who said Pakistan should not be invited," he said.

The last meeting involved former leaders including Japan's Yukio Hatoyama and Pakistan's Shaukat Aziz, serving and retired diplomats, and strategic experts from around the world for discussions on China's relations with the US, Japan, South Asia and Southeast Asia. Dr Swamy said there was "an urgent need for structuring a new paradigm" for regional ties in South Asia, with the present SAARC charter that prevents the inclusion of bilateral issues in its agenda undermining its effectiveness and making the grouping "anaemic."

Trilateral Meeting: Pakistan's "explicit and implicit complicity in terror" and illegal immigration from Bangladesh are the "roadblocks" that needed addressing. India should have trilateral meetings with the US and China considering the reality of their influence on countries in the neighbourhood. Increased political understanding with China could help address lingering issues such as the boundary dispute, Dr Swamy believed.

NaMo Buzz across the Globe

The PM Narendra Modi's invitation to the SAARC nations for his swearing-in ceremony also caught the attention of global opinion makers, international markets and the media across the world.

In the Neighbourhood: Re-aligning India's partnership with key neighbours is of vital importance. India has ceded space to China in terms of being strategically with several SAARC and African nations. The governor for Sri Lanka's central bank Ajith Nivard Cabraal, in an interview to The Wall Street

Journal as reported said that a 'business–friendly' government in New Delhi would make his work 'a lot easier'. That India and Sri Lanka are set to enjoy more strengthened relation has been affirmed by the news byte that Indian premier is quite likely to choose Sri Lanka to make his first foreign visit. At the swearing–in ceremony China was conspicuous by its absence where not even a high ranking representative of the country was present. The reason for the absence of any Chinese representative may have more to do with the presence of Lobsang Sangay, Prime Minister of the Central Tibetan Administration in Dharamsala, the Tibetan Government in exile, as stated a report in the *Watch China Times.* China's reaction to Indian premier may have been 'chilly' though the latter has extended an invite to Xi Jinping to visit India, an action that has no doubt been prompted by economic reasons rather than political and lie very much within the ambit to further diplomacy through trade.

In the Land of the Rising Sun: India may forge stronger trade bonds with Japan as the Japanese entrepreneurs look to notch infrastructure projects under their belts. *The Japan News* quotes a Hitachi Ltd official saying, "Following the launch of the stable Government, infrastructure development is expected to be promoted in India." The UPA's lack of interest in infrastructure development and lackadaisical approach to policy formation had driven many Japanese businesses away look to tap in to cater to India's massive population of 1.2 billion people. As per the report, Toshiba Corp plans to invest $50 billion in the country over the next five years, primarily in thermal power turbines and other infrastructure-related projects.

India as is evident from the *Business Daily Africa report* needs to up its game in the continent. The two regions share immense goodwill, despite the previous Indian regime slow to tap into the vast China looks to fill up. India enjoys good trade relation with African nations such as Kenya. *Kenya National Bureau of Statistics* reports 'Kenya's imports from India were worth $144 billion compared to $114 billion imports from China'. Indian banks are the biggest lenders to Kenyan businesses by as much as six times during the period 2005-12.

Europe Sniffs an Opportunity: Shifting to the European mainland, Spain eyes are set on certain Indian markets. The Spanish have a firm foothold in the Indian infrastructure sector including roads and power. According to a report in *The Corner*, Spain's major infrastructure companies have a presence in India. They have usually the upper middle-class in sight as is evident like Borges Company through its Indian subsidiary and CIE Automotive in alliance with Mahindra. The United Kingdom believes India could be crushed in on following earlier frustrating attempts to open up trade through trade mission. Mark Field, lawmaker for the cities of London and Westminster in his article for the *Conservative Home* writes, "Hopes are high that the liberalisation of broader range of industries will attract fresh foreign capital and expertise in a market of 1.2 billion." In particular, the English look towards opening of professional services sector that would allow UK law firms to enter Indian markets through alliances.

The Scoop reports that a Bipartisan Congressional Resolution passed in the United States House of Representative recognised the victory of new premier in the Indian election. It speaks of the Congress's commitment to work with "the government to advance shared values and interests," and strengthen US-India partnership in the "defence, trade, and security arenas." America's haste to patch up things has a lot to do with Russia's Vladimir Putin's growing clout. A report in the *Voice of Russia* claims, "the obvious route for India is to get closer to Russia and China". India and the Kremlin have always shared close ties, China being thrown into the mix, there is a very real chance the US may be reduced to non-player in the region. Meanwhile, Allen Meltzer in his article for the journal for Hoover Institution urges the Republicans to endorse ties with India. *World Tribune* recognises the importance of the Indian premier extending an invitation to his Pakistani counterpart.

Xi Jinping's visit to India: Top 10 priorities

Chinese President Xi Jinping is on a three-day visit to India which will focus on significantly ramping up trade and investment, besides addressing the contentious border issue that has seen occasional flare ups between the two Asian giants. Below are the 10 Chinese and Indian priorities:

- China plans to invest in bullet and other high-speed trains and work on the metro train system across 50 cities within the country, where Mass Rapid Transit System (MRTS) projects are being planned.
- Chinese investments stand at $400m, mostly in Gujarat.
- India-China trade stood at $66.4bn last year, heavily skewed in China's favour.
- Major Chinese thrust in India's railway upgrade expected.
- India will seek to learn from Chinese expertise and achievements in mass affordable housing.
- Chinese electronics and mobile companies likely to invest in parks at Gujarat's Karjan and Sanand.
- Several academic institutions in states such as Gujarat likely to tie up with Chinese institutions.
- China and India likely to set up common platforms to promote cultural exchanges.
- Beijing likely to set up several industrial parks in India.
- China promises to bring investments worth $100bn, almost triple the amount Japan has pledged.

Modi-Xi visit

The three-day visit of Chinese President Xi Jinping to India began on a positive note on with Xi and Modi sharing a rare bonhomie and the two countries signing 12 agreements on issues relating to infrastructure, railways and culture.

Key Points

- India, China signed 12 agreements including cooperation in railways, outer space.
- Will begin process of discussion on civil nuclear energy cooperation that will bolster broader cooperation on energy security—Modi.

- On the border issue, President Xi said, "Due to non-demarcation of the border, certain incidents take place but both countries have mechanisms to handle such incidents."
- Agreements on two Chinese industrial parks and commitment to $20 billion Chinese investments in 5 years signed.
- Pact on making Shanghai and Mumbai twin-cities signed.
- We (India, China) are emerging markets and should strive to achieve peaceful development—President Xi
- President Xi officially invited PM Modi to visit China.
- 2015 will be called 'Visit India' year in China, and 2016 will be 'Visit China' in India.
- Two countries proposed cultural exchange programmes covering culture, education, tourism: President Xi.
- President Xi hopes for India's support in building relations with SAARC countries.

US for Greater Indo-US Ties

Hailing the "historic victory" of Narendra Modi in general elections, several influential American lawmakers have called for rejuvenating ties with India. "What a great time! Now, we have a new opportunity in India to some of the challenges. What can be done to create a shot in the arm for more economic prosperity in India," said Congressman Ed Royce, chairman of the powerful House Committee on Foreign Affairs.

"With a clear majority, there is now a mandate for changes to address pro-growth economic policies and having watched what happened in Gujarat, we now have that opportunity to see that (at the national level)," Royce said in his remarks at an event organised by the US India Political Action Committee at the Capitol Visitor Centre.

"It (counter terrorism co-operation) is absolutely vital that the US and India, pick up, in terms of mutual co-operation and mutually beneficial economic issue another area of co-operation. "We need to do more to put India on the map of trade and investment," he said, adding India is the place to invest. Top Democratic leader and India Caucus co-chair Congressman Joe Crowley said, "The US looks forward to working with the new government."

"I am sure there would be better days ahead (in India US relationship). There will be potholes. I think the White House understands that India is on the rise. That's why it deserves a seat at the UN Security Council," the New York lawmaker said. He welcomed the initiative of the premier inviting leaders of the South Asian countries to the swearing-in ceremony. Crowley said, it is time that India has a permanent place in the United Nations Security Council. "I am very pleased that the (US) President invited the premier to the United States. We look forward to working with this new government and continue the relationship forward," he said.

Tough on Pak, China at Arm's Length

The Modi government's foreign policy seems to be pragmatic and reciprocal. The performance of any government couldn't be assessed, leave alone one that came riding on high hopes in the backdrop of apparent policy paralysis and indecisive leadership. The new government will have to fill many a pothole before it gets into the task of nation building. A year would be insufficient not to talk of one month, 100 days or six months.

Yet, in a democracy, where a large section of the populace finds it difficult to make two ends meet, expectations of fast results are neither unexpected nor unjustified. The evolutionary changes are the panacea, not radical reforms which would enhance the burden of common man. While one may have divergence of opinion on the initial steps (it would be unjustified to call it performance at this juncture) of the NDA government in reviving the nation's economy. The foreign policy and defence are areas where the Modi regime has made some successful moves within a short span. Bhutan as his first foreign destination for Indian Premier after he takes charge in office as China has lately intensified efforts to establish full-fledged diplomatic ties with Thimphu.

The visit came close on the heels of Modi's swear-in ceremony. The country's immediate neighbours, except, China, were invited. Though the apparent reason given was that only South Asian countries were invited (even Mauritius). There has been a perception that China has been gradually building close ties with India's neighbours. It was being seen by strategic experts as an attempt to encircle India though a 'string of pearls'. China has been building ports in Sri Lanka, Bangladesh and its 'all-weather ally', Pakistan. It overtook India as the biggest foreign investor in Nepal early 2014.

In yet another strong signal to Beijing regarding border disputes, the government has decided to nearly double the deployment of Indo-Tibetan Border Police personnel on the India-China frontier. The previous UPA government was often criticised for being 'soft' on the issue of Chinese incursions. Interestingly, Indian Minister of State for Home Affairs Kiren Rijiju desires to enhance forces, infrastructure and modernisation of the ITBP to secure the border with China hails from Arunachal Pradesh, which Beijing claims to be part of South Tibet and issues only stapled visas to residents from the area, over which India has been raising serious reservations. Similarly, the government has shown urgency in expediting projects along the border, held up due on grounds of environment disaster.

While the increase in deployment should not be construed as an aggressive posture on India's part, it is clear that the government is determined about securing India's territory. Chinese Foreign Minister Wang Yi has discussed the entire gamut of bilateral ties including the contentious boundary issue with the Indian Premier. The new Chinese leadership is keen to improve relation with India in the face of serious challenges it faces over its maritime disputes with Japan in the East China Sea and with Vietnam, the Philippines and other maritime neighbours in the South China Sea. A major US military push into the Asia-Pacific has alarmed the territory. In his meeting with Nawaz Sharif, the Indian PM Modi was categorical in his assertion that India expects zero tolerance from Islamabad when it comes to terrorism directed against India from Pakistani soil. The Pakistanis neither raised the 'K' word nor even met the separatist Hurriyat leadership. Some experimental border violations along the LoC were also thwarted with alacrity.

The Indian External Affairs Minister Sushma Swaraj's visit to Bangladesh reflects good neighbourly relations. Yet, in consonance with poll promise, Modi has moved fast on the illegal migration issue by restricting entry of Bangaldeshi nationals through visa on arrival regime. Similarly, the decision to go ahead with Sri Lankan President Mahinda Rajapakse's visit amply reflected that regional satraps can no more make foreign policy hostage to their whims and fancies. While regional issues are of concern to the government, regional parties cannot be allowed to determine the course of bilateral ties.

In yet another major move, India has decided to enhance transparency of its nuclear infrastructure. It has ratified an additional protocol with the International Atomic Energy Agency. It can be leveraged to boost energy security and lift international confidence. Later this year, the prime minister is expected to visit USA. He has shared an uneasy relation over the denial of visa on 2002 Godhra massacre and riots in the aftermath. It has made him closer to Asian countries such as Japan with whose leadership he has established a personal rapport during his tenure as the Gujarat chief minister. Yet, the practical Gujarati that he is, Modi would not be dogmatic in his ties with Washington. Also on the cards are major decisions and policy announcements including indigenisation aimed at beefing up the country's defence.

Modi's initial foreign policy moves have shown few major indicators:

- National interest would be paramount as against Nehruvian idealism.
- Improved trade ties would be the hallmark of bilateral ties.
- Reciprocity and not philanthropy would be the guiding principle.
- Emphasis would be on dehyphenating ties between India and Pakistan.

Focus on India emerging as a leader of South Asia before dreaming to become a superpower. Emphasis will be on reducing Chinese influence in the South Asian region. Pursue good neighbourly relations with China but not at the cost of India's territorial integrity or self-respect. Build common cause with countries having territorial disputes with China as a long-term strategy. Act tough with Pakistan on terrorism and cross-border violations. Pursue with determination the 'Look East Policy', wherein the focus is on Asia. It will be with country's immediate neighbourhood. All in all, India's foreign policy is set for a paradigm shift.

Chinese Foreign Minister Holds Talks with Sushma

At the beginning, Chinese foreign minister Wang Yi has discussed ways to strengthen co-operation in key areas including trade and investment. China is India's biggest trading partner as its two-way commerce aggregate close to \$70 billion. India's trade deficit with China soared to over \$40 billion from just \$1 billion (2001-02). Experts say Modi must bridge the deficit by seeking greater access to the Chinese market, so that annual bilateral trade reaches \$100 billion by 2015. India accused Chinese troops of intruding nearly 20 kilometres (12 miles) into Indian-claimed territory, triggering a three-week stand off, resolved when forces from both sides pulled back. The border between China and India has never been formally demarcated, although they have signed accords to maintain peace. Meanwhile, Tibet's government-in-exile, based in India, has pinned hopes on Indian government to speak up for Tibetans during Wang's visit. "This is in the interest of India, Tibet is a buffer zone between India and China. It has served the interests of all neighbouring countries," exiled Tibetan premier Lobsang Sangay said.

India, China Must Narrow Down Differences

Uphold Panchsheel: India and China have to narrow down differences and build on convergences by exploiting the potential of Panchsheel, the five principles of peaceful co-existence. It was agreed between the countries along with Myanmar in 1954.

"In our respective bilateral relations, our common interests far outweigh our differences," Ansari said while addressing a commemorative meeting of the 60th anniversary of the five principles in which Chinese President Xi Jinping and his Myanmar counterpart Thien Sein also took part.

"On the way forward, we have to build on our convergences and narrow down our differences. Panchsheel can help us exploit this potential for cooperation and come up with fresh, innovative initiatives to improve the lives of our people," Ansari said. Panchsheel was enunciated by Ex-Indian premier Jawaharlal Nehru along with his then Chinese counterpart Zhou Enlai. Myanmar subsequently endorsed it. Ansari was on a five-day visit to China. India, China and Myanmar are bound by age-old linkages and geography. "We may be at different stages of development but we can learn from each other's national experiences." "We need a new paradigm for global action. Our destinies are intertwined. Our quest is, should be, for a framework in which opportunities and challenges for the betterment of our societies co-exist," he said.

"In this endeavour, Panchsheel can act as a catalyst to help us better coordinate our efforts, enhance mutual understanding, share developmental experiences and tackle trans-national threats more effectively," he said. In his address, Ansari said besides being ancient civilisations and neighbours, India and China are also strategic partners. "Historically, there has been much that has bound us together, not merely through the exchange of goods and commodities but through a flourishing interchange of ideas, values and philosophies," he said.

"The imperatives of the 21st century propel us towards a better understanding of each other's objectives and more purposeful cooperation for mutual benefit. Greater interaction between the people of our two countries, in all fields, is a necessary condition for stronger overall bilateral relations," he said. India-Myanmar relations, which are rooted in shared historical, ethnic, cultural and religious ties with geographical proximity has helped develop and sustain cordial relations and facilitated people-to-people contacts.

"A significant population of Indian origin resides in Myanmar. Our shared history and common interests paves the way for greater mutually beneficial cooperation," Ansari said.

About the relevance of Panchsheel, he said on the global level, it preserves the right of all nations to choose their own path while interacting with others on the basis of mutual respect and equality. "It facilitates the expression of views of all members of the international community, particularly the developing countries, so that their concerns are highlighted and interests are protected in the international economic, social and political order," he said. Panchsheel provides the framework within which a just and equitable global order can be achieved to the satisfaction and benefit of all, he said. Pursuit of world peace is a fundamental tenet of India's foreign policy, he said, adding that India draws inspiration from "our ancient civilisational value of considering the world as one family". "This shapes and guides our actions in international relations," he said.

"Even before India became an independent nation, the leaders of our freedom struggle had outlined the fundamental precepts and values that embody the Five Principles of Peaceful Existence or Panchsheel." "The Constitution of India enjoins the State to endeavour to promote international peace and security and to maintain just and honourable relations between nations," he said.

"Panchsheel emanated from the civilisational matrix of Asia and is Asia's contribution towards building a just and democratic international order. Ancient ideals of Panchsheel, envisioned by our three countries, in the modern form are of continuing relevance in the changed world of today and will remain so in the world of tomorrow," he said. Panchsheel came to be accepted almost universally by countries and finally by the United Nations in the conduct of international relations. "We gather here today to reaffirm the timeless relevance of Panchsheel in establishing a peaceful, stable, prosperous and secure world. As the co-originators of Panchsheel, it is our duty to revitalise our friendly relations and to promote co-operation as the only way forward towards the realisation of our common goals of progress and prosperity for our peoples," he added.

China Map Shows J&K as its Territory

China has just released its new map. It showed the whole of Arunachal Pradesh and large parts of Jammu and Kashmir as its territories. The Chinese cartographic aggression has come days after Chinese troops made a six-km-deep incursion in Pangong Lake in Ladakh, Jammu and Kashmir, on 24th June and went back after staying put in their high speed boats for about two hours. This is the first brush of Indian premier with China, a country he admires and wants to emulate in lifting the sagging Indian economy. It applies to the manufacturing sector, where the Chinese performance has been consistently impressive. China has provoked India on several occasions in the past few years. It was on cartographic as well as military incursions. The Chinese actions this time is much different and far more significant for two reasons.

First, The Chinese cartographic provocation has come at a time when Vice President Hamid Ansari is currently in China on an official visit (26-30 June) to celebrate the 60th year of Panchsheel, the five principles for peaceful coexistence that once formed bedrock of India-China ties. The timing of publication of the controversial Chinese map is significant. It has clearly been timed to coincide with Ansari's ongoing visit to China.

Second, China has hardened its position on boundary dispute with India. It is clear by a just-published report in Chinese state newspaper *People's Daily.* Without mincing words the daily said that Chinese citizens would now be able to "fully, directly know the full map of China".

What India can do with China?

Many of those proffering ideas to Indian premier suggest that he should emulate Richard Nixon. The latter belied his reputation as a fierce anti-communist, with an audacious diplomatic breakthrough to make an

American peace with China. But a far more apt exemplar for Narendra Modi would be Mikhail Gorbachev, who assumed power in Moscow under circumstance. As far as Soviet relations with China were concerned, it was rather a great deal in with utmost deal in common with India's today.

Just as had Nehru's India previously, the USSR in the 1960s adopted an intransigent and bullying approach to China over their border disputes. It brushed aside Beijing's reasonable and practical suggestion. The differences were be subjected to negotiation with the haughty insistence—that there were no disputes, and that Sino-Soviet boundaries ran exactly where Moscow said, they ran. To its unyielding refusal to negotiate, the USSR added its own variant of a "forward policy". It began to exercise armed force to drive the Chinese off the two great continental rivers, Amur and Ussuri, which together, under the 19th century Sino-Russian Treaty of Peking, comprise the boundary features in their eastern sector. Defeat in the fierce battles fought in 1969 on the ice of Ussuri River left a bitter memory in Russia, official and popular. And Moscow followed Nehru's example again, accusing China of "unprovoked aggression" to cover up its own record of provocative bellicosity. For years Sino-Russian relations stayed frozen in hostility.

So, Gorbachev inherited a deadlocked territorial quarrel. The fact in the recent past brought the USSR and China to the point of war. Ideological differences found intensified with the estrangement. He broke out of that stalemate with a variant of Nixon's audacity. In a much heralded 1986 speech in Vladivostok, he called for friendship with China. He slipped into his text a fundamental reversal of policy. He implicitly accepted the need for general negotiations over disputed borders.

Panchasheel to Improve Ties with Neighbours

Expressing its readiness to work with the new Indian government to promote bilateral ties, China invoked 'Panchasheel' to improve relations with neighbours to settle disputes peacefully while firmly holding on to its core interests.

"China is ready to work with the new government in India in promoting continued progress of China-India relations," State Councillor Yang Jiechi said. He was speaking at the World Peace Forum organised by Tsinghua University in Beijing. Mr Yang—who is also China's special representative for Sino-India boundary dispute, is the highest ranking diplomat in Chinese hierarchy, placed higher than the foreign minister. As the two countries along with Myanmar celebrated the 60th anniversary of the Panchasheel in June 28, 29, 2014, Yang said Beijing will pursue ties with neighbours based on the five principles of peaceful coexistence as a guide.

"China committed to deepen cooperation with others on the basis of five principles of coexistence," he said. Beijing actively champions and implements the five principles and enhance co-operation with ASEAN (Association of South East Asian Nations) and SAARC (South Asian Association of Regional Co-operation).

"Adhering to a neighbourhood diplomacy concept featuring amity, sincerity, mutual benefit and inclusiveness, China wants to cooperate with its neighbours," he said.

"China is committed to settle disputes through peaceful means. It is firm in upholding its sovereignty. We will not trade with core interests or swallow the bitter fruit that undermine our sovereignty, security and development interests," Mr. Yang said referring to China's tensions with Japan and as well Vietnam and the Philippines over the South China Sea. China says 'happy to see' Modi's Bhutan visit: As Prime Minister Narendra Modi visits Bhutan. China rejected suggestions of any competition with India for strategic space in the neighbourhood. It vouched to be "happy" with the Premier's visit and "full of confidence" over the future of relations with India. Asked about perceptions among some analysts on the Premier's decision to make Bhutan his first overseas visit may have been prompted in some measure by Beijing's recent overtures to Thimphu. China does not yet have formal diplomatic relations with Bhutan. Chinese foreign ministry spokesperson Hua asserted that China was "happy to see the development of friendly, co-operative, mutually beneficial relations between our other neighbours". The countries exchange regular political, trade and cultural delegations. They have engaged in talks to settle their disputed border, holding more than 19 rounds of negotiations.

She added, "China pays high attention to developing relations with India. With consistent efforts from both sides, relations have scored substantive progress in recent years. Our strategic cooperative partnership for peace and development is advancing steadily". India has had traditionally close historical relations with Bhutan. Beijing and Thimphu were willing to take ties to a higher level. Former Bhutan Prime Minister Jigmi Thinley, who ended his term in July last year, held a first ever meeting with then Chinese Premier Wen Jiabao, on the sidelines of a United Nations conference in Brazil (June 2012). Mr Thinley then told Mr Wen that his government "wishes to forge formal diplomatic ties with China as soon as possible" – a declaration that generated much interest in India at the time. The Chinese leader said Beijing was willing to settle the boundary dispute "at an early date" and step up co-operation in all fields.

Russia for Enhanced Co-operation with India

Russia has good relations with Prime Minister Narendra Modi. It hopes co-operation between the two countries, particularly in defence and nuclear non-proliferation.

"We have good very cooperation and cohesion with the new Premier. We never introduced any black list (many western countries including the US and EU block had refused Modi a visa over the 2002 Gujarat riots)."

"He (Modi) had three successful visits to Russia. On that level we do not see any problem. With his energy and more focused attitude to cooperation projects, they will no doubt succeed," Russian Ambassador to India Alexander Kadakin said. Russia had far reaching plans in energy sector. It wanted to build 14 to 16 nuclear reactors. It is looking forward for better co-operation in the field of defence, including the fifth generation fighter aircraft, he said. Asked whether Russia was keen on leasing out Akula class submarine, Kadakin said that it had not received any formal request from India.

Leaders of Indo-Pak Holds Meeting

The Pakistani officials were optimistic about the prospects for peace between India and Pakistan. The last burst of progress came in the late 1990s, when Sharif held power concurrently with Atal Bihari Vajpayee.

"I intend taking up threads from where Vajpayee and I left off in 1999,"

Sharif said. Asked by a journalist about the outcome Sharif recited an Urdu couplet that translates as, "cling to the tree and hope, for spring is in sight."

It was the first Indian visit by a Pakistani leader since the 2008 Mumbai terror attacks. The relation between the two countries worsened. Initially, scheduled to last for 35 minutes, the meeting went on for nearly an hour. One possible concession from the Pakistani side would be the extension of most-favoured-nation status. It would allow Indian goods access to Pakistan markets, though Sharif is likely seeking a concession in return from Modi. A major topic, Indian television reported, was the trials of suspects in the Mumbai terror attacks of 2008, which killed 163 people. India has long complained about postponements and delays of the trial.

The Premiers risked displeasing hard-liners in their own countries by taking part in the meeting. Sharif has delayed for almost three days before accepting the invitation. In India, though, Modi's landslide victory in parliamentary elections this month has meant the criticism was muted. One voice of dissent came from the Shiv Sena, which has steadfastly opposed high-level engagement with Pakistan. But its leader, Uddhav Thackeray, attended Modi's swearing-in Monday and issued a statement expressing support for the new leader.

"We trust the firm and decisive leadership of Modi. We do not wish to put obstacles on his way at the very start of his term," the statement said. He added, in a kind of warning, "if, despite this gesture, Pakistan doesn't change, we expect Modi to take firm steps."

Peace and Co-operation will Accelerate Progress: Indian Premier had written to his Pakistan counterpart, saying he looked forward to charting a "new course" in the bilateral relations in an atmosphere "free from confrontation and violence". Responding to Sharif's letter (June 2, 2014) Modi has said that "a relationship between India and Pakistan defined by peace, friendship and co-operation would unleash enormous opportunities for our youth, secure a more prosperous future for our people and accelerate progress across our region." He condemned the terror strike in Karachi earlier. He conveyed his "deepest condolences" for the loss of innocent lives in this "senseless and barbaric" attack. He said he was encouraged by discussions with Sharif. The discusssion took place on bilateral relations and the convergence on views.

He thanked Sharif for attending the oath taking ceremony. "Your presence and that of other leaders from our region added a special sheen to the event. It was a celebration of the strength of democracy in our region. It reflected our collective hopes and shared destinies," he wrote.

In the letter, Modi has written, "I also take this opportunity to condemn in the strongest terms the terrorists attack in Karachi and convey my deepest condolences for the loss of innocent lives in this senseless and barbaric attack." He thanked for the letter which Sharif wrote on June and also for the gift of sari that Sharif sent for his mother. He replied it is "a gesture that she has deeply appreciated".

Mother's Love Drives Diplomacy: Sharif Sari for PM mom: If the UPA-2 government bonded over biryani with Pakistan, it is "ma ka pyar" which seems to have emerged as the driving force of India-Pak diplomacy under the Narendra Modi government. Modi's counterpart Nawaz Sharif on June 12 reached out further to Modi when he dispatched a sari, shawl and a suit for the

PM — all for his Gujarat-based mother. "Nawaz Sharifji has sent a wonderful white sari for my mother. I am really grateful to him and will send it to my mother very soon," Modi tweeted.

PM Modi Replies Nawaz Sharif's Letter: 'Look Forward to Working with You': Prime Minister Narendra Modi has replied to a letter written to him by Pakistan's Prime Minister Nawaz Sharif and said he is looking forward to working closely with him and his government "in an atmosphere free from confrontation and violence in order to chart a new course in our bilateral relations."

Modi condemned the recent terror attack at the Karachi airport in Pakistan. He is condoled the loss of innocent life. The Prime Minster has addressed Mr Sharif as "Dear Mian Sahib" in the letter and has thanked him for his participation in swear- in ceremony. He has also thanked him "for the sari that you sent for my mother, a gesture that she has deeply appreciated."

PMs Bhutan Visit

To Boost Hydropower Projects: The Indian Premier visited Bhutan on invitation of Bhutan's King Jigme Khesar Namgyel Wangchuck and the Bhutanese Prime Minister Tshering Tobgay on June 15-16, 2014. A move aimed at adding content to an early initiative taken by the country's new leadership to reinforce the idea that India's priority is its immediate neighbourhood.

Modi will be accompanied by external affairs minister Sushma Swaraj and national security adviser Ajit Doval, besides Singh. The visit comes against the backdrop of contacts established in recent months by Bhutan and China with reports suggesting that the latter could open a diplomatic mission in Thimphu. "Our relations with Bhutan are unique and especially warm. Our historical and cultural linkages make us natural friends and partners.

India had been the biggest trading partner of the tiny Himalayan country—sandwiched between India and China—was India. Bilateral trade amounted to Rs 6,830 crore (2012-13). Bhutan is one of the top recipients of India's development assistance packages. The quantum exceeds 70 per cent of the total foreign aid received by Bhutan coming from India. India has committed Rs 4,500 crore to Bhutan in assistance (2013-18).

India had "invested in hydel power in Bhutan. We get electricity at cheaper rates—this is something unique in the relationship". Modi may push for expediting the hydropower projects under construction in Bhutan. The Indian side is likely to allow higher export of edible oil to Bhutan, the government official said. Bhutan has been urging India to increase the annual import cap on edible oils from India from 2,400 tonnes to 13,000 tonnes.

According to Singh, the Indian foreign secretary, co-operation in the hydel power sector was "a classic example of win-win cooperation". "The hydropower projects generate export revenues for Bhutan, cement our economic partnership, and provide clean and low-cost electricity to India," she said. Three projects totalling 1,416 megawatts, or MW, (Chukha, Tala and Kurichu) were already operational, she said. Three others—Punatsangchu-I, Punatsangchu-II and Mangdechu totalling nearly 3,000 MW—were under construction and to be commissioned in the next two or three years, Singh said.

India and Bhutan signed a framework pact for four more joint venture projects totalling 2,120MW, she recalled. According to Amit Bhandari, a South Asia expert at Mumbai-based think tank Gateway House, "Electricity (to India) is Bhutan's single largest export. Modi's visit to Bhutan demonstrates the importance India places on furthering this relationship." "Bhutan has the potential to generate 24,000MW of hydropower. It is in India's interests to help Bhutan develop this potential—India can improve its energy security in the long term by purchasing clean, renewable energy from a politically stable and friendly neighbour," Bhandari said.

He addressed the joint session of the Parliament of Bhutan. He inaugurated one of India's assistance projects—the building of the Supreme Court of Bhutan. Ahead of his visit, Mr Modi said Bhutan was a "natural choice" as his first foreign destination because of the "unique and special relationship". In his pre-departure statement, Mr Modi said relations with Bhutan will be a key foreign policy priority of his government. "I am looking forward to my first-ever visit to Bhutan and to nurturing and further strengthening India's special relations with Bhutan," said Modi before undertaking the trip at the invitation of Bhutan's King and the Prime Minister.

"Our relations with Bhutan are unique and especially warm. Our historical and cultural linkages make us natural friends and partners," Foreign Secretary Singh told a press conference in Delhi. "Bhutan is one of our most important strategic partners ....It is a very good country to show our policy of good neighbourliness in South Asia and special token of our friendship," she said explaining why Bhutan was chosen as the first foreign destination of PM Modi. During Indian Premier's tour, both countries reaffirmed their commitment to extensive development co-operation and discussed ways to further enhance economic ties.

Key points of Modi's visit to Bhutan

1. India and Bhutan reiterated their commitment to achieving the 10,000 MW target in hydropower cooperation and not to allow their territories to be used for interests "inimical" to each other.
2. Modi inaugurated one of India's assistance projects - the building of the Supreme Court of Bhutan and laid foundation stone of the 600MW Kholongchu Hydro-electric project, a joint venture between India and Bhutan.
3. India announced a slew of measures and concessions. It included the exemption of Bhutan from any ban on export of milk powder, wheat, edible oil, pulses and non-basmati rice.
4. The two sides recalled over the free trade arrangement between them and the expanding bilateral trade and its importance in further cementing their friendship.
5. Indian Premier mooted the idea of an annual hill sports festival with India's northeastern states along with Bhutan and Nepal.
6. Modi announced doubling of scholarships being provided to Bhutanese students in India Rs 2 crore.

7. India will assist Bhutan set up a digital library. It will provide access to Bhutanese youth to two million books and periodicals.
8. India-Bhutan reaffirmed their commitment to extensive economic development. It described Bhutan as a natural choice as the two countries shared a "special relationship".
10. The fact that the Prime Minister chose Bhutan as his first foreign destination assumes significance since China has lately intensified efforts to woo it and establish full-fledged diplomatic ties with Thimphu.

Neighbours will Benefit from Strong India

Prime Minister Narendra Modi said India is committed to good neighbourly relations and assured Bhutan that change in government will not alter the dynamics of India-Bhutan ties.

"Stability and development in India will help neighbours like Bhutan," he said in his speech in Hindi. He also lauded Bhutan for the smooth transition from monarchy to democracy in a span of seven years which showed maturity in governance in that country.

Recalling India's historic ties with Bhutan, Modi said his government would work towards further strengthening the relations between the two neighbours. Noting that terrorism divides and tourism unites, he said Bhutan has immense potential in the tourism sector. Modi said development of tourism does not require large investment but can yield substantial profit and even the poor can benefit from it. Describing the Himalayas as a shared legacy of the two countries, he stressed on the need to develop the region and said India is planning to open a university for Himalayan studies. He also thanked Bhutan's Prime Minister Tshering Tobgay for attending his swearing in ceremony in Delhi last month. Modi vowed to nurture bilateral relations which he described as "B4B - Bharat for Bhutan and Bhutan for Bharat" as he held wide-ranging talks with Bhutan's King Jigme Khesar Namgyel Wangchuk and Tobgay.

2014 BRICS Summit

The Indian premier visited Brazil on invitation of its President Dilma Rousseff for BRICS Summit. He would be in the company of Russian President Vladimir Putin, Chinese President Xi Jinping and South African President Jacob Zuma as the leaders converge in the Latin American nation for the 2014 BRICS Summit (July 15, 17, 2014) in the seaside city of Fortaleza. BRICS is an association of five emerging economies—Brazil, Russia, India, China and South Africa. The BRICS summit, originally scheduled for March, 2014, has reportedly been postponed. Brazil played host more than 20 world leaders, including German Chancellor Angela Merkel, the Emir of Qatar, Prince Albert of Monaco and UN Secretary-General Ban ki-Moon, during the month-long tournament.

Prime Minister Narendra Modi met leaders from the four nations and it is expected that the blueprint for a development bank and reforms of United Nations and international financial organisations. India attaches high importance to the BRICS forum for promoting global economic growth, peace and stability. The meeting in Brazil will usher in the second cycle of BRICS Summits. We meet at a time of political turmoil, conflict and humanitarian crisis in several parts of the world, and persisting weakness and risks in the global economy. Many emerging economies have experienced a slowdown, which has increased the challenge of pursuing inclusive and sustainable economic development.

The Summit theme, "Inclusive Growth; Sustainable Development", will enable us to shape the post-2015 Development Agenda being discussed in the United Nations. The Summit provided an opportunity to interact with a number of leaders of South American countries at a meeting being hosted by Brazil. India has traditionally enjoyed close, cordial and mutually beneficial ties with these countries. We share common aspirations and challenges. The Indian Diaspora in these countries also serves as the continent's enduring link with India. South America's all round progress makes it a potentially important pole of the global economy and a land of enormous opportunities for us.

Sushma's Goodwil Visit

Talks Border, Teesta with Bangladesh Counterpart: India and Bangladesh on June 25 made forward movement on key issues like visa simplification for certain categories as well as cooperation on supply of electricity from a Tripura-based power plant. These issues figured during External Affairs Minister Sushma Swaraj's meeting with her Bangladeshi counterpart Abul Hassan Mahmood Ali and Prime Minister Sheikh Hasina in Dhaka. She discussed Land Boundary Agreement, proposed Teesta river water sharing deal and the issue of illegal immigration. The Foreign Secretary Sujatha Singh and senior officials assisted the Miniuster during her talks in Dhaka.

The Indian side assured Bangladesh of its positive intention towards Dhaka's concerns on LBA and Teesta river issues. Regarding the visa simplification, it was not immediately clear who would be covered under the relaxation regime. The two sides also discussed the gas-based power project at Palatana in Tripura and the supply of electricity to Bangladesh from the plant. Though there are no pacts to be signed and no big expectations, the trip, which is termed as a "goodwill" visit, is aimed at taking bilateral ties forward which are on a "positive trajectory" for past few years. Among other issues the meetings also discussed ways to enhance cooperation in important areas including economic and trade. Significantly, it was BJP's opposition, coupled with that of Trinamool Congress and Asom Gana Parishad which prevented the previous Congress-led UPA government from formalising the LBA and signing the Teesta water sharing deal with Bangladesh. The LBA, which is yet to be approved by Parliament, is aimed at redrawing the international boundary between India and Bangladesh by exchanging areas of adverse possession and enclaves along with population on either side, thus making the highly incongruous and porous India-Bangla border more manageable.

Modi on a Visit to Nepal

Prime Minister Narendra Modi embarked on a visit to Nepal to help speed up negotiations on a power trade pact that is at the centre of a new effort to improve ties with a neighbour that serves as a buffer with China. His will be the first bilateral visit to Nepal by an Indian Prime Minister in 17 years, though Indian leaders have routinely attended regional summits in Kathmandu.

Negotiators were trying to narrow down differences over the power pact aimed at harnessing Nepal's estimated 42,000 MW hydro-electric potential to meet domestic needs and also supply India's giant energy-starved economy.

The Himalayan nation currently has an installed capacity of 600 MW as its development has been held back by years of political instability. It is still struggling with the transition to a constitutional republic after the abolition of the monarchy in 2008. Nepal's politicians are at odds over the proposed energy pact. Opponents say it would give Indian firms a stranglehold over Nepal's energy resources and bar other countries, like China, from investment in the sector.

"We will identify steps to strengthen our bilateral cooperation in key sectors, including trade and investment, hydro power, agriculture and agro-processing, environment," he said.

A Significant Outing in Nepal

Prime Minister Narendra Modi concluded an important visit to Nepal, where he tapped all the right nodes of the relationship—political, economic and cultural—to turn around ties, which had begun to languish over the last few years. The visit seems to have caught the imagination of the people of Nepal. Partly, this was because PM Modi managed to connect with the common person through his carefully choreographed visit to the ancient Pashupatinath temple, and a generous announcement of donations to give the ancient place of worship an essential facelift. The Prime Minister's visit also created a buzz because he seemed to have fresh ideas, born out of a vision that Indo-Nepal ties can flourish only when they are connected with South Asia's promising future. Modi has re-emphasised that bilateral ties with neighbours must promote the overall well-being of the eight-nation SAARC.

In his bid to reinvigorate the relationship, PM Modi underscored his penchant for using energy as an instrument to reinforce political bonds. During his stay, India pledged to bolster Nepal's energy security by agreeing to establish a two-phase products pipeline, which will eventually carry petroleum products from Raxaul in Bihar to Kathmandu. More significantly, discussions have been held to link Nepal with a gas pipeline from India. If that happens, it would lock India and Nepal into a genuine strategic embrace, opening up the possibility of Nepal benefiting from gas that India might in the future procure from a variety of overseas destinations, including Iran and Turkmenistan.

India's energy pledge to Nepal follows a decision to build a pipeline channelling diesel and kerosene to Pakistan from its refinery in Bhatinda. Besides, India is planning to send gas, transported from Dahej in Gujarat to Jalandhar, before it is sent on to Pakistan. Nepal would be one of the beneficiaries if the project fructifies; it could also be connected with the futuristic Iran-Pakistan-India (IPI) and Turkmenistan-Afghanistan-Pakistan-India (TAPI) pipeline networks. Following improved atmospherics resulting from Modi's visit, India and Nepal decided to "once and for all" resolve the pending Nepal-India boundary issues, including differences over Kalapani and Susta. Yet, both sides have their task cut out to remove the remaining impediments in the relationship. New Delhi and Kathmandu need to quickly revise the Treaty of Peace and Friendship of 1950, so that the archaic "big-brother" tag on India is swiftly removed. Besides, the two have to learn to work together with China, which has the political heft and the economic surplus to make solid investments in the Himalayan republic.

A New Sunrise

India and Japan have enjoyed the best of relations over the decades. Yet, their trade and economic partnership has, strangely, been under-performing, belying the promise and potential. Bilateral trade at $16.29 billion in 2013-14 accounted for just 2.13 per cent of India's total trade and barely 1 per cent of Japan's. The low-profile trade relationship is especially disappointing considering how much Japan has to offer in terms of investment and technology, and how much India needs both. India may be one of the largest recipients of Japanese ODA (Official Development Assistance), but when it comes to foreign direct investment (FDI), it ranks low, well behind China. Between April 2000 and February 2014, Japanese companies cumulatively invested $15.97 billion in India, accounting for just 7.46 per cent of total FDI inflows into India, which in a way epitomises the state of the economic relationship between the second and third largest economies of Asia. All this could change for the better, post-Modi's visit to Japan, which seems to have breathed new life into economic relations. Japan has said it would invest 3.5 trillion yen ($33.5 billion) in India in the next five years in the sectors of infrastructure, manufacturing, transport and clean energy, and on smart cities, all thrust areas for development for the Modi government.

To be sure, this is not the first time we have seen positive intent in the leadership of the two Asian giants to improve trade and investment. Ever since India liberalised in the early 1990s, there has been steady interest among Japanese companies and investors—but they have often been frustrated by complicated procedures and cumbersome processes. Actually, Japanese companies willingly ceded market space in India to competitors from South Korea and China rather than deal with the red tape. It is in this context that Modi's promises of "red carpet, not red tape", and a special track in the Prime Minister's Office to facilitate Japanese investments, have to be seen. Modi harped on all the right themes including the three Ds that India can boast of, namely democracy, demography and demand, while making his pitch to Japanese business. With manufacturing costs increasing in China and given the political issues between the two countries, Japanese businesses are looking to diversify, and India presents a good choice with its huge market. New projects such as those for super-fast trains and smart cities are ideal destinations for Japanese investments. The Modi government has to now move quickly to fulfil its promises of easing procedures and facilitating investment to capitalise on the optimism and goodwill generated from what has clearly been a successful visit in economic terms.

Befriending Japan, Balancing China: Modi's Foreign Policy

Prime Minister Narendra Modi is set to put his stamp on foreign policy as he holds bilateral summits in quick succession with three powers central to Indian foreign policy — Japan, China and the United States. Modi has already bared a two-fold focus to build a pragmatic, dynamic policy that ends the era of belated, reactive diplomacy: Proactively regain India's clout in its own strategic backyard and build closer but differentially calibrated collaboration with major powers. After highly effective visits to Nepal and Bhutan, Modi now turns his gaze to the grand chessboard to underpin broader national interests.

Modi's upcoming tour of Japan is certain to deepen bonds between the world's largest democracy and Asia's oldest (and richest) democracy. But if this emerging democratic axis is to turn into a game-changer in Asia, the two countries must make their collaboration meatier through deeper strategic linkages. Some of Prime Minister Shinzo Abe's recent steps, including easing Japan's arms-export ban and reasserting the right of collective defence, open new avenues of collaboration with India. When Chinese President Xi Jinping comes calling in mid-September, Modi will have a more difficult task at hand. At a time when the India-China trade relationship is already lopsided, with Beijing exporting three times as much as it imports and treating India as a raw-material appendage of its economy like Africa, Modi must find ways to address this insidious asymmetry as he seeks to make a cash-rich China an important partner in India's development.

Another challenge for him is to balance deeper India-China economic engagement with India's strategic imperatives, like bolstering defences against China and containing increasing Chinese border provocations. According to minister of state for home Kiren Rijiju, Chinese border transgressions this year have exceeded more than one per day, totalling 334 till August 4. Given America's critical importance to India, Modi sagaciously placed national interest above personal umbrage by shaking off the US visa-related humiliation heaped on him for over nine years. After his thumping electoral mandate, he could have, given Washington's itch to woo him, waited for top US officials to come calling. Instead, he quickly accepted President Barack Obama's invitation to visit the White House, thereby leaving no room for perceptions about bilateral strains to arise and hurt India's foreign policy interests. Yet the reality is that India-US relations, after their heyday under Obama's predecessor, have gradually run out of momentum, even though America has quietly become India's largest arms supplier. Modi seems ready to reinvigorate the ties. But he will be visiting Washington at a time when Obama is already beset with multiple crises at home and abroad and appears increasingly as a lame-duck president under political siege, including from the Democrats. The contrast between a newly-empowered Modi and a fading Obama could not be starker.

In this light, it is unclear as to what the visit can accomplish, other than to drive home the message that all is well on the India-US front under Modi. Still, as if to highlight how transactional aspects overshadow strategic elements, Washington would be expecting Modi to come bearing gifts, in the form of new economic and arms contracts. Modi, with his India-first instincts, has already shown that he will unflinchingly stand up for national interests, even if it means going against a large US-led combine, as happened at the WTO talks in Geneva. Clearly, Modi's smoothest interactions will be with Japan, even though he has gone out of his way to befriend China. He received the Chinese foreign minister before welcoming any other foreign dignitary. Modi's first bilateral meeting with a major State head was with Xi in Brazil. He allowed Xi to advance his India visit to September while postponing his own Japan trip by eight weeks. He sent the country's vice president to attend the 50th-anniversary 'celebrations' in Beijing of the Panchsheel Treaty, a pact that China used to outfox and outflank India, culminating in its 1962 invasion. Modi agreed to let Shanghai host the new BRICS bank, accepting just a consolation-prize job offer for an Indian to be its first president.

Despite all this, Abe is likely to ensure that Modi's Japan visit is a resounding success. Modi is expected to return home with the much-sought civil nuclear accord with Tokyo. Although this deal will be played up in India as a diplomatic triumph, its practical value will be largely symbolic. As India is discovering through its negotiations with France's Areva, the price of imported reactors is so high that it would burden Indian taxpayers with onerous subsidies. Indeed, France—the 'poster child' of atomic power—has announced it will cut nuclear-generating capacity by a third by 2025 and focus instead on renewables. India must use its scarce resources on advancing its expertise in fast-breeder reactors and the thorium fuel cycle and building more indigenous 700 MWe reactors. The India-Japan partnership holds the potential to shape Asian geopolitics in much the same way as China's rise or Obama's 'pivot' to Asia. This win-win partnership can help to drive India's infrastructure development and great-power aspirations, while catalysing Japan's revival as a world power. India's foreign policy has never had a distinct strategic imprint, except for a period under Indira Gandhi. India has always wanted to be a state that is liked, not a state that is respected internationally. Modi recognises this failing and—as Geneva exemplified—appears intent on fixing it. His overtures to Beijing can barely conceal his resolve to build close strategic ties with Japan to put discreet checks on China's exercise of its rapidly accumulating power, which risks sliding into arrogance. Modi's vision for Asia is stable power equilibrium in which India can thrive unhindered.

Sustained US support

India and the US have penned a joint op-ed, followed by a comprehensive 3,500-word joint statement. It spoke volumes for the breadth of discussion between them in a short period of three days. Dismantle terror groups including al-Qaeda, Lashkar-e Taiba, Jaish-e-Mohammad, the D-Company, and the Haqqanis" seldom any modus operandi. The countries agree on mutual help from the US on defence and energy. Nuclear trade and WTO issues remain ambiguous. Efforts to India did not accede to the US request to join the international coalition against ISIS. The two sides agreed on several ways to enhance cooperation on terror.

India and the US: obliquely referral to China's aggression in the South China Sea, 'global crises' like the situations in Iraq and Syria, and cooperation in Afghanistan, and a confounding, long reference to North Korea. India would discuss, the possibility of joining the anti-ISIS coalition. There is silence of course on where the discussions lead. Energy, health, space, women's empowerment, trade, skills, strategy and security were being discussed Modi's visit successfully brought India-US ties, faltering for a few years, back on track.

'Thank you America': Modi says before leaving for India

"Thank You America," Modi said he concluded his last official engagement of the US Indian Business Council (USIBC). He left for the Andrews Air Force Base, from where Air India One took him off for New Delhi.

"My visit has been very successful. I am going to airport directly," Modi said. Modi met Obama in the Oval Office of the White House. The two leaders issued a joint statement that promised to take the India-US relationship to new heights.

Obama, it is understood, decided to join Modi on this visit which many analysts said reflected the close bonding the two leaders have established among themselves in such a close time. In the first leg of his five-day US trip, Modi spent four days in New York, where he addressed the annual session of the United Nations General Assembly on September 27, and stormed the Indian American community by addressing the diaspora with a packed Madison Square Garden in the Big Apple on September 28. In New York, Modi held meetings with a host of top American businessmen including breakfast with CEOs of Fortune 500 companies, while top American leaders like Bill and Hillary Clinton, and former New York Mayor Michael Bloomberg. In all he met more than 50 top US lawmakers and three Governors including South Carolina's Nikki Haley. During his trip, Modi visited the 9/11 Memorial in New York and the Gandhi Statue in Washington D.C. He held a series of meetings with the Indian diaspora, including the dinner that was hosted in his honour wherein he stood for nearly two hours to get photographed with more than 700 Indian-Americans.

They Break Ice, but not Bread

Modi managed to come up with some surprises for the guests. President Obama greeted him Gujarati, "Kem Chho?" (How are you), Modi replied "Thank you," in English, a break from the last few days where he has stuck to Hindi for his interactions. The leaders then sat down for their first face-to-face meeting. Modi handed over his carefully-chosen gifts to President Obama. It had a version of the "Bhagavat Gita according to Gandhi," based on a series of lectures the Mahatma had given on the sacred text. The book was covered in Khadi. Japanese PM Shinzo Abe as well as Emperor Akihito also received Chinese President Xi Jinping a Mandarin version of the book. It earlier the White House would not confirm if President Obama had reciprocated with any gifts.

Gandhi, Morality and Political Legitimacy

Every October 2, for the past 66 years, Indians have reflected on the legacy of Mahatma Gandhi. He was born on this day in 1869, and assassinated on January 30 in 1948. This moment of reflection has sometimes gone by in a haze of indifference. Sparked deep criticisms of flaws and contradictions in Gandhi's thought were acleat. It has been observed as a day of ahimsa, non-violence. This year after the general election and the victory of the Bharatiya Janata Party (BJP), Gandhi Jayanthi feels like a poignant crossroad. Young Indians seem not to have any particular attachment to Gandhian ideals like ahimsa, swaraj and satyagraha. Gandhi is either diminished into a parochial Gujarati figure, or reduced to a formula and a cliché. In the current rhetoric, Gandhi not been the fountainhead of India's polity. He was rather an icon to be monumentalised and trivialised in one go. Why just Gandhi, it could be Swami Vivekananda who is trotted out one day, Sardar Patel another day, and Babasaheb Ambedkar when his name temes on. The particularities of the beliefs and ideas of each individual, and their very different, often incommensurable contribution in the making of modern India, are of no relevance in an atmosphere of illiterate nationalistic jingoism and complete ideological vacuity. Gandhi's repertoire of ideas turns out to be surprising and resilient. We might realise after decades of having him be a part of our default political furniture. His ideas like non-violent sovereignty, the dignity of the poor, the power of truth, and the difficult practices of moral courage are not fashionable. There is nevertheless a key lesson Gandhi taught us. It was during the British Raj, the lesson about the true sources of political legitimacy outshone. How to recognise that, no matter what the outer garb of sovereign power or the architecture of a state. Gandhi showed Indians and the world about the political legitimacy. He proved that it comes not from brute force, not from the state apparatus. Mechanisms of political participation couldn't where in electoral choice representative self-government. All of these are limited, and fallible. The popular mandate of Hitler did not make Nazi rule legitimate. The benign despotism of the British in India did not make colonial rule legitimate. Totalitarianism or imperialism couldn't not prime political legitimacy. It is successful only in capturing power on the basis of professed good intentions. True political legitimacy has to be premised on popular will. It will sustain on the desire for self-determination, and capabilities of a government. It exceeds and transcends such factors, and resides elsewhere, in a more subtle quality. It has to do with the inherent morality of any structure of power that purports to rule the people in their name and for their own good.

Upbeat Mood Persists after Modi Visit

Business and government leaders alike or basked in the afterglow of the Premier's US visit. Then endorsed India proceeding. through less red tape and more economic openness under him. In a private briefing, senior business executives of the Federation of Indian Chambers of Commerce and Industry expressed unequivocal optimism.

"The real test for any CEO – British, American or German – to invest is to see whether Indians themselves are investing [in the Indian economy]. Indians have stopped investing although they still comprise [over] 90 per cent of the investments," said FICCI president Sidharth Birla.

"We are watch. We have a far bigger hope than before. Modi puts his money where his mouth is, and for the 'Make in India,' initiative. For example, the land and labour laws and infrastructural efficiency issues [will be addressed]," said Birla.

Similarly Y.K. Modi, a past president of FICCI, said that Modi had had "excellent track record as the Gujarat chief minister, which he is cleverly using" to prove that he is willing to "walk the talk," and deal with the "nuts and bolts," as a means to improve the macro-economic situation in the country. The foreign and Indian businesses were not necessarily waiting for a "miracle". "What people expecting is that the government does not become a hurdle, which it was so earlier."

US officials to echoed the sentiments. The Assistant Secretary of State for South and Central Asian Affairs, Nisha Biswal, briefing select media said, "We've got folks who are firming up travel plans. Whether it's on a trade policy forum to reinvigorate on trade issues, or issues like the bilateral investment treaty... the contact group on civil nuclear cooperation. It is equally true in higher education and skills, or energy or counter-terrorism. We have been lining up pretty ambitious agenda."

Philip Reiner, the National Security Council Senior Director for India Presumed the meeting between Modi and Obama who seemed to hit over a their shared experiences. Obama entered the oval office, with two catastrophe the world has seen since the depression in the 1930s. Similarly, Modi said that "India has faced a mass exodus of industrial investment. He has come in the door. You've already seen a turnaround. You've seen the stock market really explode. You've seen the growth rate increase." Reother reminisced.

Looking ahead

At the very least, this visit restored a degree of confidence to a neglected relationship. It has prepared the ground for a lift to bilateral ties, ensuring that India and the US get on with operationalising what they can from our multilayered agenda. It could bridge the differences on managing of global commons, resolving bilateral roadblocks on commercial exchanges and investments, building cooperation in science and technology and defence production, and forging a closer strategic partnership in the Indo-Pacific region. Notwithstanding shared values and interests, the real traction in India-US relations lies ahead. Perhaps with a new US President just over two years away, India begins to realise her economic potential and augments what the Chinese could have described as comprehensive national power.

Deepening Relationship

The fact that India and the US issued a vision document, Modi and Obama penned a joint op-ed, and then a comprehensive Joint Statement, speaks volumes for the breadth of discussions between them.

After a hectic, often frenetic five days in the United States, it is time to take stock of the achievements of Modi's visit. To begin with, the welcome he received, both in New York and in Washington, has firmly closed the door on a most awkward situation in bilateral ties: that of India voting in a leader proscribed by the US Modi has been received at every level in the US, and if the Obama administration didn't revoke the visa order, the gesture of President Obama right at the end to accompany Modi to the Martin Luther King Memorial came as a poignant signal that the US genuinely wants to move ahead with India's newly elected leader. Secondly, US business, clearly disaffected by the difficulties they face in doing business with India, have also signalled its desire to renew investments. The fact that the two countries issued a vision document, the two leaders penned a joint op-ed, and then came out with a comprehensive 3,500-word Joint Statement, speaks volumes for the breadth of discussions between them in a short period. Yet, while the three documents contain all the parts of the relationship, they fail to convey the whole.

On issues where the countries agree, such as defence and energy, they show only incremental progress, without any big announcements. On issues where the countries differ, like the nuclear deal, trade and WTO, they seem to have deferred negotiations, indicating that no progress was made in resolving them. In that context, even the renewal of the strategic partnership, and reference to "joint and concerted efforts" to dismantle terror groups including al-Qaeda, Lashkar-e Taiba, Jaish-e-Mohammad, the D-Company, and the Haqqanis" do not indicate any particularly new action or formulation. The statements seem most opaque when it comes to spelling out a shared worldview for India and the US: while referring obliquely to China's aggression in the South China Sea, 'global crises' like the situations in Iraq and Syria, and cooperation in Afghanistan, and a confounding, long reference to North Korea

(DPRK), they list no action or step that the two countries hope to take together. And while both sides made it clear ahead of the talks that the US would request, and India would discuss, the possibility of joining the anti-ISIS coalition, there is silence on where those discussions led. On all fronts of the 'comprehensive dialogue', that is, eight issues including energy, health, space, women's empowerment, trade, skills, strategy and security, Modi's visit successfully brought India-US ties, that were faltering for a few years, back on track. But in order to reach the finish line, Modi and Obama will need a clearer enunciation of their shared vision for the road ahead.

Modi, Sharif Break Ice with Handshake in Himalayas

It took a Himalayan retreat at Dhulikhel, about 20 km from Kathmandu, for PM Narendra Modi and his Pakistani counterpart Nawaz Sharif to break some ice after the foreign secretary-level talks debacle in August.

There was at least a semblance of a thaw as Modi shook hands with Sharif and exchanged greetings at a resort terrace overlooking a wide expanse of the Himalayas and later followed it up with an even longer shaking of hands back in Kathmandu in the evening as the 18th Saarc summit ended "successfully". At the summit venue in Kathmandu, the two leaders were cheered by other Saarc leaders as they shook hands for nearly 40 seconds and posed for the cameras. There was no substantive "one-on-one" dialogue between the two leaders at any stage but the interaction and long handshake towards the end was enough to spark hope, if not expectations, about a possible resumption of dialogue between the two countries after ties seemed to have taken a debilitating blow in August.

"We want to have peaceful relations with Pakistan, a meaningful dialogue and if this interaction or handshake leads to it, we will welcome that," said MEA spokesperson Syed Akbaruddin.

PM Modi and Nawaz Sharif were cheered by other Saarc leaders as they shook hands for nearly 40 seconds and posed for the cameras. The fact that Pakistan relented and agreed to sign a framework agreement for energy cooperation, which the Indian cabinet had cleared last week in anticipation of a Saarc agreement, also seemed to have given Modi enough leeway to be seen in public as bonding with Sharif. Pakistan seemed to have indicated in the morning that it was looking for a successful conclusion of the agreement during the day. India described Modi's first Saarc outing as a "success" after the signing of the agreement.

At the Dhulikhel retreat, the two leaders also sat close to each other while leaders bonded over a vegetarian lunch sampling delicacies from all Saarc countries in a "convivial atmosphere". At the retreat, as host, Nepal PM Sushil Koirala apparently played a role in getting Modi to shake hands with Sharif but Indian officials said Modi greeted Sharif as he did other leaders. "They exchanged greetings, courtesies were extended," said the spokesperson.

India-US N- deal could Help Clear Project Logjam

A civil nuclear pact struck at summit talks between Indian Prime Minister Narendra Modi and US President Barack Obama could help clear a logjam of stalled projects, the head of US nuclear power plant maker Westinghouse said.

Daniel Roderick, president and CEO of Toshiba-backed Westinghouse Electric Co, said a commitment by India to "channel" immediate costs arising from any nuclear accident to the plant operator marked an important step forward. But he said he was looking for more detail on a nuclear liability insurance pool that India has proposed that would involve a state insurer and be backed by the government. "The term breakthrough is appropriate," Roderick said in an interview in New Delhi. "We have been in such a logjam for such a long time that making forward progress with a large stride instead of not even a baby step is pretty significant for us."

At their first summit in September in Washington, Obama and Modi set up a contact group to address ambiguities in a 2010 liability law passed by India that put ultimate responsibility for any accident on nuclear suppliers, and not on plant operators. The law sought to prevent a repeat of the battles for compensation over the Bhopal gas disaster three decades ago, but had the effect of stalling billions of dollars in projects under a U.S.-India nuclear alliance struck in 2006. The Indian side said it was not able to change the law, but still made a convincing case that costs - such as rehousing people away from a nuclear accident site - should be borne by a plant operator and not its suppliers, said Roderick. "Legal experts have looked at and said, OK, yeah that makes sense," he said. "They believe they have that issue solved."

On the nuclear liability insurance workaround, Roderick said he looked forward to hearing more details but welcomed the commitment from the Indian side to finalise the proposal in the coming weeks. Under the plan, the state-run insurance company GIC Re and four other Indian state companies would contribute 7.5 billion rupees ($122 million) to the pool and the government would contribute an equal sum. "I am very optimistic if we can get past that hurdle, and if the insurance does what has been discussed ... then maybe we can move forward," Roderick said. Westinghouse is keen to launch its AP1000 reactor in India, where it has collaborated with Larsen & Toubro, but has not progressed beyond a $10 million feasibility study and the award of a site in Modi's home state of Gujarat. It is already building eight AP1000 reactors in China and four in the United States. The first of the 1,100-megawatt reactors should enter service in China in early 2016. The AP1000 uses a 'passive' technology in which water-cools the reactor core under the force of gravity. That means, said Roderick, that it can remain safe in the event of an accident similar to the 2011 Fukushima disaster in Japan without external power or human intervention.

8 Zero Tolerance on Terrorism, Extremism and Crime

Introduction

Prime Minister Narendra Modi is keenly aware of high expectations after BJP's stunning poll showing. With the new government takes charge under his leadership, Modi has his tasks defined. Addressing issues on the 'home' front will be one of his top priorities. MHA chalked out an agenda for safeguarding sovereignity, territorial integrity and law and order mechanism. Here are the seven top priorities of the Home Ministry under Rajnath Singh.

Top Priorities

1. Eliminate Indian Mujahideen (IM) as a foremost goal of the counter-terrorism strategy. Recent arrests of IM leaders have weakened the organisation. Now, it is right time for concerted action to root it out.
2. While there's always a political angle to violent movements like Naxalism—the MHA believes it must limit Naxalites' area of influence with coordinated action, better intelligence, improved teeth-to-tail ratio in deployment of central forces and political initiatives.
3. The National Population Register (which suffered due to duplication with the Aadhaar card). A reliable database on citizens will help tackle issues such as illegal immigration, double citizenship and prosclytisation etc.
4. The new government would like a return of migrants to J&K. This isn't an easy job as only a sense of security can trigger the process of return migration. For that, the situation in J&K will have to ease. This will require both political and security initiatives.

5. Police needs to be made people-friendly. Currently, a lot of people, especially the poor, believe the community with dread. Police is also seen as a force that works at the behest of political masters unlawfully. Its reforms have been written out to make the force more autonomous. Nothing has been made concrete. The force has become corrupt, uncouth and disloyal.
6. Turning on intelligence network–the agencies use obsolete technology for security operations. Reforming the criminal justice system ought to be required as it has been pending for so long. Streamlining the visa needs to be addressed on priority to promote tourism with complete scurity to visitors during stay in the country.

Centre-State Relations

A new State, Andhra Pradesh, with massive development plans needing Central assistance, could well be some litmus test on Centre-State relations. The chief minister N. Chandrababu Naidu's interests in the two states honed political skills over some rapprochement between the two Telugu-speaking states. The formation over sharing of power, river water, fee reimbursement to students, educational institutions, allotment of government employees and special powers to the governors of two states ended up the impose Naidu ought to bargain with the TDP. He may have to strike a balance between his party's revived relations with the TDP. If he agrees to all the demands made by Naidu, he may invite criticism of giving into coalition compulsion. It may force an avalanche of similar demands from other states.

Bihar chief minister Nitish Kumar wondered now, the special category status is being denied to his state while Tamil Nadu chief minister J. Jayalalithaa shot off a letter to thePM Modi cautioning him against granting tax breaks to Andhra Pradesh and Telangana. Modi's attempt to please Naidu may ruffle the feathers of Telangana chief minister K. Chandrasekhara Rao.

His demands include the bridging of the revenue deficit through a grant of Rs 15,000 crore, special development packages for seven backward districts, liberal funding for the capital, Polavaram as a national project, relaxation from the fiscal responsibility and Budget Management Act and a string of 11 national institutions like the IIT and the IIM. Telangana, as such will emerge as the most powerful resource mobilising state. The demands could court controversy. Former premier Manmohan Singh orally promised the SCS for five years, when the Reorganisation Bill came up for discussion. It was aimed at assuaging the pent up feelings of Congress lawmakers from Seemandhra. Dr Singh said the Planning Commission would be asked to grant SCS's while the then Union Minister representing Andhra Pradesh, Jairam Ramesh, spoke of creating a special cell in the Planning Commission. The Planning Commission being wound up, the SCS for A.P. was uncertain.

Secure Indians

Zero Tolerance on Terrorism, Extremism and Crime: Comprehensive national security is not just about borders. It includes military security, economic security; cyber security; energy, food, water and health security; as well as social cohesion and harmony. To effectively address the issues of national security, the Central govrnment needs to harness human resources, science and technology, system of governance and dynamies of money.

National security cannot be compartmentalised based on one of issues. It needs a clear roadmap to ascertain the cause. Over the past decade, lack of a strong and visionary leadership, coupled with multiple power centres, has failed to address the issue of national security. It leads to utter chaos, confusion and disbelief among the work force to dent India's image in the international arena. India has a sensitive neighbourhood. She ails from internal security issues. There have been intrusions inside the LAC (Line of Actual Control), loss of squadrons of combat aircraft by the air force, witnessing of a series of accidents by the Navy, leading to a loss in its combating capability built over many decades. Frequent communal riots without cause, maoist attacks, enhanced Pakistan-backed ambush by terror groups, illegal immigration across the eastern border, and racists' attacks in the national capital are regular feature. These reflect indications of surrendering of India's interest. This calls for a review and overhauling of the current system. With the worsening finanacial situation, the issue of national security can acquire a horrifying dimension. The government recognises the importance of identifying a clear roadmap to address the issue head-on with radical systemic changes in logistics.

Internal Security

The new government will revive the anti-terror mechanism disowned by predecessor. It will strengthen the role of NIA and put a system in place for swift and fair trial of terror related cases. Reform the National Security Council to make it the hub of all sector-related assessments. It will be accountable for real-time intelligence dissemination. Digital and Cyber security will be thrust area of insulate intelligence agencies from political intervention and interference. Completely revamp the intelligence gathering system by modernising the intelligence department.

Provide the State governments with assistance to modernise their respective police forces and equip them with the state –of-the-art technology. This will be taken up on a mission mode approach. Strengthen and expand the Civil Defence and Home Guards mechanism to create a group of citizens for community defence, self-defence and disaster management. Encourage and strengthen NCC training at the school, college level. Chalk a national plan in consultation and participation of the state governments, to address the challenges posed by the Maoist's insurgency. Talks with the insurgent groups will be conditional and within the framework of the constitution. Take urgent steps for the safety of the migrant workers and communities from the Northeast and other states.

External Security

Its Boundary, Beauty and Bounty: The new government at the centre will address the issue of reforms with regards to defence logistics, support services, organisational reforms and other related matters. Address the increasing shortage of commissioned and non-commissioned staff in the defence forces on a priority basis, in a time-bound manner. Implement one rank, one pension mode. Build a War Memorial to recognise and honour the gallantry of the country's soldiers. Take measures to make Short Service Commission more attractive. Set up the National Maritime Authority replete the State-of-art technology, and will focus on coastal security. Modernise armed forces, and increase the R&D in defence, with a goal of developing indigenous defence technologies and fast track defence purchases. Deal with cross-border terrorism with a firm hand. Review and improve the border management. Punitive measures will be introduced to check illegal immigration.

Set up four dedicated defence universities to meet the shortage of manpower. Appoint a Veterans Commission to address the grievances of veterans, including reforming ECHS and re-employment of ex-servicemen. Ensure greater participation of Armed Forces in the decision-making process of the Ministry of Defence. Implement measures to improve the efficiency of Armed Forces Tribunals, and minimise appeals by the government. Ensure that servicemen can register and vote from their place of posting. Initiate the process of digitisation of defence land in cantonment and other places.

Sharp Increase in Allocation for Internal Security

The budget earmarked for internal security has registered a sharp increase in the current fiscal, which reflects the priorities of the Narendra Modi-led government's policy as stressed in the President's address to the joint session of Parliament. The most significant proposal has been the porous border management. Finance Minister Arun Jaitley proposed to allocate Rs 500 crore, a hike by five times. It goes to barbed wire fencing along the Indo-Bangladesh border. The allocation for road construction along the border has also been hiked by over 15 per cent.

President Pranab Mukherjee in his address promised "special emphasis" on improving intra-region connectivity and border infrastructure in the Northeast as well as in Jammu and Kashmir. The issue of infiltration and undocumented migration in the Northeast region would be tackled on priority basis on completion of pending fencing along the Northeast border. In keeping with this provision, the government has proposed to allocate Rs 300 crore for works along the sensitive Indo-Pakistan border, quantum increase of more than three times, and effected an almost 75 per cent increase in the allocation for the India-China border works.

A three-fold increase, albeit from a modest Rs five crore, has been proposed for the Indo-Myanmar border works, while for the first time an allocation has been made for the Indo-Bhutan border although it is Rs 10 crore. The allocation for the Indo-Nepal border works has fallen by one-third to Rs 500 crore. Coastal security has been invigorated beyond the quantum doubling to Rs 150 crore. The expenditure on border out-posts has also gone up by nearly Rs 100 crore to Rs 287.70 crore. This apart, a sum of Rs 300 crore has been set aside for border area development programmes.

The government through the President's speech had declared its intention to "maintain utmost vigil in the area of internal security. A policy of zero tolerance towards terrorism, extremism, riots and crime" has doubled the allocation to the Land Port Authority to put in place systems which address security imperatives along the international borders. Allocation for other arms for maintaining internal security, such as the Intelligence Bureau, the Border Security Force and the Central Reserve Police Force, has been increased apparently to nullify the impact of inflation. The allocation for the national intelligence grid has more than doubled to Rs 29.97 crore, the Special Protection Group—which provides security to the Prime Minister, former Prime Ministers and their immediate families—has been aportioned Rs 408.98 crore.

National Police Memorial: The nation is equally indebted to the officers and the jawans of the Police forces, including the central armed constabulary, who are constantly engaging with the enemy from within and in the process sacrificing their lives on duty. The government proposes to set aside a sum of Rs 50 crore for this purpose in the current financial year.

More Funds for Police Modernisation

Keen to equip the police and paramilitary forces with better infrastructure and weapons, home minister Rajnath Singh sought a two-fold enhancement in budgetary allocation for police modernisation. Singh, who was briefed on paramilitary and police forces by his ministry officials, asked the latter to take up with finance ministry a proposal to double the Rs 1,500-crore budget allocation for police modernisation during the current financial year. The minister stressed on provision of best-quality training and equipment to paramilitary and police personnel. After hearing out his officials on the challenges faced by the paramilitary forces, including lack of adequate housing and low allowances, Singh sought enhanced allowances for paramilitary personnel deployed in Left wing extremism-hit areas for reinforcement. Seeking stronger police and paramilitary forces in terms of manpower as well, the Home Minister reviewed the vacancy position and called for steps to be taken for time-bound raising and recruitment of personnel. According to a Home Ministry release, Singh "desired" to pursue the proposal of 35 additional Indian Reserve battalions to help the state governments in fighting the menace of Left-wing extremism and militancy/insurgency in Jammu and Kashmir and the northeast.

Appreciating a proposal to set up paramilitary forces' Institute of Medical Sciences, the MHA sought the project to be completed in a time-bound manner on priority, enhanced number of scholarships for the wards of paramilitary forces personnel, under the PMO-welfare schemes.

Befitting Reply to Maoists

If Forces are Attacked: Warning of a massive retaliation in the event of a major attack by Left-wing extremists, Rajnath Singh stressed on the need for the Centre and affected states to adopt a uniform approach to make any counter-action effective. At the same time, he asked the states to weave in entitlement of local tribals and perception management into the counter-Maoist strategy, which so far was focused on security action and development.

While entitlement will cover distribution of pattas to local tribals in Naxal-hit districts under the Scheduled Tribes and Traditional Forest Dwellers (Recognition of Forest Rights) Act, perception management refers to publicising through the media about the hurdles posed by Left-wing extremists to development projects in dominated areas. Addressing a meeting of chief secretaries and DGPs of 10 Naxal-hit states—Chhattisgarh, Jharkhand, Odisha, Bihar, Maharashtra, Telangana, Andhra Pradesh, West Bengal, Uttar Pradesh and Madhya Pradesh Singh asked them raise special forces modelled on Andhra Pradesh's Greyhounds, from within their respective police. While the badly-hit Chhattisgarh, Jharkhand, Bihar and Odisha will take the lead in raising these Special Forces, other states may follow later. The Centre will fully fund the initiative, an official said, adding that the home ministry has already sought doubling of the Rs 200 crore allocations towards its security-related reimbursement (SRE) scheme to Rs 400 crore in the coming budget.

The Intelligence Bureau reported the states like Odisha and Maharashtra as better performers on the counter-Naxal front, followed by Chhattisgarh. Jharkhand and Bihar was ranked the lowest. According to sources, Bihar, which had earlier been at variance with the Centre and other states on tough policing against Maoists, joined other states in unanimously backing a uniform approach against Left-wing extremism. The new initiatives also include making skill building the focus of the Integrated Action Plan scheme, under which Rs 30 crore is directly given to top district officials across 88 districts every year for development works. "The young tribals will be imparted skills to help them earn a regular livelihood, which will prevent them from being poached upon by CPI (Maoist)," said the official.

For Better Centre-State Co-ordination

The Union Home Ministry has proposed revival of the Inter-State Council and Zonal Council meetings as the primary forum for discussing and resolving Centre-state issues. The suggestion, included as a priority area in the MHA presentation within the ministry that UPA proposals like NCTC and the Communal Violence Bill ran into stiff opposition from chief ministers primarily due to lack of coordination with state governments. Incidentally, the MHA presentation — listed past achievements, gaps and misses, vision and low-hanging fruits — has skipped any reference to either the NCTC or the pending anti-riots bill. The Inter-State Council compising state chief ministers, few union Cabinet ministers is normally supposed to meet once a year. The standing committee may meet more often, to consider issues with federal implications. The zonal councils address issues related to states within a specific region. The Inter-State Council had been meeting regularly under the previous NDA regime, but the mechanism remained nearly defunct under UPA.

The report mentions the recent arrests of Indian Mujahideen leaders as a key feat, but outlines the elimination of IM as the foremost goal of counter-terrorism strategy. The intelligence agencies and operations, reforming the criminal justice system, limiting Naxalites' are of influence and minimising force casualties, improved combat capabilities of the central forces in terms of manpower and equipment and the peace process with various north-eastern insurgent outfits to logical conclusion are part of the home ministry's vision for coming years. The diminished focus on the National Population Register (NPR) exercise on account of "avoidable duplication" with the UIDAI's Aadhaar scheme, gaps in intelligence gathering and collation have been highlighted as a possible area for redressal greivances.

Nirbhaya Fund Schemes

The Home Minister instructed his ministry officials to expedite a key project sanctioned under the Nirbhaya Fund. It envisages speedy police assistance in response to distress calls by women. The project, for which Rs 321 crore would be disbursed from the Nirbhaya Fund, is proposed to be implemented over nine months in 114 identified cities. Approved by the Cabinet in February 2014, the project will enable a woman in distress to generate an alarm to the police control room by pressing a button on her mobile phone. Using GPS-based tracking, the police will be able to pinpoint the location of the victim and dispatch a PCR van to the spot to assist her.

During a briefing by officials on the Centre-state division, Home Minister raised concern regarding the delay in starting Nirbhaya Fund schemes and directed it be implemented in an expeditious manner. "He desired to review it personally soon with stakeholders," India had 916 million phone subscribers and 239 million internet users, just 3,477 crimes were reported in 2012 under IT Act and relevant sections of the IPC. The incident of crime reported, it was felt, was negligible because of lack of awareness and the lack of capacity in the agencies, the minister said. He directed that an appropriate body working in the software industry be outsourced to state police forces in developing their capability to tackle cyber crimes. A few states/UTs like Rajasthan, Arunachal Pradesh, Bihar, Goa, Haryana, Lakshadweep and Manipur were found irresponsible in handling cyber crimes. The home minister offered to personally take up the matter with the chief ministers and UT administrators.

Controvresy over Circular on Hindi

Facing flak from opposition and even allies over a circular asking officials to increasingly use Hindi on social media for official communication, the Centre pointed out that the controversial circular was actually issued under the UPA government and that the order was meant only for Hindi-speaking states and non-Hindi speaking states need not follow it. BJP, however, maintained it was in favour of promoting Hindi. Its spokesperson Shahnawaz Hussain said, "Hindi is our national language and we (BJP) respect all the languages in the country. Hence we do not want to impose Hindi over other languages, but there is no harm in promoting Hindi."

Minister of state for home Kiren Rijiju, under whom the department of languages functions, said, "The March 27 circular is only a repetition of the original circular issued on March 10. We took over only on May 26 and hence it is unfair to link the incumbent government with the move." "We have not given any instructions to the states that Hindi is compulsory. The order is meant only for Hindi-speaking states and non-Hindi speaking states need not follow it. We respect all languages of the eighth schedule. We want all languages to be promoted. I have briefed the PM and HM on the issue."

The March 10, 2014 circular and its reiteration were provoked by certain government departments and public sector undertakings blanking out Hindi from official accounts on social media. The circulars pointed out that the exclusion of Hindi was violation of official language policy of the government, and instructed that Hindi ought to be used along with English on social media. However, Hindi should get precedence. Significantly, the circulars were meant for Hindi-speaking states, but don't appear to be region-specific. The circulars have created a major controversy in the past couple of days. Regional parties, including those in opposition and allies, ahead a move on part of the government to impose Hindi on non-Hindi speaking states. On the other hand, parties such as SP and BSP have appreciated the government's move to promote Hindi.

CISF may Substitute NSG

In an apparent thinking within the MHA of home, that VIP security should be gradually moved away from NSG. The country's elite counter-terror force, CISF is strengthening its VIP protection unit to become the premier agency. Efforts are being made to increase manpower in the unit under the directives of the minstry. CISF-DG Arvind Ranjan said he has asked MHA to sanction more number of personnel in the unit. At the same time, rigorous training is being provided to personnel in the unit with help from NSG and armed forces trainers. CISF is regularly holding joint exercises with NSG to adopt best practices in VIP security from the force.

Panel Moots Private Agencies

The security review committee of the state government has recommended that the government consider engaging private security for individuals with high threat perception. This comes in the backdrop of an increasing number of police personnel being deputed on VIP security duty. It leads to immense manpower shortage, affecting routine policing.

"At present, a sizeable number of police personnel are engaged in security, causing strain on core duties of the police. Except officials and persons armed, it is desirable to engage the services of private agencies for individuals who are considered to have security threat," an order issued by the home department, based on the recommendations of the security review committee, said.

Apart from the duties, over 700 personnel of the 55,000 plus police force have been deployed at the residences of retired police officials and judges, who use their services even for household works. "There are officers who had retired as early as in the 1980s, who still avail the services of the police constables," a top police source said. "The security review committee has asked ADGP (intelligence) to prepare and submit a report. As far as the police department is concerned, private security would mean that some of the security provided by the police will be on payment basis," said state police Chief K.S. Balasubrahmanian. The security review committee took strong exception to the practice of getting police security sanctioned without the approval of the committee. "Present practice of providing security without the approval of the security review committee will be discontinued.

CBI Director's for Top Interpol Post

The home ministry cleared the name of CBI director Ranjit Sinha for selection to the post of Interpol secretary general. The ministry had been asked for its views by the ministry of external affairs (MEA). India has for the first time joined the race for the Interpol post currently held by Ronald K Noble. CBI had sought MEA's help to mobilise support for its director's candidature.

At 61, Sinha is the country's senior-most IPS officer. He has been shortlisted along with three candidates from Europe, one each from Africa and the US. The executive committee comprises representatives of the US, Canada, Chile, Italy, the Netherlands, Finland, Japan, Korea, Nigeria, Algeria, Rwanda and Qatar. It is headed by Mireille Ballestrazzi of France.

The appointment will go to the 190-member general assembly. In case there is no consensus among the executive members on who will be the next secretary general. According to the Interpol, which has representatives from 190 countries, the appointment of secretary general shall be proposed by the executive committee and approved by the general assembly for a period of five years. The candidate can be re-appointed for other terms, but must lay down office on reaching the age of 65 although, he may be allowed to complete his term of office on reaching this age. The third-term of current secretary-general Ronald K Noble, holding the post since 2000, ends next year. The secretary-general heads Interpol's general-secretariat in Lyon. He is effectively the chief full-time official of the organisation. The secretary-general shall engage and direct the staff. He will administer the budget, organise and direct the permanent departments, as per directives of the general assembly or the executive committee.

National Identity Cards

End of UIDAI in Sight: The Home Minister Rajnath Singh directs Registrar-General of India to initiate effective steps to take the Rs 5,000 cr National Population Register project to its logical conclusion. He instructed that necessary proposals, including the updating of database through linkages with the Birth and Death registration system and the Issuance of National Identity Cards to Citizens, be brought for approval at the earliest.

The Union Home Minister reviews the National Population Register (NPR) scheme, the biggest security and e-governance initiative in the world. Registrar General of Citizen Registration in India C. Chandramouli made a presentation on the project outlining its importance for national security.

The Home Minister Rajnath Singh asked for the long-pending proposal for issuance of National Identity Cards to be brought for "approval at earliest", a move that could effectively end the role of Unique Identification Authority of India (UIDAI) in executing the Direct Benefits Transfer (DBT) scheme.

The UPA government had failed to approve the Rs 5,500-crore project of issuing National Identity Cards under the National Population Register (NPR) project. It was expected to benefit nearly 82 crore adult Indian residents it being mentioned in the UPA's manifesto of 2009 and also approved by the Union Cabinet. Officials of the home ministry and census office said the identity cards were imperative to address security concerns regarding illegal immigrants and could also be very useful in delivering the government's welfare programmes to the poor, in a hint towards the DBT.

The Home Minister directed that effective steps be taken to take the project to its logical conclusion which is the creation of the national register of Indian citizens. He instructed that all necessary proposals including the updating of the database through linkages with the birth and death registration system and the issuance of national identity cards to citizens be brought for approval at the earliest," the ministry said in a statement.

Endorsement for NPR project signifies UIDAI's role in authentication for DBT could be finished. The finance and oil ministries have already said UIDAI is not necessary for DBT. The national identity cards are basically meant to be smart biometric-readable cards. It carries details of each resident that can be read with handheld readers for executing the DBT programme. Census officials have issued over 65 lakh national identity cards for coastal areas residents. The scheme was disapproved by the UPA for extension to the rest of the country.

UIDAI has already enrolled biometrics of over 63 crore people. NPR scheme has captured the biometrics of nearly 25 crore people as of date. With the NPR scheme now getting precedence due to its better security processes than the UIDAI scheme, it is expected that UIDAI's role in enrolling people's biometrics and authentication for DBT will end. It will at most be a back-office for NPR. UIDAI's role may be limited to de-duplication (ensuring no two people with the same biometrics enter the system) and creating UID numbers. NPR could undertake additional vetting of credentials before admitting them to NPR. Incidentally, the NPR scheme was launched by the NDA government in 2003. It has not been completed even a decade later as UPA gave preference to UIDAI.

ID Cards for all Genuine Indians: The Home Minister said that the government would prepare a National Population Register (NPR) incorporating all genuine Indian citizens and issue them national identity cards in a time-bound manner in Lok Sabha."We have to identify who is an Indian citizen and who is not. We have to take steps to identify genuine Indian citizens," Singh told Lok Sabha in reply to a question regarding infiltration along various borders and counter-measures taken by the government.

The NPR authorities, meanwhile, seem reconciled to accepting enrollment data largely from UIDAI. A house-to-house verification may be undertaken to confirm the address of Aadhaar number holders. The NPR TIN will be matched with Aadhaar number and thereafter, biometric data will be taken from the UIDAI tech centre. Photos and other fields will ultimately be culled out for citizenship verification.

J&K High on Modi Agenda

The government wants international bodies should accept the Kashmir as Jammu and Kashmir with Leh-Ladakh region. This is holistic in approach, in the light of Pak occupied Kashmir with separate premier controlling Pakis nuclear arsenal. The territory falls south of Pir Panjal ahead of Jammu.

Jammu and Kashmir is clearly high on the Modi government's agenda. The latest move follows minister of state in the PMO Jitendra Singh's suggestion that Article 370, giving special status to the state, could be repealed, sparking vehement protests by J& K Chief Minister Omar Abdullah. A BJP leader said the proposed changing of the name from PoK to PoJK was not only a strategic move but also a psychological one.

This will send a positive message to residents of Jammu. They have always found themselves cut off from the discourse over the future of the state. They have a stake in the state as that the interlocutors appointed by the previous UPA government had ignored Jammu in their report. They recreate the offices of the 'Wazir-e-Azam' and the 'Sadar-e-Riyasat', in their report.

Coupled with a comprehensive policy separating Article 370 for rehabilitating internally displaced persons, the move is aimed at boosting the morale of the homeless Kashmiri Pandits and the people of Jammu. It will correct other perceived lop-sided treatment. There is huge discrimination against Ladakh and Jammu regions in terms of development, education, public employment, expenditure and number of elected representatives.

Development, Security to Top Agenda

The Prime Minister payed a short one-day visit, but touching both Jammu and the Kashmir Valley, with stops in Jammu, Katra, Srinagar and Uri. He is inaugurated a railway line, a power project, addressed a gathering in Katra and the troops in Srinagar. However, there will be no political outreach as in the past. There are no official meetings with the Chief Minister, his cabinet, or any public gatherings in the Valley. Officials called the visit "strictly business."

Chief Minister Omar Abdullah said it was just as well "politics was kept out of this visit." As a result, no mention is expected of the controversies over Article 370, or the Hurriyat's objection to the proposal to rehabilitate Kashmiri Pandits in segregated colonies, which they referred to as "divisive." However, Abdullah denied there was any proposal for segregation. The Prime Minister's agenda isn't the only departure from the past. He will be stopping in Srinagar for a couple of hours only, to address a 'Sainik Sammelan'.

Ahead of visit, extra security personnel have been deployed in the State and the border at Uri, where he will go, has a heightened level of alert. Sources confirmed to The Hindu that the border alert was at the DGMO level, given the incidents of firing in the past few weeks.

There was firing overnight in the Mendhar sector along the border, but officials denied any injuries. Inspector-General of Police in Jammu Rajesh Kumar claimed militants trying to infiltrate. He said the claims of Army personnel being injured were incorrect. Despite the security, traffic moved freely in Srinagar. Officials said they had given orders that common man and pilgrims in the State should not be inconvenienced. "Amarnath yatris will proceed even without restrictions on markets in the city." However, a *bandh* call by the Hurriyat leadership and other separatist groups sought extra policing for Muslims offering prayers.

Dignified Return of Kashmiri Pandits

The government has flagged the return of Kashmiri Pandits to the Valley with "dignity, security and assured livelihood," an issue on which it will lay special emphasis during its tenure. Perhaps finding a mention in President Pranab Mukherjee's joint address to both Houses of parliament on Jult 7, 2014, it was welcomed by Kashmiri Pandit organisations which have been fighting for the lakhs of people from the community who fled the Valley in 1990 due to ethnic cleansing during militancy.

"Special efforts will be made to ensure that Kashmiri Pandits return to the land of their ancestors with full dignity, security and assured livelihood," the President said while outlining the agenda of Modi government for the next five years. The BJP had mentioned return and rehabilitation of Kashmiri migrants to the Valley in its manifesto.

According to official data, 24,202 families migrated after militancy raised its ugly head in the Valley in 1990. A total number of 38,119 families are registered with the Jammu and Kashmir Revenue and Relief Ministry. The Kashmiri Pandit organisation, however, put the number of displaced people anywhere between six to seven lakh now. It was for the first time that the plight of displaced community had been flagged by the Central Government as its priority, said the general secretary of All India Kashmiri Samaj (AIKS) Romesh Raina.

"Our request to the government would be that while framing the blueprint for the return and rehabilitation of community, it should take the aspirations and needs of the displaced into the consideration. It must ensure the political rehabilitation of people through Constitutional mechanism so that it is not refouled again."

PM Condemns 'Proxy War' By Pakistan

On his second trip in two months to Jammu and Kashmir, Prime Minister Narendra Modi visited Kargil, where a massive crowd turned up to hear him speak. He is the first Indian PM in 15 years to visit Kargil. He said Pakistan "has lost the strength to fight a conventional war, but continues to engage in the proxy war of terrorism." His remarks come amid heightened tensions in Kashmir, with India and its rival Pakistan trading accusations of ceasefire violations. (Two BSF Jawans Injured as Pakistan Targets Border Outposts in Jammu)

The state of Jammu and Kashmir is meant to vote for its next government later this year, and the PM's party is hoping to win the election, riding on the momentum he generated with his high-profile campaign and stunning victory in the national election in May. The region of Ladakh, where PM Modi landed recently, has four assembly seats and the party hopes that it will win at least two of those in the state elections. The BJP had won the Ladakh Lok Sabha seat in the national elections this year, for the first time ever.

"There was a time when Prime Ministers never visited this state. I have come here two times already, your love has drawn me here," the Prime Minister said in Leh, dressed in traditional Ladakhi gear. He inaugurated a power plant; he said his three-pronged plan for the development of the region was about three Ps - "Prakash (electricity), Paryavaran (environment) and Paryatan (tourism)." In Kargil, Modi inaugurated a power project and promised industrial development of the area. He also announced Rs 8,000 crore in additional funds to complete pending projects to thunderous applause and cheers of "Modi, Modi." New Delhi and Islamabad agreed to a ceasefire in 2003. But despite the truce, firing along the disputed de facto border called the Line of Control has escalated in the last few months.

Policies on Minorities

Equal Opportunity: The new government at the Centre believes that in India's 'Unity in Diversity' lies India's biggest strength. We cherish the depth and vibrancy that the diversity in Indian society adds to the nation. It is thus committed to the preservation of the rich culture and heritage of India's minority communities; along socio-economic empowerment. It is unfortunate that even after several decades of independence, a large section of the minority, and especially Muslim community continues to be stymied in poverty. Modern India must be a nation of equal opportunity. It is committed to ensure that all communities are equal partners in India's progress. We believe India cannot progress if any segment of Indians is left behind.

Need to Prompt Steps: The government should ensure that the young and the girl child in particular get education and jobs without discrimination. Strengthen and modernise minority educational systems and institutions; dovetailing them with modern requirements. National Madrasa modernisation programme would be initiated. Empower with vibrancy in Livelihood and Entrepreneurial opportunities. Augment their traditional artisanship and entrepreneurial skill, which are a backbone of our cottage and small-scale industry, strengthening these sectors through better market linkages, branding and access to credit. Empower Waqf Boards in consultation with religious leaders; taking steps to remove encroachments from and unauthorised occupation of Waqf properties. Curate their rich heritage and culture, maintenance and restoration of heritage sites, digitisation of archives, and preservation and promotion of Urdu.

Ensure a peaceful and secure environment, where there is no place for either the perpetrators or exploiters of fear. Facilitate the setting up of a permanent Inter-faith Consultative mechanism to promote harmony and trust, under the auspices of religious leaders.

End of Minority Tokenism: Modi offers modernisation, and not sops, to the Muslims: The Muslim community in India, the second largest in the world, has seen its parliamentary representation come down to it's lowest ever since independence, at 22 MPs with not a single one from the politically important state of Uttar Pradesh. His government has not ended the ministry of minority affairs, often accused by the ruling BJP of being symptomatic of the tokenism that ruled the secularism of the previous regime, the prime minister in his utterances till date has made it very clear that a "new deal" for the most significant minority in India was what he is looking at.

In an interview to an Urdu daily Modi had categorically stated that "there is a need to strengthen constitutional and statutory bodies and not to abolish them. The need is to make them [Muslim community] productive and strong. They could do solid work instead of continuing with the existing system which takes symbolic measures." While institutions would persist the idea is to make them redundant to the discourse.

The Good Muslim: The BJP and the Jana Sangh haven't had the smooth relation with the Muslim community. For long the demographic character of most Indian states and Lok Sabha constituencies was considered so peculiarly designed. It precluded the possibility of a Hindu majoritarian party from coming to power. The earlier NDA government, which came to power on the strength of coalition numbers, did try to implement the agenda of the Sangh Parivar. It had to keep their core issues of abrogation of Article 370, uniform civil code and the construction of a Ram temple in abeyance.

On the other hand, the Vajpayee government did give good-sized Haj subsidies, hosted iftaar parties and gave India its first Muslim president in APJ Abdul Kalam to complete a full term. There are nuances of course to this engagement, which will now appear full blown in a BJP-majority government.

In the literature left behind by Sangh Parivar ideologues, there is a very clear demarcation between Indian Muslims, who are patriotic and those who cleave to pan-Islamic identity. The formation of Hindu Mahasabha from the embers of 1919 Khilafat movement is perhaps the reason for this distrust of a larger Islamic identity. Whatever it was, the BJP has always maintained, as does Narendra Modi that, Indian Muslims, like India's Hindu citizens woul be treated no better or worse than any citizen. Kalam, a veena-playing scientist who gave India its nuclear bomb and made it a nuclear power house, was a perfect example of this kind of Indian Muslim. Minority affairs minister Najma Heptullah's assertion that the fast dwindling community of Parsis were far deserving of a "minority community" title was another. The reference to madrassa modernisation in President Pranab Mukherjee's address to parliament was a reference to a more direct enunciation of this idea.

Modernisation and Islam: According to Tufail Ahmad, director of the South Asia Studies project at the Middle East Media Research Institute in Washington, the advent of the Narendra Modi government should be looked at as an opportunity by the Muslim community. "While previous governments kept Muslims embroiled in emotional issues of quota and secularism, the Modi government came to power by overcoming this type of divisive politics," he says.

"Muslims in India whose population is estimated to be up to 180 million in 2014 cannot be called a minority. They are India's second largest community. They can't persevere under this complex anymore or allow themselves to be manipulated," he adds.

Ahmad goes on to say that the opportunity that the Modi government represents is particularly important in the way that the community can free itself from the orthodoxy of the clerics. "Islamic clerics who are the most organised section among Muslims are responsible for teaching obscurantist ideas. The Modi government must confront opposition from orthodox institutions like the Darul Uloom Deoband and begin the modernisation of governmentrun madrassas," he added. It isn't clear whether or not this very optimistic prognosis is apt or that the Modi government is quite ready for that battle yet, but the electoral mandate has suggested a tectonic shift.

The subtext of Modi's mandate is not as important for the BJP or even the Muslim community. Each will learn to do business with the other. It is a time for parties which for years enjoyed support among the Muslim population to recalibrate secularism. The engagement through clerics or pandering to the most orthodox elements of the community is clearly not going to be enough in future political battles. The template of the past 62 years is broken.

Article 370

Three Key Points: Minister of state in the Prime Minister's Office, Jitendra Singh, triggered a controversy after he pitched for a debate on BJP's stand. It demanded the repeal of Article 370 guaranteeing special status for J&K. Singh, BJP MP from Udhampur in J&K, argued the debate could help convince the "unconvinced" that the article had actually worked more to J&K's disadvantage. The minister's pitch was in line with the stand that Premier took while campaigning in J&K.

Soon after, Jammu and Kashmir chief minister Omar Abdullah strongly objected to the minister's statement. Abdullah tweeted, "So the new MOS PMO says process/discussions to revoke Art 370 have started. Wow, that was a quick beginning. Not sure who is talking."

He went on to add, "Mark my words and save this tweet - long after Modi government is a distant memory either J&K won't be part of India or Art 370 will still exist."

PDP chief Mehbooba Mufti commented on the issue. She said irresponsible utterances on Article 370 should be stopped. They could lead to serious repercussions in J&K. Singh, however, retracted his earlier statement adding that the 'controversy as totally baseless'. Here, it is important to understand what actually constitutes Article 370. He said how it affects crucial aspects such as governance in Jammu & Kashmir.

(1) *What is Article 370?:* Article 370 of the Indian Constitution is a 'temporary provision'. It grants special autonomous status to Jammu & Kashmir. Under Part XXI of the Constitution of India, it empowers the state with "Temporary, Transitional and Special provisions". The state of Jammu & Kashmir has been accorded special status under Article 370. All the provisions

of the Constitution applicable to other states does not find applicable to J&K. For example, till 1965, J&K had a Sadr-e-Riyasat for governor and prime minister in place of chief minister.

(2) *History of Article 370:* The provision was drafted in 1947 by Sheikh Abdullah. He had by then been appointed prime minister of Jammu & Kashmir by Maharaja Hari Singh and Jawahar Lal Nehru. Sheikh Abdullah had argued that Article 370 should not be placed under temporary provisions of the Constitution. He wanted 'iron clad autonomy' for the state, which Centre didn't comply with.

(3) *Provisions of Article 370:* According to this article, except for defence, foreign affairs finance and communications, Parliament needs the state government's concurrence for applying other laws. The state's residents live under a separate set of laws. It includes those related to citizenship, ownership of property, and fundamental rights, as compared to other Indians. As a result of this provision, Indian citizens from other states cannot purchase land or property in Jammu and Kashmir. Under Article 370, the Centre has no power to declare financial emergency under Article 360 in the state. It can declare emergency in the state only in case of war or external aggression. The Union government can therefore not declare emergency on grounds of internal disturbance or imminent danger unless it is made at the request or with the concurrence of the state government.

India Wants Peace with China, But Not at Cost of Honour

Home Minister Rajnath Singh said that India wants peace with China but that cannot come at the cost of honour.

"*Humlog shanti chahte hai samman ki saath. Asamman ke saath shanti nahi ho sakti* (We want peace with honour. Peace cannot come at the cost of honour)," he said, referring to the recent border row with China.

"Pride is the ultimate accomplishment of a human being, of mine and yours," he said, addressing the 53rd raising day function of the Indo-Tibetan Border Police, which guards the China-India border.

Mr Singh said Prime Minister Narendra Modi has made it clear that New Delhi wants to maintain peaceful relations with all its neighbouring countries and wanted to resolve border issues peacefully.

"Our Prime Minister has told the Chinese President and requested him that if there is a dispute we should talk," he said. The Home Minister said China often raises question over the border and even had raised objections when India wanted to improve border infrastructure within its own territory. Referring to Pakistan, the Home Minister said the neighbouring country should stop firing on border posts and civilian areas. He said Pakistan had fired upon the civilian areas along the border in Jammu and Kashmir just a day before Deepawali. "When we get to know about ceasefire violations done by Pakistan or there is some dispute in the context of India-China border, we feel hurt and we feel angered," he said.

"Pakistan fired on civilians even on the eve of Deepawali festival and they did not even spare our festival. Pakistan should be wary of this. I want to tell Pakistan to stop this continuous violation of ceasefire," he said.

The Home Minister said Pakistan should know that the armed forces guarding India's border possess the "capability to give a befitting reply" during any misadventure.

Mr Singh disapproved of Pakistan's recent move of approaching the United Nations to internationalise the Kashmir issue and seeking the world body's intervention, saying all issues can be resolved through bilateral talks. He said the government will ensure India's territorial integrity and will not compromise with the country's pride.

"India wants to keep friendly relations with our neighbours whether it is China or Pakistan. We believe in the philosophy of *'Vasudaiva Kutumbakam'* which means the world is one family and India has told the world about it," he said.

9 Self-Sufficiency in Defence Technology

Introduction

The Ministry of Defence has set the agenda of seven top priorities under the control of its minister Arun Jaitley. Now, the former chief minister of Goa Manohar Parikar took the charge of Defence Ministry.

Priorities of this ministry:

1. Boost indigenous defence R&D and production. Revamp DRDO and its 50 laboratories, five defence PSUs, four shipyards and 39 ordnance factories. Encourage the private sector to enter arms manufacturing in a major way. India, embarrassingly, still imports 65 per cent of its military hardware and software.
2. Streamline cumbersome arms procurement procedures to fast-track acquisitions and reduce corruption. Also re-examine the policies for offsets, transfer of technology and ban on agents. Projects for new submarines, howitzers, fighters, helicopters, night-fighting capabilities, air defence weapons and the like have been stuck for years due to politico-bureaucratic apathy.
3. Reform the country's higher defence management, with measures ranging from creating a chief of defence staff-like post to truly integrating Service HQs with the defence ministry and "cross-staffing" (posting military officers to MoD at the director/joint secretary-levels).
4. Ensure faster build-up of both the new mountain strike corps as well as military infrastructure like the long-identified 73 strategic roads and 14 railway lines, helipads and advance landing grounds, along the Line of Actual Control to counter China. Boost force-levels and infrastructure at Andaman and Nicobar Command, apart from creating three new

tri-Service commands for space, cyber and special operations.

5. Complete India's nuclear weapons triad by faster induction of nuclear submarine INS Arihant and its follow-on sister ships with long-range missiles. Land and air legs are already in place with Agni ballistic missiles and fighter-bombers.
6. Hike budgeted defence expenditure to at least 2.5 per cent of GDP, instead of letting it wallow around just 1.7 to 1.9 per cent for adequate military modernisation and requisite deterrence against both China and Pakistan. Cut the flab in the armed forces; improve the teeth-to-tail ratio.

***Efective Steps to Get the Desired Results**:* With its skilled human resources and technical talent, India can emerge as a global platform for defence hardware manufacture and software production. The Defence Research and Development Organisation (DRDO) ought to be stengthened. Outsource some jobs on investment, including FDI in selected defence industries.

Technology transfer in defence manufacturing ought to be encouraged to the maximum. The government will find solutions to the problems hampering the growth of the defence sector. It will encourage domestic industry to have a larger share in design and production of military hardware and platforms for domestic use and exports, in a competitive environment.

Need to Self-sufficient' in Defence Tech: The Indian premier dedicated INS Vikramaditya, the largest and most powerful aircraft carrier inducted into the Indian Navy, to the nation. He termed it an "important day for our nation". A tweet from the PM's quoting Modi as saying: "We need to give immense importance to latest technology. This will help the nation." He also emphasised that India must be "self-sufficient" and manufacture the defence equipment.

"Why should we import defence equipment? We must be self-sufficient. Why can't we send our defence equipment to other nations," Modi tweeted. On board INS Vikramaditya, Modi hopped into the cockpit of a MiG-29 K fighter jet. The 44,500-tonne INS Vikramaditya, procured from Russia, has been one of the newest acquisitions of the Indian Navy. It is the most powerful symbol of its military reach. It was commissioned by then defence minister A. K. Antony at Russia's Sevmash shipyard, November, 2013.

Rs 2,29,000 Cr for Defence

The Union Government said that there can be no compromise with the defence of the country. The Finance and Defence Minister Arun Jaitley proposes to allocate an amount of Rs 2.29 lakh crore for the current financial year for Defence.

One Rank-One Pension: Modi government reaffirms the commitment to the brave soldiers. A policy of "One Rank One Pension" has been adopted to address the pension disparities. We propose to set aside sum of Rs 1,000 crore to meet this year's requirement.

Modernisation: Modernisation of the armed forces is critical to enable them play role effective in India's strategic interests. The government, therefore, proposes to increase the capital outlay for Defence by Rs 5,000 crore over the amount provided for in the interim Budget. This includes the sum of Rs 1,000 crore for accelerating the development of the Railway system in border areas.

Urgent measures will streamline the procurement process to make it speedy and more efficient.

War Memorial: The country is deeply indebted to the officers and jawans of armed forces for having made huge sacrifices to defend its honour. In doing so, a very large number of them gave up their lives. It is a privilege for the nation to erect a befitting memorial in their memory. The Union Govrnment is happy to announce that a War Memorial will be constructed in the Princes Park. It will be supplemented by a War Museum and allocated a sum of Rs 100 crore.

Defence Production: In the year 2011 a separate fund was announced to provide necessary resources to public and private sector companies, including SMEs, as well as academic and scientific institutions to support research and development of Defence systems that enhance cutting-edge technology capability in the country. However, beyond the announcement, no action was taken. Therefore, the government proposes to set aside an initial sum of Rs 100 crore to set up a Technology Development Fund to support this objective.

The Defence Minister announced that foreign companies would now be allowed 49 per cent stake in companies involved in manufacturing military equipment — a clear signal of the Modi government's aspired to infuse foreign capital to modernise the domestic defence industry.

The fresh policy direction from the government is accompanied with the Rs 5,000 crore hikes in defence allocation over the previous interim budget. However, the pattern of the modest increase reveals the government's intent to step up modernisation of the Army, along with a renewed focus on indigenously developed weaponry.

Jaitley also announced that Rs 1,000 crore were being earmarked for strategic railway projects in border areas, a decision that resonates with bouts of tension that are yet to abate along India's borders with Pakistan and China. A similar amount was allocated to fine-tune the "one rank one pension" scheme for the armed forces.

Out of the total allocation of Rs 2, 29,000 crore, the Army has got Rs 1, 18,867.23 crore, which is 51.91 per cent of the total defence kitty. But significantly, a sum of Rs 25,197.91 crore — much more than the allocation in the interim budget — are to be spent on the capital head, signalling a fresh thrust on inducting new equipment in the Army, which is in the process of raising a mountain strike corps, equipped with a "Quick Reaction Force,"armed with credible aviation assets. Significantly, the budget allocates Rs 2,127.99 crore for aircraft and aero-engines, marking a nearly 80 per cent increase over the previous budget under this head.

The capital intensive Air Force gets Rs 53, 817.02 crore — a 23.50 per cent of the total. The Navy, which is going ahead with its new submarine and aircraft carrier projects, has been allocated 15.36 per cent of the total budget, with Rs 21,190.93 crore being channeled under the capital head. Indigenously developed weaponry owes to the Defence Research and Development Organisation (DRDO) which got Rs 15,282.92 crore, amounting to 6.67 per cent of the total outlay. The combined with Rs 2, 481.99 crore allocated to ordnance factories, the combined figure jumps to 7.75 per cent of the total.

Inc Pushes for FDI in Defence

The Confederation of Indian Industries (CII) has endured the move of his government. "FDI is directly linked with core national priorities such as raising manufacturing growth to 25 per cent of GDP, significant job creation and bringing high end technology into the country. The associated benefits are the spin offs for the civilian market, a CII statement said.

CII is very keen to see very high-tech and highly complex System Integration work being done in India. Indian industry is ready to take this challenge and opportunities, it believes. Opening up various sectors have helped Indian industry grow and become globally competitive. India has witnessed a resurgence of its manufacturing sector over the last two decades. It faces robust domestic demand and increasing private sector participation. Amongst the emerging economies, India's manufacturing sector has established its name for better quality, design and innovation. The country has already made its mark in the automobile and automotive components sectors. Anumber of auto giants around the world source from India, the CII statement said.

Further, the domestic heavy and light engineering sectors have come a long way with high end innovations and capabilities. The Indian automotive sector has also started leveraging Indian industry's strengths in IT, high-tech engineering and research and design capabilities, it added.

Currently, the defence sector contributes between 2.5 to 3.0 per cent of the global GDP. However, India's share is disappointingly very low. India can leverage her purchasing power, IT infrastructure and manufacturing potential to be one of the key global manufacturing hub for defence systems and equipment, the statement argued.

A meagre $4.8 million FDI under the 26 per cent cap came to India ever since the defence sector was opened up for the private enterprises' participation. Raising the FDI in defence sector will create more opportunities within India. CII would fully endorse the Government's initiatives of linking FDI with the exports from India. No business can be sustained for long-term just on the basis of domestic orders. There is an immediate need to revisit export policy.

INS Vikarmaditya, longest warship off Goa coast in Arabian Sea, showcase India's naval prowess.

Here are six things you may want to know about INS Vikramaditya:

1. The 44,500-tonne INS Vikramaditya, procured from Russia, is one of the newest acquisitions of the Indian Navy and the most powerful symbol of its military reach. INS Vikramaditya joined the Indian Navy on November 16, 2013 and was commissioned by former defence minister A. K. Antony last November at Russia's Sevmash shipyard.
2. Vikramaditya, a floating airfield, has an overall length of about 284 metres and a maximum beam of about 60 metres, stretching as much as three football fields put together.
3. Standing about 20-storey tall from the keel to the highest point, the ship has a total of 22 decks and carries 1,600 personnel.
4. Its logistic requirements include nearly 100,000 eggs, 20,000 litres of milk and 16 tonnes of rice per month. The vessel is capable of sustaining at sea for about 45 days.
5. It is a modified Kiev-class aircraft carrier purchased from Russia. The

ship has been renamed in honour of Vikramaditya, a legendary emperor of first, century BC.

6. Originally built as Baku and commissioned in 1987, the carrier served with the Soviet (until the dissolution of the Soviet Union) and Russian Navies before being decommissioned in 1996, it being too expensive to operate.

INS Vikramaditya

Adds to India's Maritime Might: From the sky above off Goa, it looks like a tiny metallic fleck floating on the deep blue sea. The sheer size staggers as the Dhruv advanced light helicopter descends. Tall as a 26-storey building and spread over an area spanning three football fields, the 45,400-tonne aircraft carrier is now India's largest-ever warship. The menacing MiG-29K supersonic fighters, which can be swiftly scrambled from the warship's angled ski-jump to take the battle to any adversary. It will come into clear view once the rotors stop whirling after the chopper lands on the deck. The blunt message: India has taken a big step forward in the geopolitical power projection game, with the carrier's motto itself proclaiming: "Strike Far, Strike Sure".

India is steadily building a three-dimensional blue-water Navy. It will take care of her huge strategic interests in the region between the Persian Gulf and the Malacca Strait. As many as 44 warships on order in domestic shipyards at a cost of over Rs 2 lakh crore in a major boost to indigenisation are on international waters.

India still imports over 65 per cent of its military hardware and software. INS Vikramaditya, or the refitted Russian Admiral Gorshkov carrier, alone cost \$2.33 billion. With the 45 MiG-29Ks ordered from Russia costing another \$2 billion, it is the costliest single weapon platform the country has ever bought.

Indigenous Anti-submarine Warfare Ship Ready: India's first indigenously-built antisubmarine warfare corvette INS Kamorta built by the Garden Reach Shipbuilders and Engineers Ltd (GRSE), Kolkata.

The corvette is readying to sail out from GRSE's fitting-out jetty in Kolkata to join the Navy's eastern fleet at Vishakhapatnam in July, officials said. The sophisticated front line warship with stealth features will also be the first warship armed with the new trainable chaff launcher—Kavach.

With an approximate displacement of 3400 tonnes, it can achieve a maximum speed of 25 knots. It is powered by four indigenously designed 3888KW diesel engines at 1050 rpm and can cover nearly 3,500 nautical miles at 18 knots. The overall length of the ship is 109 meters and is nearly 13 metres wide at its maximum bulge. With about 90 per cent of the ship being indigenous, it is also capable of deploying a helicopter, adding considerable punch to the ship's anti-submarine capability.

INS Kolkata

When the Indian premier said no country will challenge India after the commissioning of INS Kolkata, he was only partially correct. The fact is that INS Kolkata, the largest destroyer built in the country, and the first of a class of three such ships, is not really complete. Several key weapon systems and sensors are missing, either being developed or yet to be procured.

While the INS Kolkata and its sister ships, the Kochi and the Chennai (still being constructed) may one day be genuinely world-class fighting platforms, they are not that today. In fact, the Kolkata is not fit for battle in its present state. Consider this: the surface-to-air missile suite of the Kolkata, the Barak 8 missile, is still being co-developed with Israel and is several months, if not a year from being tested, proven, fitted on the Kolkata, and again tested at sea as part of user-trials. Without the Barak, which the Navy calls the LR SAM (Long Range Surface-to-Air missile), the Kolkata has no credible defence against modern incoming anti-ship missiles, the sort of missiles which equip Chinese destroyers and frigates which are no longer strangers to our waters. The Barak is meant to intercept incoming missiles and aircraft at ranges out to at least 70 kilometers.

India's First Aircraft Carrier Slips into History

Built for the British Royal Navy as HMS Hercules in 1943, it was acquired by India in 1957 and saw action during the India-Pakistan war in 1971, playing a key role. When the electric saws were pressed upon the ship, it essentially put an end to a movement by activists to save her. Vikrant was auctioned to a ship-breaker for Rs 63 crore this year. Mumbai's IB Commercials Pvt. Ltd. won the bid on January 29 and bought the vessel on April 9. Since then, the company faced hurdles as a PIL filed in the Bombay high court towards the end of 2013 proceeded to the Supreme Court.

Save Vikrant Committee chief Kiran Paigankar, who had filed the PIL to save the ship, termed it "a sad day in the country's glorious maritime history". He said it was unfortunate that the process to expedite the end of Vikrant was initiated by the Indian Navy which once considered the vessel its 'pride'.

"I was ready to accede to the activists' demand for converting the vessel into a permanent museum. But my request to get my money back, the money that I had pumped in to buy the ship, was not granted. I had taken loans on high interest," said Abdul Karim Jaka, the owner of IB Commercials. "I had been meeting the activists even before the PIL was filed. I met them even after the PIL was dismissed on August 14. I met Admiral (retd) I.C. Rao and Aam Aadmi Party's Meera Sanyal, but nothing concrete happened. The navy handed over the vessel to us in October. On November 12, we got the go ahead from the Supreme Court to start cutting the steel." His son Zuber said, "At 2 pm , approximately 200 workers at our yard embarked upon the work to cut out 15,700 tons of steel from the vessel." "An important chapter of Indian history revolving around Vikrant has finally ended. Despite all our efforts, we could not prevent her from breaking up," Paigankar said.

Impetus to Space Programme

ISRO has so far launched 35 satellites from 19 countries around the globe-Algeria, Argentina, Austria, Belgium, Canada, Denmark, France, Germany, Indonesia, Israel, Italy, Japan, Korea, Luxembourg, Singapore, Switzerland, The Netherlands, Turkey and United Kingdom. A PMO release said that Modi on June 30 visited the First Launch Pad at Sriharikota. The Prime Minister also visited the GSLV-Mk III Vehicle Assembly Building.

Our Mars Mission Cheaper Than the Movie Gravity

Prime Minister Narendra Modi said that this is India's fourth dedicated commercial launch, but the Polar Satellite Launch Vehicle's 27th launch. The launch vehicle costs Rs 100 crore. Even today's satellites are from developed nations. Truly, this is a global endorsement of our space capability.

This is a domain where we are the international cutting edge. We have achieved excellent and cut beyond mediocrity. This fills every Indian's heart with pride and I can see the joy and satisfaction on your faces. Feel privileged to watch this in person. We are proud that our programme is indigenous. Generations of scientists have worked to make India a self-reliant space power. Our space journey has come a long way from the humble beginnings.

PM Modi congratulates the scientists. This *Sadhna* you have done in the lab has the power to change the lives of millions of people. Such technology is fundamentally connected with the common man. As a change agent, it can empower and connect, to transform his life. Space technology has also evolved into an invaluable asset in disaster management. Satellite communication channels, often end up being the only mode of communication. GIS technology has transformed policy planning, implementation. Space imaging enables modern management, conservation of water resources. India's Space programme, is driven by a vision of service to humanity. Not by a desire of power. He urged Department of Space, to proactively engage with all stakeholders, to maximise use of space science in Governance and Development.

Ten Developments in This Story

The Polar Satellite Launch Vehicle or PSLV lifted off at 9:52 am, on June 30, 2014. It carried five satellites from four countries—France, Germany, Canada and Singapore. The rocket's main luggage is the 714 kg French earth observation satellite SPOT-7. PM Modi was seen applauding as the 44.4 metre, 230 ton rocket tore into the sky with flames burning at its tail, at Satish Dhawan Space Centre, Shriharikota.

"The success of the mission fills every Indian's heart with pride and I can see the joy and satisfaction on your faces," Modi said, addressing large group of space scientists. Often switching to Hindi for an aside, PM Modi remarked, "He has heard that the Hollywood movie Gravity cost more than our Mars mission - this is a great achievement." India's Mars rocket or Mangalyaan is expected to reach the red planet on September 24, 2014. The premier has proposed to scientists that they develop a SAARC (South Asian Association for Regional Cooperation) satellite. This will help all our neighbours."

Scientists said Modi's speech reinforces that he is a space buff. As Gujarat Chief Minister, he had visited the state's remote sensing centre a record 50 times, and evinced interior in harnessing space technology for agriculture and other fields. Earlier India used to buy images from countries like the US and France. The recent launch reinforces India's success in launching satellites for the West. The countries are also buying remote sensing images from India. India has agreed to take on the first test flight of its monster rocket geo-synchronous Launch Vehicle (GSLV) MK III, which will carry as an experiment, India's first crew module.

Independent Strategic Nuke Programme

The government believes the strategic gains during the Atal Bihari Vajpayee regime on the nuclear programme. The emphasis was, and remains on, beginning of a new thrust on framing policies serving India's national interest in the 21st century. It will follow a two-pronged independent nuclear programme, unencumbered by foreign pressure and influence, for civilian and military purposes, especially as nuclear power is a major contributor to India's energy sector.

Study in detail India's nuclear doctrine, and revise and update it, to make it relevant to challenges of current times. Maintain a credible minimum deterrent that is in tune with changing geostatic realities. Invest in India's indigenous Thorium Technology Programme.

India, Australia Ink Nuclear Pact

India signed a civil nuclear cooperation agreement with Australia. Australia is rich in uranium ores. But Indian refusal to sign NPT has detracted the process. From the time of Independence, India has scrupulously followed international laws regardless of the ups and downs of the political situation in New Delhi. There is a very high level of trust between these two nations, hence they sign this agreement.

Australia will now be a "long-term reliable supplier of uranium to India," said an External Affairs Ministry press release, and will provide for the "supply of uranium, production of radio isotopes, nuclear safety and other areas of cooperation." Abbott said he would "welcome" Indian companies in the energy and infrastructure sectors. In particular, he mentioned the Gujarat-based Adani Group and the Andhra-based GVK Group for their large investments in the recent past, defending them against allegations by environmental organisations like Greenpeace.

"Environmental groups are very hard to please. We have very high environmental standards in Australia. I am confident that there can be no reasonable objection to the current proposal. Adani Group is speaking of $16 billion for this mine, and India's investments of under $20 billion will almost double the total amount," said Abbott.

Australian PM said he was keen to negotiate a Free Trade Agreement (FTA) at the earliest. Abbott said India must take the recent video by al-Qaeda chief Ayman al-Zawahiri, announcing a branch of the terror group in the Indian sub-continent, seriously.

N-deal Highlights Growing Energy Ties

The periodic Uranium supply however would tide over the India's transfer of coal for thermal power plants. Analysts believe the deeper engagement in energy and food security could pave the way for a broader strategic relation between India and Australia. A joint statement on defence cooperation signed last year had emphasised joint forays specifically in the Asia-Pacific region. The claims on South China Sea resources between China and other littoral States has been remarkable. The Indo-US nuclear deal has paved the way for countries like Australia, a major ally of the US, to emerge as India's nuclear supplier.

Queensland Project

Observers say both India and Australia aspire to be investors in a broad spectrum of areas including energy. In July, the Australian government approved a $16.5 billion investment by the Adani group in a coal and rail project in the Queensland of province. Indian industry wants urgent coal imports from Australia as thermal power plants in the country are facing acute shortage of coal. Commerce and Industry Minister Nirmala Sitharaman believed India invested more than $ 1 billion in Australia in the last decade, but the Australian contribution in India stood at a more modest $ 600 million.

Modernisation and Reforms

The combat potential of the Indian military establishment over the years calls for immediate intervention. The repeated cancellation of tenders and shying away from policy decisions by the previous government has affected certain areas of our defence preparedness. The pending contract for fighter aircraft or replacement of the aging helicopter fleet—a new dynamism is the need. Even the basic weapon of a soldier, the INSAS rifle currently in use, needs to be replaced. Our defence acquisition procedures and offset clauses need a relook. The steps required have already been in focus with the new ministry. However, to hasten up equipment induction, the whole process of lengthy, cumbersome and rigid equipment trials needs a relook.

Building domestic capability by involving the private sector is an immediate necessity. Our Ordinance Factory Board and factories need to be restructured. Aspects of accountability and productivity require institutionalisation in the entire defence production establishment. Similarly, the DRDO requires a new competitive dynamism. It ought to be pitted against government-aided research and development by the private sector. The long-term solution lies in enhancing domestic capabilities. Finally, the practice of blacklisting foreign companies for misdemeanours cannot finish with their blacklist. Such cases need to be pursued to the very end. The recipients of favours are they bureaucrats, soldiers or politicians, need to be identified and prosecuted.

The revenue expenditure consumes the larger portion of the defence budget. The funds for modernisation are inadequate. The Chinese spend liberally on force modernisation. At $39.2 billion, we spend a third of China's $119.5 billion (Pentagon 2013 figures). Defence allocations have to be pegged around 2.5 per cent of the GDP. The mountain strike corps needs to complete its raising faster. Resources for this formation need to be entirely incremental rather than a product of milking existing formations, as is often the case.

Infrastructure in the border areas has been ignored. The economic conditions degrade our societal cohesion. Economic growth will harness greater nationalistic fervour among their populace. Our missile reach, cyber capabilities, space platforms and Special Forces will be the key drivers in projecting our national interests. The early creation of inter-service commands addressing these areas is an imminent requirement.

Policy or Missile Exports

Many countries have expressed interest in acquiring missiles India has developed. A policy framework ought to be made to tap this export potential. The export of missiles is a new area that India is exploring. India's Akash and Prahaar missiles can be easily exported. BrahMos (developed in a joint venture with Russians) for which a lot of countries have shown interest. DRDO works on a programme to extend the range of surface-air missile beyond 200 kms. These have to be ship-launched, sea-launched, air-launched, submarine-launched cruise missiles. India needs supersonic air-launched cruise missiles. India needs hypersonic transportation systems. She works on anti-radiation missiles.

India to Fortify Defence along China Border

54 New ITBP Posts being Planned in Arunachal: Over 50 new border posts are being planned for the Indo-Tibetan Border Police (ITBP) force in the northeastern state of Arunachal Pradesh. A proposal for creating 54 modern posts for the ITBP is under consideration of the Union home ministry. Arunachal Pradesh shares a total of 1,126 km of its international border with China. It is second in length after Jammu and Kashmir. The latter has a 1,597 km long frontier with India's eastern neighbour. The posts will be, under the proposal, equipped with the basic gadgets that the troops require to position themselves at these icy heights.

The new border posts will be solar-powered. These have space to not only accommodate the regular ITBP guards but also to house small squad of reinforcements, in case of emergencies. The posts will have satellite phone connectivity. At present, India has 142 border posts along this 3,488 km long frontier with other Border States. These are Himachal Pradesh (200 km), Uttarakhand (345 km) and Sikkim (220 km). Arunachal Pradesh, at present, has close to 30 ITBP border posts but a need has been felt to bolster the presence of the para-military men in order to meet border challenges and future commitments.

The new posts will help reduce the distance between two ITBP locations thereby enabling the patrols to co-ordinate better and keep a tight vigil. A fresh contingent of troops will also be posted to man these locations, which are expected to be sanctioned soon by the home ministry.

ITBP has been created in the state capital of Itanagar. It has 10,000 men under its command. In 2004, the force was tasked with the job of guarding of the border. A few posts of the force are located at glacial heights of 9,000-18,700 feet in this sector. They have to face heavy snow and blizzard conditions for a number of months in a year. The ITBP, a 50,000 personnel strong force, was raised in 1962 in the wake of the Chinese aggression.

Expedite Defence Procurement

India's new Defence Minister Arun Jaitley met the top Navy brass at the Sena Bhavan. Jaitley said that the government will focus on increasing defence spend to meet growing requirements of the forces. He said funds are not a problem for defence acquisition and upgradation. Defence modernisation is a pressing issue facing the Indian armed forces, and the government stressed that it would look into the needs of the forces on an urgent basis. Later, when asked whether India was mulling to send forces to Iraq where a number of Indians are believed to have been kidnapped by ISIS militants amid a growing internal crisis, the minister only said that he "won't speculate on it".

He promised to speed up the procurement of military equipment after a series of corruption scandals under the last government brought deals to a near standstill. Following a meeting with top naval commanders, Arun Jaitley said the "slow pace of acquisition" was a matter of concern for his government. He said that there are several decisions in the pipeline and there is a good case for these processes to be expedited.

He said that significant funds must be provided to "those in the defence of the country", hinting that a lack of resources would not stand in the way of acquisitions when he unveils his first budget next week. India is one of the world's biggest arms importers but the collapse of a series of defence deals during the last decade of rule by the centre-left Congress party years has left the military short of key equipment.

Global Powers India-bound for Mega Defence Deals

Western governments are rushing to visit India, drawn by the prospect of multi-billion-dollar deals as the government prepares to open the defence industry to foreign investment. Senior politicians from France, the United States and Britain arrive over the next few weeks as PM Modi prepares to accelerate the modernisation of the country's mostly Soviet-era weaponry.

The premier intends to build up India's military capabilities and gradually turn the world's largest arms importer into a heavyweight manufacturer. On the table is a proposal circulated within the new government to raise caps on foreign investment—with one option to allow complete foreign ownership of some defence projects. Harsh Pant, professor of international relations at King's College London said that all the countries are trying to make their case, especially as there is the sense that the Indian market will undergo a shift. "They get a sense from their dealings that something dramatic is going to happen and they want first-mover advantage," said Pant, who specialises in Indian defence. French foreign minister Laurent Fabius is expected to visit in July, whose top priority is to close a stalled deal to sell India 126 Rafale fighter jets, built by Dassault Aviation, for an estimated $15 billion.

UK Still Hopeful on Fighter Jet

Britain has drawn some cheer from the slow progress of the negotiations for the Rafale deal. The Eurofighter Typhoon was shortlisted along with the Dassault fighter before India announced the French jet was the winner. Britain's foreign secretary William Hague and finance minister George Osborne met Indian premier over this deal. Cost escalations and disagreements about building the Rafale in partnership with India's state-run Hindustan Aeronautics Limited have complicated talks with France, and London has never entirely given up hope that it will return to the race. Russia, for years India's top weapons supplier, pipped all three countries to the post. It sent her deputy Prime Minister Dmitry Rogozin to visit Delhi. Washington last year replaced Moscow as India's top defence supplier, according to IHS Jane's.

The Western nations will have noted that India's foreign minister expressed displeasure with Russia's recent offer to sell Mi-35 attack helicopters to Pakistan. "I don't think it's a competition," US assistant secretary of state Nisha Biswal said after an early post-election visit to New Delhi. "India will have strong and positive relationships with different countries and that is to be encouraged," said Biswal. "We want to see India taking on a stronger and a leadership role in the region and around the world so we welcome that."

$6 Billion Spree

India imported $ 6 billion worth weapons in 2013. She makes few of her own weapons, beyond ballistic missiles and assembly lines for foreign jets. Now, she will allow manufacturers allow build more components without licences, making it easier for Indian firms to partner with foreigners. At present foreign companies can only invest 26 per cent in Indian defence projects without technology transfer. Many investors backed out on this ground.

Make a Policy for Defence: "For higher-tech intellectual property, we sould be in a position to share technology that we have significant investments," said Phil Shaw, chief executive of Lockheed Martin India Pvt Ltd. "An uplift from 26 per cent to 49 per cent maintains the status quo. It may not be sufficient incentive to make an investment."

'Happy Diwali, You Make It Possible for Indians to Celebrate'

Modi spent some time rallying soldiers at Siachen, the world's highest battlefield, where he made a surprise visit as India celebrated the Diwali festival.

"From the icy heights of the Siachen Glacier and with the brave Jawans and Officers of the Armed Forces, I wish all of you a Happy Diwali," he tweeted to the nation. PM Modi took a special Indian Air Force aircraft to Siachen and was flown by helicopter to the base camp at about 12,000 feet. Accompanied by Army Chief Dalbir Singh Suhaag, he made an aerial survey of the glacier before interacting with officers and jawans posted at one of the most inhospitable places on earth."I have come to spend my first Diwali as prime minister with you. 125 crore Indians can celebrate Diwali today and go about their lives in comfort because the jawans guard the borders, prepared to make every sacrifice for the nation," PM Modi told the troops.

India is Proud of all Three Wings of Armed Forces

Boosting the morale of the armed forces, Prime Minister Narendra Modi told the soldiers stationed at the Siachen base camp that the nation is proud of its three wings: army, air force and navy. Addressing the officers and jawans at the Siachen base camp, which is situated at a height of over 12,000 feet, Prime Minister Modi praised their valour and courage, saying that 125 crore Indians could celebrate Diwali and go about their lives in comfort because the jawans stood guard at the borders and were prepared to make every sacrifice for the nation.

He stated that the nation is proud of all three wings of the armed forces. Asserting that it is a rare opportunity to be called upon to defend the country in such difficult conditions, the Prime Minister said that he had come to the camp as a representative of the family members of the soldiers serving Mother India at the borders. He further said he is privileged that his first Diwali as the Prime Minister will be spent partly with the jawans of Siachen, and partly with those affected by the floods in Srinagar. Earlier in the day, Prime Minister Modi extended the nation Diwali greetings from Siachen, the world highest battleground, as he interacted with the troops stationed here.

"From the icy heights of the Siachen Glacier and with the brave Jawans and Officers of the Armed Forces, I wish all of you a Happy Diwali," he tweeted.

India, Vietnam Call for 'Freedom' of Navigation, Ink Seven Pacts

Strategically important oil and gas cooperation and extension of a $ 100 million credit by India for defence purchases are among the seven pacts inked between India and Vietnam as they called for "freedom" of navigation in the South China Sea, a remark that could irk China which has been claiming territorial sovereignty over the high seas. The agreements were signed during the second day of the four-day state visit of President Pranab Mukherjee who held talks with his Vietnamese counterpart Truong Tan Sang here. Both the countries decided to strengthen and deepen bilateral ties on the basis of the strategic partnership with focus on political, defence and security cooperation. They decided to step up collaboration in the economic sector, science and technology, culture and people-to-people links. In a subtle message to China, India and Vietnam, who established strategic ties in 2007, asserted that the freedom of navigation in the disputed waters of the resource-rich South China Sea should not be "impeded" and called all the parties "concerned" to exercise restraint in this context.

"The leaders reiterated their desire and determination to work together to maintain peace, stability, growth and prosperity in Asia. They agreed that freedom of navigation in the East Sea/South China Sea should not be impeded and called the parties concerned to exercise restraint, avoid threat or use of force and resolve disputes through peaceful means in accordance with universally recognised principles of international law, including the UNCLOS-1982," said a joint communique issued after the meeting.

China has been exerting its influence in these waters which is not taken well by Vietnam and other bordering countries like the Philippines. Beijing has also objected to India's exploration projects in the Vietnamese oil blocks. Among the seven pacts inked, a Letter of Intent (LoI) was signed between the ONGC Videsh Limited (OVL) and Vietnam Oil and Gas Group (PetroVietnam). The LoI is aimed at further consolidating cooperation between India and Vietnam in energy sector and pave the way for future collaboration between the two countries. The two sides urged for "collective commitment of the concerned parties to abide by and implement the 2002 Declaration on the Conduct of Parties in the South China Sea and to work towards the adoption of a Code of Conduct in the South China Sea on the basis of consensus.

"They called for cooperation in ensuring security of sea-lanes, maritime security, combating piracy and conducting search and rescue operations," it said. India and Vietnam also signed an MoU on extension of $ 100 million Line of Credit to Hanoi for defence procurement. The pact, inked between the Exim Bank of India and the Vietnamese Finance Ministry, provides a concessional line of credit for procurement of defence equipment from India. Details of equipment to be procured by Vietnam are under finalisation.

Another significant pact signed during Mukherjee's visit here is an MoU on operating and jointly promoting direct air services between Vietnam Airlines and domestic Indian air carrier Jet Airways. For the first time, India and Vietnam will have direct daily flights from November 5 with Jet Airways connecting Delhi and Mumbai to the historic Ho Chi Minh City.

"We will be beginning the operations from November 5. There will be a flight daily and it would connect Delhi and Mumbai to Ho Chi Minh City," Jet Airways chairman Naresh Goyal told PTI after signing a deal in this regard.

Apart from the LoI, the MoU on extending a credit line to Vietnam for defence purchases and the agreement on operating and jointly promoting direct air services, other pacts inked were — agreement on cooperation and mutual assistance in customs matters, MoU on animal health, MoU on setting up of Pangasius breeding and farming in India and MoU on cooperation in youth affairs and skill development.

India, Australia Establish Framework for Security Cooperation

India and Australia established a framework for bilateral security cooperation as they stepped up their defence collaboration for advancing regional peace and combating terrorism among other challenges.

Prime Minister Narendra Modi and his Australian counterpart Tony Abbott held talks and agreed to establish a framework for security cooperation to reflect the deepening and expanding security and defence engagement between the two countries. They established the framework to intensify cooperation and consultation between Australia and India in areas of mutual interest.

"I greatly welcome the New Framework for Security Cooperation. Security and defence are important and growing areas of the new India-Australia partnership — for advancing regional peace and stability, and combating terrorism and trans-national crimes," Modi said in the statement to the media at a joint press conference with Abbott. Modi, while addressing the Parliament later, also called for collaboration in the field of maritime security.

"We should collaborate more on maintaining maritime security. We should work together on the seas and collaborate in international forums. And, we should work for a universal respect for international law and global norms," he said reiterating his call for collaboration on maritime security made at the East Asia and ASEAN summits in Myanmar last week. Modi and Abbott decided that the framework will be implemented in accordance with an action plan.

A Blueprint for Defence Industry

The government needs to set up a national committee to resolve turf battles between government agencies and reconcile with competing interests of small and medium enterprises and industry majors. The government believes liberalised access is unlikely to contribute much towards the goals of self-sufficiency and self-reliance.

There are reports that the Department of Industrial Policy and Promotion (DIPP) is pushing to allow 49 per cent FDI without transfer of technology, 74 per cent with transfer of technology, and even 100 per cent in cases involving the transfer of state-of-the-art technology and equipment, while the Defence Ministry would like it to be restricted to 49 per cent. This debate is sterile because merely liberalising FDI will not help. The need of the hour is an appreciation of the characteristics of the defence industry. The co-ordination among the multiple stakeholders is a sine qua non and for it is, they who drive and have distorted often the decision-making process.

Distant Goals, Continuing Imports: The twin objectives of self-sufficiency and self-reliance have been articulated. Sometimes, interchangeably and at times separately, since the early 1950s. In 1947, India inherited the Ordnance Factories (OF) Organisation. Today consists of 41 OFs, nine Defence Public Sector Undertakings (DPSUs) and 50 or so defence Rural and Development laboratories under the Defence Research and Development Organisation (DRDO). The model followed was "production of technologies conceptualised by the DRDO; projects nominated by MoD [Ministry of Defence] after consulting the Services; and assembly and production of platforms under licence from foreign OEMs (Original Equipment Manufacturers)." Currently, with about two lakh employees, the OFs and DPSUs have a modest turnover of

$7.6 billion. The goals of self-reliance and self-sufficiency remain distant, with almost 70 per cent of defence equipment still being imported.

A task force set up in 1998 concluded that the public sector alone could not deliver. Licensed production had fostered neither indigenisation nor innovation. Frequent blame games between the Services, the DRDO and the DPSUs lead to delays in acquisition. A self-reliance review committee set up in 1992, under Dr Abdul Kalam's chairmanship developed a self-reliance index (SRI). It is defined as the percentage share of indigenous content in total procurement expenditure. It earmarked 70 per cent self-reliance by 2005, extended now to 2020.

The first instance of opening up of the defence sector came in 2001. The domestic private sector was allowed to produce defence items with FDI up to 26 per cent. It was subject to industrial licensing and security clearances. This was followed by the announcement of a Defence Procurement Procedure in 2002, a Defence Offsets Policy in 2006, a Long Term Integrated Perspective Plan (LTIPP) in 2009, a Defence Production Policy in 2011, and eight committees/ task forces set up to look into various aspects of national defence, including defence production and self-reliance, since 2000. Clearly, the issue remained a priority for various governments. However, the outcome has been meagre. Certainly, some responsibility rests with former Defence Minister A.K. Antony. He seldom endorsed decision-making, underlying structural reasons.

Growing Defence Expenditure: Since 2001, the total FDI received in the defence sector is below $5 million. Meanwhile, India's defence expenditure grew every year; today, India has the eighth largest defence budget in the world. She accounts for three per cent of global defence expenditures. She has also emerged as the largest defence importer, with nearly 10 per cent of global defence imports. Growing obsolescence and a 10 per cent annual rise in the capital budget for equipment procurement, lead the conservative estimate indicates that India spend nearly $100 billion over the next eight years to modernise and equip her armed forces.

During the 12th Five Year Plan, the defence capital account budget is expected to go up from $15.9 billion to $25.6 billion. By the end of the 14th Five Year Plan, the cumulative capital expenditures over 2012–27 are projected to exceed $235 billion. Assuming that 80 per cent is meant for platform acquisitions, of which 60-70 per cent is earmarked for committed liabilities; this still leaves 30-40 per cent for new schemes. To meet the target of 70 per cent self-reliance by 2020, she requires an indigenous defence industry worth $80-$100 billion. It could provide direct employment to some 1.25 lakh skilled workers and indirect support to that of another five lakh.

The Defence Offsets Policy, announced in 2005, requires some foreign company to invest 30 per cent of the indicative cost in the request for proposals whose indicative cost is Rs 300 crore or more. Initially, the offsets were for the defence sector. In 2009, the policy was diluted to permit offsets to civil aviation and internal and coastal security sectors. Its objectives are to improve the domestic defence R&D base; develop an internationally competitive defence industry, and an industrial base covering dual use technologies (i.e., having both civilian and defence applications). Offsets are implemented by raising domestic procurement, generating exports, bringing FDI into related services and building local supply chains, transferring technology/equipment to Indian entities. The DRDO has identified some 15 critical technologies that seek to acquire through offsets; incidentally, exports of these technologies are controlled and require special approvals by the foreign vendor's government. The 16 offset contracts, worth $4.3 billion, till 2012, were signed which is expected to cross $25 billion by 2020.

Manipulation: The Defence Procurement Policy encourages domestic private sector, including government R&D funding for product development, on special incentive. Some of the enterprises (includ TCS, Tata Power, Godrej, HCL, L&T, Mahindra, and Kirloskar) are to be classified as *Raksha Udyog Ratnas* to enable them on a par with DPSUs. In addition, there are about 6,000 Small and Medium Enterprises (SME). Many of whom feel they are nimbler and better suited to innovate in niche areas. In fact, they oppose limiting FDI to 49 per cent. The position is being supported by domestic majors and the MoD.

Many of these measures are unexceptionable. These have failed to create a military-capable, dual-use manufacturing technology-base. Different lists of defence products in the MoD, the DIPP and the Directorate General of Foreign Trade (DGFT) have messed up. Most of the technologies are controlled under the Wassenaar Arrangement (a grouping of major arms and dual-use technology exporting countries). India is not a member, which makes her more difficult to acquire such technologies. (China and Israel are also not members, but they have aligned their export controls with Wassenaar lists, and are significant arms exporters.) With multiple players pulling in different directions, it is easy for vested interests to tweak specifications of items to be procured favouring certain vendor and derail debates to the limits of FDI in defence.

Way Forward: The government needs to take charge by setting up a national defence industry committee. It should resolve turf battles between various government agencies, reconcile with competing interests of SMEs and industry majors, set targets (including for SRI, intellectual property rights (IPR) generation, integration of SMEs, technology acquisition through offsets), monitor implementation, and co-ordinate policy approaches by: (a) creating uniform lists of defence products and related technologies; (b) enabling the harmonisation of Indian lists with the Munitions List and Dual Use Technology List of the Wassenaar Arrangement, with the eventual aim of securing India's membership. An enabling framework already exists with India's Special Chemicals, Organisms, Materials, Equipment and Technologies (SCOMET) export control lists; (c) amending the Industries (Development and Regulation) Act to bring defence and dual-use technology-related Industrial Licensing into sync with the above; (d) amending the terms of the production licence for defence items to ensure that control of the entity cannot be transferred without Government of India (GoI) approval, that all exportable items and services will be available domestically, and that exploitation of IP generated will not be denied in India. These conditions would render the debate of FDI levels irrelevant; (e) promoting the clustering of SMEs with industry majors through targeted policies; (f) changing the role of the Department of Defence Production, whose structure limits it to a mere administrative unit for OFs and DPSUs; (g) integrating the working of the LTIPP with defence R&D, production, procurement and offsets policies; (h) providing a degree of continuity and predictability in the policy framework for the next 10 years instead of the annual revisions that have afflicted the sector in recent years.

Mars Mission a Historic Achievement

The success of the mission to Mars will "inspire our scientists to make even greater strides", said President Pranab Mukherjee. He congratulated the Indian Space Research Organisation (Isro) for the Mars Orbiter Mission (MOM) entering the orbit of the red planet in its first attempt.

"The success has made India the first Asian country and ISRO the fourth space agency to send a satellite to the red planet. ISRO is also the first to enter the Martian Orbit in its maiden attempt. "The nation is proud of this historic achievement which has demonstrated, yet again, India's space capabilities. I am sure that this breakthrough, which marks a significant landmark in our space programme, will inspire our scientists to make even greater strides," the president said.

In a message to Indian Space Research Organisation (Isro) chairperson K Radhakrishnan, the president said: "I extend my hearty congratulations and best wishes to you and your team on the successful Orbit Insertion Manoeuver of the Mars Orbiter Mission 'Mangalyaan' after a journey of nearly nine months.

10 24×7 Power Supply for Every Citizen

Introduction

Gujarat Model for Power: The power sector reforms follow Gujarat model state. It would energise the country to optimum capacity. The state was successful in the renewable energy sector. For this country, this accounts for eight per cent of total electricity produced in the country. The network is expected operate through separate feeders for farm and domestic sectors. It will precisely consumers metered consumption to reduce transmission loss and euphemism for theft. Power is a concurrent subject where the state governments have to agree for any initiative to go through. Most of the state governments are averse to reforming power tariff — the key component of sustainable reforms and growth — any new initiative faces the threat of getting bogged down in centre-state politics. It would be difficult to revive the idling gas-fired power plants. It aggregates to some 24,500 MW worth Rs 124,000 crore of investments. No one buys costly electricity produced from imported fuel. It needs for general tariff reforms.

Consumer is the King

The responsibility of lighting up the country today rests on Piyush Goyal's shoulders. Just a month into his new job, the minister for power, coal and renewable energy has set an electric pace to energize the sector. He says consumer is the king.

The department of coal appreciates power purchaser as king. His effort is to give a far more responsive government both to the needs and problems of the consumer. Within the system the power generator is the buyer of the coal ministry or the coal supplier. The distributor is the customer of the power producer. He is trying to get that responsiveness into the system that the coal people give the best service which means quality price, timely delivery to the generator. Generator ensures timely supplies. It includes transmission and distribution, being adequate so that the generator can satisfy his customer, which is the distribution company.

The Power Minister feels that the distribution company focusses to reduce power theft, to make sure 100 per cent metering is done, he gets conscious of the fact that he has to ensure 24×7 powers to each consumer and ultimately the consumer has to be educated that he has to pay for that power. The power theft that happens in the neighbourhood could be stopped by a joint effort. Mere policing alone cannot stop every problem. It's the people's movement that resolves more problems than policing. The public have to be conscious that the things are to be done transparently so that corruption costs seldom burden the final consumer. We cannot have a system that everything can be passed on to the final consumer in the garb of cost recovery without being sensitive to their own problems and affordability. It's need of the hour to take hard decisions, given the tight economic situation.

The department expects coal plant runs to full capacity. It claims adequate coal be mined in the country to avoid expensive imported coal. It needs efficiencies in terms of linkages. Coal is imported into Gujarat for a power plant in Korba, run by NTPC. And Coal India has given linkage to a power plant of the Gujarat government from Korba. The train may be crossing the line at the same time, going up and down. Rejigging this could save Rs 400-500 crore and the benefit will pass on to the consumer. It will also unclog the over burdened railway network.

Help me push out more coal from the mines to its final destination. He has initiated a study at the pan-India level, my gut feeling says that thousands of crore can be saved, millions of tonnes can be additionally transported through the system, and pollution can come down. Coal India board is expected to take quick decisions and action so that every piece of coal output from Coal India mine will be to international standards. Similarly, coal washing is an environmental friendly step. It has been quite neglected for years. The deadlines set by the environment ministry for a certain level of washing to be done. It will be strictly implemented and won't seek any further extension beyond June 2016. It will entail some investment and washeries.

True that Coal India has no dearth of money as it's not only about having cash in the books, it's also about improving our own efficiency. The Power Minister would prefer to put that cash to good use to open new mines, expand the mining capacity. Again something that needs people's participation. He says from his side he can assure that whoever may get displaced whenever a new mine is opened, or a forest might have some mining activity, since mining activities are in forests, he can give categorical assurance that they will be well looked after, the R&R (relief and rehabilitation) will be better than the law provides. He can assure that he will use every effort to recreate afforestation to expand the forest cover.

The government expects people's support to open new mines, for larger quantities. Certain hard decisions in certain states hold back mining production. A particular state says that you cannot move trucks from one time to the other. Any delay for 14 hours in a day could prune the mine production to 40 per cent. So, it ultimately affects power generation and then the consumer. He will need a lot of support from all the stakeholders the states, consumers, environmentalists, everybody. He wants to reach out to everyone for support.

States like Rajasthan, Andhra Pradesh have come into the 24×7 category. Rajasthan utilities have increased the loss by over Rs 50,000 crore in past five years. It is completely agnostic to run projects efficiently, don't bother about proper distribution spoilt meters were never replaced. State revenue was only Rs 10,000 crore against expenditure Rs 23,000 crore last years. Power a concurrent subject and in the federal polity. States are very sensitive to any 'diktats'. The government wants to reach out to all states uniformly. It wants 24×7 powers with every citizen. The general election is over. Now, it's time to deliver and performance for 125 crore citizens.

The states ought to be helped, tide over problems. They are eligible for incentives for good performance. Gujarat has turned from Rs 2,500 crore loss-making utility into Rs 500 crore profit-making utility over the last 10-12 years. It provides 24×7 powers with least increase in tariffs compared to any other state.

It has separated their agricultural feeder, metered every home. Governors have filed FIR's. The suppliers have prosecuted (people) power thefts. The collection efficiencies were among the finest. People get the power when they want at their homes, industries; commercial output gets 24×7 power. Agriculture gets adequate power when his demand. It's a case study worth doing.

Piyush Goyal, the power minister recently visited Gujarat. He ascertained what needs to be learnt. It was a very educative experience. He felt very good being at Sabarmati ashram. He saw the river front and the government's performance. He realised what needs to be done. He means if Mahatama Gandhi can get his freedom by spinning a charkha or Modi could clean up the water front which otherwise could have been such a sensitive subject in a communally-charged city like Ahmedabad, in a densely populated area, he thinks lot of things can be done, it needs little bit of leadership, sincerity of purpose and transparency and honesty. If he tells you transparently what his issues are like when the Delhi crisis came, he shared with the people what exactly the situation is and after that he found everybody co-operating very well.

Goyal says that despite stranded generation capacity, there won't be blackouts, if this capacity is brought on stream. These are actually an opportunity for the government because come to think of it, he knows he has the ability to produce. He needs to sort out fuel supply, transmission and finally distribution. A lot of public sector and private sector project have either come up or are on the verge of getting commissioned. They need some last-mile funding for which the government had a meeting with the bankers. A small group of people, bankers and experts, work to see what will be the best way. How to expand the output from coal mines. How to ensure more coal goes to the power producers. The previous government had all sorts of permutations and combinations that these people will get so much coal, those will get so much; these will not be eligible, these will have to import. It's quite a complicated web we've created.

Goyal's logic is simple, if a plant has come up it is now a national asset. Any waste arising that keeps it idle, is a national liability, national cost, whether the banks have funded or whosoever. Someday that cost for being stranded will be burdened on the consumers. We are in an ecosystem wherein interest is loaded into the cost of project, as interest during construction. Some day it goes in the tariff calculation directly or indirectly. So, it is his duty to quickly get them operational. Get coal production to ramp up, start supplying to every operational asset, and get them into production. May be, he will not be able to do 90 pe cent. He will start and keep cramping it up for production increases. So, he doesn't think the stranded projects are impossible to retrieve. He thinks he only has to increase their fuel supply. He is already in dialogue with states to quickly expand the transmission. He can evacuate power all over the country and of course mobilise the last mile distribution.

About the gas-based projects, the minister says it's a much smaller dimension than the coal-based projects. It's a matter of approach everyone is crying about. He looks that it as an opportunity. May be, in the very long run there could be a problem. Gas is keeping on getting expensive. Some day will become pretty much unviable. The country has a peak load problem. Gas plants can be switched on and off within 15 minutes. They can act like a spinning reserve. He can actually use them gas provide peak loads, whenever in demand. Once, the distribution and transmission sets up, a quick decision taken by the courts on some of the issues pending, and we could expand gas supplies for production of power.

Goyal thinks for some financial relief for the stranded projects as an interim measure. His effort is to see whether done within the framework of existing RBI guideline. He says it may require some small dispensation. It won't completely erode the RBI's efforts to bring in more strength to banking sector. He had a meeting with the bankers. 'It was a very good experience', as they were very co-operative.

He thinks they realise that we are making very sincere efforts. He has appealed to them that they also put one foot forward also and he has assured that he will put two feet forward for every one foot that they extend. He thinks if all the stakeholders, government, banks, generating and distribution companies, as well public at large, work together, the problem won't be daunting. Outsourcing coal sector should bring efficiency and better management. The Cabinet ought to take a decision. It also depends on the Supreme Court, on the issue of mines under litigation. None of them could be auctioned or opening up for mining. The minister believes if more competition comes in, coal reserves can be mined faster on new technologies. Coal India will stand to benefit from competition, in terms of improved efficiencies, and bench-marking. He had a meeting with Coal India officials — people have always kind of held that company to be having a lot of problems – his effort is that to take shortest possible time to bring in high standards of probity and improve their efficiency, so even a Coal India employee can hold his head high when he goes and tell somebody that he works for Coal India.

The disinvestment plan and restructuring of Coal India will be the job for the Union finance minister and other departments. He has no problem in that either way. There's no disinvestment as such. We are just asking more of the public to hold or own the fruits of Coal India because after all, it's a public company. The ministry of power plans on that line to find a possible solution from solar projects. It helps the peak load, which comes in peak hours. Storage is getting cheaper with the new technologies. At some stage, the future plan at dovetailing solar with high storage capacities could become an excellent off-grid solution for remote villages and inaccessible areas. Leh-Ladakh has some far off places where it may be difficult to move transmission lines. A solar-cum-off grid solution could be a better option. For, it is renewable energy without any environmental degradation even on barren or waste land. It doesn't affect the agricultural or irrigated land parcels. The power ministry ought to work on making it a viable alternative, despite financial constraints. Now, the ministry of power is looking at expanding the solar mission manifold. And Indian manufacturing doesn't have the capacity. The kind of tariffs and barriers, seldom help generate solar power at competitive prices. Worldwide, the prices have lowered so much that now solar power can stand on its own feet. The tariff has come down to Rs 6.50-7 per Kwh. Indigenous production will sustain on expanding the capabilities and capacity.

Provide Power 24×7 without Tariff Hike

There is enough scope for utilities to ensure uninterrupted power supply without tariff shocks but consumers too need to do their bit by willing to pay for getting 24×7 service and actively help stop electricity theft, minister for power and coal Piyush Goyal told on June 24. Union Power Minister Goyal, a chartered accountant and former investment banker, finds every entity ought to be involved in the electricity chain. It includes the generators, transmission and distribution utilities as well as coal companies. These have to improve their operations instead of covering inefficiencies. The debate over inadequate tariffs or absence of tariff revisions is futile. Our country loses 27 units in transit out of every 100 units being generated due to inefficiency and theft. The industry claims it as 'aggregate technical and commercial losses'. The regulators need to look more closely at arguments and numbers being forwarded by utilities in several states, including Delhi, for revising tariffs. Rejigging the coal supply chain can save about Rs 400-500 crore, that could save be passed on to consumers. In this direction, the state governments must do their bit by keeping a grip on expenditure and revenue. They should meter every consumer and involve people in curbing power theft. For, power is a concurrent subject and in the federal polity, states are very sensitive to any 'diktats'. It's not about politics.

Will Ensure 24×7 Power Supply for All

"Coal output was practically stagnant in the last four years"

Union power minister Piyush Goyal said that there is no coal supply shortage...The fact that coal production was practically stagnant in the last four years. I cannot increase coal production in 100 days. Using the available resources we have increased coal-based electricity generation by 21.4 per cent in the June-August period over the corresponding period in 2013. The government was committed to bring reform power and ensure affordable 24×7 power for homes, industrial and commercial establishments and adequate supply for farms, in the next few years.The state-owned Coal India Ltd. (CIL) set a target of one billion tonnes of coal production by 2019, the present of 500 million tonnes. India's dependency on coal for power generation is about 60 per cent. Additionally, the government was about to complete of three critical rail lines (at Chhattisgarh, Jharkhand and Odisha). It would help in increasing output by 60 million tonnes per annum by 2017-18 and up to 200 million tonnes by 2021-22. The CIL had taken in principle decision to purchase 250 additional rakes (for Rs. 5,000 crore) to evacuate more coal, primarily to power plants. The government had invested Rs. 7,000 crore in power grid security in States.

Power: "Ultra-Modern Super Critical Coal Based Thermal Power Technology," earmarked initial sum of Rs 100 crore.

Coal: Adequate quantity of coal will be provided to commissioned power plants to unlock dead investments. Coal linkages could optimise transport cost of power underway.

New and Renewable Energy: Ultra Mega Solar Power Projects in Rajasthan, Gujarat, Tamil Nadu, and Laddakh in J&K finds a sum of Rs 500 crore earmarked. A scheme for solar power driven agricultural pump sets and water pumping stations for energising one lakh pumps, finds a sum of Rs 400 crore with Rs 100 crore set aside for the development of 1 MW Solar Parks on the banks of canals. The Green Energy Corridor Project will be accelerated facilitate evacuation of renewable energy across the country.

Petroleum and Natural Gas: It intends to accelerate production and exploitation of coal bed methane reserves, through modern technology. India has about 15,000 km of gas pipeline system. An additional 15,000 km of pipeline completes grid. It will help increase the usage of gas, domestic as well as imported, which, in the long-term will be beneficial in reducing dependence on any one energy sources.

Mining: It is government's intention to encourage investment in mining sector and promote sustainable mining practices to adequately meet the requirements of industry without sacrificing environmental concerns. The current impasse in mining sector, including, iron ore mining, will be resolved expeditiously. Changes, if necessary, in the MMDR Act, 1957 would be introduced to facilitate the process.

State governments sought revision of royalty on minerals. Last revision took place in August, 2009. Another revision will be undertaken soon to ensure state governments mobilise revenues.

Power Projects in Limbo

Erratic power tripping added to woes of the consumers. The normal temperature hitting a 62-year high in Delhi and NCR, a dismal scenario exists across the country on the power front. As unprecedented outages have become the order of the day, the power sector warrants some quick thinking and out of the box solutions. Power shortage concerns reached such alarming levels in the national capital that LG Najeeb Jung had to instruct authorities to switch off high-mast street lamps for a few hours every day and cut supply to malls after 10 pm to 2 pm on the following day. Even as residents of Delhi and the adjoining NCR are up in arms against the unscheduled cuts being effected by distribution companies, Union power minister claims that there are various challenges that need to be addressed first. The Central Electricity Authority (CEA), a nodal agency under ministry of power, reports the country's energy shortage at 5.1 per cent, while peak shortage at 2 per cent this fiscal, against the ground reality, which is worse. Delhi and Punjab would have surplus energy in the current financial year, but on the contrary face huge power shortages.

The maximum energy shortage was recorded in Jammu and Kashmir (21.9 per cent) and Uttar Pradesh (14 per cent). Varanasi, the constituency of Premier Narendra Modi, has been added in the list of regular power supply. The daily power demand routinely breaches 13,500 MW against total availability of 11,000 MW in the state of Uttar Pradesh.

The primary cause for power outages is projects lying in limbo. Paris-based International Energy Agency (IEA) states that statutory clearances are the "greatest barrier" for power growth in India. The famous Dabhol power project of the early 1990s, later renamed Ratnagiri Gas and Power Private Ltd., has not been generating electricity since 2013 due to lack of raw material — gas. NTPC terminated a contract to develop and operate the first coal mine for power generation. It was stalled for more than three years as high compensation was sought by villagers for their land. The cabinet committee on investment formed by the UPA government in 2013 cleared 18 power projects worth Rs 83,000 crore. The major projects included Reliance Power's 4,000 MW plant at Tilaiya in Jharkand and two hydro power projects in Arunachal Pradesh. These projects were stuck facing environmental clearances. It will take yet another 2-3 years for them to actually start generating electricity.

India produces only 4,780 MW of nuclear energy, which is only 2.08 per cent of total electricity production. The Indo-US civilian nuclear agreement was signed in 2008. Six years later, no new nuclear power plants have come up. The country lacks from harnessing renewable energy resources. Currently, around 59 per cent of electricity in India is generated from coal-based power plants. The 12th five-year plan targets an addition of 76 gigawatts (GW) electricity production by the end of 2017. About 63 GW arise from coal-based generation which needs 842 million tonnes of coal every year. However, at 540 million tonnes a year, India's coal output is short of demand by over 100 million tonnes. In contrast, gas-based and hydro power projects contribute 8.91 per cent and 17.39 per cent, respectively, in total power generation.

The President Pranab Mukherjee in his address to the parliament forecasts every family will get round the clock power supply by the time nation completes 75 years of independence. The government plans capacity addition of 17,800 MW during 2014-15, comprising 14,958 MW of thermal, 842 MW of hydro and 2,000 MW of nuclear power stations. FICCI, a Delhi-based industry body, states that unavailability of power has had a huge impact on industrial production. India lost $68 billion due to power outages in 2013. Faulty transmission in the problematic areas, apart from rampant theft and pilferage, added to the woes. The World Bank cautioned the power sector faces annual losses of $27 billion by 2017, unless sweeping reforms are taken to tackle inefficient subsidies, theft and political meddling in utility companies. The annual per capita power consumption at around 800 units is among the lowest in the world. The World Bank called for ropping more private participation in the distribution. It has identified electricity distribution to the end consumer as the weak link in the sector. It recommends freeing utilities and regulators from external interference, increasing accountability and enhancing competition in the sector for higher level of service delivery.

Blackouts this summer have underlined the scale of that task. Larger parts of north India suffer from severe power cuts after sudden rise in temperature. The suppliers failed to meet demand by the antiquated transmission system. "Ominously, the recent sharp increase in private investment and market borrowing means power sector difficulties are more likely to spill over to lenders and affect the broader financial sector", the report said. Total accumulated losses in the sector stood at $25 billion in 2011 concentrated among discoms, state electricity Boards (SEBs) and state power departments, the report said.

"Revitalising the power sector by improving the performance of distribution utilities, and ensuring that players in the sector are subjected to financial discipline is the need of the hour," said Onno Ruhl, World Bank country director in India. By tackling the losses through a focused approach, it should be possible to make a marked difference in sector performance, the report added. Power Minister Piyush Goyal called for increased participation by private companies in power distribution to help ease supply bottlenecks and reinstate investor confidence in the sector. "We will look for more private participation in distribution and would require state support for this task," Goyal said after meeting bankers to resolve issues between power sector borrowers and banks.

According to a Moody's report, of all impaired loans at public-sector banks, 20 per cent are of distribution companies (discoms), with the proportion going up to 48 per cent at some of the most exposed banks. The erstwhile UPA government had approved the restructuring of Rs.190,000 crore debt of state electricity boards in a move to turn around the finances of power distribution companies. Under the scheme, 50 per cent of the short-term outstanding liabilities would be taken over by the state governments and the remainder would be restructured by providing a moratorium on the principal and most favourable repayment terms. Currently Delhi, Mumbai, Kolkata, Surat and Ahmedabad and the state of Odisha have privately owned discoms.

Power Sector Financiers

Power, coal and renewable energy minister Piyush Goyal said the stress in the electricity sector was not as severe as it was being made out to be and lenders to power projects could work on a recovery in the next few years.

Power capacity of thousands of megawatts is stranded or idling because of fuel shortage, poor health of distribution companies and environmental issues. Power producers have said in the past that the situation was also a concern for lenders to the sector. After a meeting with top lenders to the sector, Goyal said there was an opportunity in the situation. "I am told that the stress on financial institutions is not as bad as it is made out. Power is the need of the hour and personally I feel that utilities are good assets as market has demand for what they are going to provide. All we have to do is to easier the edges. For me, it is an opportunity and not a crisis," said Goyal.

He said the challenges of financial institutions for funding stranded power projects was not going to ease soon as offering any incentives or changing RBI norms for lenders was not in government's hands. Lending to the power sector, particularly to developers and distribution utilities, is risky in the present economic condition and financial institutions are seeking government support for timely recoveries, industry executives say.

Top executives of some of the largest financiers of the power sector such as State Bank of India, ICICI Bank, Citibank and Power Finance Corporation met power, coal and renewable energy minister Piyush Goyal with status report of borrowers—they have stated that design, build, finance, operate, transfer (DBFOT) model of bidding for ultra mega power projects is not bankable. The government should ensure viability of natural gas-fired power projects by using either them to meet peak demands or bundle generation with NTPC's supplies to state utilities, they suggested. The minister replied the stakeholders ought to support the system to improve the situation.

Any relaxations for lenders or borrowers are uncalled for, the minister said: "It is not an individual bank, company or ministry related issue and we have to look at it in national perspective. I believe we have to respect RBI's efforts of the last 20 years to strengthen the Indian banking system and within that system, I feel as there are more than enough avenues to resolve problems.

We are not looking for great incentives or change in RBI laws. The states are not supplying electricity at the right price due to the economic fuel supply. The problem needs to be addressed in tandem with support from stakeholders." The ministry ought to device a mechanism, where states can be motivated to outsource distribution. The ministry has appealed to commerce and finance ministries to review their possible move to impose anti-dumping duty on imported gears.

Consumer for Renewable Energy Sources

The consumers' attitude towards renewable energy sources is changing for the better. Nearly half of residential as well as commercial customers believe it as very important for India to develop and generate more solar power. Solar energy has emerged as the most recognised source of renewable energy. Nearly 58 per cent of consumers strongly favour solar energy as future source of energy generation for India. The environment was underscored as the most important benefit of solar energy by 71 per cent of commercial and 65 per cent of residential respondents that covered 1,700 residential and commercial customers. One of the survey found only six in 10 (59 per cent) commercial respondents were aware of the government-backed subsidy programmes for renewable energy. The survey covered 1,700 residential and commercial customers. Only 30 per cent of commercial respondents and 21 per cent of residential respondents were familiar with the Bureau of Energy Efficiency (BEE label) products and their benefits, it reported.

Largest Solar Power Project—A Capacity Addition of 10,000 MW by 2017

India is about to launch the largest bidding of solar power projects worth 1,500 MW under its flagship Jawaharlal Nehru National Solar Mission (JNNSM). The government claims it as the first success story of converging three energy ministries vis-a-vis coal, power and renewable energy, solar power would be bundled with conventional power at huge scale in one go. The bidding, a part of second batch of the phase two of JNNSM, aims to achieve a capacity addition of 10,000 MW by 2017. The government tendered 750 MW of solar power projects early 2014. The current solar power capacity of the country is 2,600 MW. The government hopes to cross 20,000 MW by 2022. The solar power produced could bundle with the existing unallocated quota of conventional power. The pooled power could be sold at an average rate to the distribution companies, who shy away from procuring solar power citing it to be costly.

Rooftop Solar Power Generation Projects

Residential colonies and commercial establishments could reduce the burden of their electricity bills if a study currently being carried out by Tata Power BSE 0.96 per cent Delhi Distribution finds rooftop solar power generation projects feasible and the city joins the club of such power producers that includes Gujarat.

According to estimates, 33 *km of Delhi's total area of* 1,483 sq km can be used for rooftop solar photovoltaic projects to install 2,557 mw of capacity. However, Delhi's potential to produce solar power has not been exploited yet, even as power demand touches new heights almost every successive summer, which is the most productive season for solar power installations. Tata Power Delhi Distribution—which has already installed capacity of 1.8 mw of rooftop solar power generation at its establishments—has said that due to dust across the city the performance of the set-up is about 15 per cent, compared with 20-25 per cent in large-scale projects that have come up on wasteland in Gujarat and Rajasthan.

The power distributor, armed with financial assistance of $459,238 from US Trade and Development Agency, will prepare a business case to utilise rooftops in the city to procure solar power. It will explore viability of putting up its own rooftop projects or buying power generated from the installations owned by residential colonies or bring in third parties to own and operate these projects. "We have tied up for 1,600 mw of power to meet the peak demand of our close to 14 lakh consumers in our distribution area for this year. According to projections, the same will go up by 1,900 mw in 2017 and 2,300 mw in 2020. We wish to utilise 100-200 mw of grid integrated renewables power projects and meet the balance requirements through the demand side management," said Tata Power Delhi CEO Praveer Sinha, adding that the study would also come up with a business model to partner with residents of Delhi.

Domestic Solar Cell Makers

Indigenous Products can Keep Cost of Solar Power Low

Domestic manufacturers of solar cells have said that use of indigenous products can help keep cost of solar power low, countering the government's claim that it will escalate after imposition of dumping duty.

"The fact is that cost of power will remain exactly the same or lesser than what was discovered through an extremely transparent bidding process of Jawaharlal Nehru National Solar Mission (JNNSM) Phase 2 Batch 1," a senior executive of large Indian solar cell manufacturing company said.

"From public interest perspective, it is the cost of overall energy mix which is important. Change in that will be negligible at less than two paisa per KwHr due to anti-dumping duty." According to domestic manufacturers, the cost of solar power could fall and remain at Rs 7.5 per unit by 2020 if indigenous solar cells are used, compared with the Rs 6.5–8 per unit at present.

The Ministry of New and Renewable Energy (MNRE) and power producers had expressed concern that the cost of solar power would double. For the commerce department is about to impose high dumping duty on imports of solar cells, the bulk of which comes from the US, China, Malaysia and Taiwan. More than 70 per cent of the projects across the country are built on imported solar cells and around 4,000 Mw was tendered recently. This includes 375 Mw tendered out in the second phase of the National Solar Mission early 2014. The JNNSM of announced 2009, targets 20 gigawatts of energy generation by 2022 in three phases. In its finding, the commerce department had indicated that imposition of dumping duty could see foreign players setting up manufacturing facilities in the country in order to capture the growing sector. "In fact, once it is provided a level playing field, India will have a thriving domestic manufacturing industry with its entire supply chain, bringing in FDI, saving Forex, driving employment, and above all, ensure India's energy security with a far superior energy mix," Moser Baer Solar's chief marketing officer Vivek Chaturvedi said, adding that this could push up India's solar cell manufacturing capacity to 4–5 gw in two-three years.

Solar Power Generation Mandatory in Houses

The state of Haryana has decided to implement an energy conservation action plan. The solar power generation will be made mandatory. It will be in different categories of buildings or areas with a suitable enforcement mechanism. The generation of 200 MW of power, could save of Rs 151 crore on coal and 16.60 lakh kilo litres of water, every year. The annual energy saving by implementing mandatory provisions will be 320 million units. Three lakh MTs of annual carbon emission will also be prevented in the atmosphere. Residential buildings built on a plot size of 500 square yards and above falling within the limits of MCs and HUDA/HSIIDC sectors, the mandatory installation of solar power plant to be installed will be of minimum one KWp or five per cent of connected load, whichever is higher, according to state government official release.

Solar Water Heater Makers Demand Rs 350 cr Subsidy Arrears

A grouping of solar water heater manufacturers demanded the government immediately pay them Rs 350 crore in arrears related to unpaid subsidies. The pending subsidy includes Rs 50 crore (2012-13) and around Rs 300 crore for the last fiscal, according to Solar Thermal Federation of India (STFI). "The industry is on death bed. It is Rs 800-crore industry."

The arrears have gone up to Rs 375 crore, he added. To promote solar energy, the Ministry of New and Renewable Energy (MNRE) had launched a programme under which 30 per cent subsidy would be provided to solar water heater manufacturers for every unit sold. The subsidy scheme comes under the Jawaharlal Nehru National Solar Mission (JNNSM).

Malaviya claimed that subsidies could touch Rs 500 crore in this financial year as the market for solar water heaters is expected to see a boom. "The industry is on the verge of shutdown. Government immediately needs to set deadline of setting off the pending claims."

Cabinet Clears Coal Ordinance

The Cabinet on Wednesday approved re-promulgation of an Ordinance to facilitate e-auction of coal blocks for private companies for captive use and allot mines directly to state and central PSUs.

"Cabinet has cleared the Coal Ordinance," sources said after the meeting of the Union Cabinet. The government had to go in for re-promulgation of the Ordinance as the Rajya Sabha could not take up the Coal Mines (Special Provisions) Bill. The Bill, which provides for fresh auction of 204 coal blocks de-allocated by the Supreme Court in September, remained pending in the Rajya Sabha even though the Lok Sabha passed it on December 12.

The Cabinet had on October 20 recommended promulgation of the earlier Ordinance to help e-auction of coal blocks. The move came against the backdrop of the Supreme Court in September quashing allocation of 204 coal blocks to various companies since 1993.

The re-promulgation of the Ordinance will enable the Coal Ministry to go ahead with its decision to give a total 101 mines, including 65 through auction, in the first phase. As many as 36 blocks will be directly allotted to state-owned companies. The government had increased the number of coal mines to be auctioned or allotted in the first tranche to 101, from 92. Of the 101 blocks to be allotted and auctioned in the first lot, 63 mines would be given to the power sector, while the rest would be for sectors like steel and cement.

Coal Supply to 9940 MW Plants

The department of coal has rejected supply of fuel to 9940 MW plants of companies like Essar Power, GMR and Power. The department of power has sought intervention of the minister of Coal and Power. A list of "similarly placed projects" of 4,095 MW was sent to the coal ministry for supply of coal...Further 5,845 MW has coal blocks, but mining is delayed by one-two years...Hence, tapering linkages needs to be given for one-two years. However, the department of coal has rejected it on the ground that they have coal blocks," according to an official document.

Improve Fuel Supply

Coal India, Power Producers, Railway Officials Mull Ways: The PM Modi's move to have a common minister for the power and coal ministries seems to have started showing its impact. Executives from power producers and Coal India Ltd BSE –0.09 per cent, as well as officials from the two ministries and the Indian Railways met for four hours to resolve key differences over the quantity and quality of coal supplied to power plants. They have agreed to make coordinated efforts to improve the production and supply of dry fuel that fire more than half the nation's power capacity, along with several industry executives. Coal India, the state-run monopoly struggles to meet increasing demand for coal. Power producers had accused the miner of providing low-quality fuel which seldom meets the contracted quantity. Coal India BSE –0.09 per cent had staunchly opposed the allegations. It has deflected the blame towards the railways saying that pilferage during transportation.

The Power and Coal Minister Piyush Goyal apparently directed officials from both coal and power ministries to assess the state of affairs in coal production and supply. Gujarat officials have complained against Coal India during his recent visit to Gandhinagar.

Close to 150 representatives from the government including the railways, Coal India and its consumers from the private and public sectors have attended the meeting. Power producers demanded better sampling practices to ensure desired quality, introduction of e-billing for efficient payment systems and making the railways responsible for unloading what was loaded at coal mines. The coal ministry's additional secretary AK Dubey and power ministry's joint secretary Jyoti Arora had to intervene often, the executives said. Dubey sought an explanation on differences between domestic and imported coal based on logistics and economics, while Arora suggested forming a joint committee with the railways to resolve problems related to traffic management and adulteration. The coal ministry is expected to make power-point presentation on issues.

Rural Electrification Scheme

The Power ministry would replicate Gujarat government's Jyotigram Yojna, or rural electrification scheme, in other states to provide 24×7 power supplies to every household. The scheme was started by then chief minister Narendra Modi of Gujarat. The model was successful in Gujarat. It can't be suitable for all states. This model ought to be calibrated as per each state's need. Lesson on pruning transmission and distribution losses and power theft is what other states need to learn. It is important to learn lessons from Gujarat on how to escalate power generation, cut down on transmission and distribution losses, control the every increasing cost of power and maintain efficiency.

Gujarat separated electricity feeder lines for agricultural and non-agricultural users. The farm power rationing was effective and tamper-proof. It supplied sustained reliable full-voltage triple phase power supply for restricted hours daily. The plan made it possible for farmers to keep to their irrigation schedules, conserve water, save on pump maintenance costs and use labour more efficiently. The big state like Uttar Pradesh, facing acute power crisis, could benefit from the model. About the quality of coal supplied to state power generation units and how quality of coal needs to be controlled to increase efficiency of power plants. The issue of using railways for transportation of coal was also discussed. "Given the statistics it would seem that there is not much of a gap in demand and supply of power in India. But in reality, there is a big gap. Thanks to policy paralysis that we have inherited, it will take some time to resolve the issues. In a reasonable time, there will be a revolution in the power sector.

Transmission and Distribution: Vowing to end the misery in the electricity sector, power minister has set transmission and distribution as his focus areas and is working to bring states on board for reforms. As much as 30 per cent of the power generated in India is lost during transmission and distribution. In some areas, power does not reach users — even when it is available — due to the lack of transmission capacity, most recently demonstrated when a storm snapped lines and caused lines and caused long outages in the national capital. Sources in power ministry said Rajasthan and Andhra Pradesh have agreed to work with the Centre to reform the transmission and distribution sector. He is likely to visit these states soon to ascertain their demands in the power sector and how the central government can provide the requisite assistance. The minister views transmission and distribution of electricity to the end consumer as the major challenges, rather than generation of power.

The installed capacity of power stations in the country was 2,48,509.63 MW at the end of May, according to data on the Central Electricity Authority. Rajasthan had 14,945.68 MW and Andhra Pradesh 17,731.07 MW. The country has enough generation capacity. What is needed is operationally efficient and financially healthy transmission and distribution utilities. SEBs were lackdiasical in addressing power generation supply, T&D loses power theft despite liberalisation of the power sector in 1991 by the then government.

11 MoUD Targets Housing for All by 2022

Introduction

More than 30 per cent of India's population lives in urban areas – The number of city-dwellers is increasing every day. Integrated mobility solutions, building and security systems, power distribution equipment, smart grid applications and low-and medium-voltage products offer sustainable technologies for metropolitan centres and urban infrastructures worldwide. Combining the expertise of existing businesses in our Industry and Energy Sectors, Infrastructure and Cities is well positioned to be a major player in an addressable market. The Ministry of Urban Development (MoUD), Government of India, is the apex body for formulation and administration of the rules and regulations.The ministry is under the charge of Venkaiah Naidu. It was attached on and off with the department of housing and urban poverty alleviation on many occasions, before becoming independent in 2004. It has published the National City rating, which ranked the cleanest cities in India. The government decides to initiate building 100 new cities; enabled with the latest in technology and infrastructure—adhering to concepts like sustainability, walk to work etc., and focused on specialised domains. The approach to urban development will be based on integrated habitat development. Building on concepts like Twin cities and Satellite towns will be priority. Upgrade existing urban centres, transitioning focus from basic infrastructure to public utility services like waste and water management—for a clean and healthy city life. Rain water harvesting will be given importance to reduce humidity factor.

Cleanliness and Sanitation will be given priority. Efficient Waste and Water management systems will be set up. Model towns will be identified for rolling out integrated waste management infrastructure. Wi-Fi facilities will be made available in public places and commercial centres. Urban poverty alleviation scheme would be a key thrust area. Use technology for scientific, strategic and long term town planning—including GIS based mapping.

Build quality integrated Public Transport systems, discouraging usage of private vehicles.

Housing for All: Highlighting the priorities of his ministry, Union Minister for Urban Development, Housing and Poverty Alleviation Venkaiah Naidu said private sector as part of their social responsibility should go for housing for their staff. Naidu said that employment is going to be a major challenge before the country, no government can provide employment to all through government jobs, so you need to have public private partnership, and you need to involve private sector, public sector and agencies like banks, LIC. He said he wants to motivate private sector to go for housing for their staff as part of their social responsibility because "housing for all by 2022" is the motto of the government. "We want to involve the state, local bodies, private sector, public sector in this massive ambitious programme of housing for all," he said.

Housing for All by 2022

Smart cities to have Wi-Fi connectivity, GIS-based mapping and integrated public transport systems. The smart cities will have Wi-Fi connectivity, GIS-based mapping and scientific and strategic town planning and integrated public transport systems. Jaitley said the concept of smart cities was in keeping with the times since a "neo-middle class is emerging" which aspire for better living standards.

The government would focus on providing infrastructure, including public transport, solid waste disposal, sewerage treatment and drinking water, in the urban areas. The budgetary provision for the Pooled Municipal Debt Obligation Facility has been enhanced from Rs 5,000 crore to Rs 50,000 crore with extension of the facility by five years to March 31, 2019. He said this facility was set up in 2006. Several banks were asked to promote and finance infrastructure projects in urban areas on shared risk basis. It is the vision of the government to create at least 500 habitations. These wil have safe drinking water and sewerage management, use recycled water for growing organic fruits and vegetables, solid waste management and digital connectivity through public-private partnerships (PPPs), he said.

Home owners will have tax benefit extending the additional tax incentive on home loans. This, he said will encourage people, especially the young, to own a house. He also announced the setting up of a Mission on Low-Cost Affordable Housing will be anchored by the National Housing Bank. A sum of Rs 4,000 crore has been earmarked for National Housing Bank. It will extend cheaper credit for affordable housing to the urban poor. The private sector has been asked to pitch in. The government has already outlined an easier flow of FDI in this sector. It is willing to examine other positive suggestions. Slum development has been added to the list of Corporate Social Responsibility (CSR) activities. Rural Housing Scheme has been identified as an area that needs promotion. An enhanced allocation of Rs 8,000 crore has been earmarked for National Housing Bank.

Rs 7,060 Crore for 100 Smart Cities

The cities will be developed as satellite towns of mega cities. It will modernise existing mid-sized cities. It will finally provide fresh direction and a sense of legitimacy to a concept that has long been popular but not enthusiastically implemented. The Finance Ministry has set aside a sum of

Rs 7,060 crore for the development of 100 smart cities. The basic premise of any small city is making infrastructure network and delivery of services more efficient. This is done across verticals such as telecommunications, logistics, water and gas supply through methods such as smart meters, sensors and global positioning systems. It has long gestation period, Greenfield smart cities sprucing up in and around metros — the ones in the Delhi-Mumbai industrial corridor or the Lodha Group's Palava city in Mumbai — come with greater potential and turnaround time.

Some 50 smart grid pilot projects being conducted in mid-sized cities around India. The municipal corporations move slowly as funds for technology-aided development are scarce. Greenfield satellite cities are dependent on information technology, whose cost will be somewhat five per cent of the project's total cost. Old Indian cities like Varanasi, Amritsar, Kolkata and even Delhi, could be in for a facelift over the next few years. "The focus will be on education, entertainment, employment and environment management, so that the new cities feed into the old, like in the case of Gandhinagar and Ahmedabad," said housing and urban development minister Venkaiah Naidu.

All new cities will have integrated transport — modern bus systems, trams, metro rail and bicycle tracks — aided by satellite mapping, garbage disposal and solid waste management. "You cannot build cities overnight. It takes 20-30 years to build a new city. Instead of just making new cities, our idea is to make our existing cities smart. There will be a mix. One is to convert an old city into a smart one. Two, to build new cities wherever possible."

"The idea is to focus on specialised domains and equip cities with worldclass amenities. Integrated infrastructure will rolled out in these modern towns with emphasis on sanitation. To construct a city, you need to have a river close by. That has been the experience worldwide," he said.

Naidu did not name any city that has been identified for a facelift. He said his team has already started working on the project. Cities will be picked after consultation with the state governments. The money for these projects, he said, will come from the Budget, from institutions and also from the private sector. "The private sector is ready to invest money provided clearances are made easy with absolute care for red tape," he said. Clearances for projects, he said, will be put online. It will improve the system and make it more transparent.

Naidu's team in the urban development ministry is already preparing a new programme. It will replace the UPA government's city modernisation scheme — Jawaharlal Nehru National Urban Renewal Mission (JNNURM) announced. The project ended in March 2014 after a two years extension. This is to be announced in the budget in July, 2014. Expressing concern about rising home prices, he said prices are driven by market forces so nothing much can be done about it.

"The government is bringing some regulation in the sector. Builders have to be made accountable. The real estate regulatory bill is pending. It should not become another tool for harassment. The department plans to increase housing stock and bring down prices. It will consider a proposal to provide infrastructure status to the housing sector to enable builders raise bank loans at lower interest rates and for a longer tenure. Extending infrastructure status will enable more credit money. The Union Budget has made purchase of homes more attractive. By raising deduction against interest payment on home loan from the taxable income to Rs 2,00,000 from Rs 1,50,000, middle class home buyers could save an additional amount of Rs 15,450 from his or her tax liability. It will also, in effect, lower interest rates for home loans. So say that one has taken a loan of Rs 25,00,000 to buy a house at an interest rate of 10 per cent for 20 years, the EMI will be around Rs 24,125, which adds up to Rs 2,89,500 annually. Out of this, Rs 2,50,000 will go towards interest payment and the rest— Rs 39,500 —will be used for principal repayment. Post-Budget, the buyer can avail a deduction of Rs 2,00,000 from his or her taxable income as the interest payment will be Rs 2,50,000 in the first year. This will enable the buyer to save Rs 61,800 from tax liability if his or her income is in the highest tax bracket of 30.9 per cent.

The net tax outgo after adjusting for the savings in tax will be only Rs 1,88,200. As the loan amount is Rs 25,00,000, the net interest rate will work out to only 7.53 per cent. But if the borrowed amount increases, the net interest rate will increase. So if the loan amount is Rs 1,00,00,000 at 10 per cent rate, the net interest rate will be 9.38 per cent. This is because the tax benefit remains at Rs 61,800 only.

Experts say that in big metros like Delhi, Mumbai and Bangalore, where most flats cost upward of Rs 1 crore, it would make little difference to the buyer. "In Mumbai, the average cost of a flat is Rs 1.2 crore. On this, the monthly EMI itself would be around Rs 1 lakh, of which 80 per cent goes towards interest. But, this exemption is not enough to promote housing in category one cities.

Another Budget proposal allows corporate social responsibility in slum redevelopment. It would have a big impact in Mumbai, where half the population lives in shanties. "Big companies could pump in at least a couple of thousand crores in slum projects. Experts believe the relaxation in FDI norms for real estate would also opens up a new stream of cheaper money for developers. The FDI limit has been reduced from 50,000 sq m to 20,000 sq m and minimum investment from $10 million to $ 5 million. The tax passes through status for Real Estate Investment Trusts (REITs). It will avoid double taxation and bring in more investments to the sector.

Bank Finance for Housing for Poor

There is a need to create an apex bank to monitor the financing in urban areas. The matter should be taken up with the Finance Ministry to extend the jurisdiction of NABARD to the urban areas or some agency like SIDBI," a statement from the ministry said. New schemes for slum redevelopment and affordable housing for the urban poor are on the offing, the statement said. However, the schemes must be simple in conception and actively involve various stakeholders including State Governments, Urban Local-Bodies, Civil Society/NGOs as well as banks and financial institutions. Private partners through a transparent and competitive process could inject more managerial and financial efficiencies in the execution of projects. Urban housing shortage is estimated at around 19 million. It calls for active participation of the stakeholders in a synchronous fashion. Else, the housing shortage could balloon to 30 million by the year 2020. The department has issued instructions for expeditious completion of the houses, estimated to be around 3.77 lakh, as the top-most priority under the JNNURM, which is scheduled to close in March, 2015.

Australia Keen on India Partnership

Australia has expressed its keenness for extending its expertise, technology and other cooperation in areas of mutual interest. It includes urban development, energy and defence, claimed a recent government release. The High Commissioner in India said that Australia has necessary expertise in urban design, construction of new smart cities, green and quality buildings, networked buildings, waste management and urban regeneration and would like to participate in India's urban development initiatives. It could scale up bilateral trade substantially as coal, gas; uranium, nuclear energy and defence sector hold immense prospects. Stating that the last visit of an Indian Parliamentary delegation to Australia was in 1997, the High Commissioner emphasised the need for resumption of such visits. Naidu said that various urban development initiatives would be firmed up soon and specific proposals from Australia would be considered appropriately.

Varanasi Infrastructure to Get Boost

The Union Urban Development secretary Sudhir Krishna recently held meetings with Varanasi district officials. He ought them to prepare a roadmap and send various pending as well as new proposals to the union ministry. Krishna, who is visiting for the first time after the formation of the NDA government, held closed-door meetings with the District Magistrate, officials of Varanasi Development Authority and the municipal corporation at the Commissioner compound yesterday. Projects like metro rail, sewerage treatment plants, and cleaning of Ganga River were discussed in his meeting. The concern for cleaning of Ganga River has made building of small sewerage treatment plants to retreat the water before being drained to the river. The secretary inspected a sewerage treatment plant at Binapur and a solid waste management disposal site at Karshana. The secretary believes building up of satellite townships on the outskirts of the city could ease the urban pressure from the main parts of the city.

Plan for Beautification of Delhi

The national capital, Delhi is likely to get a facelift as the Urban Development department has prepared an action plan for beautification. This will involve focus on heritage buildings, more greenery for pedestrian pathways, plantation drives outside metro stations, among others.

Agencies like New Delhi Municipal Council (NDMC), Municipal Corporation of Delhi (MCD), Central Public Works Department (CPWD) and Delhi Development Authority (DDA) operating in the national capital will get involved in this drive to make the national capital a world class city. The action plan includes improvement and beautification of roads, parks, roundabouts, pedestrian pathways. The civic agencies have started working on an action plan on issues ranging from desilting of drains to checking for mosquito breeding, he added. Plantation drive will be encouraged at entry and exit points at metro stations. Stakeholders have been asked to prepare short-medium and long term programmes. The need to construct more public toilets across the city including use of recycle waste in a big way has been given priority.

DDA Lines up Largest-ever Offer of 27,000 Flats

DDA will soon be coming out with its largest-ever offering of 27,000 flats. This marks a substantial increase from the 16,118 flats (2010). The scheme, which will have flats across all categories on offer, will have a record number of units for the economically weaker section (EWS). Almost 90 per cent of the houses on sale, or 24,000 units, will be put to draw, exclusively for the EWS.

DDA's scheme for 2014 will have 1,500 flats on sale for the middle income group and the lower income group. It will range between Rs 30 lakh and 80 lakh. There will be 1,375 HIG (high income group) flats on offer as well. These flats start from around Rs 1 crore. The EWS flats are expected to be priced from Rs 12 lakh onwards. The EWS houses have been constructed this time with substantially improved pre-fabricated technology; across Narela, Dwarka, Rohini and Sultangarhi. A survey of unoccupied and unsold flats to reconcile with DDA's existing inventory has made the offer for sale in the new housing scheme. It includes some freshly constructed flats, finished early this year.

Work on another 37,000 flats has already begun and will be completed by March 2017. In this batch, 25,700 of the flats will be MIG flats. DDA plans to begin working on 47,000 more flats. In future, DDA will announce a housing scheme only when the flats are in "ready to move-in" condition. "Learning from past experience when flats could not be handed over to allottees even months after draws held, and we faced criticism. We will announce dates only after ensuring them ready to move in," said an official.

Housing Board to Start Registration of 2,480 New Flats in UP: UP Housing and Development Board will develop two new projects in Vrindavan Yojna on Rae Bareilly Road, Lucknow. It extended administrative and financial nod to two projects one of 2BHK and the other of 3BHK in Vrindavan Yojna Registration of around 2,480 flats. The projects are named as Kailsah Enclave. A project Ganga is also coming up at Kanpur in Dr Ambedkarpuram Yojna, costing around Rs 25 to 30 lakh. The concept and layout plans of these projects are ready, calling for only formal approval. Site selection, paper work, design lay out, registration formalities were over. According to the plan, under 3 BHK type flats, around 1,368 flats would be constructed whereas under 2 BHK types, 1,112 flats would be made.

DDA Launches 'Housing Scheme-2014'

The 'much-awaited' housing scheme-2014 of Delhi Development Authority (DDA) with 25,034 flats on offer was launched recently morning by its Vice-chairman Balvinder Kumar in New Delhi who assured delivery of "good quality flats" to people. Under criticism quite often for shoddy construction and failed schemes, the DDA this time promised better results. The DDA Vice-chairman, while launching the scheme, assured that good quality of flats will be delivered to people. The land agency plans to handover the possession of flats to successful allottees by first quarter of next year.

With 25,034 flats in different categories – High-Income Group, Middle Income Group, Low-Income Group, one bedroom flats, Janta flats and those for economically weaker section — on offer, the scheme is being touted as one of the biggest. The flats are located in areas such as Rohini, Jasola, Mukherjee Nagar, Shalimar Bagh, Narela, Dwarka, Dilshad Garden and Paschim Vihar. The scheme has 811 flats from the old inventory as well as 24,223 newly constructed flats. The forms for the scheme are available at DDA office at Vikas Sadan and also at 13 empanelled banks. The 13 banks are Punjab National Bank, State Bank of India, Central Bank of India, Corporation Bank, Syndicate Bank, Union Bank of India, Indusland Bank, Kotak Mahindra Bank, IDBI Bank, ICICI Bank Ltd, Yes Bank, HDFC Bank and Axis Bank. The forms are to be submitted at these banks.

The registration fee for all other categories is Rs. 1 lakh, and Rs. 10,000 for EWS category. There is no ceiling on income for any category except EWS with a ceiling of Rs. 1 lakh. The unsuccessful applicants would be refunded the registration amount within 15-20 days after the draw of lots, Singh said. To ensure that people who need a house get the benefit of this scheme, the DDA has for the first time introduced a five-year lock in period for ownership to check speculative buying. The allottees will be given conveyance deed after five years.

PM's Dream Project

Offers Vital Learnings for 100 Smart Cities Ambition

GIFT in Gujarat: Eighteen kilometers off Ahmedabad airport, two tall buildings rise out of literally nowhere. The twin towers with cobalt blue glass facades are anomalies in the otherwise brown, dusty landscape. At 122 metres and 28 floors high, the towers are the tallest in Gujarat. But height isn't really their claim to fame. The towers are the first buildings to go up in the Gujarat International Financial Tec (GIFT) City project.

GIFT City will be India's first 'smart city' to be built from scratch. An army of workers sweat in the sweltering sun, pounding roads and erecting buildings for a school, a fire station and a cooling plant. Workmen burrow underground, dig what will eventually be a 12 km long maze of utility tunnels, through which everything from power cables to fibre optic cables to water pipelines will be routed.

GIFT City's cooling towers won't use air-conditioning but district cooling technology. It emloys a far more energy-efficient process that circulates chilled water through buildings to cool them. Solid waste will be sucked out from homes and offices at 90 km/hr using pipelines leading directly to waste processing plant. The City will have a command centre with Information and Communication Technology (ICT) infrastructure. It will manage vehicular traffic and had had a cinema hall. The price of the latest Hollywood sci-fi flick, however may change.

A Hundred Hi-tech Cities

The government is commited to build 100 hi-tech cities. The union minister said that it is not possible to build cities overnight. It takes 20-30 years to build a new city.

Instead of just making new cities, our idea is to make our existing cities smart. Seven new smart cities are being developed from scratch along the proposed Delhi-Mumbai Industrial Corridor (DMIC). "We expect the first phase [40-50 sq km] of three smart cities — Dholera [Gujarat], Shendra-Bidkin [Maharashtra] and Global City [Haryana] — to be delivered by 2019," says Amitabh Kant, secretary, department of industrial policy and promotion (DIPP). These cities home some to 2–2.5 million people by 2040. India is not the only country building such cities. Brand newsmart cities are mushrooming in China, the UAE and South Korea. Cities like Barcelona in Spain and Montpellier in France have implemented smart city solutions to deliver better services to citizens. Over $41 trillion is expected to be spent. Computing giants like CISCO, IBM, and Oracle to surveillance solutions vendors have made their efforts in India in anticipation.

12 Holistic Care System: Health for All

Introduction

Holistic Care System: India needs a holistic care system. It should be universally accessible, affordable and effective and drastically reduces the out of pocket spending. NRHM has failed to meet the objectives and will be radically reformed. The new government accords high priority to health sector, which is crucial for securing the economy. The overarching goal of healthcare would be to provide, "Health Assurance to Indians and to reduce the out of pocket spending on health care', with the help of state governments. The situation calls for radical reforms in the health care system. It includes health care programmes and delivery, medical education and training and financing of health care. India now needs a comprehensive health care policy to address the complex challenges, keeping in view the developments in this sector and the changing demographics.

New Health Policy

The government will initiate the 'National Health Assurance Mission', with a clear mandate to provide universal health care that is not only accessible and affordable, but also effective, and reduces the OOP spending for the common man.

Education and training will review the role of various professional regulatory bodies in health care and consider setting up an overarching lean body. High priority will be given to address the shortfall of healthcare professionals. Modernise government hospitals, upgrading infrastructure and latest technologies.

The allocation for the Ministry of Health and Family Welfare has been inceased to Rs 373.30 billion. This is an increase of 49 per cent over last time's 32 per cent.

The expansion of RSBY (Rashtriya Swasthiya Bima Yojana) to other categories such as rickshaw, auto-rickshaw and taxi drivers, sanitation workers, rag pickers and mine workers would also increase the demand for health care facilities. However, the decline in spending from Rs 304.77 billion as budgeted to Rs 248.94 billion. Two key initiatives—free drug service and free diagnosis service - would be taken up on priority.

The priority will be as folows:

(a) Reorganise Ministry of Health and Family Welfare: It will converge various departments dealing in health care, food and nutrition and pharmaceuticals, for effective delivery.

(b) Increase the number of medical and para-medical colleges. It will make India self-sufficient in human resources, and set up an AIIMS like institute in every state.

(c) Yoga and Ayurveda are the gifts of ancient Indian civilisation to humanity. The public investment ought to be enhanced to promote Yoga and AYUSH. Indian System of Medicine (ISM) and Modern Science and Ayurgenomics will have integrated courses.

(d) The government will set up institutions and launch a vigorous program to standardise and validate the Ayurvedic medicine.

(e) Move to pre-emptive care model. The focus and thrust will be on child health and prevention. School health program would be a major focus area. Health and hygiene will be made a part of the school curriculum.

(f) *Senior Citizens health care:* Give high priority to chronic diseases, and will invest in research and development for chronic diseases like obesity, diabetes, cancer, CVD etc. Occupational health programs will be pursued aggressively.

(g) Utilise the ubiquitous platform of mobile phones for healthcare delivery. Establish the 'National e-Health Authority' to leverage telemedicine and mobile health care. Define the standards and legal framework for technology driven care. Universalise emergency medical services-108.

(h) Re-orientation of herbal plants board to encourage farming of herbal plants.

(i) Population stabilisation would be a major thrust area and would be pursued as a mission mode programme.

(j) Programme for Women Healthcare with emphasis on rural, SC, ST and OBC in a mission mode. Mission mode project to eradicate malnutrition.

(k) National Mosquito Control Mission: Poor Hygiene and Sanitation have a far reaching, cascading impact. It will ensure a 'Swachh Bharat' drive on by Gandhiji's 150th birth anniversary in 2019. Taking it up in mission mode by onverging resources and building around *Jana bhagidari.*

(l) Create an open defecation-free India by awareness campaign. It will enable people to build toilets in their home, schools and public places.

Set up modern, scientific sewage and waste management systems. It will introduce sanitation ratings measuring and ranking our cities and towns on 'sanitation'; and rewarding the best performers. Make potable drinking water available to everybody. Check water-borne diseases, which will automatically translate into Diarrhoea-free India.

Health and Family Welfare

Move towards "Health for All", through key initiatives—the Free Drug Service and Free Diagnosis Service. Quality diagnosis and only treatment to TB patients, National Institutes for ageing will be set up at AIIMS, New Delhi and Madras Medical College, Chennai. A national level research and referral Institute for higher dental studies would be set up in one of the existing Dental institutions. The government will build six new AIIMS at Jodhpur, Bhopal, Patna, Rishikesh, Bhubaneswar and Raipur. These institutes would have been functional under Pradhan Mantri Swasthya Suraksha Yojana. A plan to set-up four more AIIMS like institutions at Andhra Pradesh, West Bengal, Vidarbha in Maharashtra and Poorvanchal in UP is under consideration, on a sum of Rs 500 crore. Presently, 58 government medical colleges have been approved. 12 more government medical colleges have been proposed besides establishing of dental care facilities in hospitals. The central government will provide central assistance to strengthen the States' Drug Regulatory and Food Regulatory Systems. It will create new drug testing laboratories and strengthen the 31 existing state laboratories. Fifteen model rural health research units shall be set up in states, which shall undertake research on local health issues concerning rural population.

Health for All

Free Drug Policy to be Streamlined: The government has asked for thorough streamlining of systems in the distribution of free generic drugs to health institutions at all levels throughout the country. The Free Drug Programme's formal launch would be preceded by working out all logistical details with respect to procurement and distribution in consultation with the state governments.

The National Health Mission (NHM) (2013) has two components—the National Rural Health Mission (NRHM) and National Urban Health Mission (NUHM). A few, big-city hospitals so far were part of the infrastructure for procurement and distribution but will be extended throughtout the country. The Planning Commission had apportioned sum of Rs 28,560 crore during the 12th Plan period (2012-17) for free generic drug. The Centre would bear 75 per cent of the cost, the states are supposed to contribute 25 per cent. Under the programme, 348 drugs under the National List of Essential Medicines are to be provided free from 1.6 lakh sub-centres, 23,000 primary health centres, 5,000 community health centres and 640 district hospitals. The states have been requested to add some medicines to the Essential List according to their local needs. The department will develop standard treatment protocols in consultation with experts and coded to ensure that unnecessary and irrational administration of drugs is avoided. In this context the Minister reminded that when he was Health Minister of Delhi (1993-98), he had implemented for the first time. The World Health Organisation's "Essential Drug Programme" support to "Delhi Model" (1993-98) accounted the essential from the fluff, and distributed medicines in the public health system. "The NHM will be heavily e-governed to ensure minimum slippage and zero corruption. Agony of poor and middle class families when a member falls ill would be looked into.

Reforms Introduced in NHM

NHM has been in existence since 2005 and two years of the 12th Five-Year Plan have passed. Dr Harsh Vardhan said that it was time to introduce some reforms so that the NHM's reliability and transparency reiterate in Modi government's "Health for All" resolve. A Standing Appraisal Group of Experts would meet frequently to take stock of reports from voluntary sector experts as well as the officials' reactions. NGO heads with proven track record will be invited to be part of the reform process. Women specialists would receive special status in the new scheme of things. "As women are the worst victims of a dysfunctional public health system, their concerns to be addressed on a priority basis. The gender-blind nature of government delivery systems is proving counter-productive", he pointed out.

Institutionalising ASHA

Young women recruited as Accredited Social Health Activists (ASHA) will be important stakeholders. They are yet to get fixed wages. There are many impediments to their smooth functioning, especially ad-hocism and duplication of authority.

Diabetes and Other Focus Areas: International experts have warned that a "diabetes epidemic" is sweeping India. S-Vyasa University, Bangalore, treat diabetes with yoga. The Karnataka Institute of Diabetology and the non-government MV Diabetes Hospital in Chennai extend low-cost diabetes treatment to thousands of people. However, massive awareness about food-intakes changing lifestyle ought to be prioritised. Combating on a war-footing Malaria, Filaria, Encephalitis, Chikungunya, Dengue, TB, Kala Azar, measles, leprosy, would henceforth be components of NHM's sub-missions for rural and urban areas.

Environmental Hazards to Health a Major Concern

Environmental degradation has made the government to tackle ordinary water borne diseases and cancers. A network of capacity building institutions all over India will be modelled on the line of All India Institute of Hygiene and Public Health, Kolkata, and the Centre for Occupational and Environmental Health in Delhi's Maulana Azad Medical College. There is scant information available on the adverse impact on health caused by ecological and environmental deprivation at local, regional and national scale, he stated. The movement of masses and a sizeable population of migrant labourers make this mission difficult without inter-sectoral and inter-state co-ordination, he said. A Management Information System using IT tools would be developed for the benefit of central and state health departments.

Green AIIMS—A Statement of Intent

The Health Minister stated that the new-look AIIMS will have water conservation and waste water recycling systems in place. There must be regular energy audits and a phased renewal plan must be developed. It will safeguard the buildings on the complex more energy efficient. Waste generation including medical waste generation must be subjected to reuse and recycle. A scavenging system to deal with nitrous oxide and other waste anaesthetic gases is the need of the hour. The plantation around the hospital should capture particulate pollution, preventing the harm to the hospitalised patients.

Public Health Institutions

For health infrastructure of India is inadequate to fight the impact of environmental degradation and consequent adverse health outcome. The government has decided to focus on expanding the human resource base. The pyramidal structure of the public health system will soon be equipped with capacities to combat diseases caused by environmental risks. The present health infrastructure is unfortunately inadequate. It needs to quickly develop more trained health workers–whether doctors with post-graduate degree, specialised doctors or nurses or public health engineers – for combating the effects of climate change.

Role of AIIH&PH: All India Institute of Hygiene and Public Health was set up in 1932 in Kolkata with funding from the Rockefeller Foundation, the United States. Plans to set up public health institutes in the six new AIIMS are in different stages of completion. Harvard School of Public Health is already collaborating with two AIIMS at Jodhpur and Raipur for public health activity. The first specialised Centre for Occupational and Environmental Health in a government hospital has been established at the Maulana Azad Medical College. (193-98)

Information is Power

The Union health minister lamented the inadequacy of data hampers the efforts of the health administrators, whether at the centre or in the states to address the emerging environmental health threats that now need urgent attention and proactive approach. A typical case of silicosis has been cited. A disease that has resulted in profound morbidity and mortality but with little information at hand as to its magnitude and size. A man arrives from eastern Uttar Pradesh, finds work in the capital's construction sector and soon gets T.B. and silicosis.

When he gets sick and cannot work anymore then he returns to native place with no one realising the true nature of his health problem. The Health Ministry and its satellites in the states need an institution like the Indian Agricultural Statistics Research Institute. A Management Information System (MIS) using Information Technology tools which would, at the click of a mouse, make available a host of valuable data gleaned from computers at every tier of the health infrastructure.

Bring Back Old Respect to Profession: The Health Ministry will soon roll out initiatives to make a social movement out of the mission to achieve high standards in public health wedded to the priorities of prevention, environmental safeguards and disease control. The respect that we gave to doctors in our childhood is no longer there in the popular perception. This is cause for introspection. Let the new generation of doctors understand that a patient's first interface with a hospital doctor should be good. The short temper of doctors ought to be controlled through proper training. The difference between good and bad behaviour in the doctor-patient interface can often be only a hair's breadth. The senior doctors had to instil in the young generation of doctors better behaviour standards", opines the Helath Minister.

Rape and Abuse Victims Need Sensitive Handling at Hospitals

"A woman who has been raped or subjected to sexual abuse needs more respect than sympathy. It is society's responsibility that she is be rehabilitated with care so that she can overcome her humiliation and move on. The Union Minister said during his recent Bhopal visit. The psychological trauma of a battered woman is greater than the physical pain she undergoes in the aftermath of her being subjected to atrocities. So, it is absolutely unconditional that all those involved in advancing her medico-legal support are sensitised, he bemoaned. He atended "One Stop Crisis Centre" (OSCC) under the aegis of the Jai Prakash Hospital, Bhopal to provide support, care, treatment, security and legal advice to women subjected to atrocities. It is the country's first single window service set up as part of the Madhya Pradesh government's "*Gauravi*" *Mahila Samman Evam Sangrakshan Abhiyaan.* The Chief Minister of Madhya Pradesh, Mr Shivraj Singh Chouhan and Hindi film industry star Aamir Khan were present on the occasion.

"Under the Indian system a battered woman's greatest agony often begins in the police station or in the hospital because of callousness and insensitivity on the part of those responsible for her quest for justice and rehabilitation. I am sure that establishing more OSCC facilities will go a long way to ending this system," said Harsh Vardhan.

Central OSCC System Soon

The Health Minister announced an advisory to all central hospitals and to the state governments to set up OSCC-like institutions under the roofs. These could enforce a tight protocol for the benefit of victims, he believed. He said the hospital authorities will be given special training on how to deal with the physical and psychological needs of a victim of abuse. While specific rules and protocols exist there is no drive to enforce, he said. Resultantly, even the rule banning two-finger tests on rape victims is ignored, and punitive clauses will be introduced to ensure the hospital staff disobey the protocol be suspended. The havoc of encephalitis continues in Muzaffarpur (Bihar) and 42 children have died so far. The 13 children affected with encephalitis were admitted in PMCH's child department, of whom four succumbed to the disease and rest are struggling for life. Asha workers and anganwadi workers have been assigned the duty to impart information about encephalitis. They will go door to door distributing ORS packets, and distributing pamphlets about the diseases, its prevention and cure. The district collector will monitor whether the awareness programme is being carried.

Sex Education should not be Vulgar

Sex education is necessary for school students but it should not be vulgar by any means. The PIB website put up the minister's statement. The statement read, "He is a medical professional who has embraced rationalism and I wholeheartedly support pedagogy that is scientific and culturally acceptable. Anything abrasive to common sensibilities and articulated as such by responsible persons should be discarded and replaced by consensually accepted learning processes." He further said that his remarks were made in context of the UPA government's 2007 decision to introduce the Adolescence Education Programme (AE) in its original form. The statement further read, "Crudity and graphic representation of culturally objectionable symbols as manifested in the UPA's so-called sex education programme cannot be called sex education. Every education system must strive to have an ideal curriculum and to that extent my stand is valid." In the 'vision document' for Delhi, the minister had said that states must integrate value education with course content. They must put strong emphasis on exposing students to India's cultural relations. Yoga education should be made compulsory, he wondered.

Need to Revitalise Social Sector

Gujarat Model: In social sector and upliftment of poor, the government of Gujarat has made special efforts to see that benefits reach the concerned beneficiaries. It is a fundamental point. Because, the beneficial schemes if it remains on paper without reaching the targetted beneficiaries then it is useless. By decentralising the state's administrative power through a milestone yojana to extend the benefits to the right people concerned. The State government recognises it as Aapno Taluko, Vibrant Taluko (ATVT). This is Gujarat government's efforts to reach the remotest areas and bring the government to the doorstep. Jan Seva Kendras equipped with computers have been set up in every taluka with GSWAN connectivity. Different kinds of applications numbering 129 are accepted at these Kendras. This revolutionary experiment is being implemented by district collectors and a team of newly appointed pranth officers. The benefits of ATVT government schemes reach to urban poor without any problem. For getting solution of every problem, the government has approached with far sightedness and political will. A concrete plan has been visualised for providing homes to urban poor under the Garib Samriddhi yojana. Gujarat is the only state in the country that has provided housing plots to BPL families which come within the 0-16 parameter. A sum of Rs 13,000 crore funds has been established for the welfare of urban poor. Under *Ummed* programme about two lakh youths have registered themselves and one lakh youth will be given skill development training for generating employment opportunities within one year.

Rural Development

Pradhan Mantri Gram Sadak Yojana: Pradhan Mantri Gram Sadak Yojana initiated during the NDA-I under the stewardship of Prime Minister Atal Behari Vajpayee has had a massive impact in improvement of access for rural population. PMGSY under the dynamic leadership of Prime Minister Narendra Modi has been earmarked a sum of Rs 14,389 crore.

National Livelihood Mission: Ajeevika, the National Rural Livelihood Mission (NRLM), aims to eliminate rural poverty through sustainable livelihood options. Under this mission, Women SHGs are provided bank loans at 4 per cent on prompt repayment in 150 districts and at 7 per cent in all other districts. SHGS in hundred more districts will be established and Rs 100 crore has been earmarked for this.

Rural Housing: The Rural Housing Scheme has benefited a large percentage of rural population, who have availed credit through Rural Housing Fund (RHF). National Housing Bank (NHB) will fetch Rs 8000 crore (2014-15) to natonal rural housing.

Watershed Development: To give an added impetus to watershed development in the country, Finanace Minister proposes to start a new programme called "Neeranchal" with an initial outlay of Rs 2,142 crore in the current financial year.

Panchayati Raj: Backward Region Grant Fund (BRGF) is being implemented in 272 backward districts in 27 States. The building of Panchayats/ Gram Sabhas in backward areas. It is proposed to restructure the BRGF to address intra-district inequalities to ensure that backward sub-districts units within States receive adequate support.

Safe Drinking Water: The drinking water sources acros the country have excess impurities like flouride, arsenic and manmade contaminations. It owes to untreated sewage, industrial effluents and leaching of pesticides and fertilizers. It is proposed to earmark Rs 3,600 crore under National Rural Drinking Water Programme for providing safe drinking water in approximately 20,000 habitations affected with arsenic, fluoride, heavy/toxic elements, pesticides/fertilisers through community water purification plants in next three years.

Children—the Future of the Nation

"There can be no keener revelation of a society's soul than the way in which it treats its children."

—Nelson Mandela

Indicators related to children welfare are an indicator of the progress of the nation, be it health, education or safety of children. The government is committed to address the issues related to children, like malnutrition and under-nutrition, problem of child labour, child-trafficking and missing children, sexual abuse, school dropouts and the increasing crime rate among juveniles have made policy makers worried. Lay special emphasis on vulnerable children and especially those belonging to the vulnerable communities like SCs, STs, OBCs, migrants, slum dwellers, street dwellers and those with disabilities. Ensure effective implementation of the Right to Education, Right to Food Security Act.

Senior Citizens

The government is committed to the welfare of senior citizens. Appropriate steps will be taken for their security and health care. The government will provide financial support, exploring ideas like additional tax benefits and higher interest rates. Invest in setting up and improving old-age homes. Harness their experience in the National Interest. Devise schemes and programmes to engage the senior citizens as volunteers/part time workers in various development programmes of the government, in urban and rural areas. This will not only help in utilising their time, but also it would be an effective utilisation of their experience and may add an additional source of income for them.

Specially Abled

About 70 million people are suffering from disability. The welfare and rehabilitation of disabled people is integral to the vision of a responsive government. The government commits to enact the 'Rights of the Persons with

Disabilities bill' (RPWD). Use technology to deliver low-cost quality education to specially-abled students 'in-home'–through.

E-learning: The government will identify each and every special needs person across the country to establishing a web-based disability registration system. It will issue universal ID for all applicable government benefits (health care, transportation, jobs, education etc). It will ensure disabled-friendly access to public facilities, public buildings and transport. Ensure maximum economic independence of the disabled by creating more income generation models. Support and aid voluntary organisations working for the care of the disabled and provide a higher tax relief for the family member taking care of the disabled.

Youth - Making India Unstoppable

The Prime Minister feels the younger generation is the new hope of the nation. Will young men respond to the call of the nation? Each one of youngman has a glorious future if he/she dares to believe in the present government. PM Modi has a tremendous faith in yourselves, like the faith he had when he was a child, and which he is working out now.

'*Have that faith, each one of you, in yourself-that eternal power is lodged in every soul-and you will revive the whole of the country.*'

— Swami Vivekananda.

The govt considers youth as the most productive asset of the nation who have played a key role in taking the country to a near double digit growth. All sectors dominated by youth are doing exceptionally well. The government will initiate nation-wide 'district level incubation and accelerator programme' for encouraging innovation and entrepreneurship among youth. Suitable steps will be taken to avail affordable student's loans. It will set up neighbourhood Children's/Youth Parliament across India that leads to vibrant student committees and will launch a programme, 'Youth for Development'.

Women - The Nation Builder

The ruling government recognises the important role of women in development of the society and growth of the nation, and remains committed to give a high priority to Women's Empowerment and welfare. All the BJP-ruled states have demonstrated this through various schemes. The government recognises the need for women's security as a precondition to women's empowerment and will undertake the following for women welfare steps.

Crisis Management Centre for women will be set up at Delhi; money from Nirbhaya fund will be utilised for it. Rs 98,030 crore announced for women welfare. The goverment has announced Rs 100 crore funds for Beti Bachao, Beti Bachao Yojana. Safety of women will be of prime importance. Women's welfare and development will be accorded a high priority at all levels within the government, and the government is committed to 33 per cent reservation in parliamentary and state assemblies through a constitutional amendment.

Beti Bachao – Beti Padhao— Structure a comprehensive scheme, incorporating best practices from past successes like Balika Samruddhi, Ladli Laxmi and Chiranjeevi Yojana to mobilise positive attitude amongst families towards the girl child. The government will launch programme on women healthcare in a mission mode, especially focussing on domains of Nutrition and Pregnancy with emphasis on rural, SCs, STs and OBCs.

It will enable women with training and skills setting up dedicated Women ITIs, Women wings in other ITIs. Strict implementation of laws related to women, particularly those related to rape. Fund for relief and rehabilitation of rape victims lies unused at the Centre as the Government has not worked out the modalities of dispensation and will clear this on priority. The government will create an Acid Attack victims welfare fund to take care of the medical costs related to treatment and cosmetic reconstructive surgeries. It will make police stations women-friendly, and increase the number of women in police at different levels and introduce self-defence as a part of the school curriculum.

By using information technology for women's safety and set up an All Women Mobile Bank to cater to women. Apart from this, the government will set up special skills training and business Incubator Park for women. It will set up special business facilitation centre for women. It will expand and improve upon the network of women/working women hostels. It will set up a dedicated W-SME (Women Small and medium enterprises) cluster in every district. It will review the working conditions and enhance the remuneration of Anganwadi worker's.

The government will remove any remaining gender disparities in property rights, marital rights and cohabitation rights. Special adult literacy initiative would be commenced for women with focus on SCs, STs, OBCs, and slum residents. It will extend loans to Women Self-Help Groups at low interest rates. Special programmes aimed at girls below poverty line, tribals and indigent women. Appropriate measures would be taken to check female foeticide, dowry, child marriage, trafficking, sexual harassment, rape and family violence. The government will transform the quality of life of women in Rural India by providing electricity, tapped water, cleaner fuel and toilets in every home.

SCs, STs, OBCs and Other Weaker Sections

The government will follow the principles of *Samajik Nyay* (social justice) and *Samajik Samrasata* (social harmony). This social justice must be further complemented with economic justice and political empowerment. Instead of pursuing identity politics and tokenisms, it will focus on empowering the deprived sections of society. Steps will be taken to create an enabling ecosystem of equal opportunity for education, health and livelihood.

A high priority for SC, ST, OBCs and other weaker sections would be given. Eradication of untouchability and manual scavenging besides it will look at more effective ways to pull these people out of the poverty line. It will ensure the funds allocated for schemes and programmes for SC, ST, OBCs and other weaker sections are utilised properly. A mission mode project would be made for housing, education, and health and skills development. Special focus would be on the children, especially the girl child, with regards to health, education and skills development.

Tribal development will be one of the focus areas. Govt. believes that half-hearted, incremental and piecemeal attempts for the development of tribals have not helped. The government is commited to make a comprehensive, all-encompassing long-term strategy to empower tribals and ensure their welfare. Gujarat, Madhya Pradesh and Chhattisgarh have successfully implemented the tribal welfare and development schemes and their model. The government will initiate a *'Van Bandhu Kalyan Yojna'* at the national level to be overseen by a 'Tribal Development Authority'. This scheme will focus on:

- Set up the entire education network for tribals;
- Upgrade housing, water and health facilities;
- Electrify tribal hamlets and provide of all weather roads;
- Initiate new economic activities;
- Promoting products associated with the tribal culture by setting tribal haats in tourist towns and
- Other centres. Facilitating access to minor forest produce and creating a network of rural haats (markets).

Drinking Water and Sanitation

Centre Asks States to Ready Contingency Plan for Water Supply: The Centre has asked the states to prepare a contingency plan on drinking water supply. The country is trailing through the drought-like situation arising out of deficit monsoon. According to a private forecasting agency, the national cumulative average for rainfall in June is deficient by a whopping 42 per cent. India had the 12th instance in the past 113 years when her shortfall has been over 30 per cent. States like Gujarat and Rajasthan face an over 80 per cent rainfall deficit. The government has been monitoring the water supply situation in the states "very closely". These plans will be available in the public domain, he added. Centre has urged the states to give this objective the "top priority".

Nearly 90 per cent of the rural water supply comes from groundwater sources. Their recharge, depend on rainfall, canals, surface water bodies, irrigated fields, water conservation structures. Data released by the World Bank states that India is the largest consumer of groundwater in the world with an estimated usage of 230 cusecs per year. Approximately 60 per cent of the demand for agriculture and irrigation and 80 per cent of domestic water needs is met through groundwater, says World Bank.

13 Education, Employment and Job Opportunities

Introduction

Education is the most powerful tool for the advancement of nation and the most potent weapon to fight poverty. Education in India needs to be revitalised and reorganised to make future generations proud of their culture, heritage and history. Every effort shall be made to ensure 'equality of opportunity in access and success' to all learners; creating a harmonious, and cohesive egalitarian society that practices democratic values. This would be possible only when education accords due emphasis on national integration, social cohesion, religious amity, national identity and patriotism. It must also be analysed how far education has contributed to moral, ethical and humanistic values in the individuals and the society. Education must create minds free from superstitions, hatred and violence and become an important vehicle to cement national unity, social cohesion and religious amity. The government desires to inculcate moral, ethical and humanistic values in the individuals and the society. India has to become a knowledge society. She has to reverberate with educated skilled manpower of high standards required to meet the challenges of 21st century. This requires a bold and visionary leadership to introduce appropriate policy and structural changes. Highest priority would be given to address the acute shortage of teachers and researchers, quality of education and research, and the employability factor associated with most of the courses. Education should not only lead to employability; but also job creation and entrepreneurship in introducing a national multi-skills orientation programme.

Gujarat Model in Education

Employment and education go hand in hand. The state government has done a lot to bring children within the ambit of primary education and access the fruits of development. The state education minister is taking care that the kids are enrolled at schools and continue with their studies whether they belong to rural or urban areas. The government provided free textbooks, notebooks. It is a matter of pride that the drop out rate in Gujarat has drastically come down in the last decade. Class I to V drop out ratio has fallen from 20.93 per cent to 2.09 per cent. Class I to VII drop out ratio is down from 39 per cent to 7.45 per cent.

Youths Access to Higher Education

In 2001, we had only eleven universities. Today, there are thirty-nine universities in Gujarat. The state government opened many world class universities towards training youth. It is not just opening new universities that are important, but specialised world-class universities such as Petroleum University, Sports University, Raksha Shatki University and Forensic Science University have also been set up. About 52 colleges have been started with new courses. In the tribal belt there are 35 colleges now functioning. For the first time in the country, a Children's University has been set up and a Commission for Education Innovation had been started. A Gujarat Knowledge Society has been providing employment opportunity to the youth of Gujarat.

A Few Simple Lessons

To Get the Education Agenda Right: The prime minister's 10-point agenda indicates seriousness about education targets even as his government will be acting under the weight of not just a national emergency in education but also pent up hopes and aspirations of a whole generation of young people. The latter are thirsting for access to quality education. It is imperative that the new HRD minister Smriti Irani acts with boldness speed and vision. The government needs radically big leaps. So, what should the new government do? Five key things, is the answer:

Allow Private Capital in Education: For decades, limited supply of schools due to self-imposed constraints on volumes by keeping private investment out of education. Estimates suggest that if private capital is allowed to participate in education, it can unleash investment of over Rs 10,000 crore over the next one year: equivalent of building 1,000 new schools.

It has taken about 60 years to create 1,200 odd Kendriya Vidyalaya schools. The argument for private investment in education makes sense. Allowing bodies, whether for profit or not-for-profit, to set up educational institutions, will overnight create an investment environment. It can attract capital, not just from India but all over the world. It is not unthinkable to assume that $ 5-6 billion of investment could flow into India in the medium term. This kind of capital will change the face of Indian education. It wil provide us the "big leap" to make up for decades of underinvestment in education.

Introduce a Reformist Regulator: The education sector in India is beset by multiple, conflicting, parallel and in many cases, superfluous regulation. A licensing-based approach to education seeks to perpetuate mediocrity and limit education choices. A regulator will put in guidelines to regulate quality. He won't have a fixed asset/input based approach to education quality. He will rather talk about teacher training, qualifications, results, accreditation, and industry-academia relationship, continuing education for professors, curriculum, innovation and research. It would be a completely different vocabulary for education transformation.

Allow Foreign Education on Shore: It sounds silly that we would be okay with Indian students spending over $ 4 billion in foreign universities rather than permitting joint ventures and collaborations and the opening of foreign institutions in India. To allay fears of an over-run, such conditions can be put in place like compulsory local equity to the extent of either 50 per cent or more for the first three years, not dissimilar to the regulations that are put in place for telecom or insurance. We should do away with restrictions or repatriation, recognition of foreign degrees.

Take Indian Education Global: It is strange to know that an estimated 25 per cent of professors in leading universities globally and a similar percentage of the student population are Indian. The "education transaction" between teacher and student, both Indians, is being carried out abroad rather than here in the country. To correct this anomaly, we must create a mindset for our institutions. It enables them globally competitive and starts targeting world students first. We must give our existing universities a direct incentive or cash credit for attracting non-Indian students. The more foreign students we get into India, the more credibility of Indian education would be established worldwide. Academics will come back to India and Indian students won't pursue abroad for quality education. Under public-private-partnership initiatives, the government needs to encourage education rather than run educational institutions directly. So, it should better invest resources in PPP ventures and bring in credible private sector partners. A buoyant capital market and a robust FDI regime is the right ecosystem. It will attract serious capital to set up and running educational institutions. The HRD ministry has set eight top priorities to herald a new beginning in education sector which holds the key to country's progress.

1. *Right to Education:* The Vajpayee government had made education a fundamental right. The first task should be to help states funded so that trained and qualified teachers are recruited. Allocation for education must go up by at least six per cent of GDP.
2. *Jobless Educated Youth:* To make education job-friendly courses should be planned in right way. Bulk of the new jobs will be in industry (manufacturing, particularly) and in the services sector. We need to produce an army of skilled personnel through private sector participation.
3. *Government must Allow Entry of Foreign Universities:* Even if Ivy Leaguers are not interested initially, many A-grade institutions like Carltech and Duke are keen. A bill is pending in the Parliament about the role of foreign universities. Once legislation is in place, FDI could flow. Already, 100 per cent FDI is allowed.
4. *Feasibility of IITs/IIMs:* IITs should be asked to reorient towards research. It has become a factory producing engineers. IIMs should be given deemed university status. It will facilitate genuine research in the fast changing economy. The situation cells for more IITs/IIMs by keeping their autonomy intact.

5. *Sarva Shiksha Abhiyan:* The vehicle of RTE should be recast. Top priority should be given to teaching English with social values, etiquette language intricacies, and tackle challenge for learning foreign language.
6. *Mid-day Meal Mission:* HRD ministry needs to get into a mission mode to ensure hygienic food reach children. Cook-cum-helpers should be given better and regular remuneration.
7. *6,000 Quality District Level Schools:* The government should make district level establish 6,000 quality-oriented schools with qualified teachers and syllabus bridging urban-rural divide.
8. *The Huge Gap between Central and State Universities Needs to be Bridged:* In this regard, UPA's *Rashtriya Uchchatar Shiksha Abhiyan* should be bolstered. This is the first time that Centre is doing something for state universities. Initial response of states has been positive.

The goverment intends to review and revise education system. It should pay attention to salary structure associated with the teaching staff and address the shortfall of faculty. The system shall be made people-friendly restoring its credibility. Investment in education yields the best dividend. Public spending on education could be raised to 6 per cent of the GDP. It sould involve the private sector. Under the scheme of 'Quality education for all', the new government at the Centre sould takes the following steps:

1. The government proposes to set up Center of Excellence in MP named after Lok Nayak Jai Prakash Narayan.
2. It will set up four AIIMS - in Andhra Pradesh, West Bengal, Vidarbha and Purvanchal and earmarked Rs 500 crore.
3. It will set up five IITs, five IIMs, four AIIMS, 12 medical colleges, 2 agriculture universities.
4. The budgetary allocation to Ministry of HRD for various schemes has been increased by 17 per cent to Rs 65, 877 crore. Further, service tax exemption has been granted for institutes offering vocational courses.
5. Under the total budgetary allocation, Rs 272.58 billion has been allocated for Sarva Shiksha Abhiyan, Rs 39.83 billion for Rashtriya Madhyamik Shiksha Abhiyan, Rs 52.84 billion for scholarships and remaining for up-gradation of existing universities.
6. Rs 100 crore for virtual classrooms (e-learning). Conduct new teacher training programmes.
7. Revive Beti Bachao scheme: Rs 100 crore set aside for it.
8. National Centre of Humanities will be set up in Madhya Pradesh.
9. Rs 100 crore for modernisation of Madrasas.

Boost for Education

To make education a powerful tool to fight poverty is a good step. Government's intent to 'revitalise and reorganise' the curriculum has met with scepticism. If the Modi government's assurance of fulfilling the promises made in the election manifesto is anything to go by, then the education sector, right from the primary level, is in for a revamp. The manifesto describes education as the "most powerful tool" for the advancement of the nation and the "most potent weapon" to fight poverty. Modi government has the intent to strengthen education for all, provide modern education for minorities, improve higher education through the setting up of new IITs and IIMs and give a fillip to research. The government announced the scrapping of the four-year undergraduate programme of Delhi University kept the government on its feet.

The government's desire to revitalise and reorganise curriculum could make future generations proud of their culture, heritage and history. However, non-governmental organisations such as the *Shiksha Bachao Andolan Samiti* seeking rewriting of textbooks kept the government on the back foot as concerns are being expressed about the authenticity of the content. The government tries to prevent the alleged "saffronisation" of education from dominating the discourse. The spotlight is also on issues that need immediate attention. For instance, with 6,06,191 teacher's posts lying vacant at the primary level both in the state sector and under the *Sarva Shiksha Abhiyan*, the government has its task cut out.

There is faculty shortage in institutes of higher learning, even the IITs. Paucity of funds for research and disconnect between the industry and the education sector needed immediate attention. Training the teachers is yet another area that needs reforms, as does the enhancement of teacher-student ratio. The policy-makers believe the link between education for the youth and employment code for skill development. The programmes ought to produce an employable workforce. India's growing need for skilled professionals will have to be addressed. Some five lakh skilled workers are needed over the next 10 years. The sectors included aviation, food processing, automobiles and healthcare. The percentage of skilled workers in India is just 6.7 per cent as compared to China's 50 per cent and European Union's 75 per cent.

School Education

Sarva Shiksha Abhiyan: the government will set up new mechanism for its performance audit and to have real time information about its performance. Programme shall be strengthened and expanded with a goal to remove illiteracy. Universalisation of secondary school education and skills development through functional school with particular focus on rural, tribal and difficult areas must be pursued. The content and process of school education shall be thoroughly reviewed to make it dynamic, stress-free, attractive and responsive to the emerging national needs. Girls shall be extended possible help to continue and complete school education. The digital divide shall not separate them in learning process. Special pedagogy sould be developed for differently-abled students. On priority, a national modernisation programme for madrasa's could be started. Mid-day meal scheme would be revitalised in terms of management and delivery. Use state-of-the-art technology for education as a mission mode project. A national e-Library should empower school teachers and students. A multi-country student exchange programme should broade the horizon of school going children. Creative talents of students should be recognised and encouraged.

Higher and Professional Education

The Department of Higher Education is responsible for the overall development of the basic infrastructure of Higher Education sector. Under a planned development process, the Department looks after the expansion of access and qualitative improvement in the Higher Education, through world class Universities, Colleges and other Institutions.

Objectives of the department of higher education:

1. *Vision:* To realise India's human resource potential to its optimum level with equity and inclusion.
2. *Mission:* Avail opportunities of access to Higher Education with equity to eligible persons, and in particular to the vulnerable sections.

Expand access by supporting existing institutions, establishing new institutions, supporting state governments and NGOs/civil society to supplement public efforts aimed at removing regional or other imbalances that exist at present. Initiate policies and programmes for strengthening research and innovations and encourage institutions—public or private—to engage in stretching the frontiers of knowledge. Promote the quality of Higher Education by investing in infrastructure and faculty, promoting academic reforms, improving governance and institutional restructuring toward the inclusion of hitherto deprived communities.

Objectives: To expand the Higher Education sector in all is modes of delivery to increase the Gross Enrolment Ratio (GER) in Higher Education to 15 per cent by 2011-12 to 21 per cent by 2016-17 and 30 per cent by the year 2020.

To expand institutional base of Higher Education (including technical, professional and vocational education) by creating additional capacity in existing institutions, establishing new institutions and incentivising State Governments and Non-Governmental Organisations/civil society. To expand institutional base of Higher Education (including technical, professional and vocational education) by creating additional capacity in existing institutions, establishing new institutions and incentivising State Governments and Non-Governmental Organisations/civil society. To avail opportunities to socially-deprived communities and remove disparities by promoting the inclusion of women, minorities and differently-abled persons.

To remove regional imbalances in access to Higher Education by setting up of institutions in unnerved and underserved areas. To enhance plan support for infrastructure and faculty development in the institutions of higher learning and to attract talent towards careers in teaching and research. To create conditions for knowledge generation through improved research facilities in universities and colleges. To promote collaboration with International community, foreign governments, universities/institutions and regional and international institutions, for the advancement of universal knowledge and intellectual property rights. To promote development of Indian languages. To promote autonomy, innovations, academic reforms in institutions of higher learning. To undertake institutional restructuring for improving efficiency, relevance and creativity in higher education.

Functions: Enhancement of Gross Enrolment Ratio by expanding access through all modes. Promoting the participation of these sections of the society whose GER is lower than the national average. To improve quality and to promote academic reforms. Setting up of new educational institutions and also capacity expansion and improvement of the existing institutions. Use of Technology in Higher Education. Development of Vocational Education and Skill Development. Development of Indian Languages. International Collaboration in the field of education. The basic objective of higher and professional education is not only rapid advancement of the affluent sector of the society, but also to improve the lot of the last man at large. The content should be designed to prepare the students to understand the current challenges and equip themselves to be able to readily adjust in a fast changing global scenario. Policy interventions would include:

> Enhancing the pivotal role of teachers by reworking the work culture for committed performance. Ooptimum utilisation of physical and manpower resources. Instituting for interface between industry (including SME), academia and community.

Needs assessment exercise will be done for identifying future needs across sectors to meet manpower requirement. Retain autonomy to ensure accountability for institutions of higher learning. The standard of education and research should be at par with the top global universities. Restoring the credibility of the regulatory bodies. The procedures to make appointments to senior positions shall be made transparent. Merit and ability shall be the sole criterion in recruiting academia. UGC will be restructured. It will be transformed into a Higher Education Commission. A nod from policy makers, institutions, and stake holders is on hold.

School Education: Elementary education is one of the major priorities of the government. There is a residual gap in providing minimal school infrastructure facilities. Government would strive to provide toilets and drinking water in all the girls' school in first phase. A sum of Rs 28,635 crore has been earmarked for Sarva Shiksha Abhiyan and Rs 4,966 crore for Rashtriya Madhyamik Shiksha Abhiyan. A School Assessment Programme is being initiated at a cost of Rs 30 crore. To infuse new training tools and motivate teachers, "Pandit Madan Mohan Malviya New Teachers Training Programme" a sum of Rs 500 crore has been proposed. To take advantage of the reach of the IT, a sum of Rs 100 crore is earmarked for setting up virtual classrooms as Communication Linked Interface for Cultivating Knowledge (CLICK) and online courses.

Higher Education: The country needs a large number of Centres of higher learning which are world class. The Finance Minister proposes to set up Jai Prakash Narayan National Centre for Excellence in Humanities in Madhya Pradesh. It intends to set up five more IITs in the Jammu, Chattisgarh, Goa, Andhra Pradesh and Kerala. Five IIMs would be set up in the States of Himachal Pradesh, Punjab, Bihar, Odisha and Maharashtra. A sum of Rs 500 crore has been earmakred.

HRDMin to Set up Eight new IITs

The HRD ministry is pushing hard for funds to quickly set up at least eight new IITs, and has already met the finance minister for funds, after bureaucrats said it would be a huge challenge to find money, land and faculty for this.

A Central university for Himalayan Technology and a national e-library are on the cards. Kerala, Karnataka, Jharkhand, Uttarakhand, Goa, Sikkim and Chhattisgarh—the states that do not have an IIT — would benefit from this proposal. The number of IITs in the country was doubled to 16 in 2009. The new ones are facing challenges such as fund crunch. About Rs 12,500 crore were allocated for the IITs in the 12th Five-year Plan (2012-17). A little over Rs 6,000 crore is set aside for the eight IITs set up in 2009. However, given rising costs, the fund requirement for new IITs, many of which are yet to operate from their permanent campuses, has more than doubled to Rs 14,000 crore.

HRD officials believe embarking on an expensive exercise of setting up as eight new IITs would not be feasible. Some of the new IITs were operating out of make-shift campuses, as land was unavailable. In some cases, construction and infrastructure development has been delayed.

Digital India: There is an imminent need to further bridge the divide between digital "haves" and "have-nots". It has been proposed to launch a pan India programme "Digital India". This would ensure broad band connectivity at village level, improved access to services through IT enabled platforms, greater transparency in government processes and increased indigenous production of IT hardware and software for exports and improved domestic availability. Special focus would be on supporting software product startups. A National Rural Internet and Technology Mission for services in villages and schools, training in IT skills and E-Kranti for government service delivery and governance scheme is proposed. The Finanace Minister has provided a sum of Rs 500 crore for this purpose. A programme for promoting "Good Governance" would be launched on a sum of Rs 100 crore and a sum of Rs 500 crore for the mission-digial India.

Beti Bachao, Beti Padhao: The government has unleashed a flurry of schemes to educate, empower and protect women and the girl child and to sensitise people to gender equality. The scheme 'Beti Bachao, Beti Padhao Yojana' focusses on generating awareness and better delivery of welfare services which has been earmarked for Rs 100 crore.

The government desires to focus on campaigns to sensitise people towards concerns of the girl child and women, even initiating a separate chapter on gender mainstreaming in the school curriculum. A special small savings instrument will address demands of education and marriage of girls will be introduced. A sum of Rs 1,000 crore Nirbhaya fund helps intensify include provision of GPRS and CCTVs in buses, panic button alert to transport and police through visual, text and voice and setting up of crisis management centres across the country.

The Quality of India's Higher Education

China has recognised the crucial importance of retaining high quality scholars and research institutions, It has adequately funded and resourced to compete with the world's best. It is making a concerted effort to entice the best of its overseas researchers back. It has been offering them exciting work conditions. It has guaranteed their right of exit and re-entry. They can keep up their scholarly connections with the world's best universities.

The average quality of India's higher education has been falling steadily behind the world average. We may be outsourcing our brains. We are far from educating them to maximum potential. There is something rotten in the state of higher education and research when overseas Indians can hold almost 30,000 patents for every one held by an Indian. Tsinghua in China n comparison has 4,600 faculties for 26,500 students, including 5,000 Ph.D candidates.

Most Westerners frankly disbelieve when told that the government appoints vice chancellors. How many bright Indian undergraduates aim for the higher education sector as their profession of choice as opposed to last resort, after the civil services, private sector, journalism, etc.?

Ideas matter. They impart vitality to a society. Universities are the marketplace of ideas. Groups may vanquish rivals through superior skills in warfare. The long-term success of the civilisations and countries is due. More often, it access the dynamism and vibrancy of ideas steady ascendancy over competing visions of the good life. A society in intellectual ferment is fertile ground for progress and advancement, provided the clash of ideas is given free play. Conversely, a society that is bereft of, and represses, new ideas is a society doomed to stagnation. Education and scholarship provide the terrain on which intellectually arid and stagnant societies encounter new worlds of ideas from foreign cultures.

The process of transformation of large and complex societies creates social ferment, disorder, dislocation, volatility, and sometimes even conflict. The comments apply to international society as well. Universities are often under siege precisely. They are at the forefront of the struggle for social and economic transformation. A university, is a repository of scholarship, is dedicated to teaching and research in the spirit of free and critical inquiry. Tolerance of diversity, and a commitment to resolution of difference of opinion through dialogue and debate glory the process. That is, to the acquisition, criticism, and transmission of knowledge from one generation to the next and to being a centre of creative and innovative learning.

University qualifications are the gateway to social mobility. It will be so far an increasingly meritocratic-technocratic society. The concomitant emphases on equitable and affordable access to quality education. Social classes and groups produce an explosion in the number of tertiary students. In an information society and world, the comparative advantage of the higher education sector lies in its identity. It will be the custodian and manager of knowledge-based networks. It will endorse global mandate and reach. Owing to frequent changes under the impact of globalisation, universities across the world are being forced to change. They became bureaucratic and risk-averse to agile and market-responsive institutions. They used to be hierarchical, governed by religious rules, subject to religious authority. Some were interested in religious scholarship amidst an essentially feudal society. Buffeted by broader social changes, universities have been transformed through:

Any significant lessening of the scale of changes in the university sector is unson in the near future. It belongs to the practical management innovation, creativity, flexibility, and entrepreneurship. Suggest new mix-and-match modes of governance, operation, financing or internal structures. The challenge however is to maintain international competitiveness. Indian universities are falling behind in the global marketplace of ideas. This is true for sciences frailties. it is embarrassingly true about the arts and social sciences. India lags not just on global but on Asian benchmarks. China in particular has made efforts to upgrade its elite institutions. It is impressive to find Beijing ranked 14th in the world and Tsinghua 28th. The first Indian universities to appear on the list are the IITs, at number 57, followed by the IIMs at number 68. There are nine Asian universities outside of China, Hong Kong, and Japan in the top 200, compared to a meagre three Indian. The Jawaharlal Nehru University, New Delhi, just squeaks in joint 183rd, while its equivalent Australian counterpart, the Australian National University, ranks 16th. Few Indians, even among academics, are likely to know about he position. Yet Indian universities ranks 79th in the world: more than twice as high as JNU. Globalisation creates winners and losers in education. It is so in trade, investment, and economic growth. Talent is in great demand in the global marketplace. Universities are becoming a major source of service exports, where talents and enterprise Speak out. The regulation and undervalued social status and economic incentives (for example promotions based primarily on seniority of service), as in India, are the source rather than destination for internationally mobile students. Indian students flood American, Australian, British, and Canadian universities. They pay huge fees that could otherwise fund significant upgrade in the quality of higher education. India ought to invest heavily in higher education as the pivot of modern-day knowledge management. Else one will be mere feeder stations in one-way educational traffic to international destinations. Education is expensive, the alternative is much costlier.

Foreign Varsities could be in India

The Minister has decided to focus on a legal framework for allowing foreign universities. It will curb unfair practices by existing education institutions as part of the human resources ministry's legislative agenda. In doing so, the minister hopes to address the questions of increasing access and improving quality of higher education institutions. "The Foreign Education Providers Bill and the Prohibition of Unfair Practices Bill are on her priority list. We will have to go through the entire process — circulating a cabinet note, discussions with the legislative department, then cabinet approval, then vetting by the standing committee, before the Bill can be taken up for discussion and passage by Parliament," claims an official of the department.

"We don't know for sure whether these can be completed in the course of the Budget session, but these bills are on the priority." The legislative measures were initiated by the previous Congress-led government, but fell off the government's legislative priority agenda in the face of political opposition, some of it from within the ruling coalition partners. The country doen't have legal and regulatory framework allowing foreign universities on Indian soil, despite efforts by the previous government.

The department decided in September 2013 to take the executive order route to open the doors for the top 400 institutions to set up campuses in the country, and award degrees, giving Indian students the opportunity to study in global institutions without leaving home or spending a fortune in dollars oversea. The proposed UGC (Establishment and Operation of Campuses of Foreign Educational Institutions) Rules required that foreign education providers set up the India campuses as not-for-profit companies, that is companies set up under Section 25 of the old Companies Act (Section 8 of the new one). The proposal had the support of the Department of Industrial Policy and Promotion besides the department of Economic Affairs.

However, the regulations were never ratified. There is a need to improve the protection available to students against fly-by-night operators and other malpractices. The intent of the legislation is to uphold legal basis to curtail profiteering in higher education institutions as well as ensure their accountability by making it mandatory for them disclose information related to admission process.

DU Agrees to Roll Back FYUP

The showdown between DU and UGC over the four-year-undergraduate programme (FYUP)—which had held up this year's DU admissions—has finally ended with the university's administration conceding defeat. Vice-chancellor Dinesh Singh, who had kept a low profile in the past few days, issued a statement announcing that FYUP would be rolled back. The mood on campus immediately changed, with heated protests giving way to raucous celebrations. A meeting of college principals, convened to deal with the deadlock, was cut short and they were summoned to the VC's office for admission-related instructions.

A 12-member committee of principals has been created to facilitate admissions as per the three-year structure, indicating that the DU administration has completely handed over even the responsibility of conducting admissions to the colleges. UGC also stated that it would not micro-manage the admissions. UGC had outright rejected the DU registrar's letter stating that the university was actively considering a "blended proposal". The commission told DU in no uncertain terms that it would have to comply with its order to restore the three-year structure. The registrar of DU writes to UGC, "The University is in the process of drafting a response in accordance with the spirit of your directives to ensure the admission process soon." Given the June 23 fiasco over Singh's 'resignation'—there were contradictory reports about whether or not he had quit even as the VC himself maintained a studied silence—protesters remained uncertain about the fate of FYUP.

However, the campus erupted in celebration after the DU administration released Singh's statement saying, "The University of Delhi recognises the need of the hour. It is of paramount importance to protect the interest of students by ensuring admission process. In line with the directive of the UGC the university has decided to roll back the FYUP. Consequently, the admission process shall be conducted under the scheme of courses that were in force in the academic session 2012-13 in all the colleges of the University of Delhi. It is expected that the principals of our colleges shall assist in devising and ensuring a speedy completion of the admission process." The brief statement ended a two-year battle that has raged within DU over FYUP.

Students Celebrate: Meanwhile, the meeting of the college principals' association at Indraprastha College was stopped and a delegation called to meet the VC. After the meeting, the registrar issued a statement saying, "The VC has appointed a committee of principals, which will devise the modalities for admissions, advise and monitor admission-related issues in colleges so that the process of admissions to the undergraduate courses for 2014-15 is completed in the shortest possible time and in a smooth manner.

UGC: 4-year B.Tech for 2013 Students

Putting an end to uncertainty following rollback of the controversial FYUP, the UGC sought the University of Delhi to continue with the four-year

B.Tech. Programme only for students admitted during the academic year 2013-14. The august body directed the university to ensure colleges obtain approval from regulatory bodies without inconveniencing FYUP students.

About 2,500 students are enrolled in six sections B.Tech programmes—Computer Science, Electronics, Food Technology, Polymer Science, Instrumentation and Electronics and Psychological Science. They have been protesting ever since the rollback of FYUP.

"The 4-year B.Tech Programmes in Computer Science, Electronics, Food Technology, Instrumentation Electronics and Polymer Science (where such students were admitted in the colleges under Delhi University). These are covered under Section 22 of the UGC Act, with respect to B.Tech, may continue in these programmes only for the students already admitted for academic year 2013-14," the UGC said. The commission was, however, silent on the psychological science course. This programme continues with the Bachelor in Management Studies (BMS) programme. However, the commission also remained silent as it is likely to be converted into three-year courses.

The directive of UGC is in line with the recommendation of its standing committee. The latter has suggested the programme should continue in the four-year format for students already admitted so that there won't be any "prejudice" caused to their interest. The Standing Committee had discussed the steps for transition from FYUP to a three-year programme. A 12-member committee of DU principals has been set up to look into the issue of admissions under three-year undergraduate course. The BJP had attacked the FYUP and alleged the implementation of such programme could be a violation of the National Policy on Education. The latter moots the 10+2+3 pattern of education. Its implementation could hurt the students by way of wasting one year of their productive output, the party had claimed. The youth wing of the BJP, the ABVP, had been lobbying hard with the HRD ministry, ever since the election of the new government attempted to scrap the FYUP.

Institutes Soon to Get Official Ranking: Indian educational institutes will be accorded official ranking soon. A national framework is getting prepared for the purpose said the HRD minister. However, the minister did not elaborate whether the framework will cover both government and private educational institutes. She addressed a gathering of students and teaching faculty at National Institute of Technical Teachers Training and Research (NITTTR) at Shyamla Hills, where she launched a teachers' training hub and laid foundation stone of golden jubilee convention centre. The idea of a national ranking framework is in line after recommendations by a committee of IIT directors on the issue of rankings.

The panel had suggested while it was important for Indian institutes to participate in global rankings, there is a greater need for India to devise its own domestic ranking that factors in India-specific criteria. In her keynote address, she said, "Accreditation of colleges and institutes in the country should be strengthened. For this purpose, accreditation board will be formed covering all aspects on the campus."

After Raman, no Indian Varsity has given Nobel Laureate

President Pranab Mukherjee expressed concern over the standard of Indian universities. Our universitites have not figured in the top 200 universities of the world. "In last 83 years, no research scholar from any Indian university has won Nobel prize after CV Raman. Scholars like Amartya Sen, Har Gobind Khorana, products of Indian universities, have obtained the Nobel Prize while working for foreign universities. It is worrying," he said.

Mukherjee said since 2012 annual convocation of IIT-Kharagpur, he has been sharing his concerns about education in convocation or annual conferences at Rashtrapati Bhavan. Of late, reputed international rating agencies have started recognising quality of our institutes, he said. "In subject-wise world rankings, two IITs, Madras and Bombay, are among top 50 institutions in civil engineering, while IIT Delhi and Bombay, are in the top 50 in electrical engineering. Five institutions are among top 20 universities in BRICS nations. The number of Indian institutions in the top 100 in Asia has increased to 10 this year from three in 2013. IIT- Guwahati is among top 100 institutes aged 50 years or less," he said.

Mid-day Meal should Include Buttermilk

The HRD minister Smriti Irani has proposed, what she calls, three big ticket ideas in school education. She has asked the department of school to look into the cost of mandatorily giving buttermilk to children as part of the Mid-day Meal scheme, opening separate model schools for talented boys and girls at the district level and declaring Saturday as sports day in schools.

The proposed menu can cure rampant amoebiasis among school children. Extra cost of giving butter milk has been worked out. Some 12 crore children across 12.65 lakh schools are benefitted. Many states like Kerala and Tamil Nadu give milk to children under the scheme. Some states even give iron tablets to girls and other health supplements. The Minister asked the ministry to look into the cost of starting model schools. Navodaya Vidyalaya Sangathan has been asked to examine the minister's proposal.

I was Referred to as Burden at my Birth

"I am sharing it for the first time that when I was born, someone hinted to my mother that *beti to bojh hoti hai* (daughter is a burden) and therefore she should kill me. My mother was brave and she did not do that because of which I am standing here in front of you," Ms. Irani said when a student asked her about the menace of female foeticide. "Such malpractice should be curbed. It was a priority programme for the government," she said.

"If you teach a girl, then you are not just imparting education to a woman, but to a family which will later help in nation building," she said. To a query on different boards and curriculum in various states, Ms Irani said the issue of uniformity in education will be addressed in National Education Policy (NEP).

She said the government is committed to linking education with skill development for addressing the problem of unemployment and also in making the curriculum more practical. The NEP will be formulated after discussing the issue at national, state, regional and also international level to address all issues. The department is creating a national e-library project so that students and other citizens have access to vast knowledge bank. For the purpose, the ministry will also collaborate with international libraries. The ministry is also focused on imparting quality training to the teachers, she said. She advised students not to feel their parents were unable to do much for them. Citing her example, the minister said she herself was brought up in a slightly lower middle class family and because of her parent's support; today she has reached this position. Ms Irani also cited the example of PM Modi, who sold tea and has now reached the country's top position, to inspire students. HRD ministry would offer scholarships to such candidates to promote them. It is working also on National Academic Depository Project and National Innovation Campaign, popularising mathematics and science streams.

Engineering Graduates' Degrees to be Recognised across 17 Countries

Engineering graduates from India could gain prospects as their degrees will now be recognised across 17 major countries. These include the United States, Japan and Australia. India became a permanent member of the Washington Accord, an international protocol for accrediting undergraduate engineering degree programmes. International mobility of engineering graduates from Indian Institutes of Technology (IITs) has not been an issue. The global fraternity has recognised these institutes. The case of graduates from the 1,300-odd other engineering colleges in the country has not been so.

India became the permanent member of the Washington Accord. Indian engineering graduates will be considered to have met the necessary academic requirements to take up the practice of engineering in any of the signatory countries. The Washington Accord aims to promote mobility and quality assurance across countries. Besides recognition for Indian engineering degrees, membership of the international accreditation agreement will ensure a minimum global quality for all engineering institutions in the country.

The decision to give India permanent membership, seven years after it acquired provisional membership, was taken at the meeting of the International Engineering Alliance in Wellington, New Zealand. The membership is effective immediately. This brings to a close India's 15-year quest for permanent membership. In 2000, the All India Council for Technical Education (the NBA was part of the council) initiated efforts for membership of the Washington Accord but no real progress was made. Another attempt was made in 2003, even though India's proposal was considered fit for appraisal in June 2003. Delays by the government in pursuing the case make India mis the opportunity, for being considered at the 2005 meeting of the Washington Accord members. Despite efforts in fits and starts, India's serious quest for membership began with a push from former HRD minister Kapil Sibal through moves including granting of autonomous status to the NBA. The Washington Accord requires countries to have a mandatory national accreditation system. In September 2013, the IITs agreed to be brought under the NBA's accreditation umbrella, a move that helped India's case enormously.

Vocational Training

The government would set up Massive Open Online Courses (MOOC) and virtual classrooms to make it convenient for working class people and housewives to further their knowledge and qualifications. Correspondence courses will be started in new domains for self-employment; family run businesses, entrepreneurship and innovation. These courses would be provided to women, free of cost. The goal would be to prepare the youth for jobs being created by the emerging sectors. Those will foster a spirit of innovation and entrepreneurship, leading to more income and job creation. The government will set up a National Commission on Education. It will report in two years about the state of education and the needed reforms. Based on the report, it will implement a National Education Policy to meet the changing dynamics of the population's requirement with regards to quality education, innovation and research, aiming to make India a knowledge superpower. It will equip her students with the necessary skills and knowledge. It is expected to eliminate the shortage of manpower in science, technology, academics and industry.

Employment and Job Opportunities

Employment and Entrepreneurship: The country dragged through decade long jobless growth by the previous government. Under the broader economic revival, the government will accord high priority to job creation and opportunities for entrepreneurship through appropriate measures to strengthen this sector. Labour-intensive manufacturing (*viz.,* textile, footwear, electronics assembly, etc.) and tourism are in the pipeline. It will strengthen the traditional employment bases of agriculture and allied industries, and retail-through modernisation as well as stronger credit and market linkages. It will harness the opportunities by infrastructure upgradation and housing, for its job generating potential will encourage and empower youth for self-employment—incubating entrepreneurship besides facilitating credit.

The government will address the employability issue by initiating multi-skills development programme in mission mode. Focus will be on job creation and entrepreneurship, in rural and urban areas. It will transform our employment exchanges into career centres connecting youth with job opportunities in transparent and effective manner through the use of technology counselling and training.

Thrust on Employment Generation: It is encouraging that creating jobs for young, skilled professionals is of paramount importance for this government. More so against the backdrop of an economy faced with daunting challenges such as inflation, low capital investment hinder growth in industrial output, slowing thrust on infrastructure. Foreign Direct Investment in insurance and defence is the need for a big push to the manufacturing sector. The emphasis on infrastructure projects using the appropriate PPP model, firm the vision for the development of smart cities. The Union budget 2014-15 focussed on investment of Rs 38,000 crore in the construction of national highways and state roads, disinvestment by banks to meet Basel III capitalisation norms, and newer investment vehicles such as the creation of Infrastructure Investment Trusts (on a modified REITs type structure) to mobilise infrastructure investments. The theme of job creation by catalysing focussed on skill development and providing a fillip to entrepreneurship. In proposing a Rs 10,000 crore fund to provide equity, quasi equity, soft loans and other risk capital for start-up companies, the government has kept entrepreneurial ecosystem vibrant.

Skills—Focussing on Productivity and Employability

Skillful hands, bright minds, discipline and perseverance makes Indian talent worldwide asset. The country has to live up to its potential, preparing the world's largest work force. The government has to take suitable steps to make youth productively employed and gainfully engaged. It has to develop

India as a Knowledge Powerhouse, train and nurture human resource. The government will take up skill development on a mission mode. It shall be an unprecedented scale like skill mapping to help scientifically plan our national human resource development India needs (like engineers, architects, doctors, nurses, lawyers, accountants, plumbers, carpenters, welders, etc.).

National Multi-skill Mission: The government wishes to run short-term courses, in the evening, focussing on employable skills. It will set up Centres of Excellence in various sectors in partnership with the Industry. To ensure industry responsive manpower, industry, universities and government work together. It will promote vocational training on a massive scale. Segregation of formal education and skill development will be broken, to give vocational qualifications of academic equivalence. It will create institutional mechanisms to refresh and upgrade abilities through continuing employable education—to make them employable. It will be on comprehensive programme in foreign languages, bringing India on par with International Labour Organisation (ILO) stipulations.

Modi's Pet Project GIFT Likely to Create 10 Lakh Jobs

"It is a pet project of Narendra Modi. He was monitoring it personally when he was the chief minister. The Rs 65,000 crore project is being developed on the lines of global financial services centres spread over three phases of development to be completed by 2022.

Gujarat's GIFT city has two components of development—domestic financial centre and international financial services centre. It is being developed on 886 acres of land, of which 673 acres is in possession of GIFT. It has multi-services Special Economic Zone (SEZ) of 250 acres and domestic finance centre and associated social infrastructure on 423 acres. The state-of-the-art GIFT city will be supported by all basic urban infrastructure comprising external connectivity by roads, metro and BRTS. It is conceptualised as a global financial and IT services hub on the lines of globally benchmarked financial centres such as Shinjuku, Tokyo, Lujiazui, Shanghai, La Defense, Paris, and London Dockyards. The project is located on the bank of Sabarmati River amidst host of IT conglomerates and banks are around 12-km from Ahmedabad International Airport. The Gujarat government is developing GIFT city through a joint venture between Gujarat Urban Development Company Ltd. (GUDCL) and Infrastructure Leasing and Financial Services Ltd (IL&FS). GIFT city aspires to cater to India's large financial services potential. It offers global firms a world-class infrastructure and facilities. The Rs 65,000-crore project is being developed on the lines of global financial services centres spread over three phases of development to be completed by 2022.

Indian Cities Top List in Attracting Tech Talent

India's Silicon Valley-Bangalore topped the list, followed by Pune, Hyderabad and Chennai, scooping up the top four spots in the LinkedIn ranking. Another Indian city Gurgaon was ranked at the 10th spot.

According to the study, 45 per cent of new residents in Bangalore had tech skills. It will be followed by 43 per cent each for Pune and Chennai. In comparison, the number was 31 per cent for San Francisco Bay Area, the highest among global cities.

"This is indicative of more people are moving to big cities than ever before, and the Indian technology sector is experiencing explosive growth," claimed Sohan Murthy, a research consultant at LinkedIn. The size of the India's information technology and business process management industry is estimated at $118 billion. Many multi-national technology companies are also showing their presence in India. For the 52 global cities LinkedIn looked at, the median percentage of new residents with tech skills was 16 per cent or just under one in six. Seattle, Austin, Melbourne and Sydney are other surveyed cities. In conducted the study by collecting information from over 30 crore member profiles and identified several cities across the globe that attracted significant proportions of tech talent in 2013. According to LinkedIn, the three most popular categories of skills among the new residents with a technology background were IT infrastructure and systems management, Java development and web programming.

1,000 km of new BRT would Save 27,000 Lives

The World Bank president Jim Young Kim believes India could save more than 27,000 lives and create over 128,000 jobs if it builds 1,000 kilometres of new bus rapid transit (BRT) lanes in the next 20 years.

Speaking at the release of a report "Climate-Smart Development", the report claimed $ 3-4 billion is needed to develop 1,000 kms of BRT corridors in about 20 cities across India within 6-12 years. India could also reduce "greenhouse gas emissions by about 42 million tons. The report focussed five countries— Brazil, China, India, Mexico and the US plus the European Union. It shows the potential economic, health and other gains from scaling up climate-smart policies as well as projects already in place in developing countries like Brazil, India and Mexico. It can deliver significant benefits to lives, jobs, crops, energy, and GDP as well as emission reductions to combat climate change. Policies promoting clean development in transport and energy efficiency will lead to global growth.

Creating New Jobs in Rural India

The Agriculture Ministry is likely to get a big leap in Modi government's economic revival and rural jobs agenda. It will be one of the most important areas for the government. It will focus on building agriculture as an industry and will free up exports of dairy products and foodgrains, etc., with full back-end support for cold storage as there is no other real way creating jobs in rural India. Apart from this dairy and other allied farm-related activities would receive a big push too. The government wishes to "globalise" India's agriculture. Given that the prices of rice and milk and other farm sector produce in the global market is several times that in India, it would like to give a big push to agricultural exports, whose output will have to expand fast.

Back-end support for the agriculture sector — cold-storage, packaging and processing — would be developed across the country. Developing the farm sector is important for creating jobs in rural India and arrest unpredictable migration from villages. India's population resides in the countryside and finds non-farm jobs, such as in the industrial sector, somewhat alien. It will revive 'Brand India', riding on its strength of five 'T's, three Ds and three Ss. The five Ts are Tradition, Talent, Tourism, Trade and Technology while the three Ds are Democracy, Demography and Demand and the three Ss are Skill, Speed and

Scale. India will also pursue such foreign policy on the basis of "enlightened nationalism" and mutually beneficial relationship. The government has announced a slew of measures. It will enhance growth and create jobs, encourage investment and create a predictable, transparent and fair environment. The government will initiate a series of social, health-care and infrastructure programmes. It will focus on 'zero tolerance' towards terrorism and extremism, besides violence against women.

14 Highest Priority to Agriculture

Introduction

Agriculture is the engine of India's economic growth. It is the largest employer, increases farmer's income and promotes rural development. It could increase public investment for the recovery and curb inflation.

The government desires to enahance the profitability, ensure minimum of 50 per cent profit over the cost of production, provide cheaper agriculture inputs and credit; introduce latest technologies for farming. High yielding variety seeds and linking MGNREGA to agriculture, welfare measures for farmers above 60 years and support to small and marginal farmers and farm labours could fetch instantaneous result.

Optimum utilisation of water resources, soil assessment-based crop planning and setting up mobile soil testing labs will be on the main agenda. Re-orient pest management and control programmes. Implement and incentivise the setting up of food processing industry sought to be on priority. The government will lead to better income for farmers and create jobs. It will to set up 'agro food processing clusters', with high value, export-quality and vacuum packed food processing facilities.

Focus on the quality, productivity and trade of spices. The Organic Farming and Fertiliser Corporation of India will promote organic farming and fertilisers, and provide incentives and support for marketing organic produce. It will introduce rotation farming for herbal products, based on geographical mapping, to enhance the income of farmers. Implement a farm insurance scheme care of crop loss from unforeseen natural calamities. Strengthen and expand rural credit facilities. Promote horticulture, floriculture, pisciculture, honey bee-keeping and poultry for generating jobs and income for rural India. Promote fish farming and aqua culture. Measures would be taken for the welfare of fisherman. Create Cluster-based storage systems (e.g., Rice cluster, Wheat Cluster, Veg - Fruit cluster, Spices cluster).

Introduce the concept of consumer-friendly farmers' market to reduce wastages, increase income and risk coverage. Reform the APMC Act. Work with the states to set up seed culture labs in each district and regional agriculture innovation labs to conserve agro-biodiversity, identify and preserve rare species of indigenous varieties. Explore setting up of regional Kisan TV channels. Give high priority to poverty alleviation in rural areas. Genetically Modified (GM) foods without scientific evaluation on its long-term effect on soil, production and biological impact on disallowed consumers will be accounted. Land acquisition is a contentious issue. The government will adopt a 'National Land Use Policy'. It will look at the scientific acquisition and development of non-cultivable land. It can protect the interest of farmers and keep in mind the food production and economic goals of the country. National Land Use Authority will monitor with the State Land Use Authorities, to regulate and facilitate land management. Its power and functions would be more or less similar to those of other regulatory bodies.

Gujarat Model in Agriculture

The state government launched a campaign for agriculture development and water conservation. It boosted agriculture growth adopting scientific farming and cattle-rearing initiative. The state has seldom seen drought in the last ten years. The farmers' agriculture income rises from Rs 14,000 crore to Rs 80,000 crore. The average agricultural growth of the country is less than three per cent while Gujarat's has crossed the double digit figure of nearly 11 per cent. It is using drip irrigation, green house, net house and sprinkler technique to maximise profit with minimum investment. The productivity of land multiplied on soil health.

Soil Health Card: Gujarat farmer has taken up modern methods of scientific farming leaving behind his old traditional approach. Soil health card has turned out to be a boon to the farmers as it helps educate them on deficiencies relating to the land and to what needs to be done to rectify these deficiencies. This has also resulted in judicious use of fertilisers on the basis of findings of the soil health check-up. Earlier, there was a tendency to overuse fertilisers which invariably harmed the composition of the land. This harmful effect has been reversed and thereby has helped to save unnecessary expenditure on fertilisers. Considering this, the state government has decided to give soil health card to every farmer in the state. Till now the lands of 42 lakh farmers have been tested. Gujarat has been the first state to achieve this enviable record. Till March 2011, 31 lakh soil health cards have been disbursed, which is a record in itself.

With Industrial Growth the Cultivable Land Decreases

Agriculture land holdings decrease due to industrial development. Gujarat has turned out to be an exception. Fallow land is now getting water for irrigation and has become fit for farming. This achievement owes to efficient and effective water management. The world and the country have taken note of this and it's a matter of pride to say that the country's apex court has recently lauded Gujarat's land policy and this innovative policy is worth emulation and can be used in other parts of the countries.

India's Agriculture Ministry will surely follow the Gujarat model under Radha Mohan Singh, who hails from Bihar and now the Agriculture Minister.

It would be his main priority to implement the measures that had taken in Gujarat for empowerment of villages and farmers in the rest of the country. The biggest challenge in front of the country is price rise of essential commodities. Agricultural growth rate has also remained very low.

Agriculture Minister is determined to stabilise prices *of* food *and essential commodities and make sure that farmers get adequate returns. He aims to use his grassroots knowledge to help the country's agriculture, which he says has trailed behind other sectors since independence. He believes farmers have access to new technology, accurate and timely weather forecasts and get remunerative prices will help in the long run.* The previous NDA government capped prices of food and essential commodities. In BJP-ruled states like Gujarat and Madhya Pradesh agriculture production has gone up.

Agriculture

Farming as an activity contributes nearly 1/6th to our National GDP and a major portion of our population subsists on it for livelihood. To make farming competitive and profitable, there is an urgent need to step up investment, both public and private, in agro-technology development and creation and modernisation of existing agri-business infrastructure. Indian Agricultural Research Institute, Pusa has been at the forefront of research in this area. However, since independence only one such centre has been established. The government will establish two more such institutions of excellence on similar pattern in Assam and Jharkhand with an initial sum of Rs 100 crore in the current financial year. In addition, an amount of Rs 100 crore is being set aside for setting up an "Agri-Tech Infrastructure Fund". Agriculture Universities in Andhra Pradesh and Rajasthan and Horticulture Universities in Telangana and Haryana finds an outlay of 200 crore in the budget 2015-15.

Deteriorating soil health has been a cause of concern and leads to sub-optimal utilisation of farming resources. The government will initiate a scheme to provide to every farmer a soil health card in a Mission mode. A sum of Rs 100 crore and an additional Rs 56 crore will be transferred for 100 Mobile Soil Testing Laboratories across the country. There have also been growing concerns about the imbalance in the utilisation of different types of fertilisers resulting in deterioration of the soil.

Climate change is a reality which all of us have to face together. Agriculture as an activity is most prone to vagaries of climate change. The governments will set up "National Adaptation Fund" for climate change. An initial sum an amount of Rs 100 crore will be transferred to the Fund. Sustained a growth of 4 per cent in Agriculture and for this it will bring technology driven second green revolution with focus on higher productivity and include "Protein revolution" as an area of major focus.

As a very large number of landless farmers are unable to provide land title as guarantee, institutional finance being denied to them and they become vulnerable to money lenders' usurious lending. Joint farming groups of *"Bhoomi Heen Kisan"* through NABARD will get Rs five lakh in the current financial year. They face price volatility in the agriculture produce creates uncertainties and hardship for the farmers. To mitigate this sum of Rs 500 crore has been earmarked for establishing a Price Stabilisation Fund.

The central government will work closely with the state governments to re-orient their respective APMC Acts, and establish private market yards/

private markets. The state governments will be encouraged to develop Farmers' Markets in town areas to enable farmers sell produce directly. A sum of Rs 50 crore has been earmarked for the development of indigenous cattle breeds and an equal amount for starting a blue revolution in inland fisheries.

Agriculture Credit: Banks extend strong credit support to the agriculture sector. A target of Rs 8 lakh crore has been set for agriculture credit (2014-15).

Short Term Crop Loans: Under the Interest Subvention Scheme for short term crop loans, the banks extend loans to farmers at concessional rate of 7 per cent. The farmers get a further incentive of 3 per cent for timely repayment.

Rural Infrastructure Development Fund: NABARD operates the Rural Infrastructure Development Fund (RIDF), out of the priority sector lending shortfall of the banks. It helps in creation of agriculture infrastructure and rural sectors across the country. The corpus of RIDF will be raised by an additional Rs 5,000 crore from the Interim Budget target to Rs 25,000 crore in the current financial year.

Warehouse Infrastructure Fund: The urgent need for availability of scientific warehousing infrastructure calls for an allocation of Rs 5,000 crore (2014-15).

Long Term Rural Credit Fund: The share of long-term investment credit in agriculture is going down as compared to short term crop loan. This is severely hampering the asset creation in agriculture and allied activities. "Long Term Rural Credit Fund" in NABARD will refinance Co-operative Banks and Regional Rural Banks with an initial corpus of Rs 5,000 crore.

Allocation of STCRC (Refinance) Fund: The Short Term Co-operative Rural Credit (STCRC) – Refinance Fund was announced in Union Budget 2008-09 with initial corpus of Rs 5,000 crore. In order to ensure increased and uninterrupted credit flow to farmers and to avoid high cost market borrowings by NABARD, an amount of Rs 50,000 crore for STCRC Fund during 2014-15 is allotted.

Producers Development and Upliftment Corpus (PRODUCE): The issue of profitability of small holding based agriculture has assumed importance. Small and marginal farmers proliferate in the country. NABARD's Producers' organisation development fund for Producer's development and upliftment called PRODUCE will have a sum of Rs 200 crore earmarked for building 2,000 producers organisations across the country over the next two years.

Food Security: Restructuring of FCI, reducing transportation and distribution losses and efficacy of PDS would be taken up on priority. The government is committed to provide wheat and rice at reasonable prices to the weaker sections of society. Inadequate rainfall leads to marginal decline in agriculture production. Stocks in the central pool are adequate to meet any exigency. The government shall, when required, undertake open market sales to keep prices under control.

Kisan TV: Kisan TV is dedicated to the interests of the agriculture and allied sector. It will be launched in the current financial year to disseminate real time information on new farming techniques, water conservation, and organic farming. A sum of Rs 100 crore has been earmarked for the purpose.

National Crop Insurance Programme

The government plans to review the National Crop Insurance Programme (NCIP)-(2013). Farmers face the spectre of failed crop in anticipation that El

Nino may reduce rainfall by 10-20 per cent. The ministry of agriculture would like to continue with the new programme or bring back the previous National Agriculture Insurance Scheme where the claims be funded equally by the central and the state governments.

New Farm Insurance Scheme in Six Months

The Centre is likely to announce new agriculture insurance scheme by January 2015, after taking inputs from state governments and farmers organisations. The recommendations made by a commission on the Minimum Support Price (MSP) for various farm produce are being currently considered by the Finance Ministry. Even farmer will soon get soil health card besides water to farm land.

PM Reviews Drought Contingency Plan

Boosting Rural Economy: The agriculture ministry presented a drought contingency plan for 500 districts to the Prime Minister. The country received just about half the rainfall it normally receives every June 2014. With a poor monsoon threatening to be a challenge for the new government that is looking to step up economic growth and revive the investment cycle, the Prime Minister urged ministers dealing with farm sector issues to focus on boosting the rural economy and reducing farmer distress.

It was a detailed stocktaking of the departments, various schemes, bottlenecks faced and what we plan as the ministries of fertilisers, food and water resources were not able to make their presentations due to paucity of time. The Central Research Institute for Dryland Agriculture had prepared a contingency plan for more than 500 districts out of 540 districts across the country that the Centre was sharing with all state governments.

Govt Plans Urea Price Hike to Curb Fertiliser Subsidies

The government plans to raise the price of urea, the fertiliser most used by the farmers, by at least 10 per cent in order to contain subsidy costs that are straining the budget. The first major price hike in four years would mark an important step pruning wasteful use of urea and ease fiscal pressures resulting from a weak economy. Government and industry officials said: "A two to three per cent rise in urea prices won't make any meaningful difference in subsidy allocation. We are pitching for at least a ten per cent hike."

Food Security Act

The government has always held that 'universal food security' is integral to national security. It will take steps to ensure that the benefits of the scheme reach the common man and that the right to food does not remain an act on paper or a political rhetoric. It will review all the laws and schemes, in consultation with the states, to ensure a corruption-free efficient implementation of food security on priority.

The successful PDS models may incorporate the best practices to revise the existing PDS, for benefitting common man. The issue of under-nutrition and malnutrition, production of cereals, pulses and oils will also be studied. The Food Corporation of India will be transformed for any exigencies arising due to natural calamities or external factors. The government will seek the participation of voluntary organisations in running community kitchens. It will review, amend and strengthen the Child and Adolescent Labour (Prohibition and Regulation) Act, 2012 and Integrated Child Protection Scheme (ICPS). Efforts will be made to address issue of anaemia, reduce the burden of books on children without compromising on the quality of education and inculcate values-system amongst children.

Govt to Set up Kisan Mandis in Food Inflation Fight

The government has drawn up plans to set up *"kisan mandis"* (farmer's markets) which will sell directly to consumers and shut out middlemen. The Small Farmers' Agribusiness Consortium (SFAC), an agency of the agriculture ministry, will set up *"mandis"*. The first such market will come up in the national capital. It is expected to be in place by September, 2014. Mandis will sell potato, onions and tomatoes. The prices of vegetables used across the country by consumers have firmed up recently, prompting the government to act. Kisan mandis sell them by at least 20-25 per cent cheaper than current retail prices. It will stock vegetables and fruits from 6 lakh farmers linked to farmers' producer organisations. The vegetables would grade and sorted before being sold to consumers. SFAC has identified a warehouse of NAFED in Delhi. It will encourage FPO's from Haryana and Punjab to bring in vegetables. A unique feature of the Kisan Mandi will be the opening up of new market segments for direct selling. There include RWAs, online retailers and the hotel and catering industry. There are even plans to convert the 2000-odd Delhi Milk scheme kiosks into mini-vegetable marts. *Kisan Mandi* could be a game changer for the supply of fresh produce in the Delhi and NCR area, if it works out.

The plan to set up markets was triggered to delist fruits and vegetables from the monopoly of the Azaadpur market. Untill now, farmers and traders had to bring their produce to the Azadpur mandi and navigate a complex web of middlemen and "red tape". The opaque system added to the price burden for retail consumers and the farmers. Anyone can organise the marketing of fresh produce. SFAC is seeking to be the first to take advantage of this major policy reform. It may provide an alternate channel of supply to retailers and consumers. It could benefit farmers through lower intermediation cost and fair practices. Fruits and other vegetables from different states could arrive through proposed special trains for these commodities.

Ganga River Project

Cleaning the Ganges will be the government's toughest task. After all, with it, the world's largest democracy's image will be scrubbed clean too. The Central Pollution Control Board (CPCB) report states that "The Ganga is the largest and the most important river of India. The 2,525 kilometres long river carries off the drainage of a vast basin area 8,61,404 kilometres. It covers 26.2 per cent area of India's total geographical area. The watershed of the river Ganga spreads over ten States of India, namely Uttaranchal, Uttar Pradesh, Bihar, Jharkhand, West Bengal, Himachal Pradesh, Rajasthan, Haryana, Madhya Pradesh and Delhi. Discharge of untreated sewage from urban centres is a major cause of river water quality degradation. As per the latest estimate out of 22,900 Mld of wastewater generated, only about 5,900 MLD (26 per cent) is treated before letting out, the rest i.e., 17000 Mld is disposed of untreated. Twenty-seven cities have only primary treatment facilities and forty-nine have primary and secondary treatment facilities. The level of treatment available in cities with existing treatment plant varies from 2.5 per cent to 89 per cent of the sewage generated, the report said.

For years, the degrading state of the Ganga River has been a matter of concern and shame for the nation. Efforts have been made by the government and projects undertaken to clean up the river, but to no avail. The 2012 Central Pollution Control Board report, claims around Rs 20,000 crore has been spent so far. The Ganga is still among the filthier rivers in the country. Plans to clean up the 2,500 km holy river date back around 1989. The first Ganga Action Plan was announced in 1986. Activists believe the stretch flowing through Varanasi is in worse condition than it was even five years ago. Late premier Rajiv Gandhi had initiated Rs 1,700 crore-worth Ganga Action Plan (GAP) project. A 2004-parliamentary committee report declared the project a failure, due to insufficient funds and monitoring mechanisms. In 2009, after the River Ganga was accorded national status, headed by Premier Manmohan Singh, Rs 7,000 crore-worth National Ganga River Basin Authority was constituted. The World Bank in 2011 sanctioned $1 billion but of no avail as it does not ensure the cleaning of Ganga.

Other major rivers of the country are also in no better condition. Yamuna was labelled at the 'filthiest' river too needs major correction plan to 'detoxify' her bed. Earlier, the concern was that the pesticides may be contaminating what's grown on the bed of the Yamuna. Recent reports suggest the harmful mix of sewage and industrial effluents affect fruits and vegetables grown on her bed, compromising the quality drastically. National Green Tribunal (NGT) sued the government detailing how the river's pollution is thwarting the health prospects of those who eat greens grown on its soil. An RTI application filed in 2013 suggested the amount of the sewage and industrial effluents discharged in the river from a number of cities upstream was at an alarming rate. Recently, the rejection of several consignments, for quality issues — of fruits and vegetables exported from India made news. Even Saudi Arabia has banned import of Indian chillies due to high-level of pesticide residues.

The recent application submitted in the NGT by *Yamuna Jiye Abhiyan* suggests large-scale pollution of Yamuna from industrial effluents and sewage. It has led to groundwater and soil pollution. Vegetables irrigated by contaminated water are laced with heavy metals and chemical residues, the plea states. The Energy and Resources Institute (TERI) -2012 study found the level of toxic metals like nickel, lead, manganese, chromium and zinc high in many water samples. It has suggested that at one location, lead levels have harmed the foetuses of many expectant mothers. At another location, near a thermal power plant, mercury concentration was about 200 times more than a United States Environmental Protection Agency standard.

In 2011, scientific data proved the level of industrial pollution in the river was nearly 13 times the permissible limit. The river, when passing through Delhi, registered the highest levels of industrial pollution in the country.

Data collected over a 10-year period by the Central Water Commission through its 371 monitoring stations across the country then revealed Yamuna has the highest level of biochemical oxygen demand (BOD) concentration when it passes through Delhi. Yamuna's level of industrial pollution based on the BOD test conducted then suggested there was 39.83 mg per litre of water as against the permissible limit of three mg during non-monsoon days.

The water bodies in different states in India are in terrible condition. Be it the Bandi River in Bali, Rajasthan that gets polluted by over 500 textile units, or the fact that sewage water freely flows in Gorewada Lake–Nagpur's drinking water reservoir—in Maharashtra, or the Narmada River in Jabalpur, Madhya Pradesh gets polluted by various dairy industries, the water bodies in the country needs to be preserved and preserved fast.

Interlinking of Rivers

Ambitious interlinking of river projects will get new impetus under the government, but the Centre would like to select the specific project for implementation very cautiously. Its focus will first be on linking rivers of sub-basins within a basin or nearby basins instead of going on for distant inter-basin river linkages. An inter-ministerial matter had to sort out drinking-water\irrigation needs of people and ecological concerns. The interlinking of river (ILR) was mooted way back in 1982. It was actively taken up during Atal Bihari Vajpayee's tenure as premier during 1999-04. The next government ignored on the arising complexities.

CAG Report: The projects on papers claim availability of water for irrigating 35 million hectares. These will generate hydro-electricity to the extent of 34,000 mw and control floods in many states across the country, if implemented.

No Dearth of Funds: Water resources minister, Uma Bharati claims fund for cleaning River Ganga would flow on its own in the form of corporate donations and contributions from various sections of the society on her single call". Bharti said the government is in the process of preparing a compact plan. We are in the process of preparing a compact plan. The ministry has not opposed to power projects on rivers, but at the same time it ought to be ensured that main river is never dry during any point of the year.

Clean-up Plan Soon: The Union ministries of water resource development, tourism, environment and forest and shipping will draft an integrated plan accordingly. She said a meeting of religious people, activists for a clean Ganga, and organisations working for the purity of the river water would be held soon. The meeting, to be called *"Ganga manthan"*, will discuss ways and means to achieve the goal of 'aviral' (uninterrupted) 'nirmal' (clean) Ganga.

'Ganga Promise' Turns into Reality with Waterway Project

Chairman of Inland Waterways Authority of India Amitabh Verma assured for early completion of Allahabad-Haldia waterways project. Union minister Uma Bharati launched a web portal on Ganga rejuvenation in New Delhi.

She said the government is committed to develop of 1620-km long National Waterways-1 in Ganga from Allahabad to Haldia. A fund of Rs 4,200 crore has been allocated for the project. It would help in cargo movement and promote cruising on this waterway. The cruise facility for tourists between Patna and Varanasi will be extended up to six month in days had. Rs 2,037 crore for conservation of Ganga. Rs 100 crores develop ghats and beautification of riverfronts in Varanasi, Kedarnath, Haridwar, Kanpur, Allahabad, Patna and Delhi. According to the Ganga portal, the ministry of urban development would spend Rs 51,000 crore to expand the sewerage infrastructure in 118 urban habitations on the banks of Ganga. Varanasi will be the beneficiary of Namani Gange and inland waterways schemes.

The Right to Education Act calls for pupils spend six hours in school every day. Irrespective of how and where they relieve themselves the government s determined to could separate toilets. The boys and girls will have their blocks. The teachers and the staff will have their own.

For they will spend even longer hours in school to complete non-teaching work. It is resident from the District Information System for Education, 2013, that 10 per cent of elementary schools (nearly 2 lakh schools) do not have functional toilets. In fact, in 2004, a civil writ petition (No (S) 631) was filed against the Delhi administration for the lack of toilets in schools. The Supreme Court sought each state submit affidavits on the status of toilets in their respective states. 18 state governments told the apex court to have met the requirement in accordance with RTE norms. Now, the issue is under dispute about the maintenance and upkey. Is the HRD Ministry or that of Rural Development (MoRD) or that of Drinking Water and Sanitation (MDWS) or together responsible? The Sarva Shiksha Abhiyan has a provision for construction of toilets. It ranges from Rs. 50,000 per toilet (Himachal Pradesh) to Rs. 70,000 per toilet (Jharkhand). The provision of sanitation facilities, however, is the responsibility of the MDWS. Scores of schools have constructed toilets — but without sanitation facilities or water supply. Their use, is limited.

Nitin Gadkari the MDWS recently announced that toilets would be delinked from the Mahatma Gandhi National Rural Employment Guarantee Act. The construction of individual toilets would Rs. 15,000, while school toilets will have Rs. 35,000 to Rs. 54,000. The construction of anganwadi and community toilets will have their share. Does this mean these toilets will be provided water supply?

River Interlinking to Aid Irrigation Facilities

Laying emphasis on the need for interlinking of rivers, Union water resources minister Uma Bharti said the ambitious project once completed would bring about 90 per cent of arable land under irrigation. "Interlinking of rivers would enhance irrigation facilities to 90 per cent of farm lands in the country," she said while inaugurating the national conference on issues for optimal use of water resources here.

According to agriculture ministry data, 40 per cent of the agriculture land is irrigated and accounts for 55 per cent of total production, while 60 per cent is rain-fed and contribute 45 per cent to total output. Minister for rural development Chaudhary Birender Singh said that 86 per cent of drinking water supply schemes were based on ground water and proper attention should be paid for water security planning.

"The ministry has taken up 15 pilot blocks in 10 states, where comprehensive planning is undertaken to promote water security with the active participation of the panchayati raj institutions," he said.

Australia Offers Assistance for Cleaning up the Ganga

Australia will offer technical support and assistance to India's mammoth undertaking of cleaning up the Ganga, Australian High Commissioner Patrick Suckling says.

"We have agreed to work with India. We have spent $350 million to develop river basin modelling technology to save one of our biggest rivers, the Murray-Darling river basin. We are sharing this technology with India," he said in an interaction here. A pilot study is already on in the Brahmani river in eastern India, he added.

"When Modi [Prime Minister Narendra Modi] was in Australia, we also announced an intensification of our water partnership in order to work with India on the PM's priority of cleaning up the Ganga. So, we are going to be looking at some areas of technical support. It's a massive exercise to clean-up an entire river system," Mr. Suckling said. Stressing that both India and Australia have huge water challenges that need to be addressed, he said effective management of river systems was essential to ensure equitable allocation of water and preservation of ecosystems.

Yamuna Clean-up Needs Another Rs 25,000 Cr

The capital will have to spend another Rs 25,000 crore to clean up the Yamuna and extend sewerage connections in unsewered areas. The figure was quoted at a review meeting on the river held by LG Najeeb Jung. The LG has asked work on several sewerage projects. It includes the interceptor sewage system, to be fast-tracked. Delhi Jal Board, PWD, DDA and other civic agencies have been asked to control the pollution load.

DJB is in the process of laying interceptor drains along three main drains. It claims around 70 per cent of the pollution load in the river will be reduced after the system is in place. It intercepts untreated sewage from Sweeper Colony, Magazine Road and Khyber Pass drain. This will be made fully functional by June 2015. Metcalf House, Qudsia, Mori Gate, Tonga Stand, Civil Military drain shall be intercepted into the existing Ring Road trunk sewer.

Plans are afoot to trap sewage being carried by the Barapullah drain intercepted at the Okhla sewage treatment plant. Work is on to augment the capacity of the sewage treatment plant (STP) at the Delhi Gate drain from 2.2 million gallons per day to 17.2 MGD. The plant is likely to be commissioned by December 2015. At present, DJB has a sewage treatment capacity of 604 MGD. DJB will also build four new plants by December to take its sewage treatment capacity to 684 MGD. Treatment standards at new STPs have been improved to reduce biochemical oxygen demand and suspended particles to below 10 parts per million. It is proposed to rehabilitate all old STPs and improve treatment standards up to tertiary levels. DJB will work towards increasing sewer network. Till date, 541 of 567 unauthorised colonies, 129 of 135 urban villages, 44 resettlement colonies, 34 of 189 rural villages and 104 of 1,639 unauthorised/regularised colonies have been provided sewerage facility. The work of laying sewers in 162 colonies is under progress and tenders have been invited for another 142.

15 Transport is Lifeline of the Country

Introduction

Indian Railways is the lifeline of the country. The government will take effective steps to modernise, strengthen and upgrade this vital sector in view of serving passengers as well as the country's economy. This will be done in a planned manner focussing on national development, rather than political exigency. In this chapter, the issues related to transport like raliways, road and sea-route will be discussed.

The Future Plans to Boost Railways: The hinterland will be connected to the ports through strategic new rail networks. Agri Rail network will be established with Train Wagons designed to cater to specific needs of perishable Agricultural products like milk and vegetables as well as light weight wagons for salt movement. Tourist rail including pilgrimage rail inducts the state-of-the-art technology. Special focus will be on developing skilled human resources to meet future demand. Prioritise safety and invest in long required overhaul of stressed infrastructure, strict norms and warning systems. Modernise and equip stations with requisite infrastructure and public utilities. Convert all unmanned crossings into manned crossings in a phased manner. Initiate R&D for indigenous railways, coach design and signals. Diamond Quadrilateral project—of High Speed Train network (bullet train) will be operational very soon.

Railways in Decline, it's Time for Overhaul

Railway, the great monolith often christened as the economic lifeline of the nation, is in for a major overhaul is both sad as well as gratifying. After all, even the most modern machines require periodic overhauls and therefore why not organisations?

Is Overhaul Possible: The recent spate of accidents and the general public perception add woes betide? Railways carry over 20 million passengers every day and over thousand million tonnes of freight every year. It has almost reached otimum limits in its present shape and structure. And that's where the nub lies. There's no longer time to beat about the bush—rather it's time to call a spade a spade. An archaic, feudal and sycophantic organisation steeped in complex processes cannot be expected to meet the expectations of 21st century India. Its three-tier structure on departmental lines, with redundant tier in the middle, aligned cadres on similar lines is the real issue that prevents a monopolised commercial organisation from meeting the country's aspirations. At one level, the reports made by persons of eminence—Prakash Tandon, Rakesh Mohan and Kakodkar—need to be acted upon. At another level, the organisational structure needs to be shaken.

Display of Message in Hindi

Information dissemination to passengers is the foremost duty and therefore from time-table to statuary information and rules, should be both in Hindi and English. This is also include the information on coach indicator boards, price rates of items at the stations and putting up direction signage and safety instructions. This was the opinion from band of officers of Northern Railway meeting held in New Delhi (June 19, 2014). Before the meeting, issue of 'Rail Sangam' was also released in which there was special edition on the signal and telecommunications department.

14.2 Per Cent Fare Hike

The national transporter, face a loss of about Rs 900 crore every month in passenger segment. A hike in passenger fares and freight rates by 14.2 per cent and 6.5 per cent respectively was effected from May 20, 2014. However, the hike notification was put on hold leaving the decision to the next Railway Minister. Railways target Rs 8000 crore through the increase in passenger and freight charges.

The railways sought to correct the long running distortion in the fare structure by hiking passenger fares by 14.2 per cent across all classes and freight charges by 6.5 per cent. It includes a flat rate increase besides fuel adjustment components as and when effective.The increase took effect immediately. Senior officials believe the hike in passenger fares will help pare down the diversion of profits from the freight to passenger segment. Successive governments have shied away from biting the bullet on passenger fares, because of fears of public wrath. The second class and suburban travel were either rolled back or were lowered. Nearly about 600 crore passengers travel every year. Opposition parties opposed the hike. Senior officials claimed this will partially restore railways financial health. The existing infrastructure ought to be replaced and build new one. In the long term, it will help stave off from financial predicament. Its employees do benefit from Sixth Pay Commission award.

Biting the Bullet

The two hikes together are expected to fetch the Railways between Rs 7,000 crore and Rs 8,000 crore in a full year. It is estimated that the monthly loss to on account of passenger fares is about Rs 900 crore. As a result, the freight rates were subsidising or diverting profits to the unsustainable passenger segment.

Indian Railways move 20 million passengers everyday. The subsidy burden was clearly hurting the system. For nearly a decade, successive ministers from alliance partners in the Congress-led UPA, found it convenient to deny any fare revision. Pawan Kumar Bansal of the Congress took charge in 2013. He effected the first increase, followed by a minor revision by Mallikarjun Kharge. Now, the new government has decided to bite the bullet and mark up the fares substantially. The freight increase could contribute to inflationary pressures. Railways find it difficult to fund major infrastructure, safety, and other ongoing projects, given the financial constraints. Excessive market borrowing was creating another burden. It wants to attract private and even foreign investment in infrastructure, including in the Railways, the financial viability of the system assumes importance. It is believed to invest in projects under implementation, to shore up safety and security on the wheels.

FDI in Railways to Attract Investments

Sparing passengers of any further fare hike, Railways attract private domestic and FDI in infrastructure projects and pursuing private-public partnership to boost the finances of the cash-strapped railways.

The railway minister in his budget plans to introduce a bullet train in Mumbai- Ahmedabad sector. The Diamond Quadrilateral network of high speed rail will connect major metros and growth centres. A sum of Rs 100 crore has been earmarked for initiating the project. The speed of trains will increase from 60 to 200 km per hour on nine select sectors. Gross traffic receipts stood at Rs 1,39,558 crore. It will short of revised estimates by Rs 942 crore over the previous year. The ordinary working expenses and pension outgo were higher. The budget estimates for 2014-15 assumes a freight loading 1101 metric tonnes, 51 metric tonnes more than the previous year, growth in passenger traffic at two per cent and freight earning at Rs 1,05,770 crore.

Passenger earnings will be Rs 44,645 crore after a revenue sacrifice of Rs 610 crore on account of monthly season ticket fares. Total receipts for the current year have been pegged at Rs 1,64,374 crore and expenditure at Rs 1,49,176 crore. Rs nine lakh crore fund is needed to complete the Golden Quadrilateral Network. Rs 60,000 crore alone will go for introducing one bullet train. Surplus funds of railway PSUs in infrastructure projects can generate attractive returns. Private investment through domestic and FDI could pave the way. Internal revenue sources and government funding are insufficient. FDI, however, will be limited to infrastructure development, but not allowed in operations, a gloomy fact.

The concept of PPP was unsuccessful in raising substantial resources for railways. Any future projects ought to be financed through PPP mode, include the high—speed rail, which requires huge investment. Holiday approach, setting timelines for ongoing projects, strategic partnership and aggressive indigenisation of imported projects could be mere sops, but not solution. The annual plan for 2014—15 has been fixed at the highest ever outlay of Rs 65,445 crore with gross budgetary support at Rs 30,100 crore, Railway Safety Fund Rs 2,200 crore, internal resources Rs 15,350 crore, external market borrowing Rs 11,790 crore and EBR—PPP Rs 6,005 crore. The budget provides higher funds for ongoing projects in North East. It includes 11 national projects. Rs 5,116 crore has been earmarked, which is 54 per cent higher than the previous year.

New Trains

Udhampur-Katra rail link in Jammu and Kashmir has left the missing link between Banihal and Katra. It needs to be completed before 2016. 18 new line surveys have been announced. It include rail connectivity to *'char dham'*—Kedarnath, Badrinath, Gangotri and Yamunetri and Shimoga—Sringeri—Mangalore. Five Jansadharan trains are being introduced along with five premium trains, six AC express trains and 27 express trains and eight passenger trains. The premium trains run between Mumbai Central and New Delhi, Shalimar—Chennai, Secundarabad—Hazrat Nizamuddin, Jaipur—Madurai and Kamakhya—Bangalore. In order to strengthen security in trains and stations, the budget proposes to recruit 4,000 women RPF constables. Already 17,000 RPF constables recruited and shall be deployed shortly. Over Rs 40,000 crore would be needed to invest in track renewal, elimination of unmanned railway crossing and road overbridge and underbridge. A provision of Rs 1,785 crore has been earmarked for railway overbridges and underbridges. The railway reservation system is being revamped. It will move into next generation E—ticketing system. It will support 7,200 tickets per minutes to allow 1,20,000 simultaneous users. Railways will move to paperless offices in five years, provide wi-fi services in A-1 and A category stations and in select trains. Real-time tracking of trains and rolling stock, mobile-time tracking.

Metro Rail Projects Coming in More Cities

Union Finanace Minister spoke about how Urban Metro Projects have proved decongesting large cities. "For two million plus cities, planning of Metro projects is a boon. The government will encourage its development, including light rail systems under the public private participation mode. The central government sill support through the Viability Gap Funding." Earlier, only three million plus population cities were considered for Metro projects. As per Census 2011, there are 19 cities with two million plus population. A sum of Rs 100 crore has been earmarked for Metro projects in Lucknow and Ahmedabad.

E-visa Facility at Nine Airports to Boost Tourism

Aiming to give an impetus to the tourism sector, the government said that e-visas facility would be introduced at nine Indian airports. The facility of Electronic Travel Authorisation (e-visa) would be introduced in a phased manner at nine airports in India where infrastructure would be put in place within the next six months. It would facilitate visas on arrival scheme that was announced earlier this year. A sum of Rs 500 crore has been earmarked for creation of five tourist circuits with specific themes in the country, he said.

Jaitley also announced the launching of National Heritage City Development and Augmentation Yojana (Hriday). It will conserve and preserve the heritage characters of cities. The programme will be initially launched in cities such as Mathura, Amritsar, Gaya, Kancheepuram, Velankanni and Ajmer with a provision of Rs 200 crore. A National Mission on Pilgrimage Rejuvenation and Spiritual Augmentation Drive (Prasad) with an outlay of Rs 100 crore was also proposed for the financial year.

Key Changes to be Made for FDI in Rlys: Two years ago, task force under Sam Pitroda, appointed by railways, showed that modernising is doable in a span of a few years. It requires a sharp focus on how less than half of existing tracks bear about 80 per cent of traffic. This modernisation project would encompass tracks, bridges and signals, thereby simultaneously improving safety standards.

More Funds Sought for Safety Upgrade: The total amount that the Railways have sought in the upcoming budget is Rs 38,000 crore. It includes money to be spent on national projects and execution of Dedicated Freight Corridor. In the interim rail budget, the Railways had received Rs 29,000 crore as GBS and around Rs 12,000 crore as cess. That the money would not be revised in the fresh budget, a case has been made for more allocation citing safety requirements. Rs 38,800 crore, incidentally, is the amount earmarked in the 12th Plan for annual GBS to the Railways.

Focus on Passenger Safety

On packages safety, the department is likely to introduce indigenous trains, collision avaoidance system on more routes. A safety cess on passengers face may be levied in place of recently announced hike, which was not effective. The budget is expected to announce projects related to harnessing solar energy and development of offshore wind energy, including those related to use of solar energy to power local trains and use of innovative technology to run AC coaches.

The focus is expected to be on electrification of around 2000 km of tracks, considering that the railways have almost 38 per cent (24,800 km) of its network electrified, carrying almost 67 per cent of the freight traffic and 51 per cent of the passenger traffic. The railways will expedite the construction of 14 strategic projects— mainly in border areas. There are struck for environment clearance and shortage of funds. These projects involve laying down of 2,888 km of railway tracks in Jammu and Kashmir, Arunachal Pradesh, Assam, Himachal Pradesh, Uttarakhand, Rajasthan and Punjab. A dedicated freight corridor will augment goods trains on important routes.

Although, former railway minister Madhavrao Scindia had mooted the idea of high speed trains in the mid-eighties, railways came out with a white-paper in December 2009. So far, six stretches have been identified and feasibility study of Mumbai-Ahmadabad corridor is underway. Former railway minister Lalu Prasad had encouraged higher-level of movement of milk by tankers from various regions of the country, besides introducing more refrigerated parcel vans for transportation of fruits, vegetables and other perishable commodities. The agenda of new government is nothing but old wine in a new bottle, but gives an opportunity to materialise plans unfinished.

The statements come at a time when the government is looking to allow FDI in certain segments of railways, such as high speed corridors. It will ensure that the weak finances of the Indian Railways does not block any attempt to modernise what has largely been inherited from the British rulers. The government, however, said that investment in railways will be increased using innovative financing methods and the network will be expanded to the hilly states and the northeast.

Apart from the railways, the President's speech suggested that there will be a push to low cost airports to promote connectivity to small cities, revival of the *"Sagar Mala"* project to connect ports with hinterland through road and rail, time-bound and well monitored highway development programme and development of inland and coastal waterways have been identified as major focus area to push infrastructure development. Realising it well that government funding will be inadequate and the private investment won't come unless there is conducive environment, Mukherjee said, "A fast-track, investment friendly and predictable PPP mechanism will be put in place."

The government also committed to evolve a model of port-led development and making the long coastline as "gateway for India's prosperity" by modernising the existing ports and developing new world class ones.

PM Opens Katra Rail Link

'Want to win people's hearts' After flagging off the inaugural train from the newly-built Katra railway station, the base camp of the Vaishno Devi shrine, to Udhampur he said the link will help in the development of Jammu. "This is a facility not only for the people of Jammu and Kashmir but also for the people of India, who want to visit Jammu and Kashmir," said Modi. The PM suggested the new train to Katra be named Shreeshakti express and said the rail link will help in the development of Jammu. "I assure you that there will be no shortage or obstacle in the development of Jammu," said Modi. The train for Jammu will chug along the newly constructed line from the Shri Mata Vaishno Devi Katra Station. It will traverse through seven tunnels and over 30 small and large bridges. There will be a small station - Chakrakhwal- between Udhampur and Katra. The 25 km-long Udhampur-Katra line has been built at an estimated cost of Rs. 1,132.75 crore.

Road Projects

Gadkari to Speed up Stalled Road Projects

The government plans to build 30 kilometres of roads every day. It will clear the backlog of stalled projects. It will switch to the EPC (engineering, procurement and construction) mode in place of the public-private partnership (PPP) mode to boost road construction. "Total road construction has gone down... Road projects worth about Rs 60,000 crore are stuck, mainly due to reasons such as land acquisition and environment and forest clearances," said minister of road transport and highways Nitin Gadkari. UPA government built roads 20 km per day, but faced environment, forest delay and land acquisition in clearance. The minister reviewed over 55 projects covering over 15,000 km over two days. A special corporation will undertake road projects in the North-eastern states of the country. He directed NHAI to take measures in 450 identified accident-prone black spots, and BRO to report on the state of its performance.

Rs 37,880 cr to be Pumped into Nation's Road Network

The Union Budget, 2014 has given importance to fast-tracking highways and improving the road infrastructure to augment the nation's arterial network. National Highways Authority of India and State roads have been earmarked an amount of Rs 37,880 crore which includes Rs 3,000 crore for the North East. The government's commitment to the Pradhan Mantri Gram Sadak Yojana launched under the prime ministership of Atal Bihari Vajpayee and allocated Rs 14,389 crore for the same.

White Paper: Nitin Gadkari said in a follow-up on the July 5, 2014 white paper, his ministry has "asked the permission from Prime Minister to clear projects of over Rs 1,000 crore. Many projects in the past delayed due to umpteen committee approvals. The Cabinet has approved 11 projects worth Rs 16,000 crore, while his office had so far cleared Rs 40,000 crore worth of projects stuck due to "inordinate delays" in clearances.

Rs 200 cr Trees to be Planted Along 1 Lakh-km Highways

The government at the Cetre plans to plant 200 crore trees along the entire 1 lakh km National Highways network across the country to employ jobless youth. The length of National Highways in the country is one lakh kilometre. A similar scheme under MNREGA (Mahatma Gandhi National Rural Employment Gurantee Act) has the potential to employ 30 lakh youth to work along village and districts roads on national highway.

Gadkari said Gram Panchayats will be taken into confidence and the unemployed youth could be assigned 50 trees each. It could fetch livelihood for them from the produce. Even 15 per cent of rainwater could be tapped out of the 60 per cent that goes to the sea; the water-scarcity could be avoided. People can be supplied with potable water besides irrigation of agriculture land. The government will lay stress on building check-dams instead of mega projects. Measures were on to save Rs 6 lakh crore on imports of petrol, diesel and gas by way of promoting bio-fuels. REC has been directed to improve power supply in inaccessible areas and villages. He said his ministry in co-ordination with others are preparing roadmaps for cleanliness of Ganga and Yamuna rivers and developing waterways in the country for environment-friendly and quick movement of cargo and passenger traffic. A project monitoring committee is looking into realignment of National Highways in calamity-torn Kedarnath region against flash floods and frequent soil erosion taking huge toll relocating.

Land Acquisition Act

With Rs 60,000 crore worth of projects stuck due to delays in land acquisition. The new amendment in Land Acquisition Act after consulting the states will be taken on priority to boost the projects. Road Ministry has set a target of awarding 7,000 km worth of road projects during the financial year (2014-15), under the BOT (build, own, operate) and EPC (engineering, procurement and construction) models. The ministry which had set a target of awarding 9,000 km of projects in 2013-14 could award less than 2,000 km projects by the end of the period, said the minister.

Rs 40,000 cr Approved to Boost Infrastructure

In a boost to the infrastructure sector, the ministry has approved worth over Rs 40,000 crore of highway projects to be implemented in time to come. These projects are in the states of Jammu and Kashmir, Himachal Pradesh, Uttarakhand and the Northeastern region.

A sum of Rs 20,000 crore has been sanctioned for Jammu and Kashmir. They include 2-laning and 4-laning of National Highways in the state some roads projects in Leh and Ladakh. It will co-ordinate with the PWD (Public Works Department) of the state for these projects.

The ministry has also announced projects worth Rs 15,000 crore in the country's north-eastern region comprising Assam, Manipur, Meghalaya, Mizoram, Arunachal Pradesh, Nagaland and Tripura. A detailed project report is expected shortly for new road network for which the work will commence a one-way road in hilly tract between Kulka and Mandis, basically widening the existing one besides those of Uttarakhand after massive floods work will start very soon. An outlay of Rs 6,000 crore has been earmarked, said the minister.

Aviation Sector

Sector's Problem: "The civil aviation sector faces crucial issues like building of airports at non-metro cities, slashing of taxes on jet fuel and turning around the ailing Air India. A detailed presentation is understood to have been made on the issues which also included downgrade of India's safety ranking by US regulator Federal Aviation Administration (FAA) and review of the rule requiring an airline to have flown domestic for five years and having a 20-aircraft fleet, before it could be allowed to fly abroad," said civil aviation minister Ashok Gajapathi Raju. The issue could be crucial to start-up carriers like AirAsia India and Tata-SIA Airlines, who would want to launch international flights no sooner as they can. His recent meeting with premier Modi centered on mobilising states to slash high sales tax rates on jet fuel, quick passage of the Civil Aviation Authority Bill, and making India a hub of aircraft engineering facilities by helping Maintenance, Repair and Overhaul (MRO) units. The national carrier seeks infusion of Rs 8,000 crore this financial year Rs 5,500 crore (2014-15) and Rs 2,500 crore (shortfall in committed equity infusion for 2013-14). It could have received a total of Rs 22,000 crore of the Rs 30,000 crore revival plans chalked out by UPA-II government. The government would focus on construction of low-cost airports in non-metro cities for deepen penetration of air connectivity. Another major issue would be the stalled process of modernising six airports, including those at Chennai and Kolkata, which were initiated and then halted by the previous government. Development of 50 no-frill airports by the Airports Authority of India in several states and greenfield airports are slated for development in Navi Mumbai, Juhu, Goa, Kannur, Pune, Sriperumbudur, Bellary and Raigarh are also part of the unfinished tasks of the erstwhile UPA-II government. The government could have to take urgent steps for restoration of the top Category-I status of the country's safety mechanism from Category- II by the US aviation regulator in 2014, January. The downgrade of India's aviation safety mechanism to Category-II by the FAA had its implications. Preparations are needed for restoration, at the earliest. The US aviation regulator had lowered India's ranking placing among countries which seldom meet the safety norms stipulated by the UN body - International Civil Aviation Authority.

Rs 49k cr Losses Put Aviation Sector on Verge of Collapse

The civil aviation sector is on the verge of collapse. It accumulated losses of Rs 49,000 crore and needs an urgent boost to prevent more Kingfisher-type meltdowns and job losses, Civil Aviation Minister Ashok Gajapathi Raju bemoaned. He pointed out that poor returns from airports, burgeoning costs and a tax structure that hurt Indian maintainance, repair and overhaul industry was burying the sector under debt. The industry could generate large revenues and enhance employment if service tax and VAT structures were made attractive. The current rates make India a 35per cent more expensive destination for MRO operations than a place like Singapore. Air India contributes a staggering Rs 30,000 crore to the accumulated Rs 49,000 crore losses in the civil aviation sector and the ministry outlined the need for a credible, result-oriented capital infusion plan.

No Decision Taken to Privatise A-I

The Civil Aviation Minister said that no decision has been taken to privatise Air India, with the government saying it was close to finalising a short-term strategy to strengthen the burgeoning civil aviation sector, including slashing taxes on jet fuel. "By and large, there is a general feeling that the aviation sector in India is no way near its potential. So we are working on that and trying to achieve that potential... We are working out a short-term strategy, setting some goals for ourselves within the Ministry."

He was responding to a question whether the Ministry had formulated a 100-day plan for the aviation sector after he recently met Prime Minister Narendra Modi. Asked whether Air India's privatisation was discussed at this meeting, he said the national carrier formed "a substantive part of our discussion. All issues relating to Air India was discussed. No decision has been taken and I would not like to stir the hornet's nest".

Aviation Sector Waiting for a Smooth Take Off

The aviation sector in India requires a terrible makeover. The thirteen major airports and sixty non-major airports handle 95 per cent of the country's external trade. They suffer from range of customs procedure and lack of inefficient operation system. Environmental clearances take upto five years before construction. Tariff issues are other set of hazards. These affect private investment severely for the sector. There are lot of changes and amendment for the sector. Here are five such issues they are expecting a solution:

A 10-year Old Tax Holiday: Though Ports Regulatory Authority Bill of 2011 has been looking into these concerns; major changes have not been made. A 10-year old tax holiday covers customs, excise and service tax to the aerospace manufacturing and MRO (maintenance, repair and overhaul) sector is a necessity. The creation of jobs and saving of foreign exchange could be larger than the national loss from the tax holiday policy.

Reduce the cost of ATF (Aviation Turbine Fuel): The cost of ATF is higher than that of Gulf and Asian countries. The soaring oil prices have avoided ATF on uniform levy of four per cent across India.

Upgrade Existing Airports: Essentials airport infrastructure require round-the-clock maintenance. Ground handling, fuel farm should be covered under the same umbrella. The passenger and cargo traffic at 15-20 per cent needs requisite support.

Ratify Civil Aviation Authority Bill: As most of the financial powers lie with Central Government financial decisions which needs to be taken immediately, does not get approved when in need. Quick passing of the Civil Aviation Authority Bill will give more independence to the Directorate General of Civil Aviation (DCCA), which will help them function better.

Allocate Money for NAU and AME: To support the upgradation of Aircarft Maintenance Engineering (AME) and to set up National Aviation

Universities (NAU) in the country, government should allocate a particular amount of money in the budget. There have also been talks about civil aviation ministry planning to impose nominal cess on some of the metropolitan airports like in Delhi, Kolkata and Mumbai, although there have been no further discussions on it.

India Expects 400 Million Air Passengers by 2020

The aviation minister said that India has witnessed a growth in number of air travellers due to liberal aviation policy and entry of small air carrier, and is likely to touch 400 million marks by 2020. The entry of small carriers has increased the number of middle class passengers to 169 million, a six per cent growth for 2013-14 in comparison to 2012-13. It is expected to rise above 400 million passengers by the year 2020. India's aviation was fastest growing market in the world, being the 10th largest. It is the domestic travel market in the world with an immense potential in maintenance, repair, ground handling and capacity building. Air connectivity to Bikaner was bound to increase tourism in the sandy desert part of the state, claimed the civil aviation minister, Ashok Ganapathi Raju.

Govt Asks States to Cut Tax on Jet Fuel

The minister and his top bureaucrats made a presentation to the prime minister on ways to are bleeding revive the sector. Many airlines are bleeding due to high interest and fuel costs. The jet fuel sold in India is nearly 50-60 per cent costlier than elsewhere else due to addition of state sales levies on the ATF which accounts for anywhere between 4-34 per cent. The previous government had tried to put the ATF under regulated regime of a declared good, thereby attracting a single value added tax (VAT) rate of about four percent nationwide. However, the move never took off. Domestic airlines could not even import fuel.

Industry–Modern, Competitive and Caring

The government at the Centre should no longer remain a market for the global industry; rather, a global manufacturing hub. It has to encourage our industry to innovate and collaborate internationally, for efficient production and effective cost. Economic freedom implies that government will not get in the way of the freedom of individuals to start and operate legitimate businesses. Increased economic freedom will break open the economic space to new entrants, especially in the form of small and medium-enterprises, creating jobs and prosperity. Particularly, it will ensure that a conducive, enabling environment is created for 'doing business' in India easy. It will focus on cutting the red tape, simplifying the procedures and removing the bottlenecks. It ensure logistics infrastructure, including stable power. It attempts to move towards a single-window system of clearances at the centre and the State level through Hub-spoke model. It will put in place a mechanism Central and state governments work in close co-ordination and synergy while giving clearances to mega projects. Decision-making on environment clearance will be made transparent as well as time-bound. It will set up World class Investment and Industrial regions as Global Hubs of Manufacturing. It will set up a task force to review and revive our MSME sector (Micro and Small Medium Scale Enterprises); enabling it with better access to formal credit and technology for modernisation.

Frame the environment laws without leading to confusion and will lead to speedy clearance of proposals without delay.

Infrastructure: Connecting the Nation

Bullet trains and aviation and port projects aims to shrink India

Nothing conveys the idea of nation-building more as the grand images of infrastructure development — men and machine at work and trucks, ships and trains driving the country forward along highways, seas and rails; it represents a vision that is visible and tangible. India's first Prime Minister Jawaharlal Nehru, credited as the architect of modern India, conveyed the idea of a nation in the making through a scientific vision based on development of infrastructure — heavy industries, big dams and a vibrant public sector. The Prime Minister Narendra Modi, too, buoyed by the popular mandate the BJP received under his leadership, would settle for nothing less than being the architect of a new India that "unhesitatingly desires to grow" and nurtures the ambition of emerging as a global superpower.

His vision for the re-imagination of India is bejewelled with a Diamond Quadrilateral of bullet trains connecting the four metros; a Sagar Mala project connecting India's coastal cities with the mainland; hundred new smart cities; and the revival of ex-Pm AB Vajpayee's ambitious river-linking project. But while Nehru's vision was driven by the public sector, Modi intends to fuel his massive infrastructure drive through foreign investment and public private partnerships, with half the $1 trillion required expected to come from the private sector. To begin with, the government is working to set up a $4-5 billion dollar infrastructure fund, with Japanese and Korean participation, to finance infrastructure projects, besides hoping to raise Rs 58,425 crore through disinvestment. The Prime Minister's Jan Dhan Yojana, while based on the broader premises of financial inclusion, is expected to prove another vehicle to fund the grand infrastructure plans by boosting household savings. In the Budget, Finance Minister Arun Jaitley set aside Rs 7,060 crore for developing hundred smart cities, which will be developed as satellite towns of larger cities and by modernising existing mid-sized cities. The first step towards this project was taken during Modi's just-concluded visit to Japan, where he inked a MoU with Japan to assist in the transformation of his Lok Sabha constituency, Varanasi, into a smart heritage city on the lines of Kyoto. Besides, Mr. Modi secured a commitment from Japanese Prime Minister Shinzo Abe to invest $33.6 billion in infrastructure projects in India over a period of five years.

Gujarat Model in Industry

Strategic planning is undoubtedly needed to bring about parallel agricultural and industrial growth. Gujarat organised five vibrant summits in the last decade. 7,936 MoUs were signed with the investment commitment of Rs 20.83 lakh crore. It created over 52 lakh for local youth jobs. In agro-based industries, MoUs worth Rs 81,600 crores have been signed. The people of Gujarat saw the dream of parallel development of agriculture and industry a decade ago. It has become a reality and is a talking point the world over. Gujarat became the auto hub of India, besides textile and petro capital. The state has a farsighted vision for small scale industries. The country's five per cent population lives in Gujarat which has six per cent of the country's land mass and its GDP share is ten per cent. The contribution of nearly four lakh small and medium industries is noteworthy. The country's 70 per cent salt production is in Gujarat. The state leads in caustic soda production (90 per cent); chemicals (60 per cent); petrochemicals (50 per cent); pharma (40 per cent); and polished diamonds (80 per cent). Salt, pharma and chemicals is largely run by small scale entrepreneurs.

Gadkari Announces Rs 2 Lakh Cr for Infrastructure Projects

Road Transport and Highways Minister Nitin Gadari claims the government to have enrmarked Rs. two Lakh crore works infrentruct we projects. He was addressing the annual convention of Society of Indian Automobile Manufacturers. The department desies to build two lakh km of roads under Public-Private-Partnership (PPP) mode. It includes the widening of existing one lakh km of highways. More funds through securitisation of toll revenue Returns about Rs 1.8 lakh crore in 15 years. The government will launch funds could also be raised through infrastructure bonds worth Rs 10,000 crore. 350 electronic toll plazas by December and build amenities for drivers and commuters on every 50 km stretch. Bids have already been floated for consultancy and design of 270 such facilities. The Motor Vehicles legislation is expected to be passed in the upcoming Winter Session. The government seeks suggestions from stakeholders. The set will be analogous to those fallowed in US, Japan, Germany, UK, Singapore and Australia. The minister appealed to SIAM on the need for introducing ethanol-friendly engines to cut on the huge Rs 6 lakh crore annual bills on import of crude in the country. Boosting waterways for transportation of cargo and planned introducing seaplanes, airport-like terminals on Ganga besides shipment of cargo through waterway would else the situation.

Govt Plans Industrial Corridors, Smart Cities to Boost Manufacturing

The government said that to boost manufacturing sector, it intends to develop industrial corridors and smart cities for providing infrastructure based on modern technology with high-speed communication. Listing its achievements and initiatives in 2014, the commerce and industry ministry also said that existing infrastructure would be strengthened. "Innovation and research activities are supported through fast paced registration system and accordingly infrastructure of Intellectual Property Rights registration set-up has been upgraded. The requirement of skills for industry are to be identified and accordingly development of workforce to be taken up," it said. Strengthening infrastructure, is one of the four pillars on which 'Make in India' is based. The other pillars include improving ease of doing business, focus on 25 identified sectors and new mindset. "Industry is accustomed to see Government as a regulator. 'Make in India' intends to change this by bringing a paradigm shift in how government interacts with industry.

The government will partner industry in economic development of the country. The approach will be that of a facilitator and not regulator," it said. Further, it said that after de-licensing of several defence sectors' products, 61 pending applications for defence industries have been disposed of, including granting of 43 licenses, and advising that 18 applications do not need license. About e-Biz project, it said that eight more central government services such as permanent account numbe (PAN) and tax deduction and collection account number (TAN) services of Central Board of Direct Taxes (CBDT), DIN, certificate of incorporation and certificate of commencement of business services and employer registration service of EPFO will be integrated shortly. Delhi Mumbai industrial corridor (DMIC), it said request for qualification proposal for the empanelment of the EPC (engineering, procurement and construction) Contractors for roads and services for activation area of Ahmedabad Dholera special investment region in Gujarat has been floated. "Final environmental clearance has already been obtained from the Ministry of Environment for three DMIC nodes," it added. Significant progress has been made in the model solar power project at Neemrana, Rajasthan and the first batch of panels have arrived at the site, it said, adding the actual commissioning of the project has been initiated. It said that things are moving for other corridors including Chennai Bangalore industrial corridor, Vizag Chennai industrial corridor and Bengaluru Mumbai economic corridor. To revamp special economic zones, it said "mixed land use in non-processing areas to be allowed" soon.

Manufacturing

A strong manufacturing sector will not only bridge the demand-supply gap leading to price stabilisation, but also create millions of jobs and increase income for the working class. Above all, it will increase the revenue for government and lead to import substitution to bring down the import bill. The government will make India a hub for cost-competitive labour-intensive mass manufacturing. To give boost to manufacturing, NDA government will accord high priority to the growth of manufacturing, so that it can create enough jobs in the country. This sector must grow fast to ensure employment and asset creation. Take steps rationalisation of interest rate and have a clear tax policy to remove uncertainty and create investor confidence. It will remove red-tapism involved in approvals, make it easy to do business, invest in logistics infrastructure, ensure 24×7 power supply and undertake labour reforms, besides embrace steps to create conducive environment for investors.

Industry

The e-Biz platform aims to create a business and investor-friendly ecosystem facilitating business and investment related clearances and compliances on a 24×7 single portal, with an integrated payment gateway. All Central Government Departments and Ministries will integrate their services with the e-Biz platform on priority by 31st December, 2014. A National Industrial Corridor Authority, headquartered in Pune, will co-ordinate the development of industrial corridors, with smart cities linked to transport connectivity. It will be the cornerstone of the strategy to drive India's growth in manufacturing and urbanisation, at a corpus of Rs 100 crore. The Amritsar Kolkata Industrial master planning will be completed for establishment of industrial smart cities in seven states. The master planning of three new smart cities in the Chennai-Bengaluru Industrial Corridor region, viz., Ponneri in Tamil Nadu, Krishnapattinam in Andhra Pradesh and Tumkur in Karṇataka will be completed soon. The perspective plan for the Bengaluru-Mumbai Economic Corridor (BMEC) and Vizag-Chennai corridor would be completed with the provision for 20 new industrial clusters. Kakinada, its adjoining area and the port will be developed as the key driver of economic growth in the region with a special focus on hardware manufacturing. Exports cannot be exponentially increased unless the states play dominant role in promotion through good infrastructure and facilitation. It is proposed to establish an export promotion mission to bring stakeholders under one umbrella.

Special Economic Zones: The Government is committed to revive the Special Economic Zones (SEZs) and make them effective instruments of industrial production, economic growth, export promotion and employment generation. For achieving this, effective steps would be undertaken to operationalise the Special Economic Zones, to revive the investors' interest to develop better infrastructure and to effectively and efficiently using the available unutilised land.

Apprenticeship: Comparing the size of the Indian economy, the unsatisfactory performance of the Apprenticeship Training Scheme and a large number of unutilised training facilities. Apprenticeship Act will be suitably amended to make it more responsive to industry and youth. MSMEs will be encouraged to avail the benefits.

Micro, Small and Medium Enterprises Sector

SMEs form the backbone of our Economy. They account for a large portion of our industrial output and employment. The bulk of service sector enterprises are SMEs. Most of them are SMEs are own Account Enterprises. A majority of them are owned or run by SCs, STs and OBCs. A committee with representatives from the finance, MSME departments abd the RBI will give concrete suggestions on how to finanace them. Promotion of entrepreneurship and start-up companies remains a challenge. There have been some efforts to encourage. One principal limitation has been availability of start-up capital by way of equity to be brought in by the promoters. In order to create conducive eco-system for the venture capital in the MSME sector, it is proposed to establish Rs 10,000 crore funds as a catalyst to attract private capital by way of equity, quasi equity, soft loans and risk capital.

A corpus of Rs 200 crore will promote innovation, entrepreneurship and agro-industry through technology centre network. The definition of MSME will be reviewed to provide for a higher capital ceiling. A programme to facilitate forward and backward linkages with multiple value chain of manufacturing and service delivery will be put in place. Entrepreneur-friendly legal bankruptcy framework will be developed for SMEs to enable easy exit. A nationwide "District level Incubation and Accelerator Programme" would be taken up for incubation of new ideas and necessary support for entrepreneurship.

Textiles: The government proposes to set up a Trade Facilitation Centre and a Crafts Museum with an outlay of Rs 50 crore to develop and promote handloom products. Varanasi could be a Textile mega-cluster. More Textile mega-clusters will spruce up at Bareily, Lucknow, Surat, Kuttch, Bhagalpur, Mysore and one in Tamil Nadu. A sum of Rs 200 crore has been earmarked. A Hastkala Academy for the preservation, revival, and documentation of the handloom/handicraft sector in PPP mode in Delhi attracts an outlay of Rs 30 crore. Pashmina Promotion Programme (P-3) and another for development of paper machei crafts of Jammu and Kashmir will attrack an outlay of Rs 50 crore.

Infrastructure

India has emerged as the largest PPP market in the world. She has over 900 projects in various stages of development. PPPs have delivered some of the iconic infrastructure. These include airports, seaports and highways which are seen as models for development. But, we have also seen the weaknesses of the PPP framework. The rigidities in contractual arrangements, the need to develop more nuanced and sophisticated models of contracting and develop quick dispute redressal mechanism. An institution to provide support in mainstreaming PPPs called 3P. India will be set up with a corpus of Rs 500 crore.

Shipping: A policy for encouraging growth of Indian controlled tonnage will be formulated to ensure increase in employment of the Indian seafarers. Development of ports is also critical for boosting trade. Sixteen new port projects are proposed with on port connectivity. A sum of Rs 11,635 crore had been earmarked for the development of Outer Harbour Project in Tuticorin under phase-I. SEZs will also be developed in Kandla and JNPT. A comprehensive policy will promote Indian ship-building industry.

Inland Navigation: Development of inland waterways can vastly the capacity for goods transportation. A project on the river Ganga called *'Jal Marg Vikas'* (National Waterways-I) will be developed between Allahabad and Haldia. It will cover a distance of 1,620 km. It will enable commercial navigation of at least 1,500 tonne vessels. The project will be completed over a period of six years at an estimated cost of Rs 4,200 crore.

New Airports: Despite increase in air connectivity, air travel is still out for appreciable number of Indians. A scheme for development of new airports under Tier-I and Tier-II will be launched trough Airport Authority of India or PPPs.

Cooperative Sector: Every effort will be made to encourage the cooperative sector. It will review the existing laws and amend the multi-state cooperative act to remove anomalies.

Handicrafts: The value chain of the sector driven will be on quality and finishing.

Market linkages: Access to credit and information and skills upgradation, value addition will be encouraged through branding, packaging and state-of-art.

Artisans: Schemes will be launched for skill-upgradation and enhancement of business opportunities for artisans like smiths, weavers, carpenters, hair-dressers, shoe-smiths, and potters. Services will be driven by quality and efficiency.

Business and Trade

The modern era is an era of exchange. Over-regulation needs to be addressed for businessmen and traders. Transparent systems will ensure credibility of our goods and services. Transport bottlenecks and export hassles have to be removed. Tradable items data ought to be made available to the rest of the world. Focus on Zero defect products. Build world class Ports; connecting them with roads and rail to the hinterland so as to drive the maritime trade of the country. Air Cargo facilities will be enhanced throughout the country. An Export Promotion Mission will integrate stakeholders. Current accounts deficit will be brought down aggressively by focusing on exports and reducing the dependency on imports. Value addition on our products will be the biggest task. It shall work with the state governments to usher in the

GST in an appropriate time-frame. A robust IT network system will be put in place. It will embark on the path of IPRs and Patents in a big way. The government will take necessary steps to protect the interest of retailers, small traders and small vendors. It will equip them with the latest techniques and methods to modernise them competitive. It will ensure that the retailers and SMEs don't have to spend time and money for seeking multiple licenses to start the business. A system in place could avoid harassment of small traders, ensuring easy availability of institutional credit. Review obsolete and multiple laws to reduce and simplify them. Remove ambiguity in rules to make way for prompt decisions without any scope for discretion. Telecom revolution has touched the length and breadth of the country. There is significant scope and necessity to improve the quality of voice and data to leverage the potential fully.

Tourism–Untapped Potential

Tourism and hospitality can play as a foreign exchange has the ability to create millions of jobs every year. It plays a key role in socio-economic progress through creation of jobs, enterprise, infrastructure development, and foreign exchange earning. A mission mode project is expected to create 50 tourist circuits affordable and built around like: (a) Archaeological and Heritage, (b) Cultural and Spiritual, (c) Himalayan, (d) Desert, (e) Coastal, (f) Medical (Ayurveda and Modern Medicine), etc. This will lead to creation of infrastructure and employment potential around each tourist circuit and help in boosting revenue generation. Specialised course in tourism will be commenced for capacity development. Safety and Security of tourists would be accorded due priority.

Labour Force—The Pillar of Our Growth

The government recognises the fact that the labour is the key to revival of economy. Labour laws do govern them. We believe in promoting a harmonious relationship between labour and the industry either will play an important role in contributing to economic growth and development. It will ensure the interests of labour in the unorganised sector. The government will propose to encourage industry owners and labour to embrace the concept of 'Industry Family'. This concept, in which industry owners and labours bond as a family is guided by the principles of efficiency, skill development and upgradation, productivity, appropriate wages and perquisites, on time and personal security. The government will issue identity cards to the unorganised sector labourers. The arrangements will be made to safeguard their health and education services. Their skills will be upgraded through appropriate training. Extend access to modern financial services to labour including the option of setting up dedicated Workers Bank. Stakeholders will review outdated, complicated and even contradictory labour laws. Strengthen the pension and health insurance safety nets for various kinds of labourers.

16 Stability, Sustainability and Good Governance

Stable Relations

India is a diverse country. Diverse communities settled in vastly different regions have their own aspirations. The centre and the states have to evolve a working system, which leads to harmonious relations. The genuine grievances of every state will be addressed in a comprehensive manner. The government will be an enabler and facilitator in the rapid progress of states. It will evolve a model of national development, which is driven by the states. Team India shall not be limited to the Prime Minister led team also, but will include chief ministers and other functionaries as equal partners. Ensure fiscal autonomy of states while urging financial discipline. Create 'Regional Councils of States', with common problems and concerns, seeking solutions applicable across a group of states. The government will encourage cooperation among states on security-related issues, inter-state disputes and for removing inter-regional economic disparities, promoting tourism. It recognises the special needs and unique problems of the hill and desert states. State-specific developmental priorities/ models will be evolved, so that the aspirations of the people are met. Given the unique status of Union Territories (UTs), they will receive special attention. It will focus on developing and strengthening the economy of UTs. Tourism will be promoted, tribal welfare and their rights will receive full attention, and infrastructure and coastal area development will be given top priority. The government reiterates its commitment to the protection and integrated development of our island territories. The moribund forums like 'National Development Council' and 'Inter-State Council' will be revived and made into active bodies. Involve the state governments in the promotion of foreign trade and commerce. Help the states mobilise resources through investments in industry, agriculture and infrastructure.

Decision and Policy Paralysis: The country has suffered a decade of maladministration and scams in addition to decision and policy paralysis;

thus bringing growth and development to a grinding halt leading to a 'Governance deficit'. This situation will be changed and the engine of Government will be ignited again with strong will-power and commitment to public interest. It will also encourage the bureaucracy to take right decisions and contribute their might in building a modern India.

Poor Delivery: Wherever we go, we encounter bottlenecks. We experience it on a daily basis in government offices for even the simplest of public services, in our courts buried in high pendency and so on. Similarly, we are known by a culture of missing links and lack of last mile connectivity. We have water but no pipeline to carry it; we have schools but no teachers; we have computers and machines but no electricity; we have scientists but no labs; we have instruments but no one to work on them. This reduces the pace of our performance resulting in wastage of time, money and energy. Intent to do the right thing and the will to do things rightly is missing. This has to be attended to on a priority basis. Whatever we do and provide for, the whole chain has to be kept in mind. With this in mind, we will remove bottlenecks and missing links in all sectors, activities and services; focus on proper planning and execution for right outcomes; strive for scale and speed with futuristic vision; build institutions for today and tomorrow.

Credibility Crisis: The biggest challenge that India faces today is to restore the credibility of, and trust in the Union Government. In recent years, the Union Government has lost every semblance of credibility. Its intentions, integrity and initiatives, all are questionable. The Congress party has not only lowered the dignity of the Government, but also the dignity of India. This is what is driving recent adversities like the falling value of rupee and countries riding roughshod over us. The BJP-led NDA government at the Centre will work for restoring the trust and credibility of the government. It will also ensure that the chain of responsibility and accountability is built in the system.

Integrating the Nation - Its Vastness and Voices: In a democratic country like India, everyone is not only free, but also encouraged to voice his or her concerns towards discrimination, biasdeness, malpracticess and corruption. It is also necessary that these voices be heard and concerns redressed. However, all this should happen within the framework of the Constitution and with the spirit of 'India First'. It's important to keep the Nation at the forefront of its thoughts and actions. Any activity, which disrupts the integrity of the nation, cannot be in the interest of any segment of the society or any region of the country. All Indians living in different regions of the country have an equal stake in the progress of the country. They have to be assured about the fruits of the progress. Presently, we see a vast regional disparity between different regions of the country along developmental parameters, particularly between the western part and the eastern part. Despite their richness in natural as well as human resources, eastern part of India still lags behind the spheres of the human activities.

So, the government shall give the highest priority towards bringing the eastern parts of the country on par with the western parts. To that extent, there shall be special focus and emphasis on the development of the eastern side of India. Government will play the role of an enabler and a facilitator to the rapid progress of the states. Planning along regional aspirations, strengths and potentials, evolving appropriate strategies for various zones of the country like hilly regions, plains, desert and coastal areas.

Regional Aspirations: The new government at the Centre has always stood for greater decentralisation through smaller States.

Northeast: Resource-rich North-Eastern states lag behind in development due to poor governance, systemic corruption and poor delivery of public services. NDA government had initiated concrete steps to address the issue of development of Northeast by setting up the Ministry of North-Eastern Region. It will empower this ministry with a broader charter and non-lapsable funds for rapid development of the region. The government will put special emphasis on enhancing the connectivity within the region and to the rest of the country. There will be special emphasis on massive infrastructure development, especially along the Line of Actual Control in Arunachal Pradesh and Sikkim.

- Address the issue of Flood control in Assam and river water management.
- Nurture more job generating opportunities like tourism and IT industry.
- Address the issue of infiltration and illegal immigrants in the Northeast region on a priority basis. This will include clear policy directions and effective control at the ground level.
- Complete pending fencing work along the India-Bangladesh and India-Myanmar border, stepping up border security.
- Take measures for the safety of North-Eastern students studying across the country including setting up Hostels for North-Eastern students at various educational centres.
- Deal with Insurgent groups with a firm hand.

Jammu and Kashmir

Jammu and Kashmir was, is and shall remain an integral part of the Union of India. The territorial integrity of India is inviolable. The government will pursue an agenda of equal and rapid development in the three regions of the state—Jammu, Kashmir and Ladakh.

The return of Kashmiri Pandits to the land of their ancestors with full dignity, security and assured livelihood will figure high on the Modi's main agenda. The long pending problems and demands of refugees from Pakistan Occupied Kashmir (PoK) will be addressed. It reiterates its stand on the Article 370, and will discuss with stakeholders and remains committed to the abrogation of this article. Steps will be taken to provide good governance, better infrastructure, educational opportunities, healthcare and more job opportunities, leading to a better quality of life in the Valley. In the context of the newly formed states like Seemandhra and Telangana, the Prime Minister is committed to do full justice and address the issues of development and governance of Seemandhra and Telangana.

Decentralisation and People's Participation

From Representative to Participatory Democracy, India is a country of immense diversity—a highly decentralised federal structure is thus crucial in meeting with varied ideas and aspirations of our diverse people. Power is currently concentrated in Delhi and the state capitals. The NDA government believes power should be genuinely decentralised. It has stood for greater decentralisation through devolving of powers to the states. A vast reservoir of People's Power has not yet been tested in the real sense. It has not been able to involve the people in governance as functionaries and facilitators.

People's Participation: Our developmental process will be a people's movement - of *Jan bhagidari*. It will make them active drivers of development rather than mere passive recipients.

People's Engagement: The ruling government at the Centre through pro-active, pro-people good governance will ensure the government directly reaches out to people, especially the weak and marginalised sections of society. It will further evolve the Public-Private-Partnership (PPP) model into a People-Public-Private Partnership (PPPP) model.

The government is committed to strengthen the self-governance at local level and empower Panchayati Raj Institutions with extensive devolution of the 3 Fs - Functions, Functionaries and Funds.

Good performers amongst the Panchayats will be rewarded with additional developmental grants. Strengthen the institution of the Gram Sabha, respecting their inputs and initiatives for development process.

It will actively involve people in policy formulation and evaluation through various platforms. It will encourage Openness in the Government, involving all stakeholders in the decision-making processes.

Mandate for Good Governance

Politicians, the argument goes, exist at the centre of a vast network of corruption and patronage; populism has replaced cogent policy-making; while parliament barely functions, constantly disrupted by noisy and undignified protests. For the past decade, stifling dynastic politics within the Congress party was pitted against a Hindu nationalist opposition that seemed to lack conviction or consistency. With both brands struggling to construct a convincing national narrative, regional and caste-based parties filled the gap.

Politics had fragmented, and an era of weak and directionless rule by coalition governments seemed to have dawned. Voters saw only their narrow interests, casting their vote only to vote for their caste. The entrepreneurial class just wanted government to leave them alone, and barely bothered to vote. In China, many people looked at Indian democracy as the greatest advertisement for decisive, authoritarian rule.

Record Turnout: While turnout has been on a long-term decline for decades in established Western democracies, turnout in India reached an all-time record of 66.5 per cent buoyed by record numbers of first-time voters, by greater participation by women, and even by new-found enthusiasm among the nation's fast-growing middle-class.

The 2014 LS election saw a record voter turn out. A large number of women participated in the polls Momentum for change had been building for years. Twenty-four-hour news television might have turned politics into a game of sensationalism and sound-bites. It had helped expose corruption and demand accountability. The Right to Information Act had empowered the poor to ask questions of India's vast, creaking bureaucracy. Young and old alike took to streets in their hundreds of thousands to protest against corruption and the treatment of women. It ran a savvy and sophisticated campaign, carefully targeting seats where it had a chance of winning and cleverly turning a 31 per cent vote share into an outright majority in India's lower house of parliament, the Lok Sabha. Regional parties fared less well; even while Congress slumped, the vote share commanded by the two main parties topped 50 per cent, up from 47 per cent in 2009.

*National Narrative: M*ore importantly, the election was not a compendium of local, caste-driven contests. It contained an important national narrative. It throw out a government widely seen as both corrupt and inept, and voting in a man who promised clean, decisive leadership, good governance and development. Modi backed away from the politics of handout and subsidies. He pledged instead to give Indians of all stripes, rich and poor, urban and rural, the chance to realise their aspirations: for education, for jobs, and for even more fundamental building blocks to a better life. He assured round-the-clock supply of electricity and clean, running water. In his campaign, he created a powerful brand, and barged in an ambitious promise. He cast himself as a Messianic figure, the knight on a white horse come to rescue the nation. His home state of Gujarat was portrayed as the *Promised Land,* where everyone could realise the Indian Dream.

Two Bold Proclamations

The international or, more accurately, SAARC underpinnings during the swears-in ceremony have been an unlikely distraction. It is healthy to bring the discussion back to the starting and finishing point of the 2014 general election. Indians voted as they did owing to profound desire to usher change in domestic politics and foreign policy, however meaningful to the small band of 'strategic experts', is no real substitute for more homely concerns. Indeed, it is on this count that the leaders' selection of his team of ministers did not match up to exhilaration that accompanied his thumping win.

First, there was the cut-off age of 75, above which an MP would not be appointed a minister. May be this was the way of tackling old guard that refuses to retire voluntarily and may be the cut-off date was needlessly generous. What is important is that a giant step has been taken to spare Indian the political gerontocracy. The principle that politics should have a retirement age has been introduced.

Secondly, this constitute somewhat remarkable change, Modi has introduced the principle of dynasty-free politics in the BJP (but not the alliance parties). This ensured individual MPs who either 'inherited' seats or whose parents were active already in the political sphere were excluded from consideration. This may have been harsh on some talented individuals, but it is important to see the principle as momentous and, indeed, radical political statement that contrasts sharply with the earlier regime's penchant for inheritors. In the coming days, many political parties, but particularly the Congress, will have to determine their attitude to this far-reaching principle.

Ten-point Agenda

A welcome step but more to be done: The electorate who gave a massive mandate to the new Prime Minister Narendra Modi welcomes his ten-point agenda for better and more transparent administration. Online auctions for government contracts, tenders and presumably, natural resources as well—should promote transparency and reduce graft. However, in the case of things like minerals, this will not be enough. Coal India's monopoly over coal will have to go. The professional miners were allowed exploring for, mine and market coal. The practice of allocating captive mines should be scrapped. An active market for coal, without the inefficiencies dragging down Coal India BSE -0.03 per cent, will immediately boost our energy sector. Empowering the bureaucracy is fine, as long as it does not turn into a hydra-headed monster slowing down development. Education, health, water, energy and roads are important sectors. These demand widespread reform and improvement. Only a skilled and healthy working population can boost India's growth.

Modi has listed inflation control as one of the priorities of his government. The Reserve Bank of India has done more than what it could. It has tightened monetary policy and coolly staving off an attack on the rupee. To attack inflation, now largely concentrated in food, the government ought to fix the farm sector. India already has a record 80 million tonnes of grain stocks. A part of this must be offloaded in small markets all over India. Vegetable, fruit, dairy and meat prices are soaring, as demand outstrips supply. To prevent wastage, cold chains must be built across India. The APMC Act, which concentrates buying in the hands of a few middlemen finds scrapped in all states. Cold chains will need power. Rural electrification BSE 4.72 per cent has to be boosted. A combination of these measures will control inflation, and boost farm productivity.

It is a good idea to liberalise foreign direct investment. It has been automatic without any porous cap in all save a negative list of sectors. In defence, where proprietary technology is involved, with implications for strategic reliability, the effort should be to develop indigenous capability, however.

***Ten-point Agenda**: Has the 'over-excited' babudom taken over the Namo Govt:* Recently, the PM announced the top ten priorities for the first 100 days, which are:

1. Build confidence in bureaucracy.
2. Welcome innovative ideas. Allow babus to be free to work.
3. Education, Health, Water, Energy and roads will be priority.
4. Transparency in the government. Promote e-auction.
5. Place the system for inter-ministerial issues.
6. Place the people-oriented system in government machinery.
7. Address concerns relating to the economy.
8. Infrastructure and investment reforms.
9. Implement policy in time-bound manner.
10. Let stability and sustainability reign in government policy.

If one looks at the list, one can clearly sees disconnect between the promises made before the election through the manifesto and the path the government has taken. By putting only education, health, water, energy and roads in the list of ministerial priorities, the government has missed out the high priority assigned to job creation, agriculture, rural development and curbing corruption, as the key promises made in the manifesto. This gives a sense that the 'over-excited' babudom has taken over the Modi government. There is a visible disconnect from the thinking on which BJP campaigned and drafted its national priorities before facing public.

Question that merits a consideration, whether there should have been priorities for the entire government across ministries, or was there a need to limit the focus to five ministries and sectors? Why should there be a laundry list of ten priorities? Why not just have simple lists of five must haves? Ideally, the first seven days must be used to look at the situation at hand. Decide the framework/working principles. Divide the urgent and the important. Align the overarching goals with the team's working. Assign the jobs. Decide the targets and KRAs. Define the supervision and monitoring process. Put in place measures for public interaction and accountability.

Ideally, the top ten priorities should have been reduced to five 'must haves':

1. Set the goals (deliverables) for the first 100 days, for every ministry.
2. Deciding the frame-work and working principles for every ministry. Let this remove ambiguity that leads to indecision; including the time to be spent in the field. Let this include a minimum number of surprise checks by minister and officials, without information.
3. Decide the team members and their responsibilities with KRAs for each team member. Let this include the supervision and monitoring process. Give the report card to the public every six months.
4. Social media plan for public interface. Spell out the grievance redressal mechanism.
5. Key objective is to remove bottlenecks. Ensure implementation, so that the policies, plans and programmes impact the beneficiaries. The top priorities should have been just procedural and systemic changes.

The 100 days work should lead to laying a strong foundation for the next five years. Key message for every ministry is to move from the policies to plans and getting into action on ground, without waiting for the 100th day. Every effort must be measurable in terms of time taken to resolve the issue. Utilisation of funds and actual ground level impact is accountable. Let the system in place for performance review. Finding out the quantum of social utilisation of funds and actual ground level impact with a system in place be subjected to performance review. Let there be social and impact audit for every programme.

Doing the right things and doing things rightly are equally important in running the nation. The strength of Modi-led Gujarat government was in bureaucracy. Steps have to be taken to ensure that the strength of erstwhile Gujarat government does not become a weakness in Delhi! Key message is to keep the heads low and overheads lower. Team members must not forget that the buck finally stops at the Prime Minister!

Jan Dhan May be Extended to Insurance, Pension Sectors

Prime Minister's Jan Dhan Yojna (PMJDY) is likely to be replicated in the insurance and pension sector to extend the financial services to the hinterland. "Given the low levels of penetration of insurance and pension, there is a case for subsequently extending or replicating a project on the lines of PMJDY, to include the provision of insurance and pension services for the common man," RBI said.

At present, penetration of insurance and pension in India is very low. Insurance penetration (premiums measured as a percentage of GDP) is just about 4 per cent. Under the Financial Inclusion Plan, banks will have to revise their targets so as to match the targets allocated to them by the Centre under the PMJDY, the central bank said.

Revised target: With revised targets for opening of basic bank accounts in place, banks will have to ensure opening of at least one account in each household by January 26, 2015. As on December 24 2014, banks have achieved the 10 crore account opening mark under the PMJDY and have issued 7.75 crore RuPay cards.

"The timeline for providing banking services in villages with populations below 2,000 under the roadmap may be advanced from March 2016 to August 2015," the RBI said.

Take Decisions without Fear: PM to Babus

The Prime Minister Narendra Modi met secretaries of government departments collectively on May 28. He asked them to take decisions without fear. It was reported that he asked the secretaries to approach him directly to resolve issues and expedite decision-making. He also told them to take decisions and assured his full support. He also "encouraged the officers to take decisions and assured them that he would stand by them," an official statement. The PM asked the bureaucrats to simplify and streamline administrative rules and procedures in order to make them people-friendly. He expressed full faith in their commitment and competence to build a better future for the country. He said that "there may be outdated rules and processes. They are leading to avoidable confusion instead of serving the process of governance. He stressed upon the need to "identify and do away with such archaic rules and procedures". Modi "listened extensively" to the top bureaucrats in 150-minute interaction. He empathised with their sentiments while noting their anguish without realising their true potential under "circumstances".

The intent behind the meeting was to give the bureaucracy a greater role in decision-making. It will be with thrust on transparency and speedy and effective governance. To ensure that implementation of decisions and programmes are not stuck in 'red-tape'. He asked them call or e-mail directly for suggestions or intervention required in resolving issues or expediting decisions.

Good Environment

The government will create a policy environment which is "predictable, transparent and fair. It will seek to heal the fractured and contentious politics of previous years and work for the eradication of corruption in the country. The people of India have voted for a united, strong and modern India -"*Ek Bharat-Shreshta Bharat*". The government will work to fulfil these aspirations, with the involvement of all the 125 crore people of this great country. In a word of assurance to minorities, the address said the new government is committed to making minorities equal partners in India's progress and just-concluded election has been an election of hope.

"The surge in aspirations and the belief that these could be realised through democratic processes, has been amply reflected in the record 66.4 per cent participation by voters. It has been a clear verdict in favour of a single political party after a gap of nearly 30 years. The electorate transcended the boundaries of caste, creed, region and religion to come together. They voted decisively in favour of 'Development through Good Governance'.

NITI Aayog will Set Policy Agenda

PM to head panel that will give strategic advice: On the very first day of the New Year (2015), the government set up NITI Aayog (National Institution for Transforming India) in place of the Planning Commission. The Prime Minister will head the new institution tasked with the role of formulating policies and direction for the Government. Its Governing Council will comprise State Chief Ministers and Lt. Governors of Union Territories.

The Prime Minister will appoint the Aayog's Vice-Chairperson and CEO. Asian Development Bank's Former Chief Economist Arvind Panagariya is tipped to be the first Vice Chairperson. The Government plans to adopt a 'Bharatiya' approach to development, states the resolution of the Union Cabinet for setting up the Aayog. India needs an administration paradigm in which the government is an enabler rather than a provider of first and last resort, it states. It will recommend a national agenda, including strategic and technical advice on elements of policy and economic matters. It will also develop mechanisms for village-level plans and aggregate these progressively at higher levels of government. The institutions of governance and policy have to adapt to new challenges and must be built on the founding principles of the Constitution, the resolution states. On the planning process, it states that there was a need to separate the process from the strategy of governance.

Transforming India, it further states, would involve changes of two types — consequences of market forces and those that would be planned. "The maturing of our institutions and polity also entails a diminished role for centralised planning, which itself needs to be redefined." A state-of-the-art Resource Centre for good governance practices is also proposed. The original Planning Commission was set up in March, 1950 through a Cabinet Resolution, which the Modi Government scrapped in August 2014.

Bharatiya governance model unveiled: The Modi government Jan 1, 2015 unveiled its 'Bharatiya' governance model in the resolution for setting up the NITI (National Institution for Transforming India) Aayog. The resolution, approved by the Cabinet, reaffirms that India is a diverse country with distinct languages, faiths and cultural ecosystems. "This diversity has enriched the totality of the Indian experience," the resolution says. Politically too, India has embraced a greater measure of pluralism which has reshaped the federal consensus, it says. "States do not want to be mere appendages of the Centre... They seek a decisive say in determining the architecture of economic growth and development."

India no longer seeks the alleviation of poverty, states the resolution, but rather its elimination. "Poverty elimination remains one of the most important metrics by which alone we should measure our success as a nation." The essence of effective governance is defined to include pro-people agenda, citizens' participation, all-round women empowerment, equality of opportunity to the youth and transparency. Inclusiveness with special attention to the socially and economically disadvantaged sections and minorities is also included in the scheme of effective governance.

Enabling legislation: The role of government as a player in the industrial and service sectors is proposed to be reduced. "Instead, government has to focus on enabling legislation, policy making and regulation." India's middle class, including the neo-middle class, is unique in terms of its size and purchasing power, says the resolution. "Our continuing challenge is to ensure that this economically vibrant group remains engaged and its potential is fully realised." The resolution also says that the Non-Resident Indian community spread across more than 200 countries is a significant geo-economic and geo-political strength. "Future national policies must incorporate this strength in order to broaden their participation in the new India beyond just their financial support."

Urbanisation has to be viewed as an opportunity to use modern technology to create a wholesome and secure habitat while reaping the economic benefits that it offers, states the resolution. Policy-making must focus on providing necessary support to the more than 50 million small businesses, which are a major source of employment creation, in terms of skill and knowledge upgrades and access to financial capital and relevant technology. Dedicated to the people of Bharat Mata for gifting to the people of India a new hope in the midst of deep despair. For having encouraged me to stand for truth and justice, no matter what the cost.

Niti Aayog Likely to Start Functioning Soon

Within hours of the government announcing a new body to replace Planning Commission, the Yojana Bhawan staff began hectic preparations to welcome new vice-chairman of Niti Aayog and other members who are likely to be appointed shortly. "Government is expected to soon appoint vice-chairman and full time members of the newly formed NITI (National Institution for Transforming India) Aayog and they may join next week," a source said. The newly set up Niti Aayog is likely to go full throttle as early as next week, they added. The formation of Niti Aayog has ended the uncertainty among the staff. They were almost without work since the resignation of the Planning Commission's deputy chairman Montek Singh Ahluwalia and other members in May last year and later the announcement of disbanding of 65-year old body by Prime Minister Narendra Modi in his Independence day speech. The Aayog will have a vice-chairman and five full time members who are likely to join next week following the announcement of their appointment shortly. The Socialist-era Planning Commission was replaced by a new think-tank, NITI Aayog, that will be headed by the Prime Minister and will have all chief ministers as members in a broad-based Governing Council to involve states in evolving national development priorities. The inclusion of chief ministers and Lt. Governors in the Governing Council is a break with the past in the structuring of Niti Aayog which Modi, has described as a landmark change that will foster spirit of cooperative federalism. The body will also have a CEO and two part-time members, while four union ministers would serve as ex-officio members.

Cutting Through Legal Muddle

Burdensome and unnecessary laws and regulations not only impose heavy economic costs, but also provide fertile grounds for corruption. Initiative of replacing archai laws-regulations is long overdue. India has been characterised as one of the most over-regulated countries in the world. No central database of laws and regulations exists in the country. If such a database existed, it would have been of encyclopaedic proportion. There are over 1,200 statutes at the Union level alone, while exact figures for Union regulations and the total number of State laws are not easily discernible. Burdensome and unnecessary laws and regulations not only impose heavy economic cost, but also provide fertile grounds for corruption. It will contribute to the perpetuation of red-tapism and the classical Indian malaise of the 'Inspector Raj.' To any right-thinking person, such laws need to be repealed.

Comparative best Practices: A survey of comparative best practices clearly indicates the need for a dedicated deregulation agency to tackle the proliferative burdensome laws. The UK's *Better Regulation Executive* aims to strike a balance between protecting people's rights and freeing them from "unnecessary bureaucracy". It could reduce red-tape across government departments. Its agenda includes adoption of a "one in, two out" rule for business regulation. It can control the creation of new rules that inflate cost for business and voluntary organisations. This rule mandates when new regulation which imposes increased cost needs to be introduced. The department has to remove or alter existing regulations, to introduce a saving of two pounds for every pound of cost imposed.

The Way Forward: Inviting suggestions from ministries about ten laws, each that are fit to be repealed is a timely move. It signals the intention of the government to create a favourable political economy for deregulation. But, this is only the tip of an iceberg. It needs to be broken through systematically. As best practices demonstrate elsewhere, an effective architecture needs to identify and weed out such laws and regulations on the basis of established criteria. One might consider it counter-intuitive to establish a new nodal body as part of a project that is aimed at less bureaucracy, not more. However, to have a body whose chief focus is on deregulation and which can be held accountable; it is essential, whether the government is serious about its intention to meet this aim on sustained basis.

Such body could have a two-fold mission: first, it would identify onerous laws and regulations for repeal. Though, the exercise must start with Union laws, it is crucial to include State and local laws where the bulk of regulatory burden lies. While recommendations concerning the former can be made to the concerned ministry of the government of India, the latter would have to be presented to state governments with suggestions for repeal. Second, the authority could have to create and implement some framework for regular impact assessment of new Union laws, and review the existing ones. This would involve designing appropriate methodology for assessment, introducing that across government departments, and acting on the results.

Entrenching Periodic Review: To ensure that the authority is effective, the importance of review must be recognised statutorily. Review clauses ought to be systematically incorporated into certain categories of laws. For example, it must be made mandatory that all laws and provisions in laws that impose a significant new cost on government, businesses or civil society organisations include some *clause* that requires review every five years. Such review will establish whether the policy objectives of the law are still relevant, and whether, and in what form the law should remain on the books. Much like clauses on the power to make rules, regulations and remove difficulties, which are standard form provisions in most laws at the Union level, the time is ripe for the statutory review provision to become part of the same standard drafting form in select laws. These systemic changes will hold lawmakers accountable. It is they who draft, curb excessive and mindless law-making. This in turn could lead to a *pruned statute book*, which could play the significant role in catalysing the government's *stated-objective* of achieving bold maximum governance through minimum government.

Engage Good People

PM Modi to His Ministers: Amid his thrust on good governance, delivery and implementation of programmes, Prime Minister Narendra Modi held a marathon meeting with his entire 45-member Council of Ministers. His objective was to emphasise on these aspects. In the meeting that lasted for more than three hours, he asked his ministers to engage good people in offices and not family members. He believed them to have shared his ideas on how to boost the economy, attract greater investment and improve infrastructure. He sought suggestions on ways to improve governance. He is reported to have suggested the ministers to be extremely cautious. He advised them to deal with unknown people under caution. He asked them to reduce expenses of their departments and use office vehicles only for official work.

Reforms Commission Instead of Advisory Councils

Former telecom and disinvestment minister Arun Shourie believes that India doesn't need multiple advisory councils, but a Reforms Commission that sets the agenda for the country.

"Everyone does similar work. Whoever is closest to Sonia Gandhi (in UPA) or Narendra Modi will get heard. The Planning Commission should be replaced by a Reforms Commission. It could tell us where to move forward and how, instead of just doing the same old fund allocations," he said. Firmly backing the Rajasthan government's decision to amend outdated labour laws to boost job creation rather than wait for the Centre to change laws, Shourie said this is the only way forward on subjects in the concurrent list of the Constitution. "Such changes will solve many of the issues where investments are stuck. Labour laws don't help labour, they are only anti-jobs. The fact you need the government's permission for retrenchment means, it's redundant as no government will grant such an unpopular move," he said. Breaking of status quo, said Shourie, is critical for India to move ahead. It is important whether to promote competition among states to attract investments, or improve working conditions and create jobs. States could similarly take the lead in the land acquisition law, which the Centre may find difficult to amend. "Under the new land acquisition law, you can't set up a factory for four years. If that is on the concurrent list, some progressive states could reduce that gestation period through state laws," Shourie said.

Let the MPs Focus on Conduct, Governance

The PM Modi asked newly-elected party MPs to focus on their conduct both in Parliament and in public. The people were observing them and directed them to nurture their constituencies and spread the message of good governance. At a workshop organised for over 150 newly-elected Lok Sabha and Rajya Sabha MPs of BJP, Modi told them realise with the transition from Opposition to treasury benches, they had bigger responsibilities. Asking them not to voice their differences in public and function as the family. He said them not to get disillusioned over small issues as "there is no full stop in politics".

"To be a Member of Parliament is an important thing. One must look at it seriously. Remember, people are observing your performance not only in the House but even outside. "Our transition from Opposition to treasury benches is not limited to moving of few seats to the other side. This is a significant transition. We must try to appreciate the meaning of this. He sressed on the importance of brevity and focus in Parliamentary speeches for the lawmakers, without being around the bush, or mixing up of language, but be brief, to the points in chaste language without using invectives. Appealing to party MPs to eschew all kinds of negativism, he emphasised that their approach to the party has to be that of mutuality and fellow-feeling. "We are a family and all are working for a common goal. Try to make new friends, learn from each other and develop a new collectivism," he said.

"Training for BJP is not just a ritual. The party has a long tradition of capacity building. The party MPs would highlight the fact that the policies nurtured by Congress in the past few decades have not mitigated the suffering of the people and solve their problems." Taking a dig at those ridiculing such training camps for MPs, Modi said, "Lack of training in political establishment is a serious lacunae, but unfortunately, many outside politics take efforts for human resource development very lightly. Sometimes such elements even try to ridicule such efforts."

I Am a Task Master

Modi believed children could help in nation-building through power saving and supporting dertness rive across the country.

Modi claimed as a "taskmaster" and a "disciplinarian", He asked professionals volunteer to teach a class in neighbourhood schools. He had two-hour long interaction with children across the country on September 5, 2014, through video conferences. "Please tell me if we agree that there are problems in the education system like lack of good teachers etc; can't this be rectified. Why can't we convert nation building into a people's movement," he asked. He asked the example of Japan where teachers and students together clean schools. He wondered why couldn't it be replicated in India? He Said environment consciousness was not an alien concept. It was part of Indian culture. "Had we continued to respect nature the way our ancestors then this degradation could have been avoided," he said; asking students whether they had ever seen the rising sun.

The interaction saw him lament the early loss of childhood these days. He rued ruing that children were no longer footloose and fancy free. The students for the most part wanted to know about change in his life after becoming Prime Minister. What kind of person he was and the mischief he had done as a child and whether he was a 'head-master'. He responded mainly in Hindi even to questions in English.

The children asked him "either/or" questions, he replied on the "tough one". Some of the children appeared to have come tutored; asking questions beyond their age. "Children should remain children," he emphasised.

View Teaching as a Way of Life

Ahead of Teachers' Day, the prime minister sent an email message to teachers stating that teaching is not just another profession but "a divine responsibility to guide and enlighten. He reminded them to be recollected as the 'Vishwaguru', Modi said: "we must once again accord such respect to teachers. India could become the beacon of knowledge for the entire world. "This is a responsibility of great significance. It depends how our present and future generations will thrive," he remained.

Goalposts for Teachers

Modi set out several goalposts for teachers. These include the widening"horizon of thinking of students"; encouraging to think critically about issues concerning the nation; society and environment; and moulding good citizens capable of preserving the past and creating the future. The teachers should support in inculcating lessons in good citizenship among children; be it in obeying traffic rules, cleanliness, gender sensitisation or showing concern for the weak and reverence for elders.

In a separate interaction with award-winning teachers at his residence, Modi urged them to view teaching as a *"jeewan dharm* (way of life)" from which one never retires. He also advised them to be always two steps ahead of time to help students keep abreast with the fast changing world. Modi said he had two wishes when he was Gujarat chief minister meet his school friends and the teachers who had taught him. She was fulfilled. The teachers shared their views on their profession, claimed an official release. On Teacher's Day, Modi will address students and then engage with those present in the Capital's Manekshaw Auditorium and others gathered at NIC centres in Leh, Port Blair, Silchar, Imphal, Bhuj, Dantewada and Thiruvannamalai. The session will be aired live on Doordarshan and webcast. State Governments across the country had been advised a week ago to ensure that schools make arrangements for children to view the address within school premises itself.

The Impact of Institutional Decay

Many Indian students went overseas in pursuit of higher education. Some of them later became leaders of the freedom movement. This trend continued after the turn of the century. Gandhi and Nehru studied in England. Ambedkar went to the United States. Lohia and Zakir Hussain acquired their doctoral degrees in Germany. Even today, we notice that thousands of our students go abroad. They never return, for the find satisfaction offshore. It is not merely the personal consequences of higher education abroad. The rich experience differs rather sharply from what is available in India.

'Politics of Waiting'

The gap between our universities and those in Europe and North America began to narrow. Established policies were ignored. A new ideology took over. The industrial policy shifted away from quota-permit-inspection raj. The system of education used precisely regulated the burgeoning private-commercial sector. The seeping corruption in the areas of professional higher education, including engineering, medicine and teacher training ended in future. Institutional decay is a common, national story. It differ from State to State. None of 700 universities figures in the list of institutions adjudged in the world. This list includes not just the American, European, Australian and

Japanese universities. It has in China, South Africa and even Malaysia. India's absence in global educational ranking is an to policy maker. What ought to concern us is the impact that institutional decay has on the young. An Ambedkar, a Ramanujan or a Jagadish Chandra Bose hidden in a young mind today would need an American or a European university to identify and nurture it. Let us imagine that such a young person returns to India after completing a doctoral degree. The first thing he or she would have to worry about is getting through the National Eligibility Test (NET) organised twice a year by the University Grants Commission (UGC).

Deprived of Dignity

You can find any number of young men and women across the country. They have been teaching for years in vulnerable positions known by various names like "temporary," "contractual," "ad-hoc" or "guest." They keep waiting for permanent vacancies to be advertised. Many parts of India, such advertisements are now outdated. In any case, getting a permanent or tenure post in an Indian university now implies managing a highly complex constellation of favourable factors. These include patronage, contacts, a desirable social background and luck. To these, the UGC has added a maze of quantifiable points. This remarkable device offers the same score whether you publish your work in bogus journals or genuine ones.

Downsizing Trend

In both higher and school education, the trend to downsize permanent staff started in the early 1990s. Economic reforms formed the background of this trend. Long before the Fifth Pay Commission explicitly ordered a reduction in posts, the process of recruitment of teachers had either been stopped or drastically modified in many States. Apparently, contractual hiring of teachers and reduction of support staff were perceived as a convenient means of meeting the fiscal crisis in many States. Once the number of low-paid, vulnerable teachers grew, they became politically useful for rival political parties and union leaders. Both these processes were quite visible across northern India.

Cultural wealth

Education signifies cultural wealth. This wealth consists of thoughtful minds. The ethos shaped by an exchange of ideas. The reading of books and creative activities facilitate the process. The happiness of teachers forms the centre of such an ethos. By denigrating the teacher, India has damaged what capacity its system of education had for producing and conserving cultural wealth. Decay of libraries has contributed to this process. Schools in our country seldom have libraries.

The institutional recovery will have to be accorded priority. Universities and undergraduate colleges determine the quality of teachers at all levels from kindergarten upwards. No matter where we look, non-appointment has become a culture. Enrolment has increased at the cost of institutional capacity. Commercial and political interests have injured the quality of education in Karnataka and Tamil Nadu. If money has indeed been saved by letting vacancies accumulate or by filling them cheaply and by cutting down support staff, this kind of saving has incurred a big price. What has India gained by doing this kind of saving? It has weakened the already limited capacity the system had for serving children. Had Dr. Radhakrishnan — whose name we invoke to honour the profession of teaching — been alive, he would have been startled to find how the teachers were glorified.

17 Vision of Modern India

Vision

Narendra Modi has outlined his Vision for the India of tomorrow which resonates with the BJP's philosophy of "*sab ka saath, sab ka vikas*".

The comprehensive vision laid out by Modi builds on the heritage of India's rich social and cultural diversity. It devolves around tradition, the talent of human resource and the aspirations of youth and women. The concept of *Brand India* encapsulates all sectors that have the potential to make India a global power. The five-Ts of Brand India are talent, trade, tradition, tourism and technology. The concept of *Rainbow of India* envisions seven key focus areas, which will be the overarching theme of initiatives to make India a developed nation. These themes are India's culture, agriculture, women, natural resources, youth power, democracy and knowledge. Finally, Modi outlined a ten-point key development model, with detailed initiatives on each, to put India back on high-growth path and deliver good governance to her citizen.

A Transformational Leader

As a result of 2014 general elections, where Narendra Modi's decisive leadership has paved the way for BJP to get absolute majority. He occupied the post of the 15th Prime Minister of India to give parliamentary democracy a new meaning after the gap of almost three decades. With this stupendous ascent, three of the world's strongest and most transformational leaders are now in Asia: Japan's Shinzo Abe, China's Xi Jinping, and India's Narendra Modi. They control a fifth of the global economy and govern two-fifths of its citizens. All have active plans to shake up their societies. The expectations and the stakes are sky-high for each of the leaders, but none more so than Modi.

Why do Indian voters find Modi so appealing—or, depending on your outlook, Congress' leadership so repulsive? As chief minister of Gujarat, his state of 60 million people, Modi unlocked economic gains reminiscent of

China. During his 12-year tenure, Gujarat's per capita income outpaced the national average, rising almost fourfold. Modi put his money where his mottos were— "less government and more governance" and "no red tape, only red carpet"—paring back suffocating state inefficiencies to unlock business potential and competitiveness. This is precisely what the Congress party has been unable to solve at national level. High inflation, sluggiest economic growth (at least by historical standards), and legislative gridlock that makes America's Congress look like a well-oiled machine. Indian voters want Modi to implement the Gujarat model on a national scale.

The question is whether Modi can do so, as quickly and dramatically as Indians demand. Unlike China and Japan, power in India remains woefully decentralised. A sweeping win won't change. We won't see a quick recovery in India's legislative output. It was at the least productive levels (2013) in history. That's because the houses of Parliament remain split. The Congress party and allies maintained a plurality of seats in India's upper house, the Rajya Sabha. Congress holds 12 of India's 28 (soon to be 29) states, which in turn elect the upper house members; Modi's BJP has only five.

The next round of elections, (where only a third of the chamber's seats will be in play), doesn't happen until 2016. And just as the BJP has derailed the Congress party agenda in an opposition role over the last decade, now we'll see a role reversal, with Congress engaging in rabid obstructionism. Modi will struggle to cut enough red tape to match voters' lofty expectation. When it comes to politically sensitive issues like labour, energy and agriculture, structural reforms that require legislative fixes will be hard to implement any time soon. But even if Modi's opponents stymie his national legislative agenda, Modi will have an immediate impact in three key areas.

First, Modi will focus his efforts on national action he can take without Parliament's assistance. He can use the power of executive to liberalise foreign direct investment. It will permit the streamlining of infrastructure and industrial projects. Second, India's decentralised system cuts both ways: even if it makes the national agenda harder. It presents opportunities for change at the state level, where many of the most dramatic structural changes occur. Modi's premiership enable the Gujarat model of development to spread to some other states, including many in India's poorer north. Infrastructure development and active efforts to speed foreign direct investment should pick up. Lastly, Modi will push for his country to play internationally more significant role. Modi will promote a revitalised India on the world stage. India welcomes the second look from multi-national corporations and major powers alike. Optimism from foreign investors in anticipation of stronger, more accommodative Modi government has helped push the rupee value to a 10-month high against the dollar and stock markets to all-time records. Modi will welcome closer relations with everyone from the US, Europe and Japan to China and Russia.

In a G-Zero World, with no single dominant voice and a lack of global coordination, India now stands out as a rare oasis of leadership. It is a prime opportunity for her bilateral engagement. Take India's direct relationship with Washington, where high-profile visa issues, including the arrest of an Indian diplomat in New York, have strained relations. The US denied Modi a visa in 2005 based on his role in Gujarat riots in 2002. But, sometimes winning really does solve everything: after Modi's election victory, Obama called to congratulate and invite him to the US. For his part, Modi is looking to put points on the board, not settle scores. Expect him to pursue an invigorated, pragmatic approach to international relations. With a resounding mandate, Modi isn't only focussed on a 10-week plan, but also a 10-year blueprint to transform India. Let's hope India can wait that long.

Modimantra

The India of tomorrow is looking at empowerment, faster connectivity, more jobs, better education and improved quality of life. The good governance model of Narendra Modi, enrapturedly referred to as ModiMantra encompasses these broad themes into simple takeaways, which have the potential of transforming India in the near future. Quadrilateral of Bullet trains will fundamentally alter the way Indians are connected. Laying of new rail lines will spur industrial growth. It will create new employment, boost rural economy and enhance productivity. Skill development will empower our youth. They will have gainful employment, not just in India but around the world. Every state should not only have IITs, IIMs and AIIMS but a host of skill development centers through ITIs. The dream of every household, farm and industry in India getting access to 24×7 powers is a powerful dream, which can transform India and its economy. Modi has delivered this dream in Gujarat and now India awaits him for such transformation.

Development

Any political party speaking about development shores on roads, ports, GDP growth, stock markets, agriculture, exports and international trade, among other issues. To Narendra Modi, however, development is all this and much more. At its core, Modi's concept of progress means Indians experiencing change that enables them fulfil their potential trigger an overall improvement in daily lives and well-being. With this primary agenda, the party armed with an incorruptible and progressive leadership aims to transform and empower the weakest and the most neglected sections of Indian society, without any bias for caste, creed or religion. Today, the BJP is the only political party in India that respects merit. It follows true secularism that says 'Justice and development to all, appeasement to none'. Narendra Modiji has already emphasised working on the principle of 'Minimum Government, Maximum Governance' after BJP-led NDA form the government at the Centre. The government's role and involvement in non-essential sectors will be reduced. The cutting of red-tape and the bureaucratic license raj will be an article of faith. These have impeded our growth and bred corruption.

Some of the changes, the new government proposes are very fundamental and basic. It could lead to India taking off in a high-growth trajectory. For instance, the government will reward area and domain experts in the field of policy-making. It will ensure the problems of today and the distant future were already accounted for. India once used to be called the 'Golden Bird' because of her indigenous production base and self-reliance. Implementing such policies will take the country back on the path of being self-reliant. It includes manufacturing, defence, agro-processing and allied services sector among others. Today's India is young Indian, where the people are willing to work hard with an assurance of being masters of their own destiny. Our model of development will let them write their own destinies. Here, the weakest Indian ever has a just and fair chance of making it big, through sheer dedication and determination. This is the idea of development that the ruling govdernment envisages. A united and vibrant nation where every citizen gets an equal share of opportunities; where merit and hard work is given due importance. Each citizen is an agent of economic change and productivity. As 1.25 billion such economic agents work together as single well-oiled machinery, there will be no milestone beyond reach.

Security

Security isn't only what soldiers fight and put their lives at risk. For, in a distant, forbidding frontier, far from the spotlight; it is also what each one of us, every man and particularly women, experiences while stepping away home. To the newly-elected government, the concept of security is dynamic one. It has many emerging challenges and opportunities. However, the most important thing for a strong and secure India is a robust economy. No nationalist government at the Centre can avoid paying attention to the Indian economy. Each time what we do is that we leave India exposed to enemies, external and internal. High GDP growth and economic development is fundamental to the idea of Indian security. For the government, the concept of national security is holistic with several aspects. First, India needs to cut down her excessive reliance on foreign arms manufacturers and focus her energies on indigenisation to become a manufacturer of technologies and equipment that can be used by our military. Not only will this effort save us crucial foreign exchange but also lead to generation of millions of jobs that will act as a catalyst for the Indian economy. Internally, India needs a stronger and state-of-the-art police force. It should have much bigger presence of women. The government is committed to modernisation of police forces across Indian states. It will extend whatever assistance, motivation and help is required to achieve this goal. It feels that a greater participation of women in the state police forces and an integration of modern investigation and forensic techniques and technology will keep in check some of the most important issues that confront us today—the safety of women, children and the elderly.

India needs to prepare her itself for the future wars. These will be fought in the virtual world. This is an area of concern for India, which, despite its undisputed leadership in the IT and services sector, hasn't been able to keep pace with developments in other countries. We need to hire, train and prepare 'armies' of such young Indian, who will ensure safety of our assets in the virtual world. It will seldom surprise that many of the changes would also have a direct and positive impact on the Indian economy. It could lead to further empowerment of a strong, united India. The vision the BJP projects gives significant weightage to security, and works towards strengthening security externally and internally.

Good Governance

Narendra Modi's definition of good governance is an administration where even the weakest and the most vulnerable sections of society have an equal stake in charting the country's growth. Everything starts and progresses from this single idea. Today, the BJP-led NDA government at the Centre is the only true merit-based democratic political party in India. In governance, it is committed to the ideals of transparency, efficiency and responsiveness. Time and again, the party has demonstrated its commitment towards these principles, wherever it has been voted to power. The Indian voters can look forward with him at the helm to a clean government, free of corruption and scandal; a leadership that hasn't reached on top on the basis of connections and cronyism, but on the basis of years of unrelenting work for masses and a youthful leadership that is in sync with contemporary India. The model of good governance ensures that even the tallest leaders and top bureaucrats are answerable to an ordinary citizen, hailing from any part of India. The government believes in operating in complete transparency, with every file and official record open for public scrutiny, except when these may endanger national security. Modi's ascendancy is an antidote to whatever has troubled the Indian political system over the last six decades– crony capitalism, feudalism, favouritism and archaic methods of governance. For us, governance is a mission that isn't complete without proactive involvement of the citizens of India. It strives to provide a clean and efficient government that invites proactive participation and involvement of citizens at every step.

Nation First

A firm belief in the ideal that a truly rich and diverse nation like India is optimally united when its people give precedence to their identity as 'Indians before everything else' is what led to the birth of the safron outfit. The party's staunch commitment to this principle is what has ensured its unparalleled rise to becoming one of the largest, most representative political parties in India. The BJP party believes in true 'National' politics, where every Indian, irrespective of his caste, creed or religion is an Indian first. It doesn't believe in narrow politics of compartmentalisation and division of society. The party's agenda is to unite people on the basis of love for the country. Primacy to this identity is what will once again chart the path for India's re-emergence as a cultural and economic superpower. This should also be looked at in light of BJP's core commitment to its guiding philosophy of 'Integral Humanism', which considers all Indians as one united entity. Our leadership has walked this path for years and believes it will ensure our precious energies aren't wasted in petty differences. Keeping the interest of the nation above everything else is what will ensure a united and powerful India, wherein each of its 1.25 billion citizens contributes in his or her unique way, and fulfils his or her unique dream.

Modi vs SAARC

Equally significant are the laudable steps he has taken to improve relations with India's neighbours. Inviting the leaders of South Asia for his government's oath-taking ceremony was a smart move. So, were some others? His first port of call abroad was Bhutan while the first port of call of his foreign minister was Bhutan. None can question about these priorities. These will doubtless become clearer once he moves to strengthen ties with Japan, China and the United States and even more so when he engages with Pakistan.

Modi's lament that his political rivals and critics have denied him a 'honeymoon period' makes little sense in a media environment that operates on a 24×7 basis. He must be given credit for generating something the country has sorely lacked these past few years: hope of an economic, social and cultural resurgence in an atmosphere largely free of caste, communal and regional conceits and petty, short-term ambitions. But none of these figures in his blog. But such modesty, if indeed it be one, is singularly misplaced.

Credit must be claimed, or given, where credit is due. Modi government needs to target 10 per cent annual GDP growth to deliver on poll promises. The UPA government has left the treasury nearly empty. Infrastructure projects worth over Rs 10 lakh crore are in limbo. The PMO is a work-in-progress. When done, the Modi government will operate through four layers: one, a strong PMO; two, a tightly run cabinet; three, empowered bureaucrats; and four, technocratic advisors with specific domain knowledge.

Centering the North-east

The North-east needs a skilful person, who can lynch out insurgency, mobilise leaders of substance and work out a decentralised multi-level development strategy. This is not Prime Minister Narendra Modi's catch-all phrase for the seven northeastern States, though the region does figure in his list of priorities for economic rejuvenation, and strategic and infrastructural development. The Northeast today needs a skilful politico-economic person, who can take the region out of insurgency, mobilise leaders of substance and work out a decentralised multi-level development strategy.

The Look East Policy

The land-locked region continues to be stuck in politico-bureaucratic status quo, even after Prime Minister Narasimha Rao placed it under special focus as part of the Look East Policy in 1991. This has since become an integral part of India's foreign policy rhetoric. It has already travelled from phase one to phase two under various Prime Ministers without addressing basic infrastructure and all-inclusive growth. Each Prime Minister has reiterated the country's commitment to take the Look East Policy forward. This has been done somewhat half-heartedly in view of strategic and logistical problems emanating from sporadic bursts of violence by terrorist and insurgent groups operating on both sides of the border. Today, the situation on the insurgency front is somewhat easier, especially along the Myanmar and Bangladesh borders. Still, "caution" has to be the mantra.

The northeastern states account for about eight per cent of the country's geographical area. They share less than two per cent of borders with other Indian states and share 98 per cent with Bangladesh, Bhutan, Myanmar and the Tibetan region (of China). The challenge is to convert this location disadvantage into an opportunity. This can be done by opening up the seven-state gateway to more than millions of ASEAN consumers for trade, commerce and education. The Northeast requires proactive, bold policies. People are alienated because of lopsided economic growth stemming from a Delhi-centric approach to issues. The leaders in Delhi ought to understand the changing lives of the tribals, who have adopted modern values, fashions and modes of living, and frame policies accordingly.

The Northeast can be rejuvenated by making the region a focal point for growth. Removing the Restricted Area Permit and Inner Line Permit would help to integrate the region with the rest of India. However, amid numerous misgivings about the existing institutional mechanism, what is reassuring is the concern among central and regional authorities and intellectuals about the future of the region and the alienation of its people. The Northeast has higher standards of living and literacy. It also has an unbalanced economy and suffers from a terrible industrial sickness. Except Meghalaya, all the States in the region face a power shortage, despite the fact that the Northeast has a huge reserve of hydroelectric potential (30,000 to 40,000 MW). Power apart, the region needs special efforts for the development of world-class infrastructural network of roads and railways, for strengthening the telecom sector, healthcare services, and tapping into the agricultural industry and the region's rich biodiversity. It can also emerge as a hub for higher education for the entire Southeast Asian belt.

There has also been concern over the involvement of non-regional entrepreneurs. We need to examine ways and means of creating a unified common market of nearly 40 million people, which will provide a big boost to the economy of the region. We also have to ensure a massive investment flow for infrastructural development on both sides of the border in order to improve connectivity for trade and commerce. This will help the emergence of local entrepreneurs. As it is, the Delhi-Hanoi rail link, trilateral highway project between India, Myanmar and Thailand, and some other initiatives have got bogged down by red tapism and a lack of political will. I would like to draw from the study of a northeast magazine that spoke of regional entrepreneurship. It said: "India needs entrepreneurs for two reasons— to capitalise on new opportunities and to create wealth and new jobs." Compared to the rest of India, the level of start-ups in the Northeast "is much lower" because of "major bottlenecks and barriers to entrepreneurship like know-how, finance, administrative burden and cultural and social factors." A few professionals, who tried to start initiatives on their own, did not get support, but this is changing.

Bridging the Gulf: At the human level, there exists a big gulf between people from the hills and people from the plains. This has resulted in creating a trust deficit. Recent ugly incidents in Delhi have only reaffirmed the distance that separates the Northeast from mainstream India. Promoting understanding at the human level apart, it is also essential to bridge the chasm in the areas of communication, information and culture. We have to provide people from the Northeast opportunities as well as honour, dignity and equality. The North-East Region Vision 2020 document states: "It is in Northeast India that Southeast Asia begins and as such, it is for the Northeast to play the arrow-head role in the further evolution of this policy. This requires a redefining of the 'Look East Policy' to resolve outstanding issues of trade, transit and investment with countries neighbouring the region. It also involves promoting Indian investment infrastructure in partner countries, especially Myanmar, particularly in respect of ports such as Sittwe and international highways to connect the Northeast Region with ASEAN." In the long run, the Northeast, as an expert put it, can become a partner in "a wider Brahmaputra-Yangtze-Mekong quadrant." Let us hope for the best.

On Priorities

Let's start with specific economic targets and how the government can achieve them. Services contribute 59 per cent to India's overall GDP. Agriculture has a small 14 per cent share. Industry makes up the balance 27 per cent. To achieve annual GDP growth of 10 per cent, the primary focus must be on boosting services. Services include IT, tourism, exports, retail, banking and finance. The Prime Minister's target would be to ensure 12 per cent growth in services by 2015-16. With services contributing nearly 60 per cent to the GDP pie, annual growth on account of services would thus be 12 per cent × 60 per cent = 7.2 per cent. Now build on that base. Industry accounts for 27 per cent of overall GDP. Growth can be accelerated with fast environmental clearances of languishing projects, investment in infrastructure and the introduction of advanced technology. Higher productivity and labour law reform can give added impetus to manufacturing.

The growth target for industry includes manufacturing, mining and power generation. It could be 8 per cent, a level reached consistently in 2004-10. With a share in overall GDP of 27 per cent (of which manufacturing comprises 14 per cent), industry would contribute 8 per cent × 27 per cent = 2.1 per cent to annual GDP growth. That leaves agriculture. The contribution of agriculture to the overall GDP pie is only 14 per cent but farm incomes have a disproportionate knock-on effect on consumption. This can affect industry, manufacturing and services. Agri reform is high on the PM's agenda and India is now relatively drought-proof. This year's monsoon is likely to be severely deficient but irrigation may suffer only slightly due to most reservoirs around the country possessing adequate water stocks. That situation could worsen though if the monsoon is delayed beyond early-July since reservoirs are depleting rapidly.

While agriculture growth in 2014-15 is likely to be two per cent or lower due to scanty rains, the target for 2015-16 should be an achievable growth rate of five per cent. Since agriculture accounts for only 14 per cent of overall GDP, its contribution would therefore be 5 per cent × 14 per cent = 0.70 per cent. This would take targeted GDP growth in 2015-16 to 10 per cent (services 7.2 per cent + industry 2.1 per cent + agriculture 0.70 per cent). However, this growth level is sustainable in the long term only if three key conditions are met: One, overhauling infrastructure; two, enhancing technology; and three, boosting productivity. All of these need deeper reforms cutting across institutions, education, labour, tax and healthcare. Without a holistic, integrated policy, GDP growth will remain hostage to extraneous turbulence, both global and domestic. India's fiscal health has been ruined by 10 years of UPA profligacy and wasteful, leaky doles. The trade deficit of $147.60 billion in 2013-14 is dwarfed by an oil import bill of $180 billion. India imports 81 per cent of its crude oil and 25 per cent of its natural gas. An immediate priority for the Modi government must be to reinvigorate the New Exploration Licensing Policy (NELP), pursue shale gas exploration as the US has done (though shale deposits and laws governing "fracking" for shale gas are less promising in India than in the US) and aim to reduce oil imports to 60 per cent, a level achieved in the 1980s when Bombay High was at its production peak.

The trade deficit would then fall to well below $100 billion. By 2019, if GDP growth averages 9-10 per cent, the economy would have grown by over 50 per cent to around $3 trillion ($7.5 trillion by purchasing power parity – PPP). The trade deficit would then be just over three per cent of GDP compared to nearly eight per cent today. The fiscal deficit has already stabilised at around 4.5 per cent of GDP. With higher revenue through the Goods and Services Tax (GST) next year and judicious cuts in non-plan expenditure, it could fall further to a targeted 3.5 per cent on a rising GDP denominator. FDI/FII funds are pouring in and the current account deficit (CAD) of $32.40 billion in 2013-14 could actually turn positive in 2014-15, boosting India's forex reserves. FDI inflows in calendar 2014 (up to June 14) have been a record $41.59 billion, according to the RBI. FDI in manufacturing, technology and infrastructure builds long-term assets in India under sovereign control and must be encouraged. Inflation meanwhile remains a serious concern. It was tackled during most of the UPA government's tenure by the RBI squeezing demand through a tight monetary policy regime. That prescription was wrong. The RBI should ease monetary policy and allow the government to use a supply-side strategy to dampen inflation. Expanding the supply of goods and services through increased productivity and better infrastructure rather than stifling demand through high interest rates is the shift in policy needed to control prices and simultaneously spur economic growth. The opportunities India affords are unique as the plane-loads of eager foreign investment bankers testify. The policies articulated in next fortnight's Budget and their execution—will determine how rapidly India lives up to its true potential, shackled for years by poor economics and poorer politics.

India to become Third Largest Economy by 2030

The London-headquartered accountancy giant said the rapid rise of the Indian economy with its young workforce would push it up from being the 10th largest economy in 2013 to the third largest by 2030, pushing the UK back into sixth place. "In the longer run, other emerging markets may overtake the UK, but only India looks set to do so before 2030 according to our latest projections," PwC said in its latest economic outlook. China, the world's second largest economy, is expected to close the gap with America by 2030, while Mexico is predicted to be the 10th largest economy by 2030, above Canada and Italy, both G7 nations. Only a couple of years ago there were forecasts that Britain would rapidly become a second-class economic power and would need to defer to the BRIC countries of Brazil, Russia, India and China in the near future. China has ranked above Japan for a decade as the world's second-biggest economy. By some calculations Brazil leapfrogged the UK in 2012, with Russia and India close behind.

Britain's fall was partly related to the costs of the banking crisis and the recession that followed, coupled with a sharp decline in the exchange rate, which knocked about a quarter off the country's value in relation to its main rivals. But since the beginning of last year the economy has recovered all the lost ground from the recession and banks have begun lending again. The pound has bounced back from about $ 1.40 in 2009 to $ 1.71.

Brazil, by contrast, has suffered a rocky couple of years that have slowed GDP growth and pushed down the value of the real. Russia will close the gap on the top eight, but its reliance on the oil and gas industry for growth and its rapidly ageing population will prevent it jumping up the table as quickly as previously thought. Only India will move ahead of the UK by 2030, though it will be sharing a projected GDP of $ 6.1 trillion among more than 1.5 billion people, only half as much again as the UK's predicted output of $ 4 trillion, produced by a population less than a 20th the size. PwC urged policymakers in the UK to implement further structural reforms to ensure that it remained ahead of emerging markets.

New Advisory to End Inspector Raj

To usher in greater ease of doing business, the government has taken steps to rein in the notorious "inspector raj". In an advisory to all ministries which is aimed to check fishing expeditions by inspectors, the department of industrial policy and promotion (DIPP) has said no inspection of business premises and factories should be done unless it is approved by the head of the department. It has also asked all ministries to shift to a system of self-certification of adherence of official norms by all companies, barring those engaged in activities that are regarded as "hazardous" or involving "risk". The DIPP has communicated that the Prime Minister wants these new measures be actioned without delay and their implementation constantly reviewed. Ministries have been told that all returns should be filed online through a unified form and a check-list of required compliances should be placed on the ministry/ department's website. They have also been asked to replace all registers that are required to be maintained by businesses with a single electronic register.

Hind Swaraj vs Hindu Rashtra

Hindutva is a historic and possibly doomed attempt to change everything about Hinduism. It concept makes what it is—its ability to accommodate mind-boggling diversity, its avoidance of strict definitions and boundaries, its amorphous, heterogeneous, tolerant and fluid character. The 2014 national election, resulting in a decisive victory for the Hindu nationalist Bharatiya Janata Party (BJP), seems to have thrown the Indian commentariat into ideological disarray. Intellectuals and opinion-makers who have professed particular beliefs and held certain positions for the longest time, appear now to be changing their views. This began happening during the campaign, continued through the election, and has become routine in the new dispensation.

Larger changes in the media, in institutions of research and higher education, and the electoral rout of the Congress and Left parties add to the general climate of confusion and mistrust. Each day it appears that one more person whose voice carries weight comes out to endorse Modi's regime. Criticism is replaced with qualified support, while in some cases the reverse is true—heartfelt enthusiasm is replaced with bitter condemnation of the Prime Minister and his team. Nobody knows any more who is with us and who is with them; who is on the left and who is on the right.

Fading Secular Opinion: Modi has begun appointing individuals who are adherents or sympathisers of the hardline Hindu fundamentalist Rashtriya Swayamsevak Sangh (RSS) to serve as ministers and as heads of cultural and educational institutions. He has shown little interest in the services of former secularists, liberals and feminists, who had indicated their willingness, even eagerness, to work with him once he took office. The fact that neither the Congress nor the Left seem any longer to be conversant with or proud of the left-liberal political traditions that dominated Indian politics since independence, drives the final nail into the coffin of secular opinion.

The Problem with Hindutva: The problem with Hindutva, which has impeded its capture of the average Hindu's political and cultural imagination, is that it is the outcome not so much of hatred for others, especially Muslims, but rather of Hindu self-hate. It's a historic and possibly doomed attempt to change everything about Hinduism that makes it what it is—its ability to accommodate mind-boggling diversity, its avoidance of strict definitions and boundaries, its amorphous, heterogeneous, tolerant and fluid character.

Hindutva wants to "Semitise" Hinduism, giving it a god, a book, a revelation, a prophet, an ecclesiastical order, a pontiff, a race, a language, a country (or a holy land), a history, a canon, doctrinal stability and missionary zeal. It's an attempt to standardise, essentialise, codify and systematise a vast universe of in commensurate beliefs, practices, rituals, theologies and narratives, to render Hinduism modern and modular.

Foreign Policy Scorecard

Prime Minister Narendra Modi has just returned from his first major foreign policy excursion. Nearly two months into his term, how well is he managing India's external relations? The report card, not surprisingly, is mixed: no gaffes, no radical departures, but also not much charm and warmth. On the positive side, the prime minister gets high marks for inviting leaders of India's South Asian neighbours to his inauguration. The ceremony itself was rather gauche, but the intent was laudable. Modi clearly wanted to signal that the region was important, after many years of relative neglect. He also wanted to reassure his fellow heads, after some rather harsh campaign rhetoric. In this, he largely succeeded, though by all accounts Nawaz Sharif went back a little offended by Modi's lectures on terrorism. Also on the positive side has been Modi's handling of the US. True to his word, he has not held the past decade of coldness and criticism from Washington against the Americans. India's relations with the US have stagnated if they have not worsened since the high point of 2008. It is clearly not in New Delhi's interest to allow relations to deteriorate any further. While Modi has not been effusive with the Americans, he has been pragmatic. To rekindle relations, he has spoken to President Barack Obama, met Senator John McCain, and agreed to visit Washington in September. In Ambassador Subrahmanyam Jaishankar, he has a first-rate "US hand" who will combine a robust defence of Indian interests with nuanced handling of difficult issues. Pragmatism should therefore prevail, with the Americans striving to put the past behind them as well.

Of course the greatest challenge for any Indian prime minister is China. Here Modi's scorecard so far is respectable, though not without blemish. He has emphasised the centrality of economic relations and more balanced trade, of attracting Chinese investment, and of setting up industrial parks that would host Chinese companies. On more political issues, he has underscored the need for a solution to the border quarrel, cooperation against terrorism and opening a second Mansarovar route for Indian pilgrims.

Any Indian prime minister would have made more or less all these points to Xi Jinping. The most important actionable item is Chinese funding and construction of infrastructure in India. UPA was all for it but didn't do much about it; let us see what Modi can deliver. The Chinese are enthusiastic and have offered up to $300 billion in investments, but Indian bureaucracy remains suspicious. Can the prime minister overcome official resistance?

The blemish in Modi's China scorecard is Delhi's rather inept handling of the New Development Bank initiative of the Brics grouping. Wrangling over the location of the bank's headquarters didn't do India much credit. China is the biggest and most powerful player by far in Brics and it is churlish to quarrel over its right to host the headquarters — just as it would have been churlish to object to the Americans hosting the UN after the Second World War when they paid most of the bills of the organisation. If Modi wanted to get his China diplomacy right, he should have graciously and quickly agreed to the headquarters being in Shanghai. Nor did it make much sense to insist that

China and the other four Brics members contribute the same amount to the corpus. In the end, there was compromise: China got the headquarters and India got to head the bank first; China will contribute the largest amount to the corpus eventually, whereas all five countries will pay in equal amounts initially. Modi to his credit finally went for the deal, after a fair bit ofhauling and pulling, but it could have been more graciously done from the start. This brings us to his persona and conduct abroad. Going by the Bhutan, Brazil trips and Nepal, he has been correct and dignified but not much more. While he is infinitely more energetic than his predecessor, he has not appeared terribly warm or charming. Admittedly, it is not easy to be attractive on the big stage amidst strangers and these are early days; but the protean Modi has work ahead.

Vajpayee's Formula on Kashmir Tweaked

Modi recalled Atal Bihari Vajpayee's call for *insaniyat* on his maiden trip to Jammu and Kashmir as PM, when he said he wanted to win the hearts of people in the state. But to a very different response, as much of the Valley shut down in a separatist-enforced strike. In reality, much water has flown down the Jhelum since Vajpayee's celebrated call. And there's an interesting difference in emphasis between Vajpayee and Modi. The former, when he called for winning hearts and minds, threw open the doors to political dialogue. But Modi has made it clear that he intends to win hearts through development. Political dialogue was indeed initiated by Vajpayee's NDA government, and Manmohan Singh's UPA government took it forward. There are credible reports—confirmed by Khurshid Mahmud Kasuri, foreign minister in General Musharraf's administration in Pakistan during 2002 to 2007–that India and Pakistan had almost reached an agreement on Kashmir barring a few commas and full stops.

I-Day Speech: About Nation and Individual

The aura around this year's Independence Day, and mood for boundless imagination nudged to take on the challenge. Journey for discovering the dreams for Independence Day with a 'Tryst with destiny' and soon hit a roadblock of lofty ideals and platitudes. There isn't a shortcut to meditated *Swadhyay* (self-study). What does independence mean? Nine 'Ss' Model for Independence to travel boundlessly and conceived *Swatantrata* (closest Hindi word for Independence, literally meaning 'a state of being within one's own system') as a focal fruition of centrifugal and centripetal forces acting in a cyclical path.

In conformity with the wisdom seeded in the words: "*Udyamenahi Sidhyanthi Kaaryani*", *Swatantrata* is not a state of being but a continuous process of spiralling towards a dream. Prime Minister's Independence Day message ought to be seen through the lens of nine 'Ss'. The Thrills *Swayambhus* (sovereigns) exist on their own terms by the force of their own innate qualities. In the speech, his body language was open and inviting and he conveyed proximity by removing the customary physical barrier. His dialogue was intimate and his thoughts streamed out effortlessly with conviction. He did a laudable job of physically radiating our country's sovereignty. It is useful to postulate here that expansion is an intrinsic quest of all *Swayambhus* and thus this exerts a centrifugal force. However, *Swayambhus* neither exist in a vacuous field of their own nor do they occupy residual spaces. *Swayambhus* need to negotiate with each other to reclaim common spaces where they collaborate for achieving goals of higher order. In fact a nation is also an example of a reclaimed common space created by *Swayambhu* individuals. When the PM chanted the Vedic mantra of *Sangachadwam Samvadadwam*, he informed the world loudly about the source of his philosophical nourishment. Later during the speech he underscored the need for consensus in governance.

The Prime Minister told us about the vastness of his vision by extending invitation to neighbouring countries for collaborating in the common goal of poverty eradication. Much of the PM's speech was about invocation of a citizen's *Swadharma. Swadharma* are self-elected properties of one's soul (innerself). Whereas his speech was multifarious and well rounded, it is analysed in the following discourse. It is started with a negotiation with our spirits. If "secular" friends will like to label this "communal" then the label is welcome. Will we continue to kill our daughters in wombs; will we continue to hold our daughters and sons to different standards; will we continue to draw salaries from government without 'serving'; will we continue to slur Mother India by perpetuating casteism and communalism? By asking these questions that each one of us has to answer for himself, he sought to establish a common denominator of *Swadharma* for all *Bharatiyas* irrespective of religious affiliations. *Swadharma* is a strong centripetal force that keeps us pulled in towards our higher goals. It had wished that the PM might emphasise on the Swaraj dimension to enable even the last person participate in governance. Indeed, he was acutely aware of the need for participatory democracy and proposed three concrete interventions—strengthening the federal structure, e-governance and model village scheme. He also mentioned the need for public-private partnerships.

At the later stage, further steps for strengthening of the Panchayati Raj institutions will also be taken up by state governments. *Swaraj* is a centrifugal force that disperses political power and expands space for collaboration. *Swarth* is generally understood by its narrow meaning to imply selfishness pursued by an individual at the cost of other people. However, *Swarth* literally means 'arth (meaning) for swa (self)'. A *Swarth* of a country is basically national self-interest. In this context Swa's definition determines *Swarth's* legitimacy. As someone who has spent considerable time in Indian rural milieu, PM took up the issue of toilets. What can be more meaningful for a person who has to relieve himself than finding a toilet? PM is rooted in ground realities and we can only wonder why no one else took it up with similar prominence before? Another important announcement that the PM made in the theme of *Swarth* was the *Jan-Dhan yojana*. A bank account is the first step towards financial inclusion of the masses. *Swarth* is a centripetal force that ensures our survival so that we can sustain the *Swatantrata chakra*.

The Prime Minister made two important announcements that address the need for *Swavlamban* or in other words the need for having assets that we can lean upon. The digitalisation he spoke of and that we are seeing penetrating every aspect of our life is not only inevitable but also desirable. It opens up opportunities that we have not known before. Another announcement was related to general skill development and enhancement in the country. These are good intentions and make us look forward to the specifics. *Swavlamban* is a centripetal force that supports our standing. During the post-independence era, the term *Swadeshi* could never find its release from its parochial nationalistic definition and then during the last two decades it was trashed. The PM redefined *Swadeshi.* 'Make in India', 'Made in India' and 'Sell to the World' set the right tempo. There is a need for global collaboration and realignment of our portfolio of economic sectors by increasing manufacturing. The direction has immense possibilities and it entails two caveats: (i) it will not happen without addressing supporting factor conditions; and (ii) we have to be strategic in approaching value-sharing arrangements. The other idea in the *Swadeshi* theme was import substitution for electronic goods. This has to be explored further. *Swadeshi* is at once both a centrifugal and a centripetal force. A strong *Swadeshi* movement of import substitution is contingent upon *Swavlamban.* Eventually, a *Swayambhu* will like to evolve from 'Make in India' to 'Conceived in India'. Speaking on *Swabhiman* (self-pride), the PM was balanced.

PM reminded us of our freedom fighters, sages, maestros, scientists, and previous Governments because of whom we are who we are today. At the same time, he did not shy away from pointing to the deficit of *Swadharma* as the biggest factor that erodes our *Swabhiman.* He reminded us of Maharishi Aurobindo and Swami Vivekananda's dream of seeing India contributing towards the welfare of the world. *Swabhiman* is a centripetal force that holds us together and propels the expansionary quest of *Swayambhu.*

The most disappointing aspect of the Prime Minister's speech was silence on *Swabhasha* — in other words, the country's language policy. In a few other articles on this forum *Sankrant Sanu*, it has argued and demonstrated that the country's language policy is a major hurdle in the way of development. It is also a major encumbrance in the way of a civilisation's self-manifestation. It suppresses *Swayambhu's* expansionary instincts. If we must wait for everyone to learn English before the aspiration of Skilled India and Digital India are realised, then progress will be marginal. The English-centric language policy of our country, just like the Planning Commission, is a vestige. It must be dismantled to pave way for fresh thinking, release of suppressed aspirations, and empowering of *Swa.* There are two changes required in the paradigm that has informed country's language policy and sporadic and ill-prepared *Swabhasha* promotional efforts. One, spirit of *Swaraj* that is now guiding strengthening of federal structure must also guide Swabhasha. Two, acceptance that unity of India does not rest upon having one langauge but upon providing a mechanism for manifestation of *Swa.* Any *Swatantrata* inventiveness that supresses Swa to promote tantra is inherently flawed. Let us be very clear tantra derives its legitimacy only as a servant of the Swa. The Swa is dispersed, it is plural and it is atomic. Call for *Yagnya* (holy enterprise) Swatantrata is not an accolade. It is very hard work. The Prime Minister appealed in his speech for more than one billion Indians to come together in unison and give their *Swaha* (may it [my offering] be good). This, he implies, is our *Swadharma.* On his part, he has promised to exceed our Swahas with no caps. The ball, my dear countrymen, is in our court.

Top Ten Welfare Schemes

In his first Independence Day speech, PM Modi unveiled his roadmap for a bold, new India—listing out key welfare schemes along with 'small ideas' that could make a big difference.

Banking for the poorest: Taking banking to the poorest, the Pradhan Mantri Jan-Dhan Yojana will give each family a bank account with a debit card and an insurance cover of Rs. 1 lakh. "Today, there are crores of families that have mobile phones but no bank accounts. We have to change this. Economic development must benefit the poor and it should start from here," the PM said. Official data puts the number of poor households in India at 6.5 crore.

Adopt a village: Modi asked all members of Parliament to adopt a village in their constituencies and turn it into a model village by 2016 using their development funds. The Sansad Aadarsh Gram Yojana strives to usher improvements in health, sanitation, greenery and cordiality.

Enter the digital age: The PM wants to connect every Indian through technology, provide governance via mobile phones and have every village on a broadband platform. "E-governance is easy governance, effective governance and economic governance," he said.

A skilled workforce: The government's mission is two-pronged—create a skilled workforce that can be employed anywhere in the world and encourage entrepreneurship to create more jobs at home. And the aim is to do this at a rapid pace.

Make in India: Modi invited global manufacturers to 'come, make in India' and sell it to the world, with an aim to strike a balance between imports and exports and create jobs. "We have the skill, talent, discipline and determination to do something," he said in his speech.

Zero defect, zero effect: The PM encouraged domestic manufacturers to adopt a policy of 'zero defect, zero effect'—make top-of-the-line products with no ill effect on the environment. He said 'Made in India' must stand for quality products.

Clean India campaign: Modi aims to clean up all the cities and villages of the country by 2019, when the country observes the 150th birth anniversary of Mahatma Gandhi. The government plans to achieve this with public and private participation.

Toilets in schools: The government's target before the next I-Day is a toilet in every school, and a separate one for girls. MPs will have to take the mission forward. Corporate participation has also been sought under their corporate social responsibility.

Planning commission out: Planning Commission set up by Jawaharlal Nehru is on its way out. It will make way for an institution that gives a new direction to the country through creative thinking, public-private partnership and optimum utilisation of resources.

Defeat poverty: Taking the war to end poverty to another level, PM called for all South Asian countries to join India. "Why not get together with all SAARC nations to plan the fight against poverty? Let's fight together and defeat poverty," he said.

Modi Moulding Digital India

As a general rule, be it a CEO or a government official, it's always better to walk into a crucial meeting with a list of three priorities and an equal number of tough decisions to be taken. A quick look at the word count of the past five Union Budget speeches will tell you that as the state of the economy has slowly worsened, our Finance Ministers have decided to compensate with more verbose and long-winded orations.

Change in Language: While prevailing wisdom would suggest that it is better to make less, and thus more believable, promises, the verbiage also sometimes hides a gentle signal as to which way the wind is now blowing. Much has been written and said over Prime Minister Narendra Modi's dream of creating a 'Digital India'. The words 'digital', 'Internet' and 'broadband' appear zero times in last year's budget, while Jaitley's speech devotes a section to it and even refers to the often-ignored "divide between digital 'haves' and 'have-nots' in India." The word 'start-up' appears once in a passing reference in the previous budget, while Jaitley has unveiled a host of incentives and measures aimed at boosting the whole ecosystem. Indeed, it seems as if Modi has laid down a lighted path, if not a specific and completes roadmap, for taking India into the digital 21st Century.

The biggest of the allotments, a decent Rs.7,060 crore, goes towards smart cities; an idea that while popular has not been enthusiastically taken up by India's poorly managed cities. Indeed, some of the biggest problems that technology companies are facing are the hesitancy of local municipal corporations in forking over or even finding funds for initial pilot projects.

A Definite Intent: There are definite statements of intent sprinkled throughout the Budget—whether it is in the Rs 100 crore allocations for virtual classrooms, the introduction of e-visas or the integration of government departments on an e-biz platform. This makes it all the more surprising, therefore, that there are very few references to fixing one of Digital India's biggest problems: the lack of high-speed broadband for all of its citizens.

To be sure, there are references to a "national rural Internet and technology mission" and "ensuring broadband connectivity at the village level" with an allocation of Rs 500 crore. In achieving this goal, there is no need for domestic production of IT hardware as the budget states; the mobile revolution, after all, has come and gone without India producing a large number of cell phones. There needs to be an admission that the UPA Government's 'National Optic Fibre Network' plan, which planned on connecting 2.5 lakh Gram Panchayats across the country with high-speed broadband, has failed. Inherent in this admission is that the top-most priority for Digital India should be to bring its Internet connectivity up to scratch. It would be a simple, easily stated goal that can be understood by everyone. As a Silicon Valley CEO was once rumoured to have said, high-speed broadband is a priority that's so simple government officials will be able to remember it even if they're exhausted, drunk and thrown out in the middle of the night by their wives.

Safeguarding Judicial Autonomy

Quite contrary to the fears propagated by its critics, the National Judicial Appointments Commission Bill will replace a failed system with a process that maintains, at the least, an element of fidelity to the Constitution's ideals.

Both Houses of Parliament have accorded their legal imprimatur to the 99th Constitution Amendment Bill. Once ratified by at least half of the country's State legislatures, and once the President's assent is secured, the amendment will establish a National Judicial Appointments Commission. The NJAC, the amendment provides, shall comprise the Chief Justice of India as its ex-officio chairperson, the two senior-most judges of the Supreme Court following the Chief Justice, the Law Minister, and two 'eminent persons' to be nominated jointly by the Prime Minister, the Chief Justice of India and the Leader of the Opposition. The NJAC will be responsible for making binding recommendations to the President for appointing judges to the Supreme Court and to various High Courts.

Disapproval of Commission: In the immediate wake of Parliament's approval of the amendment, however, criticism of the proposed commission, which will replace the collegium in making judicial appointments, has been widespread. Some, such as the Supreme Court Advocates-on-Record Association, have already moved the Supreme Court challenging the law for violating the Constitution's basic structure. The focus here has been not only on the composition of the NJAC, but also its workings as provided by the National Judicial Appointments Commission Bill, 2014, which was passed simultaneously with the Constitution Amendment Bill. Broadly, the detractors argue that the proposed laws vest excessive power in the executive, including a potential ability to veto nominations, thereby impinging on the independence of the judiciary. But these arguments overlook a number of key considerations. The new laws have their deficiencies, but they are a product of sustained discussion across all political lines and are examples of a non-partisan process of law making. What's more, they have allayed fears that the executive would exercise unbridled control over judicial appointments. And most crucially, the laws would obliterate the collegium system which is not only opaque and extra-constitutional, but also, as evidence of the recent past has shown, an abject failure.

Political Influence: When drafting the Constitution, the Constituent Assembly took great efforts to ensure that the judiciary was independent of any coercive political influence. To that end, it introduced a number of significant provisions in the Constitution. For example, the judges of the Supreme Court and the High Courts serve not at the pleasure of the President, but until they attain a fixed age; what's more, salaries and allowances of the judges are charged from the Consolidated Fund of the State (which is incapable of being a subject of a vote by a Legislative Assembly); discussion in the State legislatures on the conduct of any judge is expressly barred; powers are conferred on the High Court to punish for contempt of itself; and, significantly, judges of the higher judiciary can be removed only through a complicated process of impeachment by Parliament. But, as valued as judicial independence was to the Assembly, it did not see the vesting of the ultimate power of appointing judges on the executive as an infraction of that principle; on the contrary, it viewed such power as a vital cog in the checks and balances required to ensure a proper separation of powers. A broad process of consultation with several important authorities was mandated to further validate the system, but the ultimate authority was placed on the President. Such a system, the Assembly felt, would instil in the courts, which were given wide powers of judicial review including the power to strike down laws made by Parliament, democratic legitimacy, and would thereby serve as an effective check on judicial power.

Restore failed System: Now, through the 99th Constitution Amendment Bill and the NJAC Bill, Parliament has merely sought to realign the process of appointments in consonance with a general principle of separation of powers. It is therefore surprising to note that the Bills have met with such vigorous dissent from important quarters. Quite contrary to the fears propagated by its critics, the proposed laws will replace a failed system with a process that maintains, at the least, an element of fidelity to the Constitution's ideals. The composition of the NJAC may not be perfect, but it is, in fact, tilted in favour of the judiciary. If any two of the three judges on the panel believe that a candidate is unsuitable for appointment, they can together veto the elevation of such a nominee. The Union government, on the other hand, merely has a single vote in the NJAC, and cannot, by itself, place a proscription on any appointment. It will require the additional backing of either one of the judges or one of the 'eminent persons' for the government to thwart any nomination.

100 days of Modi Sarkar: Ten Significant Developments

Honestly, all an independent commentator could say for now is that the story of India has changed between before and after May 26, the day Narendra Modi took change as India's 14th Prime Minister. He is simply focusing on fixing the 10-year-long policy paralysis of the previous UPA dispensation. His 100 days of work shows Modi Sarkar is on the right track. The government has shouldered loads of hopes and aspirations of the people. It looks confident to fulfill those hopes and aspirations. In the last 100 days, the nation has moved from an era of policy paralysis to an era of policy priorities. In 100 days in Office, the government has successfully prepared a roadmap for India's development.

Ever since Modi took the reins, he has been continuing his focus on 'Minimum Government and Maximum Governance' in every step. Modi Government's sheet anchor for governance *'Sabka Saath, Sabka Vikas'* (Together with all, development for all) has instilled a sense of confidence among the citizens. Undoubtedly, a pro-active approach has been adopted by the Government to fulfill the aspirations of the people. There has been a major shift in work culture across Ministries. A new sense of accountability has gripped the bureaucracy. There is a tremendous amount of pressures on both the Ministers and the bureaucrats to fulfill the tide of expectations of people.

The following are the things:

1. *Bringing back Black Money:* The first decision government was setting up of a SIT, headed by the ex-apex court judge MB Shah, to unearth illegal money stashed in tax havens. The SIT has already prepared a comprehensive action plan, including creation of an institutional structure that could enable India to fight the battle against black money.

2. *Bringing economy back on track*: In a bid to arrest inflation, government asked states to delist fruits and vegetables from the Agriculture Produce Marketing Committee (APMC Act). This decision has protected farmers from the middle men and succeeded in preventing hoarding. This in turn has helped in taming inflation. With inflation on check, economic growth is picking up steadily. It is important to note that Indian economy has thrown up the best growth figures in two-and-a-half years. The GDP growth in April-June quarter is the highest in the last nine quarters. This is a sufficient indication that economy is turning around.

3. *Jan Dhan Yojana:* The government has rolled out the Pradhan Mantri Jan Dhan Yojana. The ambitious scheme aims at a comprehensive financial inclusion by opening of bank accounts of people who have been left out in the process so far. On the inauguration day, a record 1.5 crore bank accounts were opened under this scheme.

4. *Infrastructural development*: The focal point of the Union Budget 2014 was infrastructure, a sector which was neglected in the last 10 years under the

previous government. The government has attracted large-scale investments in infrastructural sector by reviving the SEZ, streamlining the PPP models and creating Infrastructural Investment Trusts (InvITs). Work for the ambitious Diamond Quadrilateral rail network—connecting major metros across the country—is in the full swing. The government has laid the groundwork for its ambitious '100 smart cities' project. To develop infrastructure in rural areas, it has launched Syama Prasad Mookerjee Rurban Mission and Deendayal Upadhyaya Gram Jyoti Yojana. It is working on strengthening and modernising the boarder infrastructure.

5. *Abolishing GOMs, EgoMs*: The government has abolished all Group of Ministers (GoMs) and Empowered Group of Ministers (EGoMs) which were set up during the UPA tenure. The move is expediting the process of decision-making in the ministries and ushering in a greater accountability in the system.

6. *Streamlining bureaucracy*: To take administration closer to people and ensure that governance doesn't get stuck in red tape, the government is streamlining the bureaucracy with thrust on transparency. The government has amended the All India Service (Conduct) Rules, 1968. The amended guidelines mandate that the bureaucrats must maintain political neutrality, take decisions and make recommendations on merit alone and take decisions solely in public interest.

7. *Disbanding Planning Commission:* Government has disbanded the 64-year-old Planning Commission. In 1950, then PM Jawaharlal Nehru formed Planning Commission on the line of erstwhile Soviet Union with an aim to formulating India's five year plans. But during the 60-year-long Congress rule, the Commission was mostly used as a parking lot for cronies of the grand old party. They did nothing apart from sucking up to Congress and its Prime Ministers. This government is in the process of replacing the Planning Commission with a new institution keeping in view of India's needs amid changing global economic scenario.

8. *Recasting judicial appointment:* In a path-breaking initiative, government has got the National Judicial Appointments Commission (NJAC) Bill passed in both the Houses of Parliament. The Bill scraps the Collegium System of appointment of Judges of Supreme Court and the High Courts and established a six-member body for the appointment of the Judges. The Chief Justice of the Supreme Court will head the NJAC. Besides, the judiciary would be represented by two senior Judges of the Supreme Court. Law Minister and two eminent personalities will be the other members of the Commission.

9. *Weeding out archaic laws*: The government is working overtime to weed out archaic rules and legislations from the statute books. Most of them are laws introduced during the colonial British rule and still prevalent in the country. These dysfunctional laws have no relevance in the present day. These are obsolete laws which only hamper governance by creating confusions. It only complicates the legislation process and stand as a hindrance within the system.

10. *Bilateral diplomacy*: Prime Minister Narendra Modi's SAARC diplomacy was indeed a bold step towards creating an atmosphere for multilateral economic cooperation. The common challenges that these nations face have made him create a common agenda of growth with mutual cooperation. During his visit to Nepal and Bhutan, he used the greater Hindu heritage as an instrument of foreign policy. The government has given a strong message to

Pakistan by calling off the Foreign Secretary-level talks after Pakistani High Commissioner to India Abdul Basit met Kashmiri separatists despite clear no from Foreign Ministry. For the first time in India's history, New Delhi under the leadership of Narendra Modi has asserted that it can't be bullied by the pressure from the Kashmiri separatists and various lobbyists. His ongoing Japan visit underlines the fact that India-Japan Strategic and Global cooperation can shift the balance of power in Asia. 100 days is too short a time to judge a Government. Let's wait and watch with patience for the India's real growth story to take shape in the days to come.

Towards a Skilled Workforce

With his twin focus on jobs and growth, Prime Minister Narendra Modi seems intent on placing renewed emphasis on skill development in the services and manufacturing sectors. In his I-Day speech, the Premier spoke of his 'skilled India' mission to promote holistic development. There is no doubt that India needs to equip its youth with greater work skills. At present, the country churns out a mostly semi-literate workforce without the requisite marketable skills in a globalised world. According to a report by the Adviser to the Prime Minister on the National Council on Skill Development, among those in the 15 to 29 years age group, only two per cent have received formal vocational training, and eight per cent non-formal vocational training. Against 128 lakh new entrants to the workforce, there were only 31 lakh seats for vocational skill training. As he stressed in his speech, with 65 per cent of the population under 35 years of age, India will have to think of reaping the demographic dividend. However, India ought to set its sights higher than what Modi envisaged when he lamented the shortage of drivers, plumbers and cooks. The real challenge is not to find low-paying jobs for the unemployed, but to equip those entering the workforce with the necessary skills in a competitive environment.

By promising to enhance the skill development of India's youth at a rapid pace, Modi spoke of forming a pool of young people who are able to create jobs. More importantly, he also talked of a workforce that will be in a position to "face their counterparts in any corner of the world" by virtue of hard work and dexterity of hands. Capacity-building was spoken of in the global context as the ability of India's youth to "win the hearts of people around the world" through their skills. The importance of promoting the manufacturing sector was highlighted both in the context of creating employment opportunities and developing a balance between imports and exports. The exhortation to multinationals to sell in any country but manufacture in India also came in the context of putting to use the education and capability of India's youth. For employment-led growth, for the "Come, make in India" slogan that Modi delivered on Independence Day to have any meaning, the government must invest heavily in education and training, in research and development. Otherwise, cheap labour will remain the only attraction for foreign investment in India.

Skill and talent are the results of education and training, and India must lay greater stress on its educational infrastructure before it can attain higher levels of growth. The skill set of India's youth have to necessarily match that of the world's best.

Give up Violence, Adopt Brotherhood to Make Progress

Striking a note of accommodation towards all political parties and acknowledging the contribution of all previous governments in nation-building, Preimer Modi made an appeal for a 10-year moratorium on "poison of casteism, communalism, and regionalism, discrimination on social and economic basis."

"We should have peace, unity and harmony. Please believe my word, if we give up the path of violence and adopt the path of brotherhood, we will make progress," he said. In an obvious reference to the unanimous approval of the National Judicial Appointments Commission Bill, 2014 in the just-concluded Budget Session of Parliament, he said his government was not interested in moving forward by virtue of its majority but on the basis of consensus. PM asserted that he was speaking not as the Pradhan Mantri (Prime Minister) but as a "Pradhan Sevak" (prime servant) and made a special mention of the services rendered by his predecessors and former governments for the country's development. Signalling his intent towards massive restructuring of the way the government functions, the Prime Minister said he was astonished to see "dozens of separate governments running at the same time in one main government."

"I was an outsider to Delhi. When I took an insider view, I was shocked at what I saw. There were dozens of governments within a government," he said. "People used to consider departments as their personal fiefdom. I saw there was disintegration and fights between departments. These fights landed up in the Supreme Court. How can you go forward in this situation?" he asked adding that he had begun the process of making the government, an organic unity, a harmonious entity with one aim, one mind, one direction, one energy.

The Prime Minister coined "zero defect, zero effect" slogan as he spoke of participation of youth in boosting the sector critical to India's economic success.

"...you [youth] decide that you will make at least one thing so that the country does not have to import it. Your policy should be 'zero defects, zero effect'. It means there would be no defect in the products you manufacture and it causes zero or no ill effect to the environment," he said.

For a WTO Stand with PDS in Hand

India should continue with its stand at the WTO to demand a permanent solution to the issue of public stockholding for food security before the protocol on trade facilitation is signed. It should also resist efforts to dismantle the Public Distribution System. In December 2013, two important items among the many others adopted at the Ninth World Trade Organisation (WTO) Ministerial Conference in Bali were the decisions respectively on the Agreement on Trade Facilitation (TF) and on Public Stockholding for Food Security Purposes. The former relates to the reduction of administrative barriers to trade—like dealing with custom barriers, documentation and transparency—while the latter concerns the procurement and storage of food grains by state agencies for the public distribution of food.

Recently, global attention was focussed on these two items as India argued that the adoption of the protocol on trade facilitation should be postponed till a permanent solution to public stockholding for food security had been worked out. Despite intense pressure from the developed countries, including the United States, India stuck to its stand even as the deadline for adopting the protocol on TF passed on July 31. Even though the developing countries have generally backed measures to enhance food security, support for India's stand was not easy to come by this time round. Only Cuba, Bolivia and Venezuela stood with India at the WTO. Later the U.N. International Fund for Agricultural Development came out in support of India's position. Many countries have openly criticised this step as India's intransigence. But is India's stand unreasonable?

Hunger and Under-nutrition

India faces serious problems of hunger and under-nutrition. According to National Sample Survey data, average calorie and protein intake have been steadily declining over the past few decades. In rural areas, the average calorie intake per person per day declined from 2,221 kcal in 1983 to 2,020 kcal in 2009-10. Over the same period, the average protein intake per person per day declined from 62 gm to 55 gm. One sees a similar pattern in urban India; the average calorie and protein intake declined from 2,089 kcal and 57 gm in 1983 respectively to 1,946 kcal and 53.5 gm in 2009-10. The vast majority of the population remains seriously undernourished. If we look at more direct measures of malnutrition, this picture is equally grim. According to the latest National Family Health Survey (NFHS, 2005-06), about 40-45 per cent of children under the age of 3 years are underweight and stunted. Close to 80 per cent of children aged between 6-35 months and 58 per cent of pregnant women aged between 15-49 years are anaemic. About 33 per cent of women and 28 per cent of men aged between 15-49 years have a below-normal body mass index. In terms of malnutrition, India fares worse than many sub-Saharan African countries.

Trade Collides with Food Security

Given this enormous burden of hunger and under-nutrition, it is only natural that India places a high priority on food security. A key mechanism to address the problem of hunger and under-nutrition has been the Public Distribution System (PDS). It involves the procurement of food grains from farmers, transporting and storing them in warehouses and then distributing them to consumers. In recent years, the price paid to farmers—known as minimum support price (MSP)—has been higher than open market prices. Also, the price at which the food grains are distributed to consumers—known as the issue price—has been lower than the market price. Hence, PDS involves providing a subsidy to both farmers and consumers. The subsidy to farmers, estimated to be about 20 per cent of the overall food subsidy, provides income support to poor agricultural families. The subsidy to consumers, by providing staple food grains at affordable prices, is necessary to increase consumption of poor families and address the widespread problem of hunger and under-nutrition.

Being a member of the WTO, India is bound by the agreements that have been signed and ratified by its members, including itself. According to Article 6 of the Agriculture Agreement, providing minimum support prices for agricultural products is considered distorting and is subject to limits. The subsidy arising from "minimal supports" cannot exceed 10 per cent of the value of agricultural production for developing countries.

PDS in India entails minimum support prices and public stockholding of food grains. It is possible that, in some years, the subsidy for producers will exceed 10 per cent of the value of agricultural production. In that eventuality, India would have contravened the Agriculture Agreement and be open to legal action by other members of the WTO. It is here that trade and food security collides for India. On the one hand, India needs to continue with the PDS to address problems of hunger and deprivation — this involves procurement and public stockholding of food grains. On the other hand, its membership in the WTO ties its hands on subsidy.

Possible Solutions Ignored

As part of the discussions on agriculture in Bali, this conflict between trade and food security came up for intense debate. Two solutions exist. The first comes from a proposal circulated by the G-33 group of countries in November 2012. This proposal argued for amending the Agriculture Agreement so that support for farmers (that comes through procurement) in developing countries is allowed without limits. The second solution was offered by India at Bali. The current method used by the WTO to compute the subsidy to producers multiplies the amount of procurement with the difference between the procurement price and a fixed reference price, which is the average of prices prevalent during the period 1986-88. This method is absurd because actual prices have increased several-fold since 1986-88. India has argued that the reference price used in the calculation should be moved forward on a rolling basis.

Both these solutions offered by developing countries have so far been ignored by the dominant forces—the developed countries—in the WTO. The developed countries are more interested in trade facilitation. As negotiations proceeded, India saw a reluctance on the part of some developed countries to deal with the issue of public stockholding. The possibility of a permanent solution to the issue of public stockholding by the 11th Ministerial Conference (i.e., within the next four years) would reduce substantially once the protocol on trade facilitation was adopted. Hence, India refused to agree to sign the protocol on trade facilitation unless there was an assurance of finding a permanent solution to the issue.

There is one area where the interests of the vast majority of India's undernourished population and genuine concerns of WTO members coincide, and the Indian government would do well to recognise and act on this. A major and genuine fear of WTO members is that India will dump its huge stock of food grains on the world market, crashing food prices. The fact that India has an unusually large stock of food grains is the result of the refusal of the government to disburse these food grains—for instance, through food for work programmes—because of the fear of increasing the food subsidy bill. The government could send appropriate signals by continuously releasing the food stocks only in the domestic market, addressing at one go, the genuine concerns of WTO members and the nutrition needs of its citizens.

Cash for Food?

While many commentators have been sympathetic to India's concern with food security, they have also argued for replacing the existing in-kind PDS with a cash transfer system. This would do away with procurement and public stockholding, and automatically solve the WTO issue of subsidy to farmers. Moreover, dismantling the existing in-kind PDS and replacing it with a cash transfer system is also a more efficient way of distributing subsidies. The current system is plagued by corruption and leakage that the cash transfer system will solve. Along similar lines, others have supported the dismantling of the PDS even as they have argued for the continuation of public stockholding to check price instability.

The key thrust of both arguments is to dismantle the existing PDS. Such arguments are problematic because they fail to engage with two important facts. First, the coverage, reach and effectiveness of the existing PDS have improved over time. Second, there is significant variation in the performance of the PDS across States. While some States like Himachal Pradesh, Kerala and Tamil Nadu have consistently performed well, others like Chhattisgarh and Uttarakhand have improved significantly. Thus, arguments for dismantling the PDS are wrong-headed. They are back door arguments for opening up the food economy to big, private capital that can have deleterious effects on the livelihood of peasants and agricultural labourers. India should continue with its stand at the WTO to demand a permanent solution to the issue of public stockholding before the protocol on trade facilitation is signed. It should also resist efforts to dismantle the existing in-kind PDS; on the contrary, it should make every effort to strengthen it.

Opportunities in Manufacturing

Manufacturing offers more scope for would-be Dalit entrepreneurs. The children of the elite simply cannot take the heat and dust. The distant locations could facilitate up a manufacturing unit. They prefer service-related occupations in metros in air-conditioned offices. If manufacturing takes off in India, Dalit entrepreneurs, will enter manufacturing supply chains. Some of them could grow into large firms in their own right. Many are willing to roll up their sleeves and do what it takes to get the job done. Small enterprises face credit constraints. It is ironic that in India, nationalised banks are on socialist principles. Today, public sector banks have lent tens of thousands of crores to big businesses. They have little money to lend to aspiring small entrepreneurs.

Social hierarchies are more rigid in rural India. Urbanising India offers better opportunities for aspiring Dalit entrepreneurs. The metros today are so expensive that entry for new entrants with few financial resources and limited social networks. An urbanisation strategy that focusses more on small and medium towns old attract large manufacturing investment (both domestic and foreign direct investment). It will create more opportunities for Dalit entrepreneurs in manufacturing supply chains.

The challenge for policymakers is to create what de Tocqueville termed “equality of conditions.” Anyone can chart his/her own course with initiative, tenacity and an enabling policy regime. We rightly take pride in our political freedoms. We are yet to ensure full citizenship rights to marginalised groups. What is required is a balance between old thinking and new wave. A coherent interlinked strategy ought to combine skill development, manufacturing and urbanisation. It has to shed old shibboleths about entrepreneurship and private enterprise. This alone could realise the promise of Dalit entrepreneurship.

Towards a Skilled Workforce

National Council on Skill Development, has reported only two per cent to have received formal and eight per cent non-formal vocational training. Against 128 lakh new entrants to the workforce, there were only 31 lakh seats for vocational skill training. Ought to some 65 per cent of the population under 35 years of age, reap the demographic dividend. India needs drivers, plumbers and cooks. The real challenge is not to find low-paying jobs for the unemployed. It had to equip those entering the workforce with the necessary skills in a competitive environment. Capacity-building was spoken of in the global context. India's youth had to "win the hearts of people around the world" through skills. Multinationals have to sell in any country but they had to manufacture in India harnessing the capability of youth. The government must invest heavily in education and training research and development. Otherwise, cheap labour will attract foreign investment in India. Skill and talent are the results of education and training. India must lay greater stress on educational infrastructure.

Recalls Vivekananda's Message of Universal Brotherhood

"There are Two images of September 11th— one of the trail of destruction in 2001 and the other — the message of Swami Vivekananda in 1893. Had we followed Swami Ji's message, history would never have witnessed such dastardly acts. September 11th, 2001 in USA is a blot on world peace history and strong cultural roots, the prime minister deserved.

Narrating his address to "Sisters and brothers of America ...", the Prime Minister said with these words of Swami Vivekananda, India's message of universal brotherhood reverberated across the world. "Let us remember the words of Swami Vivekananda. Set us dedicate ourselves to furthering the cause of unity, brotherhood and world peace," he said.

Launches 'My Clean India' Campaign

The Indian Premier Narendra Modi flagged off the mission at Valmiki Basti. It is housing society in central Delhi for sanitation workers. Mahatma Gandhi once stayed for a short while. The PM swept a small area, paid his respects at a temple. He dedicated public toilets to residents and conducted a surprise sanitation inspection on the local police station. The event was off-limits for private media, songs Indian report.

"Bapu gave us the message 'Quit India. Clean India'. His 'Clean India' dream is still unfulfilled," He pointed to the winning logo. It featured Mahatma Gandhi's round-rimmed spectacles. "When I saw that logo, I felt as if Gandhiji is looking at us through those spectacles to see if we have made India clean yet." He asked his countrymen to give Gandhi the gift of a clean India for his 150th birth anniversary. 'I am confident that Clean India will give us as much joy as Quit India," he said.

"I am not saying that our new government has done everything for sanitation. I praise all governments before me union governments and state governments, corporates and voluntary groups," Cleanliness should not be the job of sanitation workers, he said. He asked citizens to take photos of garbage, upload them on social media, cleaning the spot, and finally upload a picture of the clean spot. He invited nine people – Goa Governor Mridula

Sinha, Shashi Tharoor, cricket star Sachin Tendulkar, actors Salman Khan, Priyanka Chopra and Kamal Haasan, industrialist Anil Ambani, yoga practitioner Baba Ramdev, and the crew of the TV serial Tarak Mehta ka Ulta Chashma – to join him in his mission, seeking them more to nominate.

Salman Khan joined Modi on stage. Similar pledge was administered in government offices across the country. School children asked for a kilometer on two occasion. Open defecation kills thousands of babies and stunts the growth of children and of workforce. We should not let ourselves be distracted from it by litter, health economist Dean Spears urged the audience.

Sustaining Swachh Bharat Mission a Challenge

The first phase of the campaign ran through Diwali. It has turned will endeavour to turn it into a mass movement, requiring not just toilets but a change in the behaviour and mindset of the people. The Ministries of Urban Development and Rural Development, is expected to spend Rs. 2 lakh crore the next five years. Union Rural Development Minister Nitin Gadkari said the bulk — Rs. 1.34 lakh crore — would be ploughed into rural areas, His Urban Development collogue M. Venkaiah Naidu said the urban component would cost Rs. 62,009 crore. The States could pick up 25 per cent of the tab and corporates could dole out generously through their Corporate Social Responsibility (CSR) corpus. The key components of the campaign include eradication of manual scavenging, solid waste management and 'converting waste into wealth'. Cine stars Salman Khan and Priyanka Chopra and laumaker fom congress Shashi Thanoor became ambassadors for the cause.

The government has already contacted yoga guru Baba Ramdev, Art of Living guru Sri Sri Ravi Shankar, the Ramakrishna Mission and the Kanchi Kamakoti Peeth. It is in the process of roping in the Catholic Bishops Conference of India and Muslim clerics.

Shashi Tharoor tweeted: "Honoured to accept the invitation of PM to join Clean India campaign ... I am not a fan of tokenism. Clean India is a great campaign. The challenge will be to sustain it beyond a week of photo ops."

The Message Behind the Broom

Prime Minister Modi wanted to link his campaign to the toilet-cleaning ritual in Gandhi's ashrams. He desired to emphasise that the seemingly menial work for nation-building. The noise surrounding the mission launch was intended to draw Indians in the drive. Everyone was expected to devote two hours every week in cleaning surroundings. Surely, the drive has been successful as an event in increasing public awareness in the importance of sanitation.

If India's villages and towns are to be dirt-free, a Gandhian touch of personal involvement is sought. It could surely be a colossal waste of productive hours of skilled personnel. Political leaders, industrialists and celebrities could sweep the streets to raise general awareness on sanitation. It would be impossible for any government or civic body to ensure clean streets and public places. Everyone in the workforce ought to engage in actual cleaning. Efforts must be made to de-stigmatise the act. The participation of citizens in large numbers will have a positive effect. The government may not be able to do everything. Voluntarism cannot be a substitute for strengthening civic infrastructure. The civic bodies will need to be at the centre of the Clean India Campaign. The drive need to be sustainable. Its success ought not to depend on the hours each citizen puts in to sweep streets. A lot can be done to further the ideal of cleanliness without wielding the broom.

Launches Village Scheme

If nearly 800 MPs develop three villages each by 2019, around 2500 villages will be developed, Modi

Launching the MP Model Village Scheme today, Prime Minister Narendra Modi said if nearly 800 MPs develop three villages each by 2019, around 2,500 villages will be covered. On his part, Modi claimed that he will select a village in Varanasi area.

'I will also select a village in Varanasi area. Guidelines have been received. I'll discuss and decide," he said. Modi said the country's development model needs a change. So far, it has been supply driven. Henceforth, it should be demand driven, he said.

"Let us take interest and create an atmosphere where every person is proud of his or her village," 'Modi said.

Rolls out Labour Reforms

Modi unveiled new measures for the youth, workers and employers to ease the business for enterprises imparting skill training for workers. Modi launched the Universal Account Number scheme (UAN) for all provident fund contributors. It will allow portability of PF benefits and online tracking of benefits. Modi said the aim of the program me was to emphasise the dignity of labour. The blue-collared workers performance as *"shram yogi"*. he called them to support the graduates from Industrial Training Institutes (ITIs) across the country, who undergo vocational training after completing Class X. The government will reimburse 50 per cent of the stipend paid to apprentices during first two years of training. "ITIs are shishu mandirs of technical education. Those who have knowledge other than that of books, which of skills, must be respected. The talented among the ITI graduates msut get new opportunities," said Modi. There are 2.82 lakh apprentices undergoing training against 4.9 lakh seats. The program will increase this to 24 lakh apprentices, he said. The government in August had passed the Apprentices (Amendment) Bill 2014 in the Lok Sabha to amend the 1961 Act to regulate the conditions of work of apprentices a fresh in a wider number of trades.

UAN scheme

Modi launched the UAN for PF contributors. "More than Rs 27,000 crore is lying unclaimed in PF accounts. If mobile phones work for those traveling inter-state, or across countries, why PF accounts cannot work," he said. The PM launched an online portal that will allow employers to file returns online. It will comply with 16 labour laws and a system. Lots drawn by computers will be used to conduct inspection. He announced that to end the *Inspector Raj* which was still on, the government had decided to bring in a system based on "responsibility and trust."

"If a person driving can take care of self safety, why do we expect him as an industrial employer who could oversee the maintenance of boilers, machinery etc." said Modi. "Ease of business is the greatest requirement for India's success. Ease of business will be a priority under Make in India. Labour's problems from labour's point of view too. Shram yogis will be rashtra yogis," he said.

Applicability and Timeline

The scheme undertone ministry of labour apply only to employees and workers under central agencies and autonomous bodies. Labour is a concurrent subject. These will apply in states only after they make similar changes to their rules and laws. Twenty states' representatives have attended a consultation after the launch. It the moment, the changes will be piloted in central agencies, PSUs while the discussion goes on with states. Haryana, Karnataka, Gujarat, Bihar have expressed interest in shifting to similar system. We expect changes in this financial year," said a senior MoLE official. "A central analysis and intelligence Unit will be set up to analyse data to decide which units to inspect. Labour department staff will need to be trained in new skills for use of computers. states' staff will have to do the same," he added.

Lack of Strength in Labour Depts

Labour officials in States had a varied response. Several cited that labour departments were functioning with minuscule strength, making it impossible to carry out inspections.

"There are 25 labour inspectors in Delhi state and over 1,000 units under each inspector. I do not even know how many units there are in my area, as 90 per cent do not file returns. It is physically impossible to inspect each year even if one tried," said one district-level labour official. "Self-certification may decrease arbitrary inspections and harassment by inspectors as well as false complaints made by unions and workers. It may also lead to industries certifying without complying," he said.

A Haryana government labour official said that in his district, 11 labour inspectors were responsible for inspecting over 1200 units. "Haryana already has a system based on self-certification. Sometimes, the units themselves prefer our inspections, as they can show it to their buyers, such as in large garment units," he said.

Make for India, not just in India

The government's policies have unwittingly tilted the balance in favour of innovation for the world rather than creating conditions that encourage them for India's personal needs. India has some natural advantages in providing knowledge workers to global corporations.The government policies that have made foreign investment increasingly easy, coupled with tax holidays in Special Economic Zones that only large corporations can afford to move into, have provided excellent incentives for setting up export-oriented captives in India. In the last ten years, the number of global research and development (R&D) captives in India has been progressively increasing. A recent study by Zinnov Consulting found that nearly half of the top 500 global R&D spenders have set up shop in India. These captives and their service providers together have created a globally exposed and competent workforce in India coupled with new wealthy class of a few white collared professionals. The positive impact that this has made to the country is significant and real, even if it is limited to a small percentage of the population. To replicate success in manufacturing seems a worthy objective, but with lessons from the past, we can and should aim higher. Innovation has two beneficiaries—producers and consumers. For example, creating the light bulb was a profitable venture for Thomas Alva Edison. It also benefitted millions of consumers with the innovation.

Sharing value

In most cases, the knowledge workers pursue problems of their employers in western countries. The output of their work often tends to be irrelevant in India. Thus, one can effectively create islands of producers and consumers that are farther from each other. The value created is shared by a few producers in India and a lot of consumers in western countries. The recent 'Make in India' campaign is trying to extend this trend into manufacturing from services. There is a silver lining to this approach. The output of what workers create is being removed from the needs of their country of residence. The skills and capacity they develop in the process are transferable. For example, workers from the very same pool, using similar tools and processes, created the first of its kind Unique Identification project in India. Aadhar aimed to give a billion unique biometric IDs to Indian resident. It has already achieved half of its target within a few years.

Attracting FDI encourage as the Indian outsourcing industry. The track record in encouraging companies to innovate and make in India. India has been poor, With a dismal rank in the ease of doing business index. There is a systemic advantage that existing businesses enjoy versus the problems that new innovative companies seeking to disrupt. However, improving the country's rank on this well-established score doesn't seem to be an important priority for the government. Apart from many sound bites, no concrete action is forthcoming. The track record in encouraging companies to make in India and for India has been poor. The initiative of implementing a uniform Goods and Services Tax will do more to create an integrated domestic market. The ability to move goods across state borders without being subjected to harassment is equally important. However, an export-oriented manufacturing policy sidesteps this issue. For the goods produced will mostly go out. Another key issue in India is a broken credit system. The issue makes it difficult for new businesses to raise debt. The 'Make in India' initiative will even further tilt the balance in favour of large domestic firms that hog credit. It can tap international markets or foreign firms that have better access to capital in their home country. These are barely two in a long list of reforms that India awaits.

Software as a Service

We can see examples that frustrate businesses trying to make the software. The recent trend of delivering software as a service has proved to be an ideal solution for a capital-scarce country. Here consumers and small businesses are happier with a pay-as-you-go system rather than investing upfront for using software tools. However, the one thing that such businesses need — an ability to easily collect recurring payments online — is tedious in India. This makes it is easier for an Indian company to serve customers in the US than in India. This is no doubt tragic apart from being strange. The collateral advantage of learning from exposure to western markets comes with the inherent bias for creating products. The inherent services more relevant for the richer countries. Innovations have perfected in India on that scale. It would also find relevance in emerging economies all over the world.

However, that is an unlikely scenario given the current policies we pursue. Right now, we are trying to encourage creation of figurative islands in India for setting up factories and exporting those goods. We have done that successfully in services and seen the limitations. A focus on 'Make for India' will spur 'Make in India' export-oriented businesses. However the reverse doesn't happen automatically. We have the opportunity to get it right this time.

Come, Make In India

Modi, in his maiden Independence Day speech, articulated his vision of several social and economic policy objectives of his government. It is generally agreed that the objectives so forcefully expressed by him are unexceptionable. What is required, and often difficult, had been their effective translation into practice. The Prime Minister must be commended for stating domestic manufacturing as the core and central tenet of his foreign investment policy. The process puts job creation or employment generation at the top of the objectives for FDI in the country.

Global Manufacturing Hub

This welcome emphasis in our foreign investment policy on efficient and competitive domestic manufacturing will serve multiple objectives. First and foremost, it will enhance job opportunities within the country; second, it will minimise the imports of such products into the country, thereby mitigating the pressure on our trade deficit; third, in the long run, if not in the near-term, it will help augment and diversify our exports from the manufacturing sector; fourth, it will help in bringing latest technologies into the countryand lastly, such domestic manufacturing will help minimise some of the trade frictions we have with other countries. The importance of domestic manufacturing with foreign investment in reducing trade frictions with other countries is at present ignored or underestimated. As a corollary, the focus on world-class domestic manufacturing may be the best way to cope with globalisation and to maximise the possible benefits. The size of our domestic market and the abundant availability of skilled and technical manpower at low cost is a leverage that we need to consciously induce foreign investors to make India as a manufacturing hub in their operations. If there is any lesson we can learn from the Chinese. It is how the size of the domestic market and the availability of skilled and disciplined manpower could be put to effective use for industrial and technological development of the country with foreign investment.

If the policy is put into practice them co-ordinated action is needed on several fronts. First, it is of paramount importance that the foreign investment, foreign trade and Intellectual Property Rights (IPR) policies are viewed in a holistic manner to ensure that they mutually reinforce each other in achieving the policy objective ofworld-class domestic manufacturing.

Second, it needs to be remembered that investment opportunities, as reflected by our large domestic market and low-cost skilled and unskilled manpower, may be a necessary, but not a sufficient condition, to induce foreign investors come to India with capital and technology. The congeniality of the investment climate or environment, as reflected in the stability of the policies and the rules as well as the conditions attached to the approval of the investments is even more important to assure foreign investors of fair and non-discriminatory treatment. The focus of our foreign investment policy should be on the positive aspects. What is being produced in India, with what kind of technology and skills. How efficiently and competitively it is produced. Whether it is of world-class standards? Whether bound by negative aspects such as ownership and control? Whether it is enterprise-specific performance requirements, or other conditions interfere with the internal commercial decisions of the enterprises?

Competitive Environment

The best way to ensure that foreign investment should be of a high quality yield value to the country to have a policy framework. It had to operate in an unprotected, open and competitive environment. It should not be behind high tariff walls or import restrictions, nor with subsidies or other giveaways.

Third, with respect to the contours of the foreign trade policy. It is by and large confined now to dealing with exports and imports compartmentally. The encouragement of exports with various kinds of subsidies and prop-ups, and curtailment of imports by high tariffs and other so-called trade remedy measures like anti-dumping or countervailing duties or other import restrictions. Encouragement of domestic manufacturing of world-class standards, either by domestic or foreign investors or both, has not been a major objective of our foreign trade policy so far. Our foreign trade policy must recognise that encouragement of domestic manufacturing of world-class standards. It should cater solely to our own market, as a preferable alternative to protection and subsidisation through high tariffs. The trade remedy measures and financial giveaways are to be accented for. Rather, the policy must encourage freer imports of capital goods. industrial raw materials, components, tools and devices, as well as technology-laden imports, had to be upgraded for the quality and competitiveness of domestic manufacturing. Fourth, the importance of protection of Intellectual Property Rights (IPRs) in the scheme of attracting foreign investment and establishing high quality domestic manufacturing must not be overlooked.

Ensure IP Protection

IPRs do not consist only of pharmaceutical patents as is commonly understood in our country. They include as well copyright (computer software in our country is protected by copyright), trademarks, trade secrets, geographical indications, designs, trade secrets, business confidential information and data, and the like. IPR policies do not have domestic manufacturing as a central objective They need to be implemented in such manner that do not impede or deter technology-oriented domestic investments from foreign investors. The protection of patents, trademarks, trade secrets, layout designs and the like is crucial to these and other sectors, where we want foreign investment of high quality with modern technologies. Our intellectual property laws are largely in conformity with international standards. It is reflected in the TRIPS Agreement of the WTO and other international conventions to which we have subscribed. Yet we tend to create an impression around the world that we seldom value intellectual property or respect its adequate protection.

Address Local Woes

The competitive domestic manufacturing needs to be touched. Among the major reasons for our domestic industry being competitively disadvantaged vis-a-vis the rest of the world, two options stand out prominently: first, the inadequacy and poor quality of our infrastructure, and second, the high cost of our capital. The protection and subsidisation is not the solution, The huge disadvantage faced by the domestic industry requires to be addressed with priority and ways and means found to mitigate it.

'Make in India' digital economy

In the last month, India has seen something it's never seen before: Leaders of the world's largest technology companies – Jeff Bezos (Amazon), Satya Nadella (Microsoft), Mark Zuckerberg (Facebook) and Sunder Pichai (a top 3 Google-ite) all visited India in the span of one month. This week Softbank's Masayoshi Son is touring India, and has committed to invest $10 billion into digital India.

And last week a delegation of Indian digital entrepreneurs toured China, meeting companies like Baidu (worth $75 billion), Alibaba (worth $200 billion) and TenCent (worth $140 billion), all home-grown in China. The Chinese digital economy now contributes 4.4 per cent to the Chinese economy, directly employing hundreds of thousands of people, and indirectly giving white-collar jobs to millions more. Digital China is now a major driver of China's growth story. So when today, more than ever before, global technology companies are eyeing India, the question the Indian government should be asking is: Should the Indian digital economy be "Make in India", or "Expand into India"? We can take a cue from China. China's digital boom story is, at least partially, due to China's interest in incubating domestic digital business growth by limiting access of global majors to the Chinese market. India, conversely, has been an open door for global companies, which has led to Google and Facebook's domi-nance in India (which today capture more than 75 per cent of India's digital advertising pie, despite minimal operations here). Even India's largest digital company, Flipkart, is over 80 per cent foreign owned by investors. The truth is that India's Baidu is Google, India's TenCent is Facebook, and India's Alibaba is Flipkart, owned by Tiger Global and Naspers. And most of that development, except for Flipkart, is being done abroad.

In comparison to China, India's digital revolution is just beginning. If Prime Minister Narendra Modi wants the digital revolution to be an Indian phenomenon and a major driver of India's economic growth story, he should outline measures that enable and encourage domestic digital business growth, including domestic investment incentive schemes and measures that help Indian companies compete with global ones, including potential FDI restrictions. Doing nothing, as has been done thus far, is a passive way of encouraging global companies to earn more globally out of India's growth story, and may be a massive missed opportunity for a key driver of India's growth in the coming decade.

G20 Backs for Repatriation of Black Money

In a victory for India, the G20 endorsed Prime Minister Narendra Modi's strong pitch for repatriation of black money at its summit in Brisbane, echoing the government's line on the need for transparency and disclosure of tax information. Modi while voicing India's support for a new global standard on automatic exchange of tax information urged every jurisdiction, especially tax havens, to provide information for tax purposes in accordance with treaty obligations. The new global standard will be instrumental in getting information relating to unaccounted money hoarded abroad and enable its eventual repatriation, Modi said, utilising the forum of G20, which accounts for 85 per cent of world's GDP. The Prime Minister while flagging his concern over cross border tax avoidance and evasion also noted that increased mobility of capital and technology have created new opportunities for avoiding tax and profit sharing. The three-page communiqué was released at the end of the two-day summit of Group of 20 industrialised and leading emerging economies hosted by Australia. Welcoming the "significant progress" on the G20/OECD Base Erosion and Profit Shifting (BEPS) Action Plan to modernise international tax rules, it said, "We are committed to finalising this work in 2015, including transparency of tax-payer specific rulings found to constitute harmful tax practices."

Briefing newsmen, Railway Minister Suresh Prabhu and External Affairs Ministry spokesperson Syed Akbaruddin said the reference to transparency, which was not there in the draft communiqué, was incorporated in the final communiqué after Prime Minister's strong intervention in plenary session. After Modi's intervention, several countries, notably Brazil and South Africa wanted a reference to be made to transparency in the final communiqué, Akbaruddin said. "After the Prime Minister's own and strong intervention (on repatriation of black money), several countries shared his sentiments and wanted the views to be reflected in the final communiqué," he said.

RSS Quietly Dumps 'Ghar Wapsi' Programme after PM xpresses Annoyance

Rashtriya Swayamsevak Sangh has quietly dumped its functionary at the centre of the controversial 'Ghar Wapsi' reconversion into Hinduism programme in Uttar Pradesh that derailed last month's winter session of Parliament and has dented the Narendra Modi-led government's pro-development image in recent weeks. Rajeshwar Singh, a 55-year-old RSS pracharak who single-handedly steered the Ghar Wapsi or reconversion programme and has also led its Dharm Jagran campaignsince 1996, has been removed as coordinator of programmes in western UP and Uttarakhand. This, Sangh Parivar sources said, was a fallout of a meeting between RSS leaders and Modi during which the PM is said to have expressed his annoyance at the high-decibel campaign that took the focus away from development and scuppered his government's ambitious legislative agenda. Singh confirmed to ET that he had decided not to work on any Sangh-related work now. "There has been much pressure on me in the past few days. It has spoiled my health. I want to rest at home now," said the long-time RSS pracharak.

"I don't think I have done anything wrong. Everyone including RSS top leaders had assured me of support earlier," Singh said. "But the Sangh is not strong all the time. They may not want me now, but they may want me tomorrow," he said.

Several state RSS leaders said Singh's removal was a fallout of top-level interactions between the RSS and BJP leadership including P M Modi in recent weeks. BJP leaders complained to the RSS leadership that the controversies surrounding conversion were taking the sheen off the government's "development agenda" and prevailed upon the Sangh to send out a message by removing Singh, they said RSS spokesman Manmohan Vaidya confirmed Singh's removal, but said it was a decision made by the UP unit of the Sangh and not because of any pressure. "The Sangh doesn't work under pressure from anyone. It gives responsibilities to people at various times, makes decisions to remove them too, depending on its own issues," he said. The Ghar Wapsi programme, in which Christians and Muslims are "encouraged" to "return" to Hinduism, has been going on for decades, but mostly under the radar. However, Singh's brazen mass conversion programmes in Agra and his provocative public statements put a spotlight on it, triggering a controversy that was eventually used by Opposition parties to disrupt Parliament.

Singh has also been removed from the helm of the Sangh-affiliated Dharma Jagran that he has been leading since 1996. However, he continues to be a pracharak with the Agra unit of RSS. Although Singh has been conducting Ghar Wapsi campaigns every December for many years now, he had intensified it this year and had planned for the conversion of 20,000 Muslims to Hinduism in UP alone this year. Many of his planned programmes, including one scheduled on Christmas Day, could not be held as planned because of the controversy it triggered.

******